Humanism and Calvinism

For my parents

Humanism and Calvinism

Andrew Melville and the Universities of Scotland,
1560–1625

STEVEN J. REID
University of Glasgow, UK

ASHGATE

Published by
Ashgate Publishing Limited
Wey Court East
Union Road
Farnham
Surrey, GU9 7PT
England

Ashgate Publishing Company
Suite 420
101 Cherry Street
Burlington
VT 05401-4405
USA

www.ashgate.com

British Library Cataloguing in Publication Data
Reid, Steven J.
   Humanism and Calvinism : Andrew Melville and the universities of Scotland, 1560–1625. – (St Andrews studies in Reformation history) 1. Melville, Andrew, 1545–1622–Influence. 2. Universities and colleges – Scotland – History – 16th century. 3. Universities and colleges – Scotland – History – 17th century. 4. Church and college – Scotland – History – 16th century. 5. Church and college – Scotland – History – 17th century. 6. Reformation – Scotland. 7. Humanism – Scotland – History – 16th century. 8. Humanism – Scotland – History – 17th century. 9. University of St. Andrews – History. 10. Education, Higher – Europe – History.
   I. Title II. Series 378.4'11'09031–dc22

Library of Congress Cataloging-in-Publication Data
Reid, Steven J.
   Humanism and Calvinism : Andrew Melville and the universities of Scotland, 1560–1625 / Steven J. Reid. p. cm. — (St Andrews studies in Reformation history) Includes bibliographical references and index. ISBN 978-1-4094-0005-9 (hardcover : alk. paper) – ISBN 978-0-7546-9846-3 (e-book) 1. Universities and colleges—Scotland—History—16th century. 2. Universities and colleges—Scotland—History—17th century. 3. University of St. Andrews—History. 4. Melville, Andrew, 1545–1622. 5. Education, Higher—Scotland—History—16th century. 6. Education, Higher—Scotland—History—17th century. 7. Reformation—Scotland. 8. Scotland—Intellectual life—16th century. 9. Scotland—Intellectual life—17th century. I. Title. LA657.R45 2010
   378.411'09031—dc22

2010041851

ISBN 9781409400059 (hbk)
ISBN 9780754698463 (ebk)

Printed and bound in Great Britain by the
MPG Books Group, UK

Contents

List of Tables

List of Figures

Abbreviations and Conventions

Acta	*Acta Facultatis Artium Sancti Andreae,* ed. A. I. Dunlop (single volume edn, Edinburgh, 1961)
Acta Rectorum	St Andrews University Library Special Collections, UYUY350 (3 vols). All references are to vol. 2 unless otherwise specified.
Balcarres Papers	National Library of Scotland, Advocate's Manuscript 29.2
BUK	*Acts and Proceedings of the General Assemblies of the Kirk of Scotland from the year MDLX,* ed. T. Thomson (3 vols, Maitland Club, 1839–45)
Calderwood	David Calderwood, *The History of the Kirk of Scotland,* ed. T. Thomson (8 vols, Wodrow Society, 1842–9)
Cameron, *Letters*	*Letters of John Johnston and Robert Howie,* ed. J. K. Cameron (St Andrews, 1963)
Cant	Ronald G. Cant, *The University of St Andrews: A Short History,* fourth edn (St Andrews, 2002)
Durkan and Kirk	John Durkan and James Kirk, *The University of Glasgow 1451–1577* (Glasgow, 1977)
Early Records	*Early Records of the University of St. Andrews: the Graduation Roll 1413–1579 and the Matriculation Roll 1473–1579,* ed. J. M. Anderson (SHS, 1926)
Evidence	*Evidence, Oral and Documentary, taken by the Commissioners appointed by King George IV, for visiting the Universities of Scotland* (4 vols, London, 1837). All references are to vol. 3 unless otherwise specified.
Fasti Aberdonenses	*Fasti Aberdonenses: Selections from the Records of the University and King's College of Aberdeen,* ed. C. Innes (Spalding Club, 1854)
FBD	*The First Book of Discipline,* ed. J. K. Cameron (Edinburgh, 1972)
FMA	*Fasti Academiae Mariscallanae Aberdonensis: Selections from the Records of the Marischal College and University, MDXCIII–MDCCCLX,* ed. P. J. Anderson and J. F. Kellas Johnstone (3 vols, New Spalding Club, 1889–98)
Hannay, *Statutes*	*The Statutes of the Faculty of Arts and the Faculty of Theology at the Period of the Reformation,* ed. R. K. Hannay (St Andrews, 1910)

IR	*Innes Review*
JMAD	James Melville, *The Autobiography and Diary of Mr James Melvill*, ed. R. Pitcairn (Wodrow Society, 1842)
Munimenta	*Munimenta Alme Universitatis Glasguensis*, ed. C. Innes (4 vols, Maitland Club, 1854)
ODNB	*Oxford Dictionary of National Biography* (Oxford University Press, 2004) (http://www.oxforddnb.com/view/article/)
Original Letters	*Original Letters Relating to the Ecclesiastical Affairs of Scotland, 1603–1625*, ed. B. Botfield (2 vols, Bannatyne Club, 1851)
RCP	*Registres de la Compagnie des Pasteurs de Genève*, ed. R. M. Kingdon and J. F. Bergier (Geneva, 1962–)
RPC	*The Register of the Privy Council of Scotland*, ed. J. H. Burton and others (Edinburgh, 1877–)
RPS	*The Records of the Parliaments of Scotland to 1707*, ed. K. M. Brown and others (St Andrews, 2007–2010) (www.rps.ac.uk)
RSS	*Registrum Secreti Sigilli Regum Scotorum*, ed. M. Livingstone and others (8 vols, Edinburgh, 1908–82)
RStAKS	*Register of the Minister, Elders and Deacons of the Christian Congregation of St Andrews, 1559–1600*, ed. D. Hay Fleming (2 vols, SHS, 1889–90)
SHR	*Scottish Historical Review*
SHS	Scottish History Society
StAPR	Mark Smith, 'The Presbytery of St Andrews 1586–1605: a Study and Annotated Edition of the Register of the Minutes of the Presbytery of St Andrews' (Unpublished PhD Thesis, University of St Andrews, 1985)
UYSL	St Andrews University Library Special Collections, Records of St Leonard's College, University of St Andrews
UYSM	St Andrews University Library Special Collections, Records of St Mary's College, University of St Andrews
UYSS	St Andrews University Library Special Collections, Records of St Salvator's College, University of St Andrews
UYUY	St Andrews University Library Special Collections, Records of the University of St Andrews

All dates are given assuming the New Year begins on 1 January. All sums of money are given in £ Scots (£), shillings (s.), and pence (d.). A merk is equal to two thirds of £1 Scots. All quotations from primary sources have kept original spellings. Contractions and abbreviations in primary sources have been silently expanded. All translations from Latin are my own, except where stated.

Acknowledgements

The narrative in this monograph relating to the University of St Andrews was largely compiled during my Masters and PhD research on the St Andrews History of the University Project under the aegis of Professor Roger Mason, and it is to him that I owe the greatest debt of thanks. Roger has been an exemplary mentor, friend and sounding board since my MA degree, and has the dubious distinction of having read full drafts of both my thesis and what follows. For this, and everything else, I thank him.

Research into the broader picture of Scottish higher education after the reformation, and the monograph itself, was completed at the University of Glasgow, where I have had the singular good fortune and privilege to find myself teaching since my PhD. My colleagues have been the most welcoming and supportive group of academics a young lecturer could ask for, especially in providing me with sufficient research time and space to write the text, and my colleagues in Scottish history and the early modern research group have been a receptive audience to several chapters delivered as seminar papers over the past two years.

This study has benefited materially from the expert advice of Professor James K. Cameron, Dr Peter Maxwell-Stuart, Mrs Rachel Hart, Dr Robert Smart, Mr Giovanni Gellera, Dr John McCallum, and Professor Alexander Broadie, and the latter two deserve a special mention for reading drafts of the various sections on ecclesiastical politics and university curricula and teaching sources. As in all things, however, any errors of interpretation or mistakes arising in this work remain my own.

I happily acknowledge the financial support provided for my Masters and PhD by the Arts and Humanities Research Council and by a St Andrews School of History Scholarship. Dr Barbara Crawford and The Strathmartine Trust not only provided me with an office to call home during my studies, but also supported the post-doctoral phase of my research with a generous fellowship, for which I am very grateful.

The support and care of the people around you sustains your research as much as the work itself, and with that in mind I'd like to thank Bryce Aitken, Paul Roarty and all the other members of Fife Athletic Club for taking my mind off early modern Scotland with countless runs across the length and breadth of the Kingdom of Fife, and for their community, camaraderie, and banter. My other half, Lesley Welsh, put up with a partner who was often distracted, distressed and downright depressed during the writing process over the long winter of 2009–10, and I'm thankful for her patience, encouragement and love, then and always. Finally, my parents

John and Jacqueline Reid have been a source of continual support, even if they've never quite understood my fascination with the nuances of Scottish intellectual culture, for which they have my love and gratitude.

Introduction

Education was the cornerstone of any Protestant society. This was a fact recognised by Luther in his earliest writings, by Phillip Melanchthon in his wide-ranging work as an educational reformer, and by Calvin in his foundation of the Genevan Academy.[1] It was also recognised by the earliest Scottish reformers in their blueprint for the Scottish Kirk, the *First Book of Discipline*. Noting that there should be a school in every parish and that education would inculcate reformed beliefs in children (and by extension in their families), one of the largest sections in the *First Book* was an extensive overhaul of the three Scottish Catholic universities – St Andrews, Glasgow, and King's College Aberdeen – accompanied by an urgent plea that this should be a priority for the Kirk.[2] Yet while the ideal of creating a Protestant system of higher education in Scotland, one that would produce 'godly' and civic-minded citizens and ministers well versed in reformed doctrine, was inherent from the onset of the reformation in 1559–60, this was not fully realised until the end of the reign of James VI and I. Moreover, while two new and wholly Protestant foundations were established in Edinburgh in 1583 and at Marischal College in New Aberdeen in 1593, the 'ancient' universities underwent a rather circuitous process of casting down their medieval and Papally-sanctioned constitutions in favour of radical new Protestant ones, only to have all their original foundations (excluding that at Glasgow) restored by 1621, albeit modified to omit any overtly Catholic teaching. At the heart of this transformational process was Andrew Melville, and although the Protestant universities that emerged in Scotland in the early seventeenth century did owe something to him intellectually, they were in many ways completely different to the institutions he had first envisaged when he began the process of reform at Glasgow in 1574. His role in producing a network of Protestant seminaries from the remains of a very Catholic system of higher education, and the

---

[1]   Martin Luther, 'To the Councilmen of All Cities in Germany That They Establish and Maintain Christian Schools' (1524), trans. A. Steinhaeuser in *Luther's Works*, ed. H.T. Lehman and J. Pelikan (55 vols, St Louis, Missouri, and Philadelphia, Pennsylvania, 1955–86), vol. 45 (1962), pp. 347–78; Martin Luther, 'Sermon on Keeping Children in School' (1530), trans. C.M. Jacobs in *Luther's Works*, vol. 46 (1967), pp. 209–58; Philip Melanchthon, *Orations on Philosophy and Education*, ed. S. Kusukawa and trans. C.F. Salazar (Cambridge, 1999); Gillian Lewis, 'The Geneva Academy', in Andrew Pettegree, Alastair Duke and Gillian Lewis (eds), *Calvinism in Europe 1540–1620* (Cambridge, 1994), pp. 35–63, at pp. 36–8.

[2]   *FBD*, pp. 129–55.

effect this process had on intellectual life in the Scottish universities, is the subject of what follows.

Some explanation is perhaps required as to why a full-length study should be devoted to assessing Melville as an educational reformer, given that there is still little consensus about his better-known contribution to Scottish society in the field of church politics. Melville (1545–1622) has been seen by most historians as the successor to John Knox and George Buchanan in the tradition of Scottish radical intellectuals, and was the leader of the Presbyterian faction within the Kirk from his return to Scotland in 1574 (after a decade of study on the Continent), until his imprisonment in the Tower of London in 1607. Much of Melville's reputation was until recently dominated by Thomas M'Crie's monumentally influential *Life of Andrew Melville*,[3] which although meticulously researched relied heavily on the near-hagiographical image of Melville found in seventeenth-century Presbyterian historical narratives written by the likes of James Melville (Andrew's nephew) and David Calderwood. However, recent historians have all been sceptical of the extent of Melville's role in the Kirk in the reign of James VI and I. Alan MacDonald has argued that the existence of a group of hard-line Presbyterian ministers, centred on Melville, is a myth, and that the line between Presbyterian 'Melvillians' and Royalist 'Episcopalians' was extremely fluid. He also argues that the first 11 years of the adult reign of James VI (1585–96) saw opposition to the wider royal religious policy arising not from concerns with Episcopalianism but rather with the young king's vacillating policies towards the Catholic earls of Huntly, Errol and Angus. James took decisive action against the Catholic earls between 1594 and 1596, and between 1596 and 1603 developed a Kirk polity which was acceptable to the majority of the ministry. This resulted in Melville and a small group of hard-line Presbyterian ministers being increasingly marginalised.[4] The work of David Mullan on the evolution of Episcopacy in the Kirk, developing the ideas of Gordon Donaldson, largely

---

[3]   Thomas M'Crie, *Life of Andrew Melville*, (2 vols, Edinburgh, 1819); re-issued in a revised and expanded version in 1824, and as a single volume edition in 1856. All references to M'Crie's work are to the single volume edition, unless otherwise indicated. The main contemporary accounts of Melville's life are James Melville, *The Autobiography and Diary of Mr James Melvill*, ed. R. Pitcairn (Edinburgh, 1842); David Calderwood, *History of the Kirk of Scotland by Mr David Calderwood*, ed. T. Thomson (8 vols, Edinburgh, 1842–49); John Row, *History of the Kirk of Scotland from the Year 1558 to August 1637*, ed. D. Laing (Edinburgh, 1842); William Scot, *An Apologetical Narration of the State and Government of the Kirk of Scotland since the Reformation*, ed. D. Laing (Edinburgh, 1846).

[4]   Alan MacDonald, *The Jacobean Kirk: Sovereignty, Polity and Liturgy, 1567–1625* (Aldershot, 1998), esp. pp. 31–4, 58–65, 171–80; Alan MacDonald 'James VI and the General Assembly', in Julian Goodare and Michael Lynch (eds), *The Reign of James VI* (East Linton, 2000), pp. 170–85.

corroborated this assessment,[5] and the majority of modern historians are agreed that Melville's role in the development of this church was at best as a leading *influence* and at worst inconsequential.[6]

However, only James Kirk, who strongly supported the idea of a 'Melvillian' party within the Kirk, has commented briefly on Melville's other role in Jacobean Scotland, that of developing and reforming the Scottish universities.[7] Melville revitalised the near-defunct Glasgow University between 1574 and 1580, and from 1580 to 1607 was principal of St Mary's College, St Andrews, Scotland's only divinity college. He was also rector of the University of St Andrews between 1590 and 1597 when the Presbyterian faction enjoyed its greatest favour at the Scottish court, and his ideas can be seen at work in the early curriculum at Edinburgh University and in the constitution of Marischal College. This study sets out to provide a detailed account of Melville's personal role in the reform and expansion of the Scottish universities. It evaluates the intellectual content of his reform programme as it developed during his time in Paris, Poitiers and Geneva; it analyses his direct work at Glasgow and especially St Andrews; and it assesses what impact his reforms had on the development of the universities elsewhere.

There is also a purely narrative justification for this study. No detailed account exists of the process by which the Scottish universities shed their Catholic heritage, and in the case of St Andrews there is only a basic understanding of developments at the university in the half century after the reformation.[8] St Andrews comprised three separate colleges in the late sixteenth and early seventeenth century – St Salvator's (founded 1450), St

---

[5] Gordon Donaldson, *Scotland: James V to James VII* (Edinburgh, 1965), pp. 198–207; David G. Mullan, *Episcopacy in Scotland* (Edinburgh, 1986), pp. 78–9.

[6] See, for example, Michael Lynch, *Scotland: A New History* (London, 1992 edn), p. 228; Jane E.A. Dawson, *Scotland Re-formed 1488–1587* (Edinburgh, 2007), pp. 223; Jenny Wormald, 'Confidence and Perplexity: The Seventeenth Century', in Jenny Wormald (ed.), *Scotland: A History* (Oxford, 2005), pp. 143–76, at p. 149; Roger Mason, 'George Buchanan, James VI and the Presbyterians', in Roger Mason, *Kingship and the Commonweal: Political Thought in Renaissance and Reformation Scotland* (East Linton, 1998), pp, 187–214, at pp. 198–9, 204–5.

[7] Durkan and Kirk, pp. 262–346; James Kirk, '"Melvillian" Reform in the Scottish Universities', in Alasdair A. MacDonald, Michael Lynch and Iain B. Cowan (eds), *The Renaissance in Scotland: Studies in Literature, Religion, History and Culture* (Leiden, 1994), pp. 272–300; James Kirk, 'The Development of the Melvillian Movement in Late Sixteenth Century Scotland', unpublished Edinburgh University PhD thesis (2 vols, 1972); James Kirk, 'John Knox and Andrew Melville: A Question of Identity?', *Scotia* 6 (1982): 14–22; *The Second Book of Discipline*, ed. J. Kirk (Edinburgh, 1980), esp. pp. 51–7.

[8] Cant, pp. 60–78; Ronald G. Cant, 'The New Foundation of 1579 in Historical Perspective', *St John's House Papers* 2 (1979); James K. Cameron, 'The Refoundation of the University in 1579', *St Andrews Alumnus Chronicle* 71 (1980): 3–10; James K. Cameron, 'St Mary's College 1547–1574 – the Second Foundation: The Principalship of John Douglas',

Leonard's (1512), and St Mary's (1525, and re-founded 1537/8 and 1555) – and the total number of students at St Andrews in any given year between 1560 and 1625 outnumbered the total number of students combined at the other Scottish institutions.[9] Melville also spent a little over 26 of the 32 years of his career as an educator in Scotland at St Andrews. Consequently, any discussion of Melville's reform of Scottish higher education must place St Andrews at the centre, and a new and detailed narrative is required to do this, which occupies several chapters in this book. This narrative draws on the printed sources for the post-reformation period, including the Acts of the Faculty of Arts up to 1588, the post-reformation re-ordering of the statutes of the arts and theology faculties between 1560 and 1570, and the university's matriculation and graduation records, along with a selection of the key early charters and records of the university published for the wide-ranging Royal Commission to the Universities in the early nineteenth century.[10] In the main though, it is taken directly from manuscript material, including the Acta Rectorum (the statutes produced by the rector and his court of assessors on a range of disciplinary and legal matters), and the extensive collections of records for each of the university's colleges held in the university archives. Particularly important to this study are a collection of St Andrews visitation records for the period 1574–6 held in the National Archives of Scotland, and volumes seven and eight of the Balcarres Papers in the National Library of Scotland, which contain over 200 folio pages of material relating to the post-reformation university, particularly in relation to the 1588 and 1597 royal visitations.[11] These sources are richer and more informative than anything extant for any other university in the period, and contain detailed depositions by the masters (often against one another) which vividly recreate the internal turmoil and schism caused by Melville's programme and presence.

Unlike St Andrews, King's College, Marischal College and Glasgow University each benefit from comprehensive printed collections of their early modern records, including their statutes and laws, foundation and endowment charters, matriculation and graduation records, and biographical sketches of notable staff and students.[12] Edinburgh has similar collections for its charters, statutes and early graduation records,

---

and 'Andrew Melville in St Andrews', in D.W.D. Shaw (ed.), *In Divers Manners: A St Mary's Miscellany* (St Andrews, 1990) pp. 43–73.

[9]   See Appendix.

[10] *Acta*; Hannay, *Statutes*; *Early Records*; *Evidence*.

[11] National Library of Scotland Advocates MS 29.27.7.

[12] *Fasti Aberdonenses*; *FMA*; *Munimenta*; Peter J. Anderson (ed.), *Officers and Graduates of University and King's College, Aberdeen* (Aberdeen, 1893); *Roll of Alumni in Arts of University and King's College of Aberdeen, 1596–1860*, ed. P.J. Anderson (Aberdeen, 1900).

and has a number of printed narrative accounts of its institutional history.[13] Several recent studies produced from these sources have clarified our understanding of Melville's involvement outside of the universities where he was personally active. James Kirk, in the history of Glasgow University from its foundation up to 1577 he co-authored with John Durkan, provided a detailed study of Melville's work as principal there between 1574 and 1580.[14] A survey of King's College, Aberdeen between 1560 and 1641 by David Stevenson[15] concluded that, although Melville's curricular reforms were adopted in a planned re-foundation of the college in 1582/83, they were never implemented to any great extent. A number of short articles by Michael Lynch on the foundation and early development of Edinburgh University have argued that it had very little 'Melvillian' influence, and was in fact a 'toun [town] college' erected to provide cheap and effective education for the sons of the local citizenry, wholly controlled by the town council.[16] The narratives for King's and Edinburgh by Lynch and Stevenson are broadly accepted here, owing to the systematic study by each author of what is in both cases a very fragmentary body of evidence. Augmenting these narratives, however, is detailed research into the foundation and early development of Marischal College and of the developments at Glasgow, as far as they can be traced, in the decades following Melville's departure from the university. Completing this overview is a systematic study of the teaching sources surviving for each university to provide as full an account of intellectual life in the 'Melvillian' period as can be reconstructed, and a focus on the role that civic, royal and ecclesiastical authorities played in their development.

---

[13]   *University of Edinburgh Charters, Statutes, and Acts of the Town Council and Senatus 1583–1858*, ed. A. Morgan (Edinburgh, 1937); *A Catalogue of the Graduates in the Faculties of Arts, Divinity, and Law, of the University of Edinburgh, since its Foundation*, ed. D. Laing (Edinburgh, 1858); Alexander Bower, *The History of the University of Edinburgh* (3 vols, Edinburgh, 1817–30); Thomas Craufurd, *History of the University of Edinburgh from 1580 to 1646* (Edinburgh, 1808). Craufurd, writing in the seventeenth century, is particularly useful as a contemporary eyewitness. *History of the University of Edinburgh from its Foundation*, ed. D. Laing; with a memoir of the author by Cosmo Innes (2 vols, Edinburgh, 1862); Alexander Grant, *The Story of the University of Edinburgh During its First Three Hundred Years* (2 vols, London, 1884); David B. Horn, *A Short History of the University of Edinburgh, 1556–1889* (Edinburgh, 1967).

[14]   See note 7.

[15]   David Stevenson, *King's College, Aberdeen, 1560–1641: From Protestant Reformation to Covenanting Revolution* (Aberdeen, 1990), esp. pp. 20–60.

[16]   Michael Lynch, 'The Origins of Edinburgh's "Toun College": A Revision Article', *IR* 33 (1982): 3–14; Lynch, 'The Creation of a College', in Robert D. Anderson, Michael Lynch and Nicholas Phillipson, *The University of Edinburgh: An Illustrated History* (Edinburgh, 2003), pp. 1–49, esp. pp. 9–18; Steven John Reid, 'Aberdeen's "Toun College": Marischal College, 1593–1623', *IR* 58.2 (2007): 173–95.

By looking in-depth at Melville's programme we are able to locate post-reformation Scottish education more securely in the Continental reformed context in which it should be seen. In the fifty years since John Durkan published his seminal article 'The Beginnings of Humanism in Scotland',[17] considerable work has been done in tracing the flowering of humanist culture in Scotland and its impact on Scotland's royal court, its nobles, and its leading thinkers and statesmen.[18] But while the European understanding of both late medieval scholasticism and Renaissance humanism has grown considerably over the past few decades, particularly in terms of their interaction after the reformation, this has not been fully reflected in Scottish scholarship. Individual studies of the new reformed educational institutions of northern Europe, and general studies of early modern European education, have revised our understanding of the curriculum and of the role of the works of Aristotle within it.[19] Studies of the development of logic and rhetoric in the sixteenth century in particular indicate that, despite developments at the hands of educational reformers including Rudolph Agricola, Juan Luis Vives, Philip Melanchthon and Petrus Ramus, there was nevertheless a fundamental continuation of the scholastic and Aristotelian intellectual

[17]   *IR* 4.1 (1953): 4–24.

[18]   See, for example, Barbara E. Crawford (ed.), *Church, Chronicle and Learning in Medieval and Early Renaissance Scotland* (Edinburgh, 1999); John MacQueen (ed.), *Humanism in Renaissance Scotland* (Edinburgh, 1999); Sally L. Mapstone and Juliette Wood (eds), *The Rose and the Thistle: Essays on the Culture of Late Medieval and Renaissance Scotland* (East Linton, 1998); L.A.J.R. Houwen, Alasdair A. MacDonald and Sally L. Mapstone (eds), *A Palace in the Wild: Essays on Vernacular Culture and Humanism in Late-Medieval and Renaissance Scotland* (Leuven, 2000); Mason, *Kingship and the Commonweal*; Andrea Thomas, *Princelie Majestie: The Court of James V of Scotland, 1528–1542* (Edinburgh, 2005); Katie Stevenson, *Chivalry and Knighthood in Scotland, 1424–1513* (Woodbridge, 2006).

[19]   Amy Nelson Burnett, *Teaching the Reformation: Ministers and their Message in Basel, 1529–1629* (Oxford, 2006); James M. Fletcher, 'Change and Resistance to Change: A Consideration of the Development of English and German Universities during the Sixteenth Century', *History of Universities* 1 (1981): 1–36; Lewis, 'The Geneva Academy', pp. 35–63; Karin Maag, *Seminary or University? The Genevan Academy and Reformed Higher Education, 1560–1620* (Aldershot, 1995); Charlotte Methuen, 'The Teaching of Aristotle in Late Sixteenth-Century Tübingen', in Constance Blackwell and Sachiko Kusukawa (eds), *Philosophy in the Sixteenth and Seventeenth Centuries: Conversations with Aristotle* (Aldershot, 1999), pp. 189–205; Helga Notker-Hammerstein, 'The University of Heidelberg in the Early Modern Period: Aspects of its History as a Contribution to its Sexcentennary', *History of Universities* 6 (1986): 105–33; Helga Robinson-Hammerstein (ed.), *European Universities in the Age of Reformation and Counter Reformation* (Dublin, 1998); Anthony Grafton and Lisa Jardine, *From Humanism to the Humanities: Education and the Liberal Arts in Fifteenth- and Sixteenth-Century Europe* (London, 1986); Hilde de Ridder-Symoens (ed.), *A History of the University in Europe, volume II: Universities in Early Modern Europe (1500–1800)* (Cambridge, 1996).

heritage.[20] As Erika Rummell noted succinctly in her discussion of the shifting paradigms and patterns of the humanist and scholastic debate:

> Our examination of the humanistic approach to dialectic reveals a number of common characteristics: a critical attitude toward Aristotelian doctrine; rejection of medieval technical terminology; a shift from formal to informal modes of inference; and a concern for the practical applicability of dialectical skills. Humanist criticism of traditional dialectic did not, however, issue in significant new constructs.[21]

At the end of the sixteenth century the works of Aristotle, though presented in the original Greek rather than Latin and freed from the constraints of the medieval commentators, still provided the underpinning of university curricula. More importantly, Aristotle's logical terminology and methodology provided the common ground and tools for learned debate across Europe, especially in theology. Catholic theology, reacting against the early reformers and coalescing around the debates of Trent, never truly relinquished its Aristotelian heritage.[22] Initially there was a strong reaction against Aristotle amongst reformed theologians, particularly towards his metaphysical teachings which were abhorred for their overly speculative tendencies and their attempt 'to construct a rational science of God'.[23] By the end of the sixteenth century, however, Beza and other leading reformers had re-embraced Aristotelianism and metaphysics had begun to reappear in Protestant education, heralding the great age of a systematic Protestant theology in the seventeenth century.[24]

---

[20]   Lisa Jardine, 'Inventing Rudolph Agricola: Cultural Transmission, Renaissance Dialectic, and the Emerging Humanities', in Anthony Grafton and Ann Blair (eds), *The Transmission of Culture in Early Modern Europe* (Philadelphia, 1990), pp. 39–86; Lisa Jardine, 'Humanistic Logic', in Charles B. Schmitt and Quentin Skinner (eds), *The Cambridge History of Renaissance Philosophy* (Cambridge, 1988), pp. 173–98; Peter Mack, *Renaissance Argument: Valla and Agricola in the Traditions of Rhetoric and Dialectic* (Leiden, 1993); Charles B. Schmitt, 'Philosophy and Science in Sixteenth-Century Universities: Some Preliminary Comments', in John E. Murdoch and Edith D. Sylla (eds), *The Cultural Context of Medieval Learning* (Dordrecht-Boston, 1975), pp. 485–530, esp. at pp. 489–495; Charles B. Schmitt, 'Towards a Reassessment of Renaissance Aristotelianism', *History of Science* 11 (1973): 159–93.

[21]   Erika Rummell, *The Humanist–Scholastic Debate in the Renaissance and Reformation* (Cambridge, Mass., 1995), p. 189.

[22]   Wilhelm Schmidt-Biggemann, 'New Structures of Knowledge', in *A History of the University in Europe* vol. 2, pp. 489–530, esp. pp. 489–95, 503–7.

[23]   Burnett, *Teaching the Reformation*, pp. 116–17; Laurence Brockliss, 'Curricula', in *A History of the University in Europe* vol. 2, pp. 578–9.

[24]   Schmitt, 'Philosophy and Science in Sixteenth-Century Universities', 491–3; Charles H. Lohr, 'Metaphysics and Natural Philosophy as Sciences: The Catholic and the

However, in discussions of Scottish reformed education, there is still a conception that humanism was a radical intellectual force that obliterated a backward-looking, conservative scholasticism, and that there was nothing of merit in the latter and nothing but merit in the former. This is particularly the case in the most recent assessments of both Melville's reform programme, and the role of the works and ideas of Petrus Ramus within it. James Kirk and Hugh Kearney both used phrases such as 'anti-Aristotelian' and 'anti-scholastic' to describe Melville's reform programme, and portrayed Ramism as an ideological tool used by Melville to recruit young students to radical Presbyterianism.[25] It is certainly true that Melville brought Ramism and intellectual innovation to the methodology underpinning the Scottish university reforms, but his motivations for doing so are more complex than is generally appreciated. Chapter 2 shows that his own intellectual training in Scotland and across France and Geneva gave rise to a reform programme that syncretised a broad range of the latest developments in European humanist studies but retained Aristotelian training at its core. This broad and dynamic approach is clear in the constitutions that he developed for the universities of Glasgow and St Andrews and likely helped produce for Aberdeen, discussed in chapter 3. There was no particular intellectual bias towards Ramism in this programme, save that Melville used Ramus' universal 'method' as a pedagogical tool to disseminate teaching quickly and effectively across all levels of the arts and divinity course to students in educational settings where he had limited support and resources. The organisational clarity of the Ramist 'method' was especially crucial to furthering Melville's aim of producing an articulate and able Protestant ministry who could effectively preach and expound reformed doctrine, and the use of Ramism is clearly at work in the teaching materials and lecture notes produced under Melville at St Andrews, discussed in chapter 6. While the sum total of extant material for Melville's theological teaching comprises just seven sets of theological disputations defended between 1595 and 1602 and a set of lecture notes on Romans from 1601, there is a clear blend in these texts of Ramism and Aristotelianism, working together to give divinity students a firm and logical grounding in the articulation of doctrine. This was supported in St Andrews by an extensive and rigorous system of doctrinal exposition

---

Protestant Views in the Sixteenth and Seventeenth Centuries', in *Philosophy in the Sixteenth and Seventeenth Centuries*, pp. 280–95; Richard A. Muller, *After Calvin: Studies in the Development of a Theological Tradition* (New York, 2002); Carl R. Trueman and R. Scott Clark (eds), *Protestant Scholasticism: Essays in Reassessment* (Carlisle, 1999); Brian G. Armstrong, *Calvinism and the Amyraut Heresy: Protestant Scholasticism and Humanism in Seventeenth-Century France* (Madison and London, 1969).

[25]   Hugh Kearney, *Scholars and Gentlemen: Universities and Society in Pre-Industrial Britain, 1500–1700* (London, 1970), esp. chapter 3, pp. 46–70: '"Melvillian" Reform'.

and preaching within the local presbytery, and in particular was geared towards training students to combat the spectre of Catholic dogma.

However, Melville's use of Ramism as a pedagogical tool was not universally accepted, and the surviving evidence of the intellectual reception of Melville's programme elsewhere in St Andrews and at Edinburgh and Aberdeen, discussed at length in chapters 4–8, shows how resistant masters were to his new approach. Although the surviving body of evidence for arts teaching in this period is small, it clearly shows that although the masters across the Scottish universities did flirt briefly with Ramus' ideas, they retained a near-monolithic focus on Aristotle, albeit with clear evidence of Renaissance ideas on rhetoric and oratory incorporated into this teaching, and a commitment to Greek teaching alongside Latin.

In the same way that a growing sophistication has characterised our understanding of the interaction between old and new modes of thought at the early modern universities, our understanding of the role of religion in these institutions has grown. Recent studies of Oxford and Cambridge have shown that behind a united front of 'anti-Romanism' a diverse range of theological opinion was accommodated, particularly in the nuances of reformed doctrine and polity.[26] New reformed academies like Leiden and Heidelberg also suffered from shifting confessional identities, in the latter due to the confessional predilection of the reigning prince and in the former due to the predominance of lay interests over education in the university.[27] Kirk plays down the importance, for want of better terms, of 'royal' or 'Episcopalian' influences in the Scottish universities, but a similar mix of shifting confessional affiliations is apparent at Glasgow and St Andrews in the 'Melvillian' period. Chapter 1 shows how even two decades after the official adoption of Scottish Protestantism elements of Catholic recusancy still existed at both Aberdeen and in St Mary's, alongside moderate attempts at change. In this vein, the role of bishops as royal agents at Glasgow and St Andrews in the 'Melvillian' period is another under-researched area. Following his elevation to the archbishopric of St Andrews in 1576, Patrick Adamson engaged in heated and bitter conflict with Melville and the Presbyterian party. However, it seems likely, as Alan MacDonald has suggested, that he had a considerable hand in helping Melville consolidate

---

[26]   Mark H. Curtis, *Oxford and Cambridge in Transition, 1558–1642* (Oxford, 1959); David Hoyle, *Reformation and Religious Identity in Cambridge 1590–1644* (Woodbridge, 2007); S.L. Greenslade, 'The Faculty of Theology', and Jennifer Loach, 'Reformation Controversies', in James McConica (ed.), *The History of the University of Oxford, volume 3: The Collegiate University* (Oxford, 1986), pp. 295–334, 363–96.

[27]   Notker-Hammerstein, 'The University of Heidelberg', pp. 105–33; J.J. Woltjer, 'Introduction', in Th. H. Lunsingh Scheurleer, G.H.M. Posthumus Meyjes and others, *Leiden University in the Seventeenth Century: An Exchange of Learning* (Leiden, 1975), pp. 1–7.

the financial settlement at Glasgow.[28] Furthermore, as archbishop of St Andrews he was not only *ex officio* chancellor of the university but was also installed as a theology lecturer there during Melville's exile between 1584 and 1586. The conflicts he had with Melville in this decade, outlined in chapter 4, dominated university politics and hampered any real progress in the reform of divinity studies at St Mary's.[29]

Research into the intellectual and religious allegiances of the majority of other masters and regents at the universities in the 'Melvillian' period has been minimal, and what little has been done has shown a considerable divergence of opinion between teaching staff.[30] This is seen in the example of John Johnston and Robert Howie, two scholars who, though fellow students at Aberdeen and at a number of Continental universities, returned to university careers in Scotland in the 1590s on completely opposite ends of the Presbyterian–Episcopalian spectrum.[31] It is perhaps best reflected in the person of James Martine, a previously obscure name in the history of St Andrews who figures prominently in what follows. As provost of St Salvator's between 1577 and 1620 Martine pursued a career at the college centred upon familial nepotism and self-aggrandisement through Royalist and Episcopal support. Martine survived and thrived in what has always been seen as a radical Presbyterian environment, eventually outlasting Melville and his educational reforms. Moreover, Martine's fortunes rose in direct opposition to his Presbyterian colleague in St Salvator's, the law professor William Welwood. The story of the protracted dispute between them involves not just their religious affiliations but also their allegiances to opposed kin networks in the town and their own professional grievances within the university.[32] It is this blend of religious, social and personal factors that shows how complex university politics were at St Andrews in the post-reformation period, and paints a very different picture from that of a 'Melvillian' and Presbyterian supremacy.

Studies of both Oxford and Cambridge have shown the rise of a 'Tudor interventionist policy' in both institutions in the sixteenth century, binding them ever closer to crown interests. Cambridge was reformed via letters patent in 1561, new statutes in 1570, and an act of Parliament in 1571. These measures greatly increased the power of the *caput senatus* and the

---

[28]   Alan MacDonald, 'Best of Enemies: Andrew Melville and Patrick Adamson c. 1574–1592', in Julian Goodare and Alasdair A. MacDonald (eds), *Sixteenth-Century Scotland: Essays in Honour of Michael Lynch* (Leiden and Boston, 2008), pp. 257–76, at pp. 260–6.

[29]   M'Crie, pp. 123–7.

[30]   Kirk, 'The Development of the Melvillian Movement', vol. 2, p. 371.

[31]   Cameron, *Letters*, pp. xiv–lxxx.

[32]   John Cairns, 'Academic Feud, Bloodfeud, and William Welwood: Legal Education in St Andrews, 1560–1611', *Edinburgh Law Review* 2 (1998): 158–79, 255–87.

heads of colleges, who were directly answerable to royal government, against the more democratic diffusion of power and decision-making that had existed previously among the wider body of teaching regents.[33] While Oxford was not fully reformed until the 'Laudian' statutes of 1634, considerable attempts were made to restrict power there along similar lines in the 1560s during the Earl of Leicester's chancellorship, including the relegation of university business to a committee of the vice-chancellor, doctors, heads of houses and proctors.[34] Recent studies of Scottish state formation in the early modern period have discerned the development of an embryonic Stewart absolutism and a centralised Scottish bureaucracy,[35] and these findings are to some extent mirrored in the rise of greater crown interference in the Scottish universities. In this respect, the importance of royal commissions of visitation in shaping the Protestant educational settlement across Scotland is discussed here at length. Commissions of visitation were occasionally sponsored by the General Assembly but were mainly ordered by Act of Privy Council or Parliament on an *ad hoc* basis to enact major reform at the universities or to correct (and in some cases punish) when standards of education or behaviour were deemed to have fallen too far. The first commission was organised by Parliament to St Andrews in 1563,[36] and almost twenty others, to one or more of the universities, followed in the period discussed here. These commissions were often decisive in shaping policy at the universities. For example, as chapter 1 shows, a commission to Aberdeen in 1569 purged the university of Catholic staff who had refused to leave in 1560, and replaced them with moderate men who could smooth the disruption to distressed students.[37] Likewise, many new operating statutes were introduced to St Andrews by the commissions of 1574 and 1576, and the 'New Foundation' of the university in November 1579 was notably achieved by Act of Parliament. An increasingly critical tone can be seen in the 1588 visitation commission to the university, and a decade later the commission's jurisdictional power had grown to such an extent that they were able to remove Andrew Melville from his role as rector with no complaint and to alter radically

---

[33] Victor Morgan, 'The Constitutional Revolution of the 1570s' and 'Cambridge University and the State', in Victor Morgan and Christopher Brooke, *A History of the University of Cambridge, volume 2: 1546–1750* (Cambridge, 2004), pp. 63–146.

[34] Penry Williams, 'Elizabethan Oxford: State, Church and University', in McConica, *History of the University of Oxford 3*, pp. 397–440.

[35] Julian Goodare, *State and Society in Early Modern Scotland* (Oxford, 1999); Julian Goodare, *The Government of Scotland, 1590–1625* (Oxford, 2004).

[36] *RPS* A1563/6/26 [accessed 4 April 2010].

[37] W.S. Watt, 'George Hay's Oration at the Purging of King's College, Aberdeen, in 1569: a Translation', *Northern Scotland* 6 (1984–85): 91–6, and commentary by John Durkan, ibid.: 97–112, at p. 97.

the supervisory relationship between central government and university in the process. Outside St Andrews, royal commissions helped establish new university foundations at Edinburgh and Marischal College, and competition for control of Glasgow at the turn of the century between the university masters and the town council was also adjudicated by the royal government. Finally, it was royal intervention in the closing years of James VI and I's reign that saw St Andrews become more closely aligned with the educational and ceremonial practices at Oxford and Cambridge, and the traditional collegiate foundations at both St Andrews and Aberdeen reasserted as a result.

In addition to reassessing Melville's reforms of the Scottish universities in general, and St Andrews in particular, the appendix to this study will hopefully lay some foundations for a wider study of the student body across the universities in the post-reformation period. Thanks to the work of Robert Smart we now have a detailed biographical register of the student body at St Andrews between 1579 and 1747, which reveals that over 3,600 students passed through the gates of the university in the period covered by this study. The key data relating to these students – the courses they took, their length of study, and how many of them there were in any given year – are tabulated in the appendix, and compared against similar evidence, where available, for students at the other universities. Some high-level commentary on the student populace is provided on this evidence in the following discussion, but it is beyond the scope of this book to undertake a full analysis of the range of demographic trends among students, or their careers post-university. However, a recent and penetrating study of the graduate population among the ministry in post-reformation Fife has shown how much can be learned from undertaking such an analysis,[38] and the materials for charting the evolution of the broader university population from reformation to enlightenment are now more accessible than they have ever been, and are clearly deserving of further research.

Finally, what follows will hopefully go some way towards reassessing Melville himself. There has been a considerable resurgence in research into Melville's life in the recent past, particularly in studies of Melville's surviving neo-Latin poetry and what it reveals about his intellectual outlook.[39] However, a complete re-evaluation of his life must wait until

---

[38]   John McCallum, *Reforming the Scottish Parish: The Reformation in Fife, 1560–1640* (Aldershot, 2010), pp. 121–51, esp. pp. 134–45.

[39]   James Doelman, 'King James, Andrew Melville, and the Neo-Latin Religious Epigram', chapter 4 of his *King James I and the Religious Culture of England* (Cambridge, 2000), pp. 57–72; Steven John Reid, 'Early Polemic by Andrew Melville: *The Carmen Mosis* (1574) and the St Bartholomew's Day Massacre', *Renaissance et Réforme* 30.4 (2006/07): 63–82; Steven John Reid, 'Andrew Melville, Sacred Chronology and World History: the

his considerable corpus of surviving poetry and correspondence has been translated and analysed, and a full re-assessment has been undertaken of his involvement in both the Scottish and English Presbyterian movements. Until then, perhaps the most important aim of this study is to show that there was another dimension to Melville beyond the purely religious one – as an educator and teacher of some standing, whose university reform programme attempted to transform early modern Scottish intellectual culture.

Carmina Danielis 9 and the *Antichristus*', *IR* 60.1 (2009): 1–21; Ernest R. Holloway, 'Andrew Melville and Humanism in the Reign of James VI' (unpublished University of Aberdeen PhD thesis, 2009). Translations of some of Melville's key poems, and commentary on them, can be found in *The British Union: a Critical Edition and Translation of David Hume of Godscroft's* De Unione Insulae Britannicae, ed. P.J. McGinnis and A. Williamson (Aldershot, 2002), pp. 9–19, 136–9; and in *The Political Poetry of George Buchanan*, ed. P.J. McGinnis and A. Williamson (Edinburgh, 1995), 276–82.

CHAPTER 1

Between Reformation and Reform: The Scottish Universities, 1560–1574

The intellectual forces of humanism and Protestantism had a very limited impact on the Scottish universities prior to 1560, and the two decades following the reformation were precarious and unsettling times for what were at heart three very medieval and Catholic institutions. Cut off at a stroke from the papal authority that had created them, they not only had to re-orient their teaching and curriculum towards the new Protestant status quo, but had to find a new identity for themselves.

They had only partial success in achieving this. Aberdeen remained largely Catholic and Glasgow almost ceased to exist. St Andrews managed some measure of reform, and what was achieved was down largely to the work of university staff, with occasional help (and sometimes interference) from the civil government and minimal involvement from the General Assembly, the governing body of the new Protestant Kirk.

At all three, however, the overriding impression is one of paralysis followed by stasis. All the universities were unwilling or unable to shed overnight the legacy of their medieval and scholastic past, and the vast majority of their pre-reformation academic framework (particularly at St Andrews) was retained wholesale or modified with the minimum of effort. Looking collectively at the picture of Scottish higher education in the immediate aftermath of the reformation, it is clear that the process of university reform only gained real momentum with the arrival of Andrew Melville in Glasgow in 1574. However, one trend that does emerge in this turbulent period, and which would dominate events at the universities for the following half century, was the involvement of both national and civic government in the earliest attempts at Protestant reform. An attempt to revitalise Glasgow under the aegis of the town council in 1573, though abortive, would be a prescient model for similar attempts by town councils in Edinburgh and Aberdeen to provide their citizens with a Protestant 'arts college', where they could ensure their children received a decent and 'godly' education; and the limited progress and development at Aberdeen and St Andrews, despite a range of competing social, political and religious tensions within both universities, owed much to the interference of the royal government in their affairs.

The Scottish Universities, c. 1410–1560

By 1560 there were three universities in Scotland, and all three owed their existence to the Catholic Church. Each founded by bishops, they were all members of the elite class of institution known as *studium generale*, authorised by papal bull to teach arts and the higher faculties of theology, law and medicine, to examine students for masters or doctoral degrees, and for their chancellor (*ex officio* the bishop or archbishop of the diocese) to confer the *licentia ubique docendi*, the universally recognised qualification allowing a graduate to teach at any other university in Europe. The University of Glasgow was established by a papal bull of Nicholas V on 7 January 1451, and although its founder, Bishop William Turnbull, had placed an especial focus at its outset on the teaching of canon and civil law, within a year of its foundation the university also included a range of masters and students in theology and arts.[1] In 1495 papal approval was given to Bishop William Elphinstone to erect a university possessing the full range of faculties in the 'physical remoteness' of Aberdeen. The foundation charter of King's College (as the collegiate foundation at the core of the university was known), drawn up on 17 September 1505 and supported by a broad range of endowments and annexed parishes, provided for 36 staff and students. These included a principal and sub-principal who would teach theology and philosophy respectively, dedicated teachers in canon law, civil law, medicine and grammar, 18 bursars in theology and arts, and 12 priests and choirboys.[2] The oldest Scottish university, St Andrews, began life when a small group of graduates, mostly from Paris and without a fixed residence in the city, started teaching in early 1410. By February 1412, this peripatetic group had grown to such an extent that Bishop Henry Wardlaw was willing to grant them legal privileges and exemption from taxation in a charter of incorporation, and the university was formally ratified by Pope Benedict XIII in a series of six papal bulls in August 1413.[3]

By 1560 St Andrews had, unlike Glasgow and Aberdeen, developed from a single pedagogy into a federation of three distinct colleges (each almost as large as the foundations elsewhere) administered as a single university. The first of these, a centre for theology and arts dedicated to the Holy Saviour, or St Salvator, was founded by Bishop James Kennedy

---

[1]   Durkan and Kirk, pp. 3–20, esp. 12–16; pp. 127–8.

[2]   Leslie J. MacFarlane, *William Elphinstone and the Kingdom of Scotland 1431–1514: The Struggle for Order* (Aberdeen, 1985), pp. 290–402, at p. 347. The foundation was revised and augmented in August 1514 to include a further 2 theology students, one in canon law, two in civil law, and a further two choirboys, bringing the staff complement to 42.

[3]   Cant, pp. 3–7.

in 1450. Kennedy's foundation was an attempt to provide fresh impetus to studies in the university on a new site away from the original foundation in the south quarter of the medieval city, where squabbles over precedence and privileges, inherent resistance to change on the part of the masters, and inadequate endowment made the idea of reforming it unpalatable. The corporate structure of St Salvator's – symbolically mirroring Christ and the twelve apostles – comprised three masters in holy orders who were to be a master, licentiate and bachelor in theology respectively, four masters of arts studying towards their theology degrees, and six poor scholars who would serve as choristers in the ornately gothic collegiate church that Kennedy created as part of his foundation.[4]

On 20 August 1512 Archbishop Alexander Stewart and the prior of the Augustinians in St Andrews, James Hepburn, erected the hospital and church of St Leonard, with funds from a number of lands belonging to the priory, into a further university college, to be known officially as the 'College of Poor Clerks of the Church of St Andrews'. Better known as the College of St Leonard, it comprised a principal and theologian, four chaplains (two of whom were regents in arts), and 26 poor students in arts and theology, and was founded with the express aim of better educating novices of the local Augustinian order.[5] However, by the early 1520s the works of the 'heretik Luthere and his discipillis', outlawed in Scotland by Act of Parliament on 17 July 1525, were circulating and being widely debated at the college.[6] John Knox noted that St Leonard's was central to the early dissemination of Protestant doctrine in the city and that several of the staff and students, along with a number of the 'novices' of the abbey, were persecuted as heretics by Archbishop James Beaton in the 1520 and 1530s.[7] The most famous of these was Patrick Hamilton, who had come back to St Andrews after a brief spell at Philip of Hesse's newly-established university at Marburg in 1527 espousing a number of Lutheran beliefs, and was burnt outside the gates of St Salvator's College on 29 February 1528.[8] However, Hamilton's fellow student Henry Forrest, tried and executed by

---

[4]   Cant, pp. 26–33; Ronald G. Cant, *The College of St Salvator: Its Foundation and Development* (Edinburgh, 1950), pp. 1–80.

[5]   John Herkless and Robert K. Hannay, *The College of St Leonard* (Edinburgh, 1905); *Acta*, pp. xliii–l; Cant, pp. 34–41.

[6]   *RPS* 1525/7/32 [accessed 30 March 2010].

[7]   *John Knox's History of the Reformation in Scotland*, ed. W. Croft Dickinson (2 vols, London, 1949), vol. 1, p. 15.

[8]   Iain Torrance, 'Hamilton, Patrick (1504?–1528)', *ODNB* [12116, accessed 30 March 2010].

Beaton in October 1533, had also studied at St Leonard's, entering the college in 1526.[9]

The final college established at St Andrews before 1560 was the 'College of St Mary of the Assumption' or St Mary's. Established in rather piecemeal fashion between 1525 and 1555, the first stage in its foundation took place under Archbishop James Beaton between 1525 and 1538 and was sited on the remains of the original university buildings.[10] Founded for the 'instruction of our lieges in the Catholic faith, the opposing of heresy ... [and the] instruction of able men in culture, science and policy within our realm', Beaton aimed to counter the heresy he saw within Scotland with a college that would act as a vehicle for Catholic reform.[11] The plans for his foundation were heavily influenced by his nephew, the Parisian-trained humanist Archibald Hay, who argued in his *Oratio Pro Collegii Erectione* (1538) and in his *Panegyricus* (1540) to Beaton's nephew and successor Cardinal David Beaton that the college should incorporate the humanist subjects of poetry, rhetoric and history into the curriculum at the college, as well as the works of Cicero and Plato alongside those of Aristotle.[12] Most importantly, Hay argued that the college should follow the example of a growing range of foundations on the Continent, including the University of Alcala founded around 1500 and the *College des Lecteurs Royaux* founded by Francis I in Paris in 1530, which placed a central emphasis on training students in classical Latin and in the original source languages of the Bible – Hebrew, Aramaic, Chaldaic and Greek – so that Christian humanists could better engage with the source text of their faith.[13]

The plans for St Mary's stalled following the murder of Cardinal Beaton at the hands of Protestant reformers in 1546, but the college was

---

[9]   John Herkless and Robert K. Hannay, *The Archbishops of St Andrews* (5 vols, Edinburgh, 1907–15), vol. 3, pp. 204–6; James Cameron, 'Aspects of the Lutheran Contribution to the Scottish Reformation 1528–1552', *Records of the Scottish Church History Society* 22 (1984): 1–12; James Kirk, 'Forrest, Henry (d. 1533?)', *ODNB* [9887, accessed 26 March 2010]. T.S. Freeman, '"The reik of Maister Patrik Hammyltoun": John Foxe, John Winram, and the Martyrs of the Scottish Reformation', *Sixteenth Century Journal* 27 (1996): 43–60.

[10]   James K. Cameron, 'A Trilingual College for Scotland: The Founding of St Mary's College', in Shaw (ed.), *In Divers Manners*, pp. 29–42.

[11]   UYSMB1/P2/14 (translation by Dr Robert Smart).

[12]   Archibald Hay, *Ad ... D. Jacobum Betoun ... pro collegii erectione ... oratio* (Paris, 1538); Archibald Hay, *Ad ... D. Davidem Betoun ... de foelici accessione dignitatis cardinalitiae, gratulatorius panegyricus* (Paris, 1540).

[13]   P.S. Allen, *Erasmus: Lectures and Wayfaring Sketches* (Oxford, 1934), pp. 140–5. Brockliss, 'Curricula', pp. 571–2; Cameron, 'Trilingual College', pp. 31, 34–9; Euan Cameron, 'Archibald Hay's *Elegantiae*: Writings of a Scots Humanist at the College de Montaigu in the Time of Bude and Beda', in J-C. Margolin (ed.), *Acta Conventus Neo-Latini Turonensis* (Paris, 1980), pp. 277–301.

re-founded by Archbishop John Hamilton between February 1554 and February 1555 on a much larger scale with a complement of 36 staff and students.[14] Hamilton's re-foundation of St Mary's was part of a wider series of initiatives for Catholic reform that he implemented in Scotland between 1549 and 1559, including a series of reforming provincial councils enforcing new standards in clerical behaviour and education in line with the decrees of the Council of Trent, and the publication of a vernacular catechism in August 1552 that tried to appeal to both Catholics and moderate evangelicals in tone and content.[15] Hamilton's re-foundation proposed three theologians and three philosophy professors with a canon lawyer at its core, alongside a grammarian, rhetorician and several ancillary staff, and although it made no mention of the 'trilingual' foundation proposed by Hay, it did closely follow the plan for a school of divinity at Bonn laid down by another proponent of Catholic church reform, the Archbishop of Cologne Hermann von Wied.[16] With the different strands of his reform programme, Hamilton aimed to produce qualified, literate preachers who could strengthen the Scottish Catholic Church while appealing to as broad a base of moderate reformers as possible. Unfortunately, St Mary's was still in largely embryonic state when the reformation gained momentum in Scotland and overtook all of Hamilton's attempts at reform, including the teaching programme at the college.

Beyond the programme of Catholic reform envisaged at St Mary's and the evidence of evangelical fervour at St Leonard's, the penetration of humanism and Protestantism into the pre-reformation Scottish universities was limited. The core arts courses at both St Andrews as laid down in the minutes of the Faculty of Arts on 12 May 1419 and in the statutes drawn up for Glasgow on 28 July 1452 are almost identical in every respect and based on that of Paris, where Aristotle, in Latin translation and supported by a range of medieval scholastic commentators, formed the basis of teaching at every level.[17] This curriculum was especially daunting given that the age of the typical entrant was around 13, although *bejans* (as first years were known) slightly older than this and as young as 11

---

[14]   James K. Cameron, 'St Mary's College 1547–1574 – The Second Foundation: The Principalship of John Douglas', in Shaw (ed.), *In Divers Manners*, pp. 43–57.

[15]   Alec Ryrie, 'Reform without Frontiers in the Last Years of Catholic Scotland', *English Historical Review* 119 (2004): 27–56; Thomas Winning, 'Church Councils in Sixteenth-Century Scotland', *IR* 10 (1959): 311–37.

[16]   *Evidence*, pp. 362–6; Hermann von Wied, *A Simple, and religious consultation of us Herman by the grace of God archbishop of Colone ... by what meanes a Christian reformation ... may be began* (London, 1548), fos cclxvi–cclxxi.

[17]   *Acta*, pp. lxxxi–lxxxix, 15; Durkan and Kirk, pp. 67–108, esp. 84–91; *Munimenta*, vol. 2, pp. 25–6; Hannay, *Statutes*, pp. 11–15.

were regularly incorporated as well.[18] These young students began with the rudiments of Aristotelian logic (known collectively as the *Organon*), comprising Aristotle's *Categories* and *On Interpretation*, the *Prior* and *Posterior Analytics*, the *Topics* and the *Sophistical Refutations*,[19] and this was supplemented by several explanatory texts on basic logic, including Porphyry's 'Introduction' (*Isagoge*) to Aristotelian predicables and works by Gilbert de La Porre and Peter of Spain. Having thus been fitted with the correct tools for rational enquiry into all other branches of study, students then moved on to natural philosophy, reading eight books of the *Physics* and (either in whole or in part) *Generation and Corruption*, *On Heaven*, *On Sense and Sensation*, *On Memory and Remembering* and *On Sleep and Wakefulness*. Astronomical and mathematical study, ethics and metaphysics rounded out the course, with students reading a selection from *On the Soul*, *Metaphysics* and the *Nicomachean Ethics*, Johannes de Sacrobosco's 'On the Sphere' (*De Sphaera*), the *Meteorics*, and several rudimentary texts on geometry, perspective and fractions.[20] This outline of texts, unaltered in its fundamentals, would continue at St Andrews and Glasgow throughout the fifteenth century and was still in operation at the time of the reformation.

The other central component of the arts course at all three universities was logical disputation and argumentation. Often likened in intellectual terms to the equivalent of a chivalric trial of strength in a knightly tournament, opponents would verbally argue on a range of logical and philosophical issues arising from their studies with the aim of providing formally valid arguments or 'proofs' couched in Aristotelian terms, rather than informally convincing their audience through shows of rhetorical strength.[21] Students regularly practised and audited disputations, and in third year would undergo their first major trial to receive their bachelor's degree, comprising a set of disputations before Christmas and a further set of examinations at Lent. Having completed the bachelor's degree, students would study for the licentiate to receive their MA, which comprised a series of disputations in the winter known as great responsions. This was followed at Lent by the 'trial' or *temptamen*, where students were scrutinised before a series of four masters elected by the faculty on all the books they had heard lectures in, and were ranked in order of merit according to

---

[18]   Cant, p. 21; Durkan and Kirk, pp. 183–4.

[19]   Though at Glasgow only books I, II, VI and VII were taught, and the *Sophistical Refutations* was omitted from the course.

[20]   The first book of *Geometry* at St Andrews; *De Perspectiva* at both Glasgow and St Andrews; and the *Algorismus* and *Principia Geometriae* at Glasgow. All these mathematical texts, along with the *Ethics*, were read as 'extraordinary' at Glasgow, if time permitted outwith the core lectures in the course.

[21]   Durkan and Kirk, p. 85.

their proficiency. The final *examen in cameris*, which took place after Easter, derived its name from the fact that students were held within the bounds (*in cameris*) of the university so that each could be examined in turn privately before the masters, a process that could last over a week in some cases depending on student numbers. However, as the *examen* rarely altered the pass list agreed at the *temptamen* and was often used merely to satisfy the masters on outstanding areas of a student's knowledge, the two began to lose their separate identities from the beginning of the sixteenth century and the latter was gradually incorporated into the former.[22]

While the faculty of arts thrived and indeed became the predominant part of each university, the higher faculties had more variable fortunes. Although canon and civil law were taught initially in all three universities, by the time of the reformation teaching had either been liquidated (as was the case at Glasgow) or had dwindled to a handful of isolated practitioners with few students (as was the case at Aberdeen and St Andrews).[23] Nor had medicine made any lasting impact, save for the chair at Aberdeen which was still occupied in 1560.[24] Theology was a much stronger discipline, but the record of its teaching at the pre-reformation universities is extremely patchy. No acts of any faculty of theology survive, and the only extant theological statutes are a defective copy of those produced at St Andrews in 1439, revised by the reformers in 1560.[25] It is difficult even to know how long the actual course was. At Paris it took 14 years from entrance through the various stages of bachelor to the doctorate; at St Andrews it took somewhere between eight and 12 years, and it is likely that a similar length of studies applied at Glasgow; and at Aberdeen, where Elphinstone had a mind to produce literate clergy as rapidly as possible, a reduced course was offered that initially comprised seven and then six years.[26] What is clear, however, is that the divinity course across the universities was in every way as medieval as that of arts, focused exclusively on the Bible (divided into the legal, historical, 'sapiential' and prophetical books of the Old Testament, and the books of the New Testament) and the *Sentences* of Peter Lombard, whose four books formed an integral part of late medieval Catholic theology.[27]

---

[22]   MacFarlane, *William Elphinstone*, pp. 370–1; Durkan and Kirk, pp. 88–100; *Acta*, pp. lxxxix–cxvii.

[23]   Durkan and Kirk, pp. 127–38, esp. p. 132; MacFarlane, *William Elphinstone*, pp. 387–82; *Acta*, pp. cxlix–clvii, esp. clv–vi; Stevenson, *King's College*, p. 13.

[24]   Durkan and Kirk, pp. 328–9; Stevenson, *King's College*, p. 13; *Acta*, pp. clvii–ix, MacFarlane, *William Elphinstone*, pp. 382–5.

[25]   Durkan and Kirk, pp. 110–11, 115–16; Hannay, *Statutes*, p. 67.

[26]   Durkan and Kirk, p. 116.

[27]   Nicholas of Lyra's commentaries were also studied at Aberdeen. Durkan and Kirk, p. 116; Hannay, *Statutes*, p. 71; MacFarlane, *William Elphinstone*, pp. 374–5.

Before being allowed to determine as bachelors in divinity, students served a period of at least four year's apprenticeship under a regent master of their choice hearing lectures from both the masters and the various bachelor students attached to the faculty. On admission to the bachelorship, students were expected to provide two years of lectures on books of their choice from the Old and New Testaments before moving on to the *Sentences* in their seventh year and beyond, and each year was to be opened by the student with a formal lecture or *principium* addressing a broad theological theme that the student returned to as he progressed through his studies. As in arts, regular disputations were an integral part of the degree, most notably in the vacation disputations particular to theologians that lasted for several hours every weekend between July and October. Students also had to preach regularly on Sundays and on holy days, in both vernacular to the local community and in Latin *sermones ad clerum* to the university.[28]

Despite the entrenched medieval curriculum at St Andrews and Glasgow, there was some evidence at Aberdeen of a more sustained engagement with the new learning, owing in part to the civic-minded humanism of its founder William Elphinstone (who was also a committed diocesan and ecclesiastical reformer), and in part to Aberdeen's first principal, Hector Boece, and his colleagues, the sub-principal William Hay and the Grammarian John Vaus, who had all studied in Paris during the first flowering of humanist learning there between 1470 and 1510. Together they expanded and augmented the medieval arts curriculum at Aberdeen with a range of Renaissance texts. The traditional introduction to Aristotelian logic in first year saw the replacement of Peter of Spain's *Summulae Logicales* with Thomas Bricot's shorter and more accessible *Textus abbreviatus totius logicae*, and the Grammarian Vaus taught students the precepts of Latin prose and grammar from a range of Renaissance authors and commentators, including his own *Rudimenta*, a primer published in Scotland in 1507 that taught the basics of Latin grammar from the vernacular. This focus on humanist Latin was bolstered by selections in poetry and rhetoric from Virgil, Terence, Quintilian and Cicero, and additional lectures on Roman history. Students studied logic and the *Physics* in their second year, supported by Pliny's *Historia Naturalis*, an edition of *De Sphaera* with commentary by Pierre d'Ailly, and commentaries and reference texts by Lambertus de Monte and Bartolomeus Anglicus. Aristotle's *Ethics* and *Politics* were the order of the third year, along with Ptolemy's *Cosmographia* and works by Martin Lemaistre and Jean Buridan, and fourth year was devoted entirely to Aristotelian metaphysics. It is certainly fair to state, as one commentator has, that this curriculum was a course both 'basically

---

[28]   Durkan and Kirk, pp. 116–22; Hannay, *Statutes*, pp. 69–79.

Aristotelian' and 'Christian and humanist, neo-Platonic and neo-Classical, [and] which owed almost everything to the activities of French and Italian renaissance scholars'.[29]

The work of John Durkan, Leslie Macfarlane and others has shown that a number of gifted Latinists were produced under this regime at Aberdeen, most notably in the students Adam Mure and Florence Wilson, who both produced works of outstanding literary merit.[30] There is also evidence that a considerable number of staff and students at Aberdeen could read and understand Greek in the two decades prior to the reformation. In 1540, shortly after the death of both of James V's sons, the King, Mary of Guise and the court went to Aberdeen and specifically to King's College as guests of Bishop William Stewart for the space of fifteen days. An account by Bishop John Leslie (who was likely present as a student) of how the court was entertained notes that 'na day past by quhen outher tha had nocht a comedie, or sum controuersie, or orisounis in Greik or latin toung artificiouslie said', and suggests that Greek was well known among the scholars at Aberdeen before any teaching of the subject is officially recorded.[31]

The later works of John Vaus further confirm that men at Aberdeen had more than a passing acquaintance with Greek. His copy of his own *In Primam Doctrinalis Alexandrini Partem Commentarii* (1522) features a number of Greek marginalia, and his *Rudimenta Puerorum in Artem Grammaticum* (1531) has a frontispiece showing Jesus and the two thieves being crucified, with the words 'Jesus of Nazareth, King of the Jews' written in Hebrew, Greek and Latin, and several Greek phrases embedded in the text.[32] Unfortunately, no such evidence survives for the other Scottish universities in this period, and the first recorded instance of formal tuition of Greek in Scotland was the appointment of Edward Henryson in 1556 by Bishop Robert Reid to give a series of public lectures on the subject in

---

[29] MacFarlane, pp. 369–70.

[30] John Durkan, 'Early Humanism in King's College', *Aberdeen University Review* 163 (1980): 259–79, John Durkan and Anthony Ross, *Early Scottish Libraries* (Glasgow, 1961), introduction; Leslie J. Macfarlane, 'The Library of Bishop William Elphinstone', *Aberdeen University Review* 37 (1958): 253–71; Alasdair A. MacDonald, 'Florentius Volusenus and Tranquillity of Mind: Some Applications of an Ancient Ideal', in Alasdair A. MacDonald, Zweder R.W.M. von Martels and Jan R. Veenstra, *Christian Humanism: Essays in Honour of Arjo Vanderjagt* (Leiden and Boston, 2009) pp. 119–38.

[31] John Leslie, *History of Scotland*, ed. E.G. Cody (2 vols, Edinburgh, 1895), vol. 2, p. 247. J. Durkan, 'Early Humanism and King's College', pp. 263, 275 (n. 30).

[32] Aberdeen University Library Lambda2 Vau C; Aberdeen University Library Lambda2 Vau R3.

Edinburgh.[33] Surveying the evidence, one is forced reluctantly to conclude that the considerable advances in humanist studies at Aberdeen in the early sixteenth century were achieved largely in isolation.

Big Ideas: *The First Book of Discipline* and University Reform

As the evidence suggests, engagement with humanist ideas at the universities in the first half of the sixteenth century was limited; and an unfortunate triple assault of plague, civil disturbance by Protestant reformers, and ravages caused by English military invasions in the 1540s and by skirmishes between the Lords of the Congregation and the forces of Mary of Guise in 1559–60 conspired to plunge all three universities into a sudden downward spiral of decay and disrepair. At Glasgow, the matriculation records show that after 1539 entrant numbers dropped to a lower level than at any time in its history. Only four students were incorporated in 1550 and 1551, one in 1552, nine in 1553, one in 1554, 13 in 1555, three in 1556, 17 in 1557 and none in 1558.[34] The situation at the university was so dire in December 1551 that two of the students taking their bachelor degree chose to go to St Andrews to finish their course.[35] The university buildings were in a very poor state as well, and from 1475 onwards the minutes of the *munimenta* are full of small sums for repairs to the college fabric.[36] At St Andrews there were only 13 graduations recorded between 1545 and 1553, with no graduations at all in 1545 and 1546, and between 1553 and 1559 graduation numbers barely rose to double figures.[37] The matriculation roll reveals a similar pattern, with blanks for 1546, 1547 and 1549, and only a handful of names registered in 1548; however, numbers of entrants picked up between 1552 and 1558, and remained consistently above 30 per year. There was also a record total of 64 new entrants in 1555, likely due to the re-foundation of St Mary's.[38] At Aberdeen a visitation in 1549 ordered by the Provincial Council recorded material decay of the university on a broad scale, showing that a near total collapse in standards had taken place in

[33]   William Forbes-Leith, *Pre-Reformation Scholars in Scotland in the Sixteenth Century* (Edinburgh, 1915), p. 8; John Durkan, 'The Royal Lectureships under Mary of Lorraine', *SHR* 62.1 (1983): 73–8.

[34]   Durkan and Kirk, p. 240.

[35]   Durkan and Kirk, pp. 213–14.

[36]   John D. Mackie, *The University of Glasgow, 1451–1951* (Glasgow, 1954), p. 46.

[37]   *Early Records*, pp. 148–57.

[38]   *Early Records*, pp. 250–3.

a very short space of time.[39] This decay was compounded by low student numbers, with only seven masters entering between 1546 and 1548, along with three students in law and nine in theology.[40]

It was with a mind to this rather bleak situation in 1560 that a university reform scheme was produced by a commission of ministers, who had been appointed by the Lords of Council to write a broader programme 'touching the reformation of Religion' in Scotland.[41] The commission began work on this polity, now known as the *First Book of Discipline*,[42] in April 1560, and on 17 January 1561 it was accepted in an 'Act of Secret Counsall'.[43] While the *First Book* contained proposals for reforming all aspects of religious life in Scotland, by far the most detailed were those for university reform. The members of the commission charged with writing the section on the universities were likely John Douglas, principal of St Mary's College and rector of the university between 1547 and 1572, and John Winram, the pre-reformation sub-prior of St Andrews Priory and post-reformation superintendent of Fife, who was closely connected with St Andrews from his student days in 1513 until his death in 1582.[44]

Entitled 'of the Erection of the Universities', the scheme proposed a complete reorganisation of the three existing foundations.[45] At St Andrews the three colleges were to be kept but allocated to different areas of study. One college was to provide a three-year arts course covering mathematics, logic and natural philosophy, and a five-year course in medicine. The second college would offer a one-year moral philosophy course which taught 'Ethicks, Oeconomics and Politicks', and a four-year course in Roman and statute law. The third college was to provide a one-year course in Greek and Hebrew, and a divinity course teaching the theological exposition of the Old and New Testament over five years. Outside St Andrews the reformers advocated expansion, with Aberdeen and Glasgow each to be divided into two colleges. The first college at both would teach the same arts course as the 'first college' at St Andrews, without the course in medicine. The second college was to combine the functions of the second

---

[39] Bruce McLennan, 'The Reformation in the Burgh of Aberdeen', *Northern Scotland* 2 (1974–77): 119–44, at 121.

[40] Gordon Donaldson, 'Aberdeen University and the Reformation', *Northern Scotland* 1 (1972–3): 129–42, at 135.

[41] *FBD*, pp. 3–4.

[42] The *Second Book of Discipline*, an attempt to revise the Scottish polity along Presbyterian lines, was produced by the General Assembly in 1578; *Second Book*, ed. Kirk.

[43] *FBD*, pp. 210–11.

[44] *FBD*, p. 57; *Acta*, pp. ccxlvii–ccxlviii. Douglas was rector from 28 February 1551 to 17 March 1574.

[45] *FBD*, pp. 26–7, 137–55.

and third colleges at St Andrews, and offer courses in Hebrew, divinity, moral philosophy, and Roman and statute law.

The constitution, administrative processes and personnel outlined for each university borrowed heavily from the extant constitutions of St Mary's and St Leonard's. Each college was to be overseen by a principal, who would manage the college funds and exercise discipline over the youths in his charge. As in the pre-reformation period, each university was to be regulated by a rector, chosen annually by the principal and regents of each college, who was also to carry out monthly inspections of each college and be responsible for elections to vacant principalships. Another change was the abolition of the traditional system of a regent taking a class through all stages of a course from their entrance to examination and graduation, which had been the standard practice on the medieval arts course. They were to be replaced with 'specialist' readers who would each be responsible for teaching the subjects in only one year of study.

In another section, entitled 'For the Schooles', the reformers advocated the setting up of colleges in 'every notable town' that would teach a basic arts course and the biblical languages 'for the virtuous education and godly upbringing of the youth of this realme'.[46] If the reformers' plans had been carried out in full, the 'first college' at St Andrews, Glasgow and Aberdeen would have fulfilled these functions for the towns. Instruction in the higher faculties to qualify lawyers and ministers would have been concentrated in the remaining two colleges at St Andrews and the remaining college at Aberdeen and Glasgow, in what could be termed 'post-graduate' colleges.[47] The prime hope of the reformers was that education would disseminate Protestant belief in Scotland, ensuring that all children would be 'brought up in virtue in presence of their friends', and would 'within few years' act as catechists to their elders and provide new ministers to undertake Protestant missions across Scotland.[48] All these motives were imperative for the furthering of the reformed cause in Scotland, as it was only with English military aid in March 1560 that the Scottish Protestant nobility had removed the pro-Catholic regent Mary of Guise from power. In August they held a parliament without royal consent, where they adopted a Protestant confession of faith and outlawed the Catholic religion.[49] By adopting a broad programme of education, the reformers aimed to embed

---

[46]   FBD, pp. 129–36.

[47]   Mackie, *The University of Glasgow*, pp. 57–8.

[48]   FBD, p. 135.

[49]   Michael Graham, *The Uses of Reform: 'Godly Discipline' and Popular Behaviour in Scotland and Beyond, 1560–1610* (Leiden, 1996), p. 38; Dawson, *Scotland Re-formed*, pp. 200–215; Donaldson, *Scotland: James V–James VII*, pp. 85–106; Alec Ryrie, *The Origins of the Scottish Reformation* (Manchester, 2006), pp. 161–195; Jenny Wormald, *Court, Kirk, and Community: Scotland, 1470-1625* (Edinburgh, 2001 edn), pp. 109–121.

the newly established religion in Scottish culture as quickly as possible, especially amongst the young.

'Arts colleges' similar to those proposed in the *First Book* were established at Bordeaux in 1534, Strasbourg in 1538, Nimes in 1542 and Lausanne in 1547 and, as noted above, the precedent of 'trilingual' arts colleges on the Continent was one well known in Scotland.[50] It was from these examples that the Scottish reformers had taken the idea for the abolition of regenting and the emphasis on biblical languages in the curriculum, as well as the requirement that each student undertake a three-year arts course. However, it was the Academy of Geneva, founded by Jean Calvin in 1558, that played the largest role in influencing the reformers. The Genevan Book of Common Order was to be used for teaching children the Catechism and the statutes of the Academy were the chief source used to plan the 'third college' at St Andrews.[51] Research by Karin Maag into the Academy for the period 1559–64 has shown that it trained new ministers with remarkable speed to meet the needs of the rapidly expanding Calvinist movement in France, as well as 're-training' ex-Catholic ministers.[52] When the reformers laid out their plans for reform in 1560–1, they must have had high hopes that the Genevan experience would be replicated in Scotland.

The scheme of university reform in the *First Book* ends with an appeal to the Lords to 'set forward letters in the sort prescribed', and ultimately laid responsibility upon the civil power to carry out the ambitious reform plan they proposed.[53] In truth, the General Assembly in the decade after 1560 took little interest in pursuing this scheme. The only reference made to the universities in the 1560s and early 1570s in the assembly minutes was the token proclamation repeated in June 1563, 1565 and 1567 that all teachers and lecturers must 'profess Chrysts true religioun', and an exemption in June 1563 for university benefices from the remission of thirds for ministerial stipends.[54] Events at the three Scottish universities between 1560 and 1574 took very different turns, but it was the civil government that initiated the process of reform at each of them.

---

[50] Durkan and Kirk, pp. 285–6; Willem Frijhoff, 'Patterns', in *A History of the University in Europe* vol. 2, p. 57.

[51] *FBD*, pp. 58, 137.

[52] Maag, *Seminary or University?*, pp. 16–21.

[53] *FBD*, p. 155.

[54] *BUK*, vol. 1, pp. 33–5, 60, 109–10.

Catholic Recusancy: Aberdeen, 1560–74

At King's College, the university and its staff remained sympathetic to the Catholic cause until at least 1568. This entrenched recusancy stemmed from a number of factors. Although across post-reformation Scotland there were initial difficulties in establishing a working Protestant church structure and community, the resistance to reform was particularly apparent in the north-east, where an attempt in 1559 to cast down the churches in Old Aberdeen by an overly zealous reforming mob from Angus and the Mearns was successfully repelled. Resistance to the reformers was spearheaded by the twin figures of George Gordon, fourth earl of Huntly, and his uncle William Gordon, the bishop of Aberdeen and chancellor of the university.[55] The Gordons were resolutely Catholic and offered protection to the Aberdeen populace to maintain their faith, and the fact that Bishop Gordon refused to relinquish his palace near the university must have given considerable strength to the staff and students to remain steadfast in their beliefs. In January 1561, the sub-principal of the college, Alexander Anderson, the canon lawyer John Leslie and several of their fellow teaching staff were cited to appear at the Tolbooth in Edinburgh before John Knox and a range of other Protestant ministers for an examination of their doctrine.[56] Although both sides claimed intellectual victory at the resulting debate, the university staff were still forced to spend time in ward before being allowed to return to Aberdeen, and then only on the condition that they should not preach.[57] However, in August 1562 they gained an ally in Queen Mary, who during a visit to the university saw first-hand the exigencies it faced. On 2 November she issued a letter of protection to the university for the safeguarding of its revenues, with the threat of 'all hiest pane charge and offence' to anyone who broke this protection.[58]

Mary became increasingly hostile towards Catholic recusancy in the north-east in the first half of her short-lived personal reign, leading an armed force against Huntly which resulted in his death on the battlefield at Corrichie in 1563 and the imprisonment and execution of his son, and ordering Bishop Gordon to desist from saying Mass in Old Aberdeen in 1565. However, following her marriage to Henry Stewart Lord Darnley her domestic and foreign policy became increasingly pro-Catholic; and the ambiguity caused by this stance allowed the remote university to operate

---

[55] Stevenson, *King's College*, p. 8.

[56] Duncan Shaw, *The General Assemblies of the Church of Scotland 1560–1600* (Edinburgh, 1964), p. 189.

[57] Stevenson, *King's College*, p. 9; *Knox's History*, ed. Dickinson, vol. 1, p. 352–353; Leslie, *History*, vol. 2, pp. 449–451.

[58] *Fasti Aberdonenses*, pp. 126–7.

apparently unmolested until 1569, two years after Mary had been forcibly deposed by a coalition of pro-Protestant and pro-English lords. In the summer of that year the Earl of Moray James Stewart, Mary's Protestant half brother and regent for the infant James VI, put down an armed rebellion by the fifth Earl of Huntly, who was attempting to restore Mary to the throne. After receiving Huntly's submission Moray stopped on his return south to deal with the university, with the assistance of John Erskine of Dun, superintendent of Angus and the Mearns and commissioner for the shires of Aberdeen and Banff.[59] On 29 June, principal Alexander Anderson, sub-principal Andrew Galloway and the regents Andrew Anderson and Duncan Norie were summoned to sign the reformed Confession of Faith. They appeared the following day and bluntly refused. All four were summarily deprived of their posts in the college by Moray as 'persons dangerous and unmeet to have care of the instruction of the youth', and the college and its property was handed over to the provost of Aberdeen for safe-keeping. Alexander Arbuthnott and James Lawson, ex-teaching staff from St Andrews and committed Protestants, were appointed as principal and sub-principal on 3 July, followed shortly after by the appointment of two Protestant regents in arts, George Paterson and Hercules Rollock.[60]

George Hay, chaplain to the Regent Moray and to the Privy Council, delivered an oration on 2 July to the students of King's College between the expulsion of the old staff and the appointment of the new.[61] Hay's oration was notable for several reasons, firstly because of the profound distinction it made in terms of the quality and intellectual rigour of the curriculum under the Catholic masters at the university and the one that the new Protestant staff would put in place, which focussed on the path from humanist philology to the pure source texts of ancient philosophy, the church fathers, and the Bible itself, freed from centuries of accretion and emendation. Although Hay knew that there was a far greater pedigree of humanist studies at Aberdeen than at any other Scottish university, he also made it clear that the programme of Catholic theology and education at the university, focussed as it was on Latin commentaries and texts by medieval scholastic authors, gave students only 'barren, jejune, and dull precepts ... put before them in the driest possible manner, not derived by a process of reasoning from the springs of Aristotle and the ancient logicians but drawn off by a process of sophistry'.

Hay also emphasised the fact that it was the civil authority, and not the ecclesiastical, which had taken action to reform the university. While Moray was changing a foundation 'firmly based on great antiquity', and

---

[59]   Stevenson, *King's College*, pp. 15–19.

[60]   Durkan, 'George Hay's Oration: Commentary', p. 97.

[61]   Watt, 'George Hay's Oration', 91–6; Stevenson, *King's College*, pp. 20–24.

change was 'rightly detested by all men of wisdom' for the upheaval it caused, Hay believed there was great sense in the state's interference in the university. Hay's greatest hope was to:

> achieve one purpose, that of winning approval for my eagerness to obey and for my conscientiousness from those whom, on account of their merit, I would gladly oblige and whom, in view of the position which they occupy in the state, I neither can nor should oppose.

Hay portrayed the Regent Moray as the powerful catalyst behind the reform at King's College. The regent had seen the reformed religion accepted at St Andrews and Glasgow, and had tried a policy of 'complaisance and gentleness' with the college in Aberdeen in the hopes that it would do the same. However, Moray saw that, through 'the cunning and fraudulent pretences of crafty men' and the 'carelessness of good men' (the same men who impeded the true intake of knowledge at the university), reform had been delayed to a point where he had decided that Aberdeen 'might be curbed by the severity of the law'. It was thus through the regent, and by extension the civil government, that the university was to be reformed.

Both trends outlined in Hay's *Oration* – the reorientation of the axes of learning at the Scottish universities towards a purer version of ancient philosophical and biblical knowledge in line with the tenets of Renaissance humanism, and the intervention of the civil authority in this process – would become central to the attempts at university reform in Scotland over the following two decades. However, following Moray's initial foray in this direction at Aberdeen, little in the way of progress was recorded there in the following decade. While the Catholic masters teaching arts and theology had been removed, the canon lawyer Alexander Cheyne, the civilist Nicholas Hay, the mediciner Gilbert Skene and the grammarian Theophilus Stewart were all continued in their offices.[62] While they all taught in areas of the curriculum that did not directly affect the Protestant mission, and each likely had few if any students by 1569, the fact that they were left untouched shows again the ambiguities in educational reform left unresolved a decade after the reformation. This issue was compounded by the fact that Bishop Gordon continued to hold his post as both prelate and university chancellor until his death in 1577, and indeed by the fact that Mass was still being practised covertly in Old Aberdeen until 1578, the date at which the old sub-principal Andrew Galloway finally went into exile in France.[63]

---

[62]   Stevenson, *King's College*, p. 17; Anderson (ed.), *Officers*, pp. 30, 31, 35, 45, 91. While the sacrist, Alexander Wright, was also kept in office, he had no teaching responsibilities.

[63]   Durkan 'George Hay's Oration: Commentary', p. 103; Stevenson, *King's College*, pp. 18, 26.

These ambiguities were compounded by the strains placed upon the staff at the embryonic Protestant foundation. Alexander Arbuthnott had been minister of Logie Buchan at his appointment in 1569, and continued to exercise this ministry along with the parishes of Forvie and Arbuthnot, while James Lawson was made minister of Old Aberdeen at the same time, a post which he then transferred to Arbuthnott on his resignation to take up a ministerial post in Edinburgh in 1572.[64] Modest progress was made by these two men and the associated regents under them in their initial tenure in office. Lawson had apparently taught Hebrew in St Andrews prior to his appointment, and if he introduced the language during his brief three-year tenure at King's he would have met one of the key curricular requirements of the reformers. Arbuthnott also managed to acquire several small financial grants to bolster the college revenue, including the rectory and vicarage of the Spital in 1574, the parish of Forvie, and in 1579 the rectory and vicarage of St Machar.[65] However, the fragmentary evidence that survives does not suggest that any wholesale or sweeping change was enacted at the university following the purge of 1569, and the discussion of constitutional reform along Protestant lines, a process that would lead to one of the most turbulent periods of administrative chaos in the university's history, only got under way when Arbuthnott's friend and colleague, Andrew Melville, held discussions with him about the issue in 1574.

Collapse and Civic Intervention: Glasgow, 1560–74

While all three of Scotland's 'ancient' Catholic universities were deeply affected by the fallout from the events of 1559–60, it was perhaps Glasgow that suffered the most. Unlike its counterparts, the university had never received a sufficient endowment as its founder, Bishop William Turnbull, had died suddenly before he was able to annex sufficient ecclesiastical funding to it, and it had struggled throughout the later medieval period to remain financially solvent.[66] As noted above, the matriculation records show that in the 1550s entrant numbers dropped to a lower level than at any time in the university's history,[67] and while no statutes or teaching evidence survives for the university in the 15 years after the reformation, the few extant records confirm that it was in crisis. The majority of the staff at the reformation followed the lead of the Chancellor, Archbishop James

---

[64] At which point Arbuthnott resigned from Forvie and Arbuthnot. Stevenson, *King's College*, pp. 26–7.

[65] Stevenson, *King's College*, pp. 26–9; *Fasti Aberdonenses*, pp. 129–31.

[66] Durkan and Kirk, pp. 16, 21–39.

[67] Durkan and Kirk, pp. 240–1; *Munimenta, vol. 2*, pp. 171–177.

Beaton, and deserted the university, leaving the newly-converted Protestant principal John Davidson to maintain teaching. Davidson had perhaps been given this post owing to his humanist interests – he had experience of Hebrew and Chaldaic, and was a student of biblical philology[68] – but any teaching he undertook must have been highly limited, as he was aided only by Robert Hamilton, on record as regent between 1562 and 1565.[69]

In the absence of aid from the church, the limited support Glasgow received before Melville's arrival in 1574 came partially from the crown, but mainly from the local burgh council. A visitation to the university in July 1563 by Queen Mary confirmed the dire straits it had fallen into, and because it 'apperit rather to be the decay of ane universitie nor ony wyse to reknit ane establisst fundatioun', Mary handed over the manse and kirkroom of the black friars in Glasgow, along with about thirteen acres of land and some money and meal worth a little less than £100 Scots, for the maintenance of five poor children.[70] On 16 March 1567 Mary made a further grant to Glasgow, of all the properties of every chantry, altarage and prebend in Glasgow, along with all the former possessions of the black and grey friars of the city.[71] Mary had made this grant with the intended purpose of supporting ministers and providing hospital care within the city, but on 26 January 1573 the town provost and baillies, with the consent of parliament, used the endowment to re-found the college and provide it with a new civic constitution.[72]

This 'town foundation', signed by the town provost John Stewart of Minto, his baillies and other council members, was modest both in size and scope of teaching. In addition to a chancellor, rector and dean of arts, the head of the teaching staff was to comprise a principal who would be a professor of theology, and who each day would read and lecture upon a passage from scripture. The principal was to be supported by two regents whose role was rather vaguely defined as teaching 'the whole of philosophy'. While no detailed list of authors is mentioned, it is clear from the fact that their teaching was to comprise 'dialectic, logic, physics, moral philosophy, and metaphysics' that the focus of the curriculum was entirely upon the Aristotelian corpus traditionally studied within the university.[73]

---

[68]   Durkan and Kirk, pp. 216–18.

[69]   *Abstracts of Protocols of the Town Clerks of Glasgow*, ed. R. Renwick (10 vols, Glasgow, 1894–1900), vol. 3, no. 683; vol. 5, no. 1515; Durkan and Kirk, p. 239.

[70]   *Munimenta*, vol. 1, pp. 67–9.

[71]   *Munimenta*, vol. 1, pp. 71–4.

[72]   *Munimenta*, vol. 1, pp. 82–90; Durkan and Kirk, pp. 247–54; *Charters and Other Documents Relating to the City of Glasgow, A.D. 1175–1649 Part 2*, ed. J.D. Marwick (Edinburgh, 1894), pp. 149–62.

[73]   *Munimenta*, vol. 1, pp. 85–6.

Twelve poor foundation bursars were also to be provided for, who had to complete their degree within three and a half years, who would live *collegialiter*, and who would publicly accept the Protestant confession of faith when swearing to obey the university statutes. Beyond the teaching outlined in theology and philosophy, there was no mention of either the broader range of liberal arts that had been taught on Glasgow's medieval foundation, nor was there any mention of law, mathematics or languages beyond Latin, which students were expected to have a competent knowledge of prior to entry.

The 'town foundation' was a greatly reduced and narrowed version of Glasgow's original constitution, and most recently has been described as 'the first significant step in restoring the university's fortunes ... [that] ... was superseded four years later by a royal foundation which averted any threatened domination by the town council'.[74] However, this reading does not give due credit to the very real intent of the council to provide a pragmatic re-foundation of the university, that could function on the basis of extant college finance and the limited augmentation it had received from Queen Mary. It also ignores the fact that the 'town foundation' established a pattern of civic involvement in the university which would repeat itself over the next three decades, even after the establishment of the *Nova Erectio* in 1577.

The 'town foundation' stated that the key teaching staff were to be appointed by a committee from within the university – in the case of the principal by the chancellor, rector and dean of faculty of the university, along with the rectors of the churches of Glasgow and Hamilton, and in the case of the regents by the rector, principal and dean. The principal also had 'all ordinary jurisdiction' over both the foundation bursars and regents, and the day-to-day running of the college and its discipline. However, the central interest of the burgh, to use the university to educate local children, was made clear when it stated that it reserved presentation of the twelve poor bursaries explicitly to the baillies and city council who would then be accepted for admission by the university staff, and who were to be 'sons of the burgesses of the burgh of Glasgow' wherever possible.[75] Ensuring this finance was carefully preserved and maintained was the top priority for the council – the college was to be subject to twice-yearly visitation in March and September by a joint committee of the rector and dean of faculty and the town baillies, who would have power to remove staff if they were failing to accomplish their duties, and who were to audit the college accounts. Any surplus rents found in this audit were to be used to provide additional teaching staff or augment the number of poor bursars, who would again be presented by the council. Furthermore, the foundation

74 Durkan and Kirk, pp. 249–50.
75 *Munimenta*, vol. 1, pp. 87–8; *Charters and Other Documents Part 2*, pp. 156–7.

also contained a clause expressly stating that if any of the chaplainries or prebends granted within the gift of Queen Mary fell vacant in future, the council had the right as patrons to present them to 'scholars sons of our co-burgesses to be conferred for their maintenance and sustentation in schools within the said city', again increasing the number of bursaries at its disposal.[76]

It would be going too far, on the basis of constitutional evidence alone, to say that the 'town foundation' was a complete civic recasting of the university, nor would it be fair to say that the foundation had any success upon its implementation. The only member of staff found at the university on Andrew Melville's arrival in late 1574 was the regent Peter Blackburn, who had been appointed from St Salvator's at some point in the preceding year and had taken it upon himself to teach 'conform to the ordour of the course' where he had been previously.[77] However, it is striking that Glasgow took the initiative in trying to undertake civic control of higher education in their locality, particularly in the fact that the council focussed intently in their foundation on the areas of financing and presentation of bursaries, which they knew would most directly benefit local burgesses and their children.

It has been noted that this trend likely drew its inspiration in part from the Continental civic colleges of Geneva, Strasbourg and Lausanne, and the Protestant academies established throughout France in the later sixteenth century, showing that Glasgow's citizenry were aware of the civic dimensions of Protestant humanism and the benefits they could bring to the city.[78] However, it is also clear that, when viewed in line with the foundation of higher educational institutions at Edinburgh in 1582, in Fraserburgh in 1592 and in New Aberdeen in 1593, the Glasgow re-foundation of 1573 should perhaps be seen as an embryonic form of the later trend of Protestant 'tounis colleges' that tried to provide a 'godly' education for children in a range of Scottish urban centres.[79] While Glasgow's 'town foundation' did not fully relinquish control of the university to the city council in the way that these other foundations did, its focus on finance and provision for local students certainly reflects the trend of growing involvement by Scottish local government in higher education. It also further supports the idea that we should not simply dismiss the Glasgow 'town foundation' as a mere stop-gap on the way to the 'Melvillian' re-foundation in 1577, but take it seriously as a statement of civic intent regarding the university that continued to hold currency in the decades after the *Nova Erectio*.

---

[76]   *Charters and Other Documents Part 2*, pp. 158–60.

[77]   Durkan and Kirk, p. 254; *JMAD*, pp. 48–49.

[78]   Durkan and Kirk, p. 249, and n. 185.

[79]   See chapter 7, below.

Moderation and Schism: the University of St Andrews, 1560–1574

St Andrews was one of the earliest towns in Scotland to profess allegiance to Protestantism, and had wholly adopted a reformed church settlement by 25 July 1559, when the St Andrews Kirk Session records begin.[80] Around this same date there is a period of disruption clearly visible in all the main administrative records of the university. Regular entries in the acts of the faculty of arts cease abruptly after the entry of 7 December 1558.[81] Only two statutes are recorded for 1559 and 1560. The first on 25 November 1559 continued John Rutherford, the newly-elected provost of St Salvator's College, in his post as dean of arts along with the current examiners; and the second on 15 May 1560 stated:

> The university determined that all who ought to have graduated in this year should be held as licentiates, as due to the whole disruption of the country and the reformation of religion the old customs [of graduation] were unable to be carried out.[82]

In 1561 the situation had barely improved. The only statutes in that year comprised one on 8 January stating that John Rutherford should continue in his office as dean without further election 'until further reformation', and an act of 7 November re-electing Rutherford and electing Archibald Hamilton as quaestor, who promised 'all labour and aid in reforming the Faculty and in discharging lawful administration'.[83]

Student numbers were low in the same period. The matriculation records for the year 1558/9 show only three names for St Mary's, with no entries for the other two colleges, explained by a terse note that 'in this year, on account of the religious conflict … very few scholars came to this university'.[84] The Bursar's Book records only eight graduates in the period between 23 November 1560 and 6 November 1562, and in the following year only four graduates, from St Leonard's, are recorded.[85] An annual account of the finances of the arts faculty does not resume until 1565, and

---

[80]   *RStAKS*, p. 1.

[81]   *Acta*, p. 414.

[82]   *Acta*, p. 415: 'Statuit Academia omnes laureandos huius anni pro laureatis haberi, quod universa reipublicae perturbatione et religionis reformatione veteres ritus serviri impedirentur.'

[83]   *Acta*, p. 416.

[84]   *Early Records*, pp. 266–7: 'Hoc anno propter tumultus religionis … paucissimi scholastici ad hanc universitatem venerunt'.

[85]   *Acta*, p. lxvii, *Early Records*, pp. 157–9.

the single entry between 1560 and 1562 states that the net income to the arts faculty stood at just £6 14s.[86]

Nonetheless, the university quickly adapted to the Protestant regime. Statutes began to assume more normality and regularity in 1562, and in November of that year full staff elections began to take place again. The numbers of matriculating and graduating students also began to stabilise and rise after 1562. The total number of entrants recorded for 1561–3, although over 30 per cent lower than the totals for the years prior to the reformation, still averaged more than 20 students per year.[87] Eight graduates are recorded in 1563 and ten graduates in 1564 from all three colleges, and after this point separate entries for each college are once again maintained. Matriculation and graduation entries steadily increased between 1562 and 1574, with overall student numbers increasing above those of pre-reformation levels. This growth was reflected in the faculty accounts, with the annual net income at the end of 1573 standing at £48 3d.[88]

The ease with which the reformation was accepted at St Andrews in the early 1560s is in part due to the relative stability of teaching staff during this transitional period. Some members of staff did resist the Protestant regime and left in protest, including John Black and Richard Marshall, both masters of St Mary's, and the provost of St Salvator's, William Cranston, and his colleague Simon Simson.[89] However, out of 21 men certified as fit to minister in St Andrews by the General Assembly, 12 of these were members of the teaching staff, suggesting that many at the university were at least sympathetic to the reformed cause prior to the reformation.[90] The teaching staff also took an active role in the reformed Kirk, both at the national level of the General Assembly and at the local level of the St Andrews Kirk Session. In addition to his suspected contribution to the *First Book of Discipline*, the principal of St Mary's John Douglas was involved in numerous committees established to discuss doctrine and church polity between 1565 and 1574, along with the St Mary's master Robert Hamilton, the principal of St Leonard's James Wilkie, John Rutherford and the St Leonard's regent James Carmichael.[91] The principals of each

---

[86]   The Faculty of Arts Bursar's Book, UYUY412, fos 46r, 47v.

[87]   *Early Records*, pp. 267–70. The student numbers totalled 23, 27 and 20 respectively, though this does not include a potentially missing entry for St Salvators in 1560.

[88]   UYUY412, fo. 53r.

[89]   Shaw, *General Assemblies*, p. 184.

[90]   *BUK*, vol. 1, p. 4. The names of those certified with known connections to the university were John Rutherford, William Ramsay, James Wilkie, Robert Hamilton, Patrick Constance (Adamson), William Skene, Archibald Hamilton, Alexander Arbuthnott, David Collace, Thomas Buchanan, John Winram and David Guild.

[91]   *BUK*, vol. 1, pp. 61–2, 77, 97, 191, 238–9, 244–5, 260–1, 293.

college were elected to the eldership of the kirk session in every recorded election between 1561 and 1574,[92] and numerous entries in the Kirk Session Register show Douglas, Rutherford, Wilkie and others as members of the panels on cases in the 1560s taking their duties seriously.[93] In addition to acting as elders, the university masters also served as judges,[94] and William Skene, teacher of law at St Mary's between 1556 and the late 1570s, acted as commissary to the town and can be found in the records as procurator for a number of cases.[95]

The revision of the statutes of the faculties of arts and theology in the early 1560s suggests that the same teaching staff who maintained the university post-reformation also actively discouraged any radical alteration, despite the recommendations of the *First Book*. Statutes for the faculty of arts hastily revised in 1561–2 and then again in 1570 have survived in defective copy, as have a copy of the statutes of the faculty of theology, which were revised immediately after the reformation in 1560.[96] The theology statutes, described by the reformers in their heading as being 'in part unchanged and in [part] better reformed to the rule of the word of God' (*in parte immutata et juxta normam verbi Dei in [parte] melius reformata*) retain almost untouched the same constitutional apparatus laid down for the faculty at its inception, right down to the opening rubric attached to the statutes by Bishop Henry Wardlaw and others in 1438–9. Students still had to meet the minimum age of 25 for entry to the bachelor course, and the age of 30 for the licentiate and doctorate, showing that creating a short divinity course to produce Protestant ministers rapidly was not on the reformers' immediate list of priorities. The faculty curriculum maintained the near-exclusive focus on the books of the Bible and their division into five thematic categories, with the only substantial alteration to the course being the complete removal of the teachings of Peter Lombard that had been used '*sub Papismo*'. Students still had to study within the theological faculty for four years prior to petitioning for acceptance to the bachelor programme, and the traditional programme of disputations at all levels of the course, and of regularly preaching in vernacular in public and in Latin to the assembled university masters, was also maintained.

---

[92] *RStAKS*, pp. 1–5, 323, 342, 350, 368, 382, 399–400.

[93] The earliest recorded case is that of 21 March 1560 when Douglas, William Skene and John Rutherford assisted in the divorce case of William Rantoun and Elizabeth Gedde, *RStAKS*, pp. 25–6, 38–9. See other cases, e.g. pp. 101–3 (an act legitimising Sir John Borthwick, 1561), 155–6 (Gyb–Hyllok divorce trial, 1563), 169 (Boyd–Masterton marriage reconciliation, 1562), 220–1 (Thomson–Moffat marriage case, 1564), 249–50 (dispute over contested marriage banns in Kinghorn, 1565).

[94] *RStAKS*, pp. 33–5 (McKie–Adie blasphemy case, 1560), pp.101–3.

[95] *RStAKS*, pp. 25–6, 38–9, 158–9.

[96] Hannay, *Statutes*, pp. 112–35.

Also kept, largely untouched, was the basic structure of the latter half of the course between attaining the bachelor's degree and studying towards the licentiate. In place of a mix of lectures on the Bible and the *Sentences*, students would begin with a *principium* followed by a year of lectures on the 'legal' books of the Old Testament, a second year on the 'historical' books, a third on the remaining parts of the Old Testament and a fourth year on the New Testament, at which stage they were allowed to proceed to the licentiate and doctorate. Even the degree rubric used for the licentiate in theology was largely based on the pre-reformation one, which had invoked the authority of God, the Apostles Peter and Paul, and the Apostolic See, and now instead called upon God, his holy Catholic Church and the reigning monarch. The overwhelming impression one gains from these statutes is that theological studies at the university, though clearly acknowledging the fact that Protestant reform necessitated some change to the course, still clung largely to forms and patterns established in the university's Catholic and medieval past.

The revisions made to the arts statutes suggest a similar reluctance to effect widespread change. An act of 7 January 1562 set out laws for the faculty of arts which were to be read three times before an assembly of all staff and students, and were to be 'held up, approved and confirmed ... until a more perfect form is prescribed'.[97] The statutes, supervised by the dean John Rutherford and the rector John Douglas, are fascinating for their complete absence of discussion relating to matters of religion and for the fact that they set out a practical operating framework for the faculty in as expedient a manner as possible, and with the minimum concession to change. Instead the statutes focussed upon the duty of students to be obedient and the fees they ought to pay, the role of principals and teaching staff in overseeing their education and discipline, re-establishing the procedures for examinations and the dates for terms and holidays, and forbidding the migration of students from one college to another. While a tighter focus on entry qualifications laid down that students had to be able to write a Latin poem or speech before admission, the course itself retained unaltered its focus on Aristotle. Prior to obtaining their bachelor degree, students were to be taught the whole of the *Organon* and at least two books of the *Ethics*, while students in their fourth year would study a selection of Aristotle's texts on natural philosophy with some supplementary tuition in mathematics, although metaphysics was apparently omitted from the course. A concession to humanist teachings was clear in the fact that the 'gymnasiarch' (the college principal) was allowed to choose additional texts containing 'pure philosophy in Latin and Greek', such as those of Aristotle, Plato, Zenophon, Cicero 'and writers of this type' (*id genus*

---

[97]   *Acta*, pp. 416–21; Hannay, *Statutes*, pp. 60–65.

scriptorium), but no mention is made of tuition of the languages of the Old Testament, or of the system of specialised regenting discussed in the *First Book*, or of dividing subject areas among the colleges.

Further attempts to consolidate the constitution and statutes of the university were spearheaded first by William Skene and then John Rutherford in successive terms of office as dean of arts. On 15 and 25 January 1567, while Skene held the position, there was a specially convoked meeting of the faculty which appointed a committee of the 'most prudent' men of each of the three colleges to make a digest of the old laws.[98] Between 3 November and 22 December 1570, under the supervision of Rutherford, the laws of the Faculty were subjected to detailed excision and were copied down. Six assessors were appointed to examine the old laws, in order to adopt those that were 'in agreement with religion and honesty'. Seven days later the old laws were read in the presence of the rector and staff, where those that were 'superstitious and worthless' were excised and the rest transcribed and sent to each college, which were publicly read on 22 December. Like those revised in the early 1560s, these statutes were highly conservative and continued the apparatus of the faculty as it stood before the reformation. They were adopted in March 1571 without issue, except for a minor dispute over the acceptance of thrice-yearly visitations to each college.[99]

The account of James Melville of his time at St Andrews between 1571 and 1574 confirms the view that no curricular innovations had occurred at the university in the 1560s.[100] Melville entered the college in 1571, and his first-year tuition comprised his regent's own primer on philosophical definitions, the *Rhetoric* of Cassander and Aristotle's *Organon*. His final three years focussed on other works of Aristotle, parts of Sacrobosco's *De Sphaera* and passages from Samuel and Kings, with tuition under William Skene in Cicero's *De Legibus* and Justinian's *Institutes*, and the viewing of Skene at work in the local courts. Most telling of all, no language tuition in Hebrew or Greek was given to Melville, emphasising the moribund nature of the curriculum.

In 1563 Queen Mary visited St Andrews, where a petition was presented to her government that the 'properties' of the colleges of St Andrews were in dreadful condition. To this end Parliament granted a commission to enquire after their revenues, and to offer their opinion and advice with respect to possible reforms St Andrews should undertake.[101] They were

---

[98] *Acta*, pp. 425–6.

[99] *Acta*, pp. 434–6.

[100] *JMAD*, pp. 24–30.

[101] Cant, pp. 54, 57; *Bannatyne Miscellany*, ed. W. Scott and D. Laing (3 vols, Edinburgh, 1827–55), vol. 2, p. 83; *RPS* A1563/6/26 [accessed 1 April 2010]. The committee

ordered to prepare a report for the next session of Parliament, but the only report that we have record of is the 'Opinion' of George Buchanan, a member of the committee.[102] Buchanan advocated that the three colleges be retained and form the basis of the teaching system, but that each should offer tuition in a different subject. The first college was to be a college of humanity staffed by a principal and six regents, where students would receive a thorough grounding in Latin and Greek before embarking on their proper university course. The second college was to be a college of philosophy with a principal and four regents but also having a reader in medicine. The two teaching staff of the third college, a principal who would teach Hebrew and divinity, and a lawyer, were to provide the sum total of higher faculty tuition at the university. It has been argued that Buchanan's programme was a serious contender for university reform and the reason nothing was done with it was due to general turmoil in the period, but it is clear that St Andrews was well on the way to recovery by 1563. No record of the work is found in the university statute books, and the work itself seems too radical to have been taken seriously, especially against the evidence of moderate reform taking place at the university. It seems more likely that Buchanan's 'Opinion' was quietly dismissed by the staff, owing to its attempts to alter radically the fabric of the university, and to their natural vested interest in keeping their own jobs within the multi-disciplinary collegiate system.

At the macro level, the trend of consolidation and repair following the reformation proceeded apace in the later 1560s and 1570s. The business of staff elections and yearly faculty accounts continued regularly, the purse of the Arts faculty grew steadily, and matriculation and graduation numbers, though fluctuating, did grow on the whole, with a record number of 29 entrants at St Mary's in 1566.[103] However, a string of squabbles and disputes marred the peace at the university, and while some were minor, others appear to have been more serious, and in the case of St Mary's related to charges of sedition and Catholic recusancy.

While John Rutherford was clearly one of the central figures maintaining order at the university after 1560, a visitation to his college early in the same decade shows that he was having considerable difficulties managing it. Rutherford had taken over the administration of the college in 1560 when his predecessor, the Catholic William Cranston, had absconded into

---

included the Earl of Murray, the President of the College of Justice, the Secretary of State, the Clerk Register, the Justice Clerk, the Queen's Advocate, George Buchanan, John Winram and John Erskine of Dun.

[102]   *Bannatyne Miscellany*, vol. 2, pp. 87–100.

[103]   See Appendix, Table 1.

exile with a large portion of the college goods and moveables.[104] On 15 September 1563 a committee comprising the rector John Douglas and his council of assessors visited the college, along with John Winram and James Lamont from St Leonard's, and Robert Hamilton and William Skene from St Mary's.[105] The visitation produced 22 separate points of order condemning the running of the college. The first three statutes criticised the other two masters, William Ramsay and David Guild, and the regent Thomas Buchanan for not following the commands of Rutherford, and issued three separate statutes warning the other regents to cease being overly familiar with the students, to stop mingling indiscriminately with them at meals, and to support the three principal masters in disciplinary matters. Rutherford and the other two masters had aroused anger among the students for failing to teach any theology and were ordered to include it within the timetable, and they were also to appoint an *oeconomus*, or rental officer, for the college within 15 days of the visitation to deal with the rents of Kilmany, the main parish annexed to the college. Student behaviour and moral standards were also lax. In addition to the janitor being warned to stop the students wandering outside the college without permission, a statute ordered that the 'multitude of women' (*pluralitate foeminarum*) who were apparently constantly visiting the college were to be restricted to just Rutherford's wife and a servant woman.

The majority of complaints were directed at Rutherford, who was condemned in a number of separate statutes for failing to oversee the correct care of college finances and goods, for installing a number of bursars and carrying out financial transactions without the consent of the other masters, and for failing to provide adequate victual for the poor students of the college. There was also very obvious tension between the masters and Rutherford, whose aggressive temperament was well known. A statute exhorting the masters to treat each other with 'mutual love' (*mutuo amore*) also admonished Rutherford to 'do all things with humility' and to 'learn rather to be loved than feared' (*monentque praepositum ut omnia agat cum humilitate, et discat potius amari quam timeri*), while another warns the 'exceedingly headstrong and impatient' Rutherford, 'in accordance with the doctrine of Paul not to let the sun set upon his

---

[104] *Acta*, p. cclxiv. The story that Cranston had absconded with many of the college moveables, often believed to be apocryphal, is actually shown to be true in the tenth statute made by the visitation to St Salvator's in 1563 that legal action be pursued against his family for his theft: 'ITEM rector et deputati intelligentes iocalia argentea loci, aulea, capeles, et alia vestimentia ad ecclesiam pertinentia, et utensilia domus magna ex parte fuisse distracta per Gulielmum Cranstoun, monent praepositum ut executores magistri Guilielmi Cranstoun vocat in ius et cum iis pro rebus ab eo intromissis iure contendat ut recuperentur.'

[105] *Balcarres Papers*, vol. 7, fos 98r–99v; see also transcription in UYUY172/2, pp. 90–105.

wrath, and [to] strive to hold his tounge so that he conducts himself more humanely and sweetly in all things'.[106] Rutherford was forced to hear and sign this humiliating list, and was given until the following January to deal with the main issues arising from it.[107] However, as no further record is found it appears that the findings of the visitation were allowed quietly to pass, with the point being made very publicly to Rutherford to take tighter control.

In the early 1570s, John Knox, Richard Bannatyne and James Melville all noted a number of factions at the university, primarily arising from a split between St Leonard's, whose staff and students were zealous for the 'guid cause', and the apostate and 'evill myndit' masters of St Mary's. These allegations may well have some truth to them, as St Mary's was still the preserve of the pro-Catholic Hamilton family who had re-founded the college in the 1550s. The Hamiltons had quickly rallied to the support of Queen Mary in June 1567 after her capture at Carberry, and remained loyal to her, fearing the loss of their place in the succession following the birth of James VI into the Lennox line. The Hamiltons also believed that the right to the regency belonged to their kinsman the Duke of Châtelherault, not to the decision of a council of nobility. The entire kin network supported the Marian faction, with 46 Hamilton lairds and 26 Hamiltons of lesser rank traceable among the lists of Marian supporters. Hamilton unrest reached fever pitch on 23 January 1570 when James Hamilton of Bothwellhaugh, with the connivance of the Archbishop of St Andrews, murdered the Regent Moray at Linlithgow. This action resulted in the capture of the Archbishop by the Earl of Lennox on 2 April 1571, and his execution four days later. Unrest caused by the Hamiltons and their allies the Gordons continued through the short regencies of Lennox and Mar until the regency of James Douglas, fourth Earl of Morton.[108]

These political events had their impact on the relations between the colleges in St Andrews. The Hamiltons exercised great influence in St Mary's, accounting for just under 15 per cent of the total number of students within the college in the 14 years after the reformation, and supplying the majority of teaching masters in the early 1570s. On 16 April 1570, the St Andrews Kirk Session Register recorded a complaint by James Carmichael 'and his complices' against Robert Hamilton, the second regent of St

---

[106]   Statute 8: 'ITEM rector et deputati intelligentes praefectum ex multorum delationibus in omnibus negotiis obeundis esse nimis praecipitem et impatientem, monent praepositum iuxta doctrinam Pauli ne sol occidat super iracundiam suam, et studeat refrenare linguam ut humanius et melius in omnibus et per omnia se gerat.'

[107]   A vernacular note with the text states Douglas caused this 'charter of regress retroscript be read in presence of Mr John Rutherford provost of the said college and deliverit to him the double thereof in deu form signit and subscrivit'.

[108]   Gordon Donaldson, *All the Queen's Men* (London, 1983), pp. 83–116.

Mary's and the minister of St Andrews parish, relating to the soundness of his doctrine.[109] The source of this offence is obscured in the kirk session records, but a full narrative of the events behind this issue is elaborated by Richard Bannatyne, Knox's secretary in St Andrews.[110] He affirms that immediately after the murder of the Queen's husband, Lord Darnley, Hamilton 'began to grow cauld in his sermondis, and neuer spake a word of these materis'. This in turn led the students of St Leonard's to desire him to pray for the Regent Moray and his safe return from a diplomatic mission to England. Hamilton refused, which resulted in a complaint to the General Assembly that he and his colleagues said 'sundrie thingis ... tending to the derogatioune of the Kingis authoritie'. The students also alleged that William Ramsay, second master of St Salvator's, had been 'seducit be the Hammiltounes factioune' with the promise of marriage to a daughter of the Hamiltons 'whome he ernestly desyred'. Ramsay was called up to the General Assembly to stand trial for seditious comments, and on 21 and 22 June 1570 both men asked the kirk session for testimonials as to the veracity of their doctrine and standing in the community. In July of that year Ramsay died,[111] and the dispute between Hamilton and Carmichael was indeed escalated to the General Assembly.[112]

The seriousness of the charge brought against Hamilton is reflected by the fact that James McGill, the Clerk Register, Lord John Ballantyne, Justice Clerk, and Archibald Douglas of the College of Justice asked the Assembly to withhold adjudication of Hamilton's case until it could be discussed before a convention of the nobility.[113] No record of the case passing to civil government or Parliament is recorded, however, and the issue appears to have blown over without further incident.

Further problems arose with Robert Hamilton's ministry over the next two years. In 1571 John Knox, out of favour in Edinburgh, took up a preaching post in St Andrews. In November of that year Hamilton, once a good friend and travelling-companion of Knox, was alleged to have said to the St Mary's regents James Hamilton and John Carnegie that Knox was 'als greit a murtherer as ony Hammiltoun in Scotland, gif all thingis wer well tried', and that he had been one of the conspirators involved in the murder of Darnley. Knox wrote to Hamilton on November 15 demanding

---

[109]   *RStAKS*, pp. 334–5.

[110]   Richard Bannatyne, *Memorials of Transactions in Scotland, A.D. MDLXIX–A.D. MDLXXIII*, ed. R. Pitcairn (Edinburgh, 1836), pp. 255–63.

[111]   UYSS150/2, f. 154v.

[112]   *BUK*, vol. 1, p. 179.

[113]   *BUK*, vol. 1, pp. 181–2.

to know whether he had been making such slanderous comments, which prompted Hamilton to visit Knox but did little to resolve the issue.[114]

Discipline within St Mary's also showed signs of breakdown. On 4 January 1570 a number of the students of the college alleged exemption from the ordinary disputations that formed part of the examination process. This prompted a statute stating that in future no immunity would be given and that traditional order would be upheld. The following day the St Mary's students Thomas McGie, Walter Lindsay and James Ogilvie, who were scheduled to take their masters examination, organised a meeting of students in protest at the exemptions, stating that they would refuse examination 'quhill every ane of ther masterrois be resavit with thame in thair ordor'. This meeting was broken up and the three ringleaders were ordered to undergo public discipline in St Mary's.[115]

More serious were the assaults involving regents of the college. On 7 February 1570 John Hamilton, a regent in St Mary's, had attacked a student, James Lindsay, with a knife in the middle of supper. Hamilton was allowed to apologise and keep his teaching position.[116] On 2 February 1570 another violent attack had been attempted by John Arthur, Hamilton's fellow regent in the college. With the aid of three other conspirators Arthur had attempted to sneak into the chamber of James Hamilton, and had been caught by the masters 'with swordis andrawin' in an attempt to injure him. Prior to this, Arthur had taunted Hamilton in the communal dining room by throwing an egg in his face and calling him a knave. Arthur's co-conspirators were allowed to remain at the university, but Arthur himself was removed immediately from his regenting post and expelled from the college. While violence of this kind was not at all uncommon in early modern universities, it is interesting that both cases featured Hamilton involvement.[117]

It has been alleged that the John Hamilton involved in the assault against James Lindsay was the Catholic controversialist and writer of *Ane Catholik and Facile Traictise ... to Confirme the Real and Corporell Praesence of Chrystis Pretious Bodie and Blude*.[118] Principal Lee identified this John Hamilton as entering St Mary's with Archibald Hamilton in 1552 and as being the regent who attacked James Lindsay in 1569.[119] James Melville also identified the regent during his time at St Andrews as the same man as

---

[114] Bannatyne, *Memorials*, pp. 255–63.

[115] *Early Records*, p. 273; *Acta*, pp. 430–1.

[116] Acta Rectorum, pp. 75–6.

[117] Acta Rectorum, pp. 77–9.

[118] Paris, 1581.

[119] John Lee, *Lectures on the History of the Church of Scotland: from the Reformation to the Revolution Settlement* (2 vols, Edinburgh, 1860) vol. 1, pp. 305, 345–8.

the apostate Hamilton.[120] Lee alleged that this John Hamilton served in the college until April 1575, but his certainty in this fact and his belief that the John Hamilton who wrote the *Facile Treatise* did not actually go to Paris in 1573, as has been asserted by other researchers, is unclear.

However, the third regent of St Mary's in the early 1570s, Archibald Hamilton, definitely did become a Catholic controversialist. From late 1571 until at least July 1572 he had refused to attend John Knox's sermons, resulting in his having to explain his absence at a meeting in Knox's house before John Douglas, John Winram, James Wilkie, John Rutherford, and the Bishop of Caithness. Hamilton stated that Knox 'affirmed, in his teiching, that Hammiltounes were murthereris', to which Knox answered in protest that the university staff were attempting to censor his sermons. Hamilton responded that Knox refused to submit his sermons to ministerial 'ordore and godly discipline', in particular that they be examined in disputation.

Knox left St Andrews on 17 August 1572 with the issue unresolved,[121] but there were further allegations made regarding Hamilton's religious convictions by the minister and polemicist Thomas Smeaton, and Hamilton was alleged to have acknowledged the writing of a satire on papal primacy. Hamilton left for Paris soon after November 1576, and his Latin treatise *On the Confusion of the Calvinist Sect in Scotland* appeared the following summer.[122] In 1581 Hamilton also published another Catholic tract, entitled *Against the Scurrilous Response of the Ministers of Scotland*.[123] By 1584 he had become a priest and doctor of the Sorbonne, and following the outbreak of civil war again in France in that year withdrew to Rome, where he took employment as a librarian in the Vatican. He died in 1593 in the apartments assigned to him by Gregory XIII.[124]

A very public dispute involving the Regent Morton and the Privy Council took place at the March 1574 General Assembly. The dispute was between John Rutherford and John Davidson over the latter's *Ane Dialog or Mutuall Talking Betuix a Clerk and ane Courteour*,[125] published anonymously without Davidson's consent. Davidson had matriculated at St Leonards in 1567 and was a regent at the college when he wrote this poem, a satirical attack on Morton's reorganisation of stipends by grouping

---

[120] *JMAD*, p. 26.

[121] Bannatyne, *Memorials*, pp. 260–3.

[122] Archibald Hamilton, *De confusione Calvinianae sectae apud Scotos ecclesiae nomen ridicule vsurpantis, dialogus* (Paris, 1577).

[123] Archibald Hamilton, *Calvinianae confusionis demonstratio, contra maledicam ministrorum Scotiae responsionem* (Paris, 1581).

[124] Alasdair Roberts, 'Hamilton, Archibald (d. 1593)', *ODNB* [12049, accessed 16 November 2010].

[125] Edinburgh, 1574.

several adjacent parishes together under the oversight of one minister.[126]
Maintaining an enmity of St Leonard's to the other two colleges, the poem
also contained unfavourable references to Rutherford (whom he called a
'crusit [irritable] goose') and to the university:

> Thair is sum Colleges we ken
> Weill foundit to uphold leirnit men ...
> Lat anis the Counsell send and se
> Gif thir places well gydit be,
> And not abusit with waist rudis
> That dois nothing bot spendis yai gudis ...[127]

Morton summoned Davidson to a justice-ayre at Haddington, and
Davidson was prosecuted by the Privy Council in June, forcing him into
hiding. In March 1574 Davidson beseeched the assembly to examine the
work and see if it contained any unsound doctrine. At the same assembly
the moderator was informed that Rutherford had written a response to
this work called 'Ineptias', which he was ordered to present. Rutherford
refused to do so, stating that the only manuscript was with the regent.
Rutherford was so keen not to show his work that he left the assembly
under a cloud, wishing to seek the further advice of the rector on the
matter.[128]

Perhaps aware of the Catholic recusancy at St Mary's and angered by
the episode with Davidson, Morton went to St Andrews with a commission
on 16 April 1574 to examine the rents and the discipline of the university
and to provide interim statutes until 'sum better and mair perfite ordour'
was made.[129] Notably, the prime act urged by the commission was that:

> [in] all dispensations, propositions, lessonis, writingis, tickettis or otherwyiss,
> thair be na fals doctrine, frivolous questiones, slanderous libellis ... that may
> move onie, in doctrine or religioun, seditioun aganis the prince, or scisme,
> hatreiit, or invy amangis the memberis of the universitie ...

Every principal was to read weekly public lectures in theology, in Latin,
from the first Monday of May. St Mary's was to provide four lessons per
week in the subjects of Hebrew, mathematics and law, while St Salvator's
was to provide four in Greek and a daily lesson in rhetoric. Where these
lecturers in the biblical languages were to come from is unclear, given

---

126   Charles Rogers, *Three Scottish Reformers* (London, 1874), pp. 31–3.

127   Rogers, *Three Scottish Reformers*, p. 63.

128   *BUK*, vol. 1, pp. 289–91, 297–8.

129   *Evidence*, pp. 188–9.

the limited evidence of Greek tuition, and none for Hebrew or Syriac, in St Andrews before the arrival of Melville. Each of these lectures was to be made with no fee to any who wished to listen, perhaps reflecting a similar recommendation that had been made in the *First Book*. Owing to the scarcity of ministers, anyone who had studied theology for any length of time and had not been able to take exams to confirm themselves as bachelors or doctors were given the option of presenting themselves before 31 October 1575 for trial and examination, where they would then be awarded with the relevant degrees.

Attempts were also made to equalise the colleges. The arts degree in every college was to be standardised at three and a half years, and regents were to serve in their posts for two courses, so that 'inequalitie of tyme and late tarrying mak not ane college to prejuge ane uther, in libertie, or in honour'. Prices and fees were to be fixed for all colleges in a yearly convocation on 1 October, and the duties of the rector, chancellor, and deans of faculty were to be researched by the office holders and sent to the regent by 1 September. The thrice-yearly visitation of each college was to be upheld, and by 1 October the principals of each college were to notify who was to be presented by the king, and when the same presentations were vacated, so that accounts for those presentations could be paid at either Martinmas or Whitsunday.

Morton fully intended to see these statutes enforced. On 29 April he ordered James Balfour of Pittendreich and John Winram to visit St Andrews and ensure the adoption of the statutes on Monday 1 May, and to report back on any member of the university who did not comply and on anything necessary to ensure the execution of the statutes.[130] While it appears that these statutes were not immediately adopted and ultimately had no lasting impact on the university settlement, what is clear is that the five years between Morton's visitation and the broader Protestant 'New Foundation' of the university were ones of considerable infighting and turmoil as attempts were made to consolidate these initial mobes toward reform.[131] These statutes also paved the way for the parliamentary visitation and reform of the university in 1579, and began a trend of state visitation that formed an integral part of the reformation of education at St Andrews in the 'Melvillian' period.

---

[130] Acta Rectorum, pp. 85–6.
[131] See Chapter 3.

Conclusion

While the conspectus of university education in the aftermath of the reformation is somewhat bleak and muddled, with no real evidence that successful or broad reform was suddenly enacted post-1560, this is perhaps not something we should be surprised at. As in so many parts of Scottish culture in the immediate post-reformation era, acclimatisation and gradual change outweighed sweeping and violent cultural transformation; and the traditions of a century and a half of Scottish university education, rooted in the structures of medieval knowledge and the Catholic Church, could not simply be torn down and thrown away. The reasons for maintaining these traditions varied from university to university, but they all contributed to a sense of stagnation. At Aberdeen religious opposition clearly played the biggest part in resistance, at an institution that, ironically, had since its inception been willing to embrace the latest in intellectual advances from the Continent. At Glasgow, the bare facts of woefully inadequate staffing and funding put paid to any attempt to create a Protestant institution on what were little more than the remains of the Catholic university for the whole of the 1560s. However, with the 'town foundation' of 1573 we see an interesting shift in the role of the civic government in the development of the university that would have significant repercussions in the following two decades at Edinburgh and beyond. St Andrews presents the biggest paradox among these three institutions; on one hand the university had a staff that was largely Protestant and supportive of reform, but on the other these men were entrenched in the traditional modes of learning and teaching that they had come to know, and were unwilling to relinquish any aspect of this if they could help it. The fact that the university was so riven with controversy in the early 1570s suggests that there was considerable dissatisfaction at the unsettled state of affairs, but also that many of its leaders, like John Rutherford, were more concerned with protecting themselves than with taking real steps to reform it. This inherent conservatism and self-protectionism would be the biggest impediment in the way of true intellectual and structural reform, and would provide for some truly explosive conflicts at the university over the following two decades. Overall, however, the universities in the 1560s and early 1570s were stuck between reformation and reform, and it would take the catalysing figure of Andrew Melville to inject a new dynamism into an otherwise static system of higher education.

CHAPTER 2

Humanism and Calvinism: Melville's Education, 1545–74

Andrew Melville (1545–1622) has often been likened to a second father of Scottish university education. It was following his return to Scotland in 1574 that the universities collectively gained 'a new lease of life' with a programme of studies in keeping with the latest educational provision on the Continent.[1] However, the so-called 'Melvillian' reform programme faced massive resistance in Scotland, both as it was directly implemented at Glasgow and St Andrews between 1574 and 1580, and indirectly in the influence it had on teaching elsewhere. What were the key tenets of this reform programme, and why did it cause so much controversy? At its core, the 'Melvillian' reform programme comprised a humanist refocusing on Aristotle in the original Greek instead of in Latin translation, alongside a raft of new humanist subjects such as history and sacred chronology; a thorough grounding in scriptural study and exegesis, including tuition in the full range of biblical languages; and the use of the works of the French educational reformer Petrus Ramus as a framework to teach these subjects, but particularly to teach the rudimentary elements of logic and philosophy. It is this last component that has been the most discussed, and least understood, part of Melville's teaching programme, and in what follows we will try to delineate what Ramism actually was and why Melville found it so attractive.

In tracing Melville's own formative years studying both at St Andrews and on the Continent between 1559 and 1574, what emerges is that while Melville held Ramus' 'method' in high regard, this was only one part of a far broader education including intensive study of ancient languages, philology, and authors (including Aristotle), and of the traditional forms of disputation and rhetorical exercise that formed part of the training of any young early modern intellectual. It was also while on the Continent that Melville picked up a deep suspicion of both Catholics in general and Jesuits in particular, and the thread of deep anti-Romanism that we find pervading the divinity course in St Andrews under Melville stems in part from his time abroad. However, the final stop of his intellectual *grand tour* at Geneva, where he was resident between 1569 and 1574, was in

---

[1]   Durkan and Kirk, p. 254.

many ways the one that defined him. It was there for the first time that he studied divinity in depth and learnt the tenets of Calvinist Presbyterianism under Theodore Beza, and there that he forged links with the leading English Presbyterians Thomas Cartwright and Walter Travers. The cumulative effect of all this training was to give Melville the skills to create a programme on his return to Scotland that blended the latest advances in humanist technique and study with the fundamental tenets of Calvinism.

Early Years in Scotland

Andrew Melville was born at Baldovy, near Montrose, on 1 August 1545 to Richard Melville, a cadet of the house of Glenbervie, and Giles Abercrombie, the daughter of a burgess of Montrose.[2] Melville was the youngest of nine children, and his family were clearly adherents of some form of reformed religion prior to the widespread adoption of Protestantism in 1560. Three of his brothers became ministers in the reformed church, including the eldest, Richard, who accompanied John Erskine of Dun to the Lutheran University of Greifswald in 1546 to study under Melanchthon for two years, and then proceeded to Denmark to hear John Maccabeus, a Scottish professor of Divinity at the University of Copenhagen.[3]

There was a focus in Melville's academic career from the outset on Christian humanism, and another early Protestant influence on him was Thomas Anderson, his teacher at the grammar school of Montrose. If the curriculum at the school was the same as that which his nephew James Melville studied a little over a decade later, it would likely have included instruction in Latin and French and the *Eclogues* of Virgil, the *Epistles* of Horace and Cicero, and the *Minor Colloquia* of Erasmus, thus introducing Melville at a very early age to some fundamental classical and humanist texts.[4] Melville took the precocious step of using part of his inheritance to fund two additional years at the grammar school to learn Greek under the tuition of the Frenchman Pierre de Marsilliers, a scholar invited to Montrose by John Erskine of Dun.[5] Melville must have began this tuition no later than 1557, presumably unaware that undertaking such a course

---

[2]   Melville himself confirms his birthday in the marginalia of his copy of Abraham Bucholtzer's *Isagoge Chronologica, id est: opusculam ad annorum seriem in Sacris Bibliis contexendam, compendio viam monstrans ac fundamenta indicans* (In Officina Sanctandreana, false imprint, 1596), NLS, E.84.f.16, f. OO VIIIv, entry for the year 1545: 'And: Melvinus natus, circa Calend. Augusti.'

[3]   Durkan and Kirk, p. 263; M'Crie, pp. 1–2. Holloway maintains that this chronology is reversed: Holloway, 'Andrew Melville and Humanism', pp. 44–5.

[4]   Holloway, 'Andrew Melville and Humanism', p. 53; *JMAD*, pp. 16–17, 21.

[5]   *JMAD*, p. 39.

put him at the forefront of Scottish intellectual developments in the 1550s, given the limited evidence of Greek tuition at the Scottish universities at that time.

Melville matriculated at St Andrews in either 1559 or 1560, entering the New College, or St Mary's, on the eve of the reformation.[6] The fact that Melville chose to enter St Andrews is unsurprising given its geographic proximity to his home. It also requires equally little explanation that he should enter a college re-founded five years earlier to promote Catholic orthodoxy, given the level of widespread support for Protestant reform in St Mary's at the time of his entry, and that it was the largest and best-endowed college in the university in a period of otherwise greatly reduced student numbers and extremely poor administration.

While no account survives of Melville's personal experience at the university, if the arts statutes of the 1560s and the experience of Melville's nephew James in the following decade are any indication, Melville would have learnt a broad range of the corpus of Aristotle in Latin translation, with works in philosophy by Plato, Xenophon, and Cicero, in rhetoric by Cassander, and in law by Cicero and Justinian, with exposition of some scriptural passages by teaching staff and perhaps a range of other humanist texts chosen by Douglas as the college principal.[7] That no Greek or training in other biblical languages was given, however, is evinced by the well-known anecdote that Melville amazed his tutors by reading Aristotle direct from the Greek, which 'his maisters understud nocht'.[8]

There are no records showing when Melville graduated, as there is only a partial list of graduates for the period from 1560 to 1565,[9] but he had clearly left no earlier than October 1563 and no later than autumn 1564 after what must have been a fairly rudimentary education. This would have made him 18 or 19, a fairly standard age for the average graduate in the period.[10] However, an encomiastic verse to the young Melville by the Italian reformer and poet Pietro Bizzarri, who was in attendance at the Scottish court between February and summer 1564, shows the promise that Melville was clearly seen to hold.[11] The poem, making a play of Melville's name, states that 'no sweeter honeys' (*nulla magis dulcia mella*)

---

[6]   The matriculation roll of the university states that Melville entered St Mary's in 1559 (*Early Records*, p. 267), but Melville himself says that he began his studies in October 1560 (Bucholtzer, *Isagoge Chronologica*, f. QQ IIIr, entry at 1560: 'And. Melvinus Andreapoli ad philosophos Octobri ineunte').

[7]   *Acta*, pp. 416–21; *JMAD*, pp. 24–30.

[8]   *JMAD*, p. 39.

[9]   *Early Records*, pp. 157–9.

[10]   Durkan and Kirk, pp. 183–4.

[11]   I.D. Macfarlane, *Buchanan* (London, 1981), pp. 227–8. It is unclear though whether the two actually met in Scotland, or during Melville's time studying in Paris.

or wines could be collected than those 'whom you, a sweet man, present before me, with sweet discourse, and with your honied words, and ways, and with a natural innate talent'.[12]

Paris and Poitiers, Buchanan and Ramus

Sources for Melville's time in Paris and Poitiers between 1563/4 and 1569 give nothing but the barest account of what he studied and to whom he chose to listen. The *Acta Rectoria Universitatis Parisiensis* and associated sources have no record of Melville matriculating at the university, nor is there any documentary evidence for his time as a regent in Poitiers.[13] The only real evidence we have for this highly formative period of his intellectual development comes from the short account written by his nephew, James Melville:

> [At] Paris, whar he remeanit in the Universitie twa yeiris at his awin studies, heiring the lichtes of the maist scyning age in all guid letters, the King's publict professours, Andreas Tornebus in Greik and Latine Humanitie; Petrus Ramus in Philosophie and Eloquence; Jo[hannes] Mercerus in the Hebrew langage, whereupon he was speciallie sett.[14]

This account has to be treated with caution, as it was written long after Melville returned from the Continent. However, it is clear from the names given, as James Kirk has suggested, that Melville chose to pursue the public lectures in languages and philosophy offered at the Collège de France,[15] founded by Francis I in 1530 for the study of Latin, Greek and Hebrew.[16] The names of Adrien Turnébe and Jean Mercier, two of the foremost philologists of the age, suggest that the central focus of Melville's time in Paris was to develop his interest in classical philology and biblical languages, two interests that would form key components of his intellectual reform programme on his return to Scotland.[17] Melville likely came into contact for the first time at Paris with George Buchanan,

[12] Petri Bizzari, *Varia Opuscula* (Venice, 1565), f. 109. The poem is reprinted in its entirety in M'Crie, p. 8. 'Quam mihi dulcis ades, dulci sermone, tuisque/ Mellitis verbis, moribus, ingenio.'

[13] W.A. Macneill, 'Scottish Entries in the *Acta Rectoria Universitatis Parisiensis* 1519 to c.1633', *SHR* 43 (1964): 66–86.

[14] *JMAD*, pp. 39–40.

[15] Durkan and Kirk, pp. 266–7.

[16] Abel Lefranc and others, *Le Collège de France 1530–1930* (Paris, 1932), pp. 3–58.

[17] On Turnèbe, see John Lewis, *Adrien Turnèbe (1512–1565): A Humanist Observed* (Geneva, 1998).

whose literary skills influenced Melville's own efforts in neo-Latin poetry. It was also at Paris that he first met Petrus Ramus, the man whose work in educational reform greatly informed his own teaching methods and intellectual approach.

Why was Melville so interested in Ramus' works, and what specific role did he envisage them playing in his educational reform programme? To answer these questions, we have to first understand who Ramus (or Pierre de la Ramée in the vernacular) was and what his work in educational reform entailed, a subject that since the publication in 1958 of Walter Ong's *Ramus, Method and the Decay of Dialogue*[18] has been the focus of intense academic scrutiny.[19] Since Ramism was a central part of the pedagogical method employed by Melville in his approach to teaching and in the exposition of his own texts, and since much of the analysis in later chapters hinges around identifying strains of Ramist thought alongside Aristotelian ones in the texts produced by Scottish students and masters, it will also be worthwhile here establishing some of the key components and terminology of the Ramist 'method'.

---

[18]   Walter Ong, *Ramus, Method and the Decay of Dialogue: From the Art of Discourse to the Art of Reason* (Cambridge, Mass., 1958); idem, *Ramus and Talon Inventory* (Cambridge, Mass., 1958).

[19]   The most thorough accounts of the vast array of literature on Ramus are the invaluable summaries by Peter Sharratt: 'The Present State of Studies on Ramus', *Studi Francesci* 16 (1972): 201–13; 'Recent Work on Peter Ramus (1970–1986)', *Rhetorica* 5 (1987): 7–58; 'Ramus 2000', *Rhetorica* 18 (2000): 399–445. The most comprehensive account of Ramus and Ramism is Ong, *Ramus* – but see the cautionary comments below. A short and accessible account of his reforms of logic and their context can be found in Lisa Jardine, 'Humanistic Logic', in Charles B. Schmitt and Quentin Skinner (eds), *The Cambridge History of Renaissance Philosophy* (Cambridge, 1998), pp. 173–98. For Ramus' work on educational reform see James V. Skalnik, *Ramus and Reform: University and Church at the End of the Renaissance* (Missouri, 2002); Peter Sharratt, 'Peter Ramus and the Reform of the University: The Divorce of Philosophy and Eloquence?' in Peter Sharratt (ed.), *French Renaissance Studies, 1540–1570: Humanism and the Encyclopedia*, 1976), pp. 4–20; and Kees Meerhoff and Marcel Magnien (eds), *Ramus et l'Université* (Paris, 2004). For the impact of Ramus and his teachings across Europe, particularly in Sweden, Switzerland, England and at Trinity College Dublin, see Mordechai Feingold, Joseph S. Freedman and Wolfgang Rother (eds), *The Influence of Petrus Ramus: Studies in Sixteenth and Seventeenth Century Philosophy and Sciences* (Basle, 2001). Older studies of Ramism in England, though equally valuable, are Wilbur S. Howell, *Logic and Rhetoric in England, 1500–1700* (Princeton, 1956), and Kearney, *Scholars and Gentlemen*. For Ramus' impact on central Europe, see Joseph S. Freedman, 'The Diffusion of the Writings of Petrus Ramus in Central Europe, c. 1570– c.1630', in his *Philosophy and the Arts in Central Europe, 1500–1700* (Aldershot, 1999), pp. 98–152; Joseph S. Freedman, 'Melancthon's Opinion of Ramus and the Utilization of Their Writings in Central Europe', in *The Influence of Petrus Ramus*, pp. 68–91; and Howard Hotson, *Commonplace Learning: Ramism and its German Ramifications, 1543–1630* (Oxford, 2007).

Ramus's reforms to the teaching of dialectic and logic had their roots in the criticisms of scholastic logic made by Lorenzo Valla and Rudolph Agricola. Valla's *Dialecticae Disputationes* and *Elegantiae* focussed on the relationship between grammar and logic, and argued that most of the overly complex problems of medieval scholastic logic could be resolved by proper consideration of grammar and syntax. Rudolph Agricola's *De Inventione Dialectica*, completed in 1480 and first published in 1515, built on this and became a central textbook on logic used at universities across Europe from the 1530s onwards. Agricola challenged the necessity of the rigour of Aristotelian logic, particularly in the requirement of the syllogism and the other highly technical methods of proof that flourished in the logic schools of the Middle Ages. He placed far greater emphasis on the importance of practical argument and the ability to create rhetorical strategies and techniques to influence an opponent.[20] Agricola thus began the process by which humanist dialectic would concern itself with creating arguments that were more rhetorically convincing than provable by Aristotelian logic, a process that Ramus would in turn complete.

In 1543 Ramus published his first works, the *Aristotelicae Animadversiones* ('Remarks on Aristotle'), and the first edition of his *Dialecticae Institutiones* ('Training in Dialectic').[21] Both works heavily criticised the authority of Aristotle, and by extension the central role the traditional university curriculum afforded him. However, the 'rampant anti-Aristotelianism' of Ramus' reform is often overblown, and in fact his reputed MA thesis on Aristotle, entitled *Quaecumque ab Aristotele dicta essent, esse commentitia* most likely attacked the late-medieval scholastic baggage that had accrued around Aristotle rather than Aristotle himself.[22] It is true that Ramus did subject the logical and rhetorical works of Aristotle, Cicero and Quintillian to great reduction and criticism, but his central aim in his initial reforms was to remove the redundancy in the medieval trivium of logic, rhetoric and grammar where invention (the 'discovery' or elucidating of material for argument) and arrangement (the construction of arguments from this material) were covered multiple times.[23] The final revisions after 1555 structured logic under these two headings, with no recourse to rhetoric. This reduced rhetoric from a separate art to the 'handmaiden' of logic that confined itself to the teaching

---

[20]   Jardine, 'Humanist Logic', pp. 181–4.

[21]   Published initially as the *Partitiones Dialecticae* ('The Structure of Dialectic'). Freedman, 'Melanchthon's Opinion of Ramus', p. 71.

[22]   As explained in detail by Ong, *Ramus*, pp. 36–47. Howell, *Logic and Rhetoric in England*, pp. 146–7.

[23]   Howell, *Logic and Rhetoric in England*, pp. 153–5; Ong, *Ramus*, p. 270.

of style and delivery.[24] Moreover, the reduction of a need for formally valid proof, initiated by Valla and Agricola, was carried to its logical conclusion by Ramus – the Aristotelian predicables were seen as no longer necessary and all except the most basic form of the syllogism, the central tool of Aristotelian logic, were removed.

The reforms of logic and rhetoric were only part of the wider unified 'method' for teaching all arts and sciences developed by Ramus in successive editions of his works, particularly in the 1555/6 French and Latin versions of his most famous work, the *Dialecticae in Libri Duo*, and the 1557 *Quod sit unica methodus*.[25] The central concern of the Ramist discussion on method was that Aristotle had approached an understanding of this process in his works on logic, but that it had lacked proper organisation. To remedy this, Ramus created 'three laws' derived initially from discussions on the requirements of a middle term in a syllogism in the *Posterior Analytics*, known in English as the law of truth, the law of justice and the law of wisdom. The law of truth established that the rules and precepts connected to an art be proven and 'true' in a universally accepted sense rather than via syllogistic reasoning, thus describing a subject via a series of axioms rather than through a series of formally proven statements. The law of justice allowed only those statements directly connected to an art to form part of the discussion or methodisation of it. The law of wisdom, the centrepiece of the Ramist 'method', organised these definitions and associated material on the basis that some statements are naturally more evident or conspicuous than others.[26] According to the Ramist method, propositions of utmost generality are placed first, then those of lesser generality, scaling down through a topic to specific teaching examples in a subject. Thus a statement of the cause of a thing is more evident than a statement of its effect, and a general and universal statement on a subject is more evident than a particular or singular detail regarding that subject. An oft-quoted example, in this case from Ramus' earliest discussion of method, is that of grammar. The most general statement that can be made regarding grammar is that it is 'the doctrine of speaking well'. The next most general statement that can be made is that it has two parts, etymology and syntax. Then the student would rank third separate statements of the definition of etymology and of syntax, and rank the next most general

---

[24]   Skalnik, *Ramus and Reform*, p. 47.

[25]   Ong, *Ramus*, p. 30; Skalnik, *Ramus and Reform*, p. 43.

[26]   Ong, *Ramus*, pp. 245–57; Skalnik, *Ramus and Reform*, p. 44; Hotson, *Commonplace Learning*, p. 45; Howell, *Logic and Rhetoric in England*, pp. 150–1, 160–1.

statement about each, and so on until specific detailed examples of the usage of grammar would appear at the bottom of the list.[27]

These three laws provided the basis for what Ramus saw as the ideal method of preparing a subject for teaching. Ramus has been understood, as a result of this ordering via axiomatic statement, as structuring all discussion on a subject into a series of 'either…or' dichotomies, but this is a process that was developed by his disciples, including the British followers of Ramism, Melville among them.[28] What Ramus did argue, however, was that the ordering of subjects should be qualified as 'natural' and 'prudential'. The 'natural' ordering came out of a subject following strictly the doctrine of the three laws, but the 'prudential' was when, for the sake of the audience being preached to or the class being taught, material could be organised into the order that would most effectively get the message across to them.[29] The 'prudential' method was one used by poets, orators and historians intent on achieving a rhetorical and emotional effect, but where the speaker also educated the audience while he spoke as a secondary process. It was thus a highly practical form of pedagogy, which could be geared around the audience in front of the teacher or lecturer as and when necessary.

Finally, Ramus acknowledged two types of argument. Those that were 'artistic' stemmed from indirect or circumstantial evidence and took greater rhetorical skill to put forth. 'Non-artistic' arguments comprised direct evidence such as witnesses, documents, and the divine testimony found in scripture or axioms generally held to be eternally true of human nature. The 'artistic' grouping was of far greater interest to Ramus than the 'non-artistic', and he devoted the vast majority of his work to it. However, the total grouping of ten types of artistic and non-artistic argument may have been meant to reflect the ten categories of Aristotle, just as the three laws reflect elements within the *Posterior Analytics*. The 'artistic' arguments comprise six 'primary' causes of causes, effects, subjects, adjuncts, opposites, and comparatives, and three 'derivative' causes of reasoning from name, from division and by definition. Further parallel with Aristotle is seen by the division of 'causes' in Ramism into the headings of final (the limit or end that a cause is expected to reach), formal, efficient (the driving

---

[27]   Ong, *Ramus*, pp. 245–6; Skalnik, *Ramus and Reform*, pp. 44–5; Petrus Ramus, *Dialectique* (1555), ed. M. Dassonville (Geneva, 1964), pp. 122–3.

[28]   Hotson, *Commonplace Learning*, p. 46; Howell, *Logic and Rhetoric in England*, pp. 162–3. See, for example, the earliest translation of the Ramist logic into English, by Roland MacIlmaine (possibly MacIlvannie), *The Logike of the Moste Excellent Philosopher P. Ramus Martyr* (London, 1574), which uses dichotomy and scriptural examples instead of poetic ones to illustrate points.

[29]   Ong, *Ramus*, pp. 252–4.

or impelling force behind a cause) and material (the actual matter that makes up a cause).[30]

The fundamental ideal at the heart of Ramus' reforms centred on his belief that practical usage was the ultimate end of all arts and sciences. This idea was largely dismissed by Walter Ong but has been recently developed by modern commentators on Ramus' works, particularly James Skalnik. Each art had three aspects which determined its form and content, namely *natura*, *doctrina* and *usus* or *exercitatione* ('nature, doctrine and use'). Ramus believed every man was born with the innate ability to reason, and formal logic should build on this through observation of naturally-occurring, practical wisdom. All the examples given for understanding logic and philosophy in the *Dialecticae* were drawn not from dense philosophical texts, but from the inherent wisdom found in quotations of Virgil, Horace, Ovid and the other great classical Roman writers. This was not a process Ramus confined to his Latin version of the text, as the French *Dialectique* used the works of Ronsard, du Bellay and the other members of the Pléiade as examples. Ramus believed that students could unite the concepts of 'philosophy and eloquence' to understand both the technicalities of an author's style and the moral overtones of their work. Borrowing from discussions by Galen, Ramus called this two-step process 'analysis' – where a detailed understanding was gained of how a work was logically, grammatically and rhetorically composed – followed by that of 'genesis', whereby students would develop the wherewithal to create their own works on a similar basis. This emphasis on practical use was reflected in Ramus' own classroom practices, where he gave just two hours of lectures per day. The rest was devoted to study, memorisation of key concepts, and practical conversation and discourse.[31]

While Ramus' ideas may seem unremarkable to us, the furore generated among scholastic Aristotelians and scholars of classical philology alike was massive. It was triggered by Ramus' direct attack on the authority of Aristotle and his attempt to replace teaching methods with such an abbreviated and pragmatically focussed course of tuition. That controversy has been replicated in the scholarship surrounding Ramus and his works today. While Walter Ong's work underpinned the foundations of modern Ramus scholarship, it also hampered objective assessments of the significance of Ramism by portraying it as the 'passive indicator' of a shift in western culture from the written to the printed word.[32] As such, the only possibility that Ong was willing to countenance for the vast popularity

---

[30]   Howell, *Logic and Rhetoric in England*, p. 156.

[31]   Skalnik, *Ramus and Reform*, pp. 47–52; Hotson, *Commonplace Learning*, pp. 47–8.

[32]   Hotson, *Commonplace Learning*, pp. 9–16.

of Ramus' works was their visual appeal on the printed page, with their tables of dichotomies and bracketed expositions. Anthony Grafton and Lisa Jardine, charting the development of humanism into the foundations of the modern systematised liberal arts education in their *From Humanism to the Humanities*,[33] shared Ong's viewpoint that Ramus was the 'most pragmatic and applied' of arts educationalists. They believed the success enjoyed by Ramism could only be explained by its being a cynical brand of packaged education. For example, the works of Ramus were used by schoolteachers like Claude Mignault, master at the Collège de Reims, the Collège de la Marche and the Collège de la Bourgogne in the 1570s, who created a course where Ramist logic was the 'universal skeleton key' that gave students destined to work as priests, civil servants and teachers the skills they needed for careers in public life. They showed the flamboyant Cambridge rhetorician Gabriel Harvey as an example of this kind of careerist, who adopted the 'somewhat voguish intellectual stance' of Ramism in the same way he adopted Italian styles of clothing to project an image to impress the right people for promotion in Elizabethan England.

In contrast however, the most recent research into the pedagogical success of Ramism in central Europe, particularly in Switzerland,[34] has shown that where it was popular it was precisely because Ramism was such a pragmatic system. This process began with the detailed analysis of texts used for teaching at public schools in Germany between 1570 and 1630 compiled by Joseph Freedman, who showed that teaching staff across the German-speaking lands mixed a bewildering array of texts for the purpose of *ad hoc* teaching. Teachers combined Ramist textbooks on the trivium and quadrivium with similar works by Melanchthon, to which were added the works of Aristotle, Zabarella and Keckermann for teaching in philosophy, and excerpts from scripture for religious teaching.

Howard Hotson's study of the context behind the unrivalled popularity of Ramist works in Germany,[35] the most developed and full account of the influence of Ramism in a national framework, has confirmed the pragmatic and popular nature of the Ramist method. Ramus' works were not

---

[33]   Grafton and Jardine, *From Humanism to the Humanities*, especially pp. 161–209.

[34]   Wolfgang Rother, 'Ramus and Ramism in Switzerland', in *The Influence of Petrus Ramus*, pp. 9–37; Theo Verbeek, 'Notes on Ramism in the Netherlands', ibid., pp. 38–53; Thomas Elsmann, 'The Influence of Ramism on the Academies of Bremen and Danzig', ibid., pp. 54–67. Ramus was popularly received across the Swiss cantons between 1568 and 1570, especially at Zurich. The most committed Swiss Ramists were Theodore Zwinger and Johannes Thomas Freigius, both of whom produced encyclopaedias based on Ramist principles. However, in the Netherlands Ramism was never a strongly discernible force beyond the teaching of the Mathematician Rudolphus Snellius at Leiden from 1575, and in the theological teaching of William Ames at Franeker from 1622.

[35]   Hotson, *Commonplace Learning*, pp. 51–98.

imported into Germany by the German universities, but by the hundreds of small schools in the Hanseatic cities and the *academia illustria* of the imperial counties where Ramist textbooks were a cheap and accessible way of providing a varied education. The schools were often too poor to attract top-flight philologists and philosophers who would actively defend a humanist programme of study that focussed exclusively on immersion in classical authors. The need for competent local ministers and civil servants in areas like Nassau-Dillenberg, afflicted on all sides by varying confessional identities, prompted territorial rulers including Johann VI to found academies like the 'paradigmatic example' of Herborn, a Ramist centre *par excellence* under the noted theologian Johannes Piscator. Despite a reaction against Ramism in England, France and the Netherlands in the last quarter of the sixteenth century, the Ramist tradition continued to evolve in German-speaking areas and gave rise to a wider 'methodical' pedagogical tradition that spawned advances in systematic theology and philosophy.

Despite these more positive interpretations of Ramus and his work, Ramism has also been unduly – and wrongly, in many cases – identified with religious extremism, particularly being portrayed as an intellectual 'badge of honour' worn by Continental Calvinists, Scottish Presbyterians, and English Puritans.[36] James Kirk and Hugh Kearney are the key proponents of this idea in a Scottish context, arguing that Melville's reform programme was geared around 'anti-Aristotelian' and 'anti-scholastic' elements, and that Melville utilised Ramus' 'method' as part of an ideological programme to recruit young students to radical Presbyterianism. Kearney's own work on the social history of the early modern English universities argued that Ramism underpinned the development of an 'urban intellectual wing' of Puritanism that was much more radical than its counterpart among the 'country' gentry.[37] He applied this model wholesale to the conflicts he saw between Presbyterian and Episcopalian wings in the Scottish Kirk, arguing that Melville aimed to use the universities as centres from which to drive a Presbyterian 'urban revolution' in Scotland, with Ramism as the unifying ideological tool used by the radical intelligentsia. James Kirk built heavily on this thesis in his highly influential work on the reformed Scottish universities. Playing down the limited successes of the 'Melvillian' reform programme at St Andrews and Aberdeen, and logically extending

---

[36] Elsmann, 'The Influence of Ramism on the Academies of Bremen and Danzig', pp. 54–67; Hotson, *Commonplace Learning*, pp. 16–25 ('Ramism and Calvinism: an Overworked Explanation'). Hotson shows that Ramus' mixed reception in reformed academies between 1568 and 1570, most notably at Geneva, and the dissemination across so many confessional areas in Germany, indicates that the perceived link between Ramism and Calvinism is not sustainable. Durkan and Kirk, pp. 262–346; Kirk, '"Melvillian" Reform', pp. 276–300.

[37] Kearney, *Scholars and Gentlemen*, pp. 46–70.

his argument on the basis of the evidence of success he saw of Melville's reform programme at Glasgow and of Ramist influence at Edinburgh and Marischal at their foundations, Kirk drew the conclusion that Melville was in effective control of theological education in Scotland in the last quarter of the sixteenth century. He was thus able to cultivate a body of ministers and students loyal to the Presbyterian movement who shared Ramism as part of their intellectual outlook and methodology.

It is true that Ramus' ideas and works were utilised by Melville in his educational reforms on his return to Scotland, and it is certainly true that in the colleges where Melville directly taught there was a firm adherence to radical Presbyterianism, which he likely inculcated in his students. Yet it was precisely the 'pragmatism' of Ramism that Melville found attractive, not its radicalism. Working almost single-handedly at Glasgow and St Mary's, the Ramist 'method' gave him the framework to disseminate teaching quickly and effectively across a range of subjects with the minimum amount of resources, and also provided an ideal methodology for teaching divinity students to preach and effectively expound doctrine.[38]

However, in the 1560s his work as a teacher in Scotland lay far ahead of him, and in the two years he spent in Paris his study of Ramus's 'method' was only a small part of the wider spectrum of ideas that he absorbed from the public lecturers at the college. Melville was equally drawn to Ramus for his fame as a commentator on Cicero and Virgil, the latter being Melville's favourite author and often his poetic model, as he was to his educational methods. An obsession with Greco-Latin literature united the lecturers that Melville chose to listen to, and Melville's lecturers at Paris represented the zenith of philological studies at the Collège de France. His residency there occurred during the brief cessation of hostilities between the first and second civil war, and by the time he left a number of these great minds had died or had moved on to other universities. Melville attended the last course of lectures delivered by Adrien Turnébe before his premature death in June 1565. Turnèbe had been royal reader in Greek between 1547 and 1561, and then reader in Greek and Latin philosophy in the final four years of his life. During his time there he produced over fifty works including editions of Plato, Aristotle and Homer, translations of Oppian, Theophrastus and Plutarch, and extensive commentaries on Cicero and Quintillian. Turnèbe also directed the *Imprimerie Royale* from 1551 to 1556, and supplemented his own editions with texts and translations of many other classical authors, including Hermes Trismegistus and Aretaeus.

---

[38] For more on the use of Ramism internationally as a pedagogical tool, see Steven J. Reid and Emma A. Wilson (eds), *Ramus, Pedagogy and the Liberal Arts: Ramism in Britain and the Wider World* (Aldershot, 2011), and my 'Andrew Melville and Scottish Ramism: A Re-interpretation' in the same volume.

His most famous work was the *Adversaria*, an encyclopaedia of classical readings and emendations, first published as a two-volume set in 1564–65. As a neo-Latin poet his style was held by Montaigne to rival that of Buchanan.[39] Buchanan enjoyed a life-long friendship with Turnèbe after meeting him in the 1540s, continuing to keep in touch with him even after his return to Scotland, and likely introduced him to Melville.[40]

Melville also began to develop his learning in Old Testament languages while at Paris under Jean Mercier (professor from 1547 to 1570) and Jean de Cinquarbres (professor from 1554 to 1587), conjunct professors in Hebrew and Chaldaic. Mercier produced one of the earliest separate treatises on Chaldaic, printed at Paris in 1560, and was highly regarded for his commentaries on the Old Testament. Cinquarbres produced a treatise on Hebrew grammar that was published in a number of editions in the sixteenth century.[41] The lectures Melville heard on mathematics by Pierre Forcadel (1560–73) would have undoubtedly centred on the works of Euclid, whom Forcadel had translated into French in the year of Melville's arrival in Paris.[42] While James Melville noted that his uncle had listened to lectures on mathematics under Pascal Duhamel's successor Jacques Charpentier, he must have done so briefly and not learnt a great deal. Charpentier took over from the Sicilian Dampestre Cosel, and was woefully unqualified for the post. Charpentier's seizure of the seat without due trial by his fellows prompted considerable legal wranglings, led by Ramus, which would have inhibited teaching.[43] Melville also apparently attended the lectures of François Baudoin in law, when he was giving unpaid public lectures at the Collège, and may have heard lectures in medicine by Louis Duret, though the latter likely started teaching only after Melville left for Poitiers.[44]

---

[39]   Lewis, *Adrien Turnèbe*, pp. 15, 20–22, 334–7.

[40]   Lewis, *Adrien Turnèbe*, 35–40; MacFarlane, *Buchanan*, p. 97. The tradition, however, that Turnébe and Buchanan taught together at the University of Toulouse between 1545 and 1547 has been largely discredited by both authors.

[41]   M'Crie (1819 edn), vol. 1, pp. 22–3. *Tabulae in Grammaticen linguae Chaldaeae, quae et Syriaca dicitur-Johanne Mercero Hebraicarum literarum professore regi* (Paris, 1560); *De re grammatica Hebraeorum opus, in gratiam studiosorum linguae sanctae, methodo facillima conscriptum, authore Johanne Quinquarboreo Aurilacensi, linguarum Hebraicae et Caldaicae regio professore.* Editions were published at Paris in 1549, 1556 and 1582, though there appears to have been another edition before 1556. Dates for lecturers are taken from Skalnik, *Ramus and Reform*, appendix 1.

[42]   M'Crie (1819 edn), vol. 1, p. 24. *Les six premieres livres des elements d'Euclide trad. et commentez par Pierre Forcadel de Bezies* (Paris, 1564).

[43]   Skalnik, *Ramus and Reform*, pp. 80–87.

[44]   Holloway, 'Andrew Melville and Humanism', p. 72.

It was at Paris that Melville had his first encounter with the Jesuits, whose relations with the faculty of the university were exceedingly fraught. The Jesuits were formally recognised by Paul III in the 1540 Bull *Regimini militantis Ecclesiae*. The aims of this bull, and of their founder Ignatius Loyola (himself educated at the Collége de Sainte-Barbe in Paris), were to propagate and bolster the Catholic faith by education of the young. By the mid-1550s the Jesuits had expanded the scope of their original mission as roving preachers to include the public teaching of theology, and the right to grant degrees from their colleges even to those not intending to enter their order. This circumvented the traditional Parisian practice of sending members of religious orders to the Faculty of Theology, and the Jesuits' free arts tuition threatened Paris' central role in providing secular education. Supported by the Cardinal de Lorraine and Guillaume Duprat, Bishop of Clermont, the Jesuits succeeded in obtaining legal recognition of their order in France on 13 February 1562. By February 1564 they had convinced the rector of the university, Julien de Saint-Germain, to provide them with the *lettres de scolarité* required to teach classes. By October the Jesuits' courses in the Collège de Clermont, which had the ostentatious title above the doorway of *Collegium Claromontanum Societatis Jesu*, proved to be draining so many from the fee-paying classes that their *lettres* were revoked by the new rector, Jean Prévost. A legal trial ensued between 29 March and 5 April 1565 where the Jesuits defended their rights against the jurist Etienne Pasquier.[45] On 29 May 1565 Paul IV intervened on their behalf with Charles IX and the Jesuits were given further letters patent allowing them to open houses across France. They were also allowed to accept boarders at Clermont, which would grow in popularity to become the most famous of all Jesuit colleges.

Turnèbe's best-known poetic work, the *Ad Sotericum gratis docentem*, was a blistering attack on the Jesuits written just before his death at the height of the unrest caused by the trial. Turnèbe's poem was one of a number of polemics produced at Paris in these years which show the distrust and suspicion in which the Jesuits were held.[46] Melville's witnessing of this trial and exposure to the polemic associated with it must have greatly informed his desire to create an 'anti-seminary' to combat the Jesuits on his return home.

---

[45]   Lewis, *Adrien Turnébe*, pp. 77–104.

[46]   Lewis, *Adrien Turnèbe*, pp. 79–90, 94–7. Other anonymous attacks on the Jesuits include the *Complainte de l'Université de Paris contre aucuns estrangers nouvellement venus* (1564) and *Complaintes des escolliers contre les nouveaux viollateurs des lois, surnommez Jésuites* (1565). A poem from the same period entitled *In Jesuitas Parrhisiis gratis docentes* has been attributed to Patrick Adamson (Bibliothèque Nationale Fonds Dupuy 951, f. 87r., attributed to Adamson in Étienne Pasquier, *Le Catéchisme des Jésuistes*, ed. C. Sutto, p. 256, n. 134). The full text is given in Lewis, p. 97, n. 48.

A letter from Melville to Peter Young, the future tutor of James VI, shows Buchanan played a formative role in Melville's education at Paris. Written while Melville was at Geneva in 1572, it also indicates he placed a high value on Buchanan's poetry:

> For when he [Buchanan] was in Paris, he courteously explained to me the more difficult passages in his Psalm [paraphrases] and epigrams: and having lovingly embraced me, as if I were his son, he willingly admitted me to his rich companionship and to his learned talk. I have never once forgotten so much kindness: reading privately and commenting publicly in the schools [on] this splendid, almost divine work.[47]

The fact that Buchanan 'willingly admitted' Melville to his companionship suggests this was the first time that the two had met, and the assertion that Melville and Buchanan met at St Andrews before the latter left for Paris is highly unlikely. Buchanan returned to Scotland after more than two decades on the Continent in 1561, and worked for Queen Mary at court in the early 1560s as a tutor and translator. He also made appearances at the General Assembly from 1563, and was appointed to a committee charged with reforming education at St Andrews. However, although Buchanan did produce an abortive reform plan for the university in the early 1560s, it is unlikely that he lectured in any way until his appointment to the principalship of St Leonard's at some point after 8 November 1566.[48] Much has been made of the fact that Melville calls Buchanan his *praeceptor* in a dedicatory epistle recorded in the edition of Buchanan's *Opera Omnia* edited by Thomas Ruddiman. However, this allusion is either figurative, or relates perhaps to the connection between the two at Paris.[49] This letter informs us that Melville was well-versed by Buchanan himself in the technical construction and exegesis of Latin poetry. Melville's future skills as an epigrammatist and poet would have benefited immensely from this, and there is on occasion a traceable influence in Melville's work that can be attributed to Buchanan.[50] This time with Buchanan also informed

---

47   Andrew Melville to Peter Young, Bodleian, Smith MS. 77, 27 (Letter dated pridie Id. Aprilis 1572), trans. and pub. in MacFarlane, *Buchanan*, pp. 256–7.

48   MacFarlane, *Buchanan*, pp. 208–25.

49   M'Crie, p. 7; *Georgi Buchanani … opera omnia*, ed. Thomas Ruddiman (2 vols, Edinburgh, 1714–15), vol. 1, p. 21. The line in question states 'Andreas Melvinus Geo[rgio] Buchanano Praeceptori suo & Musarum parenti', and the epistle dates from the early 1580s.

50   There are several epigrams where Melville is either consciously imitating Buchanan or both are drawing from the same classical source: see Buchanan's 'Ite, Missa Est', and Melville's 'Ire, licet, missa est', and further below, p. 74. Also, Melville wrote a series of psalm paraphrases during his time in the Tower of London (1607–11) which no doubt were

Melville's skills as a teacher, as James Melville states that his uncle used the psalm paraphrases on his return to Scotland to educate him in Latin grammar.[51] Finally, this letter sheds light on the origins of a friendship that would last between the two men until Buchanan's death and inform much of Melville's involvement in literary affairs in Scotland in the 1580s.

In 1566 Melville decided to follow the path of a number of contemporary Scots by travelling to the University of Poitiers to take up the study of law. Poitiers, founded in 1431, was ranked as second only to Paris in the sixteenth century as a centre of legal teaching, and by the time of Melville's arrival the town possessed both a royal *sénéchausée* court and a local 'presidial' court, which acted as the definitive legal authority in the region.[52] Poitiers had a sizeable Reformed community by the late 1550s and on 10 March 1561 the second National Protestant Synod was held in the city. Following the taking up of arms by the Prince de Condé and the publication of the Edict of January in April 1562, Protestant forces seized control of the main gate into the city. A month later Lancelot du Bouchet, sieur de Sainte-Gemme, arrived at the city as governor for Condé and placed it under Protestant control. The following years saw an uneasy peace in Poitiers and the Poitou region more generally. Catholics refused to honour the Peace of Amboise (March 1563) and Protestants fled from their homes during the second religious war (September 1567–March 1568). They were only allowed to return under strict supervision in the ensuing peace (March–September 1568).[53]

There was a strong Scottish connection in the law faculty at the university. The Scot Robert Ireland settled in Poitiers at the end of the fifteenth century and taught law at the university until his death in 1561.[54] James Kirk has shown that James Beaton, the exiled Archbishop of Glasgow, had considerable influence at the university and may have awarded Melville a bursary or some financial assistance. Kirk has also shown that a Ramist influence could be seen at the university in the person of the law regent and Scot, Duncan MacGruder, who had edited an edition

---

conceived in imitation of Buchanan. Pierre Mellon, *L'Académie de Sedan* (Paris, 1913), pp. 202–7.

[51]   *JMAD*, p. 46.

[52]   Hilary J. Bernstein, *Between Crown and Community: Poitiers and Civic Culture in Sixteenth-Century Poitiers* (Ithaca and London, 2004), pp. 1, 7, 10; J. Plattard, 'Scottish Masters and Students at Poitiers in the Second Half of the Sixteenth Century', *SHR* 21 (1924): 82–6; Prosper Boissonnade and others, *Histoire de l'Université de Poitiers, Passé et Present (1432–1932)* (Poitier, 1932), pp. 148–54. Sebastian Munster in 1550 and the student Jacques de Hillerin in 1589 remarked on the pre-eminence of the university. The student population was steady at around 4,000 in the first half of the sixteenth century.

[53]   Bernstein, *Between Crown and Community*, pp. 153–60.

[54]   Plattard, 'Scottish Masters and Students at Poitiers', 83.

of Ramus' *Tabulae in Rhetoricam* in 1559. MacGruder, or Aelius Donatus Macrodorus, was a committed Calvinist, and took up arms when Coligny besieged Poitiers in 1569.[55]

According to James Melville, his uncle spent three years there as a regent at the Collége Royal de Sainte-Marthe, although there is no mention of him as a member of staff in the history of the university by Prosper Boissonade.[56] There is also no student record of Melville as the surviving Register of Graduates for the period begins in 1576.[57] Despite his nephew's assertion that at Poitiers Melville 'haid the best lawers, and studeit sa mikle thairof as might serve for his purpose, quhilk was Theologie', it seems unlikely that Melville would have had many dealings with the highly orthodox theological faculty at the university. However, the law faculty had a number of Calvinists in addition to MacGruder.[58] James Kirk thus raises a valid point in stating that Melville appears to have had no desire to study theology prior to his arrival at Geneva, and that his choices of study at Paris and Poitiers indicate that at this stage in his academic career he may not have had a clear intent to enter the full-time study and practice of divinity.[59] However, Melville was forced to flee Poitiers in the summer of 1569 when a siege of the town by Protestant forces disrupted the university, and a stray cannonball killed the young son of a parliamentary councillor whom Melville had found alternative employment tutoring.[60] It was to Geneva that he fled, and there that he appears to have found the religious calling that would dominate his future career in Scotland.

Geneva

Melville's role as a teacher in humanity in Geneva, and his achievements there between 1569 and 1574, were more modest than either James Melville or Thomas M'Crie have made out. Melville arrived at Geneva at the height of the second war of religion with many other French refugees, when the city was overpopulated and suffering from yet another bout of plague.

---

[55] Durkan and Kirk, pp. 268–9; Plattard, 'Scottish Masters and Students at Poitiers', 84; Boissonnade, *Histoire de l'Université de Poitiers*, p. 171, entry 56.

[56] Boissonade, *Histoire de l'Université de Poitiers*, p. 96, entry 4. Boissonade describes Melville as a 'précepteur du fils d'un conseiller au Parlement et étudiant'.

[57] Plattard, 'Scottish Masters and Students at Poitiers', 83.

[58] *JMAD*, p. 40; Boissonade, *Histoire de l'Université de Poitiers*, p. 111. These included 'le Picard Ch.le Sage, ami de Calvin' and 'les professeurs Babimot et Vernou'.

[59] Durkan and Kirk, pp. 269–70.

[60] Durkan and Kirk, p. 269; *JMAD*, p. 40.

Melville was appointed on 18 November 1569 as the regent of the second class of the *schola privata*, along with the appointment of Hugues Roy to the first class. This came about partially because of a display of natural talent on Melville's part, but in the main because the plague had killed Bertrand de Salis and Antoine Salomon, the regents of the second and fifth classes, in the preceding July.[61] The plague, recurring often between 1567 and 1572, caused considerable disruption to the Academy, and Beza, writing to a number of contacts in June 1570, pointed out that the *schola privata* was almost bereft of students as a result.[62] It would seem that the pastors in 1569 were keen to fill the vacant posts and Melville, though showing some skill as a tutor, had the good fortune of being in the right place at the right time.

The Genevan Academy, officially inaugurated on 5 June 1559, was split into two distinct *schola* or schools. The *schola privata* provided entry-level arts and Latin grammar courses, and the *schola publica* provided higher-level courses and training in divinity and biblical languages. It was the *schola publica* that trained Protestant ministers and re-trained former Catholic priests for use in the missionary movement in France, while the teaching in the *schola privata* was largely given over to providing a solid education for Genevan youths.[63] Melville's role as regent of the second class in the lower school would have seen him teaching youths near to the end of their studies, as the classes ascended from entry in the seventh class to completion of studies in the first. The first five classes focussed on mastering Latin, Greek and French grammar, while the top two classes developed proficiency in dialectic, reading and textual commentary, with a brief introduction to the art of rhetoric. The statutes of the Genevan Academy outline in detail the curriculum and teaching responsibilities Melville would have had, which included the teaching of history using Livy, Xenophon, Herodian and Polybius, tuition in verse form using Homer as a model, and the use of the *Paradoxes* of Cicero in dialectic. Melville would also have read the Gospel of Saint Luke, in Greek, to the students on Saturday afternoons from three until four, and have supervised the attendance of the children at Catechism and at the numerous church services in the school week.[64] With such comprehensive teaching in

---

[61]   *RCP*, vol. 3, p. 23.

[62]   Letters to Peter Melius and Christopher Thretius, 18 June 1570, quoted in A.F. Scott Pearson, *Thomas Cartwright and Elizabethan Puritanism, 1535–1603* (Cambridge, 1925), p. 48.

[63]   Maag, *Seminary or University?*, p. 10.

[64]   Gillian Lewis, 'The Genevan Academy', pp. 41–2; S. 'L'ordre estably en l'escole de Geneve ... veu et passé en Conseil le Lundy vingt neufz de May 1559', in S. Stelling-Michaud (ed.), *Le Livre du Recteur de l'Académie de Genève* (6 vols, Geneva, 1959–80), vol. 1, pp. 67–77.

religion and the liberal arts on offer, Melville would have had considerable standing with local citizens, grateful for providing their children with a sound education.

However, his involvement in the divinity faculty and its role in the Protestantisation of France and wider Europe would have been minimal. This is borne out by the paucity of references to Melville in the *Registres du Compagnie du Pasteurs*, save for an episode on 20 June 1572. Melville approached Beza to ask him if it would be possible to assist (*qu'il assistast*) with the teaching of theology, whereupon he was sharply rebuked by the Compagnie:

> To which the Company has advised that he cannot do, in the interest of the class and of the others: also that he should not make the same request if it [the teaching post] is given to one of the regents, and that he should be encouraged to follow simply his vocation. [65]

Melville was overextending his reach into a subject matter that the Genevans felt he was poorly qualified to teach, suggesting his zeal for the subject was matched by little in the way of practical experience. However, the following week, on 27 June, Melville and another regent, Antoine de la Faye, were admitted to 'hear' (*ouyr*) lessons in theology under Beza.[66] The fact that Melville was also allowed to return home with no protest from the *Compagnie* in 1574, when other members of the teaching and ministerial staff such as Simon Goulart and François Portus were refused leave for temporary periods, shows that Melville was deemed easily replaceable.[67]

Notwithstanding Melville's relative insignificance at the Academy, he did move in the right intellectual circles, and it is clear that several of the staff had a profound impact on him. He held a deep and lasting affection

---

[65]   *RCP*, vol. 3, p. 78: 'Ce que la Compagnie a advisé qui ne se pouvoit faire pour l'interest de la classe et des aultres aussi que ne faudroyent à faire la mesme requeste sy elle estoit accordee à un des regens et qu'il seroit accouragé à suivre simplement sa vocation.'

[66]   *RCP*, vol. 3, p. 80. 'L'affaire aussi des deux premiers regens du College qui demandoyent de pouvoir ouyr les leçons de Monsieur de Besze a esté remise sus. Et après qu'on a faict parler à eux particulierement et le tout consideré, leur requeste leur a esté accordee.'

[67]   *RCP*, vol. 3, pp. 61, 76, 82, 111–12. Simon Goulart was refused leave to go home in April and June 1572 to settle the affairs of his father because the number of ministers had been severely reduced by the plague, He was allowed eventually to go in August for a month. Corneille Bertram managed to extract permission to go to France in 1573 with great reluctance from the Compagnie owing to the potential dangers in France. See also Lewis, 'The Genevan Academy', pp. 52–3, n. 21 for a list of other teaching staff called away to pastoral posts just prior to Melville's arrival between 1562 and 1567, and the company's 'ambivalent response' to their leaving.

for the city and for the ministers and teachers that he befriended there,[68] but perhaps the most influential initial contact he had at Geneva was a familial one, in the person of Henry Scrimgeour. Scrimgeour was originally a native of Dundee and the maternal uncle of James Melville. He was thus extended kin to Andrew. Scrimgeour had studied at St Salvator's and Paris, and in addition to publishing a translation of Plutarch's *Septem Sapientum Convivium* in 1551 and a highly respected edition of Justinian's *Novellae* in 1558, was also renowned as a book collector and buyer. The greatest part of the Greek, Latin and Hebrew manuscripts of the Fugger collection were gathered by Scrimgeour, who frequently travelled between Augsburg and Italy in the 1550s and early 1560s. Scrimgeour also acted as agent in buying books for Otto-Heinrich, the elector palatine.[69]

It was Scrimgeour who, along with Domain Fabri, the procurator-general of the city, introduced the teaching of law to Geneva in free public lectures in 1565. The following year Scrimgeour and Pierre Charpentier were appointed to the *schola publica* teaching staff as professors of law, with Scrimgeour continuing the lectures he had started on Justinian's *Institutes* in the previous year.[70] Scrimgeour was removed from his teaching post in October 1568, but remained in Geneva with his second wife Catherine de Viellet in an old property called the 'Villete' that James Melville states Andrew made frequent use of during his time in Geneva.[71] Melville would have benefited immensely from access to Scrimgeour's exceptional collection of books, which included Greek editions of Strabo, Demosthenes, Athenaeus and Eusebius and a range of Latin works, many of which had been carefully emended by Scrimgeour following his examination of variant manuscripts during his travels.[72]

In addition to theology, Melville's education at Geneva focussed on furthering his knowledge of biblical and oriental languages. Melville studied under the famed Hebraeist Corneille Bertram, who had been born at Thouars in France in 1531. Bertram, a nephew of Beza by marriage, had studied at Poitiers, Paris, Toulouse and Cahors, before taking over the post of teacher of Hebrew at Geneva on 13 January 1567 from Antoine-

---

[68]   See his encomiastic verses on the city and his teachers there in his 'Epitaphium Jacobi Lindesii, Qui Obiit Geneva, 17 Cal. Jul. 1580', in *Delitiae Poetarum Scotorum*, ed. A. Johnstone (2 vols, Amsterdam, 1637), vol. 2, pp. 122–4.

[69]   John Durkan, 'Henry Scrimgeour: Renaissance Bookman', *Edinburgh Bibliographical Society Transactions* 5 (1978): 1–31, at 1–3, 15.

[70]   Maag, *Seminary or University?*, pp. 25–7.

[71]   *JMAD*, p. 42. I am grateful to Professor Bill Naphy for searching the Genevan Notarial Records for 1569–1574 for references to Melville while researching there, unfortunately to no avail, although he did find several references to Scrimgeour.

[72]   Durkan, 'Henry Scrimgeour', 21–5.

Rudolph Chevalier.[73] Bertram is best known for his work on the civil and ecclesiastical government of the ancient Hebrews entitled *De Politica Judaica*, and his *In Linguae Hebraicae & Aramicae Comparationem* which was published at Geneva in 1574.[74] The *Comparationem* was, as the title suggests, a comparison of the grammatical structures of Hebrew and Aramaic, which was highly advanced for the period. Melville wrote four short encomiastic verses, three of which aimed solely at praising Bertram and his work, describing him as the 'father' who had renewed the 'mother and child' languages of Chaldaic and Syriac. The fourth poem, entitled 'On the pre-eminence of holy language' (*In Linguae Sanctae Praestantiam*), shows the importance that Melville placed on the understanding of the scriptural languages:

> Whereby the certain stands apart from the uncertain, the eternal from the fallen,
> the divine from the human, the light from the darkness,
> and heaven from the lands: so great a division of things!
> This separates this pious tongue from other tongues:
> Which alone revealed the way to the life of the father, and the blessed seats
> and the brilliant kingdoms of heaven.[75]

Another linguist Melville worked closely with was François Portus, a Greek scholar. Portus was a native of the Greek island of Candia. Portus spent eight years between 1546 and 1554 at the court of Renée de France, the Duchess of Ferrara and daughter of Louis XII, where he was named a member of the Academy of the *Filareti*. He accepted the chair of Greek at Geneva in 1562. Portus is best known for his polemical exchanges with the ex-Genevan professor of law and royal apologist Pierre Charpentier between 1572 and 1574, where he refuted the claims made by Charpentier that the royal government was justified in ordering the St Batholomew's Day massacres.[76]

---

[73]   Jean Senebier, *Histoire Littéraire de Genéve* (3 vols, Geneva, 1786), vol. 1, p. 309; Émile Haag, *La France Protestante* (5 vols, Paris, 1877–96), vol. 2, pp. 229–31; Charles Borgeaud, *Histoire de l'Universite de Genéve: L'Academie de Calvin* (Geneva, 1900), p. 102.

[74]   Charles Borgeaud, *Histoire*, p. 103; Corneille Bertram, *In linguae Hebraicae and Aramaicae comparationem* (Geneva, 1574).

[75]   Bertram, *Comparationem*, f. 1*r–2*v. 'Quo distant certa incertis, aeterna caducis/ Divina humanis, denique lux tenebris/ Et Coelum terris: Quanto discrimine rerum!/ Hoc praestat linguis haec pia lingua aliis:/ Ad vitam quae sola viam, sedesque beatas,/ Et patris pandit lucida regna poli.'

[76]   Robert Kingdon, *Geneva and the Consolidation of the French Protestant Movement, 1564–72* (Geneva, 1967), pp. 112–13.

Melville also befriended the linguist and internationally renowned classical philologist Joseph-Juste Scaliger when the latter arrived in Geneva after the massacres. Only five years older than Melville, Scaliger had studied intensively under his father, the great Latin philologist Julius Caesar Scaliger, and at the prestigious Collège de Guyenne, which he entered at the slightly precocious age of just 12. By 1563 Scaliger, who had converted to Calvinism in the preceding year, had become part of the circle of textual emendators around Jean Dorat and Turnèbe, offering emendations for the latter's *Adversaria* and for Jean Lambin's second edition of the works of Horace, before publishing his own *Coniectanea* on Varro's *De lingua Latina*. This was a hugely learned exegetical analysis that showed off not only his mastery of Latin, but his understanding of the Greek and Near-Eastern etymology of many Latin words.[77] Scaliger took up a position in the *schola publica* on 31 October 1572, having just produced his own edition of the *Appendix Vergiliana*, and lectured on Cicero and Aristotle's *Organon*. During his two-year tenure at Geneva he also published an edition of the works of Varro and of Ausonius, and a collection of the works of his father with an edition of his own translation of Sophocles' *Ajax*.[78]

Although he had a reputation as a poor lecturer,[79] Scaliger had a great impact on Melville's views on both textual exegesis and on world chronology and history, with Scaliger's *Thesaurus Temporum* and *De Emendatione Temporum* two of the central sources that Melville used in his poetic commentary on the prophecies of Daniel 9 that survives in a single manuscript in Trinity College Dublin.[80] Melville also attached a series of encomiastic verses to the collection of Scaliger *père*'s poems that praised the elder Scaliger as one begotten by Aristotle, Caesar and Virgil, and the three gods Apollo, Pallas and Major.[81] In one of Scaliger's letters there is a rare insight into Melville's ability as a textual emendator, where Scaliger notes that for his commentary on Manilius' *Astronomicon* Melville

---

[77]   Anthony Grafton, *Joseph Scaliger: A Study in the History of Classical Scholarship, vol. 1: Textual Criticism and Exegesis* (Oxford, 1983), pp. 102, 109–11, 118–20. It has been mistakenly asserted that Melville was taught Hebrew by a Scaliger at Paris, but this is impossible – neither Scaliger *père* or *fils* studied Hebrew, and Julius Caesar Scaliger died in 1558. Durkan and Kirk, p. 267.

[78]   Maag, *Seminary or University?*, pp. 36–7; Grafton, *Scaliger*, vol. 1, pp. 123–9.

[79]   Grafton, *Scaliger*, vol. 1, pp. 126. In a letter to Josias Simler just after Scaliger left Geneva, Simon Goulart wrote: 'Scaliger will not return to us. For he suffered from a perpetual illness here; and if he lectured now and then, the audience was scanty.' Leonard C. Jones, *Simon Goulart, 1543–1628* (Geneva, 1917), pp. 326–7.

[80]   Steven John Reid, 'Andrew Melville, Sacred Chronology', 10–15.

[81]   *Iulii Caesaris Scaligeri viri clarissimi poemata in duas partes divisa* (2 vols, n.p. 1574), vol. 1, sig. [*3v].

advised him to read 'lapsumque diem' for 'nascentemque ipsumque diem' at line 588 of book IV.[82]

It is worth noting incidentally that Scaliger, like a number of Melville's other tutors at Paris, had little time or respect for the teachings of Ramus. While at Leiden in 1594, Scaliger responded to Nicholas Nancel (Ramus' biographer) that although Ramus had become a good orator during his life he did so against his own 'slow, rough and stupid' intellect (*repugnante ingenio tardo, rudi et stupido*). He also remarked to his students that the continued popularity of Ramus' works was disproportionate to their worth: 'these days only the Ramists are praised, but such praise is beyond measure'. This dislike of Ramist teachings continued throughout Scaliger's life.[83]

Despite the misgivings of a number of his friends, Melville heard Ramus lecture again during his short-lived tour of a number of European cities in 1570, even following him out of Geneva. Ramus took a sabbatical from his position at the Collège de France in 1568 to take a two-year tour around Switzerland and Germany as a royal commissioner of French culture. During this period he lectured in the Rhine valley, at Basle, Zurich, Berne, Strasbourg, Heidelberg, Nuremburg and Augsburg.[84] On 8 May 1570 a number of the senior ministers had asked the city council to give permission to Ramus to teach 'to help the university's reputation' (*pour donner bruit a l'universite ce quil a accorde*).[85] Ramus was duly given a place and began lecturing on his 'method', but was asked on the last day of May to 'change the way' he taught in public lectures, which he refused to do. This sudden revision of attitudes on the part of Geneva is unsurprising, as Beza had in no way been comfortable with the appointment of Ramus as a temporary lecturer. Beza had declared in letters to Ramus both before and after the latter's brief teaching appointment that he would never be given a permanent teaching post at the Academy because of his arbitrary revisions of the teachings of Aristotle and other classical authors in logic, revisions which Beza could not countenance as a proponent of traditional Aristotelian method.[86] A compromise was agreed whereby Ramus would

---

[82]   Grafton, *Scaliger*, vol. 1, pp. 126, 289, n. 157. Scaliger, *Commentarius*, in *M Manilii Astronomicon libri quinque* (Paris, 1579), p. 235, where he states 'Andreas Melvinus Scotus, iuvenis eruditus admonuit me hic legendum esse.'

[83]   Hotson, *Commonplace Learning*, p. 58, n. 75, citing *Scaligerana* (Cologne, 1695), p. 333.

[84]   Ong, *Ramus*, p. 28.

[85]   Kingdon, *Geneva and the Consolidation of the French Protestant Movement*, p. 101, n. 5.

[86]   Charles Waddington, *Ramus: Sa Vie, Ses Ecrits, et Ses Opinions* (Paris, 1855), p. 213: Beza to Ramus, 30 September 1569: 'Je m'etonne, disait-il, que vous me demandez ce qui a ete si bien dit et ecrit par tant de savants qui, d'un common accord, vous ne l'ignorez

lecture on Cicero's *In Catilinam*, but this conflict roused a number of students to post dedicatory verses supporting Ramus, protesting that he be allowed to continue his lectures as originally planned.[87] We can be reasonably sure that Melville and his fellow Scot Gilbert Moncrieff, future doctor to James VI, were among them, as they chose to follow Ramus to Lausanne to hear him continue his series of lectures there in July of the same year. The records of the Council of Lausanne record that Melville and Moncrieff left Lausanne on 5 September 1570.[88]

It is worth noting some important intellectual nuances in the dispute between Beza and Ramus over teaching methods, as it has significant bearing on the understanding of Melville's approach to teaching on his return to Scotland. Beza's dislike of Ramus' 'method' was in no way due to his being rigidly 'scholastic' or 'Aristotelian' in a pejorative sense of opposing the intellectual progress of the Renaissance and contemporary developments in logic and rhetoric. Rather, it is because, despite the considerable advances in Renaissance logic and rhetoric made by Valla, Vives and other scholars of the sixteenth century, Aristotelian logic still continued at Geneva and elsewhere as the foundation for enabling students to reason and to discuss scripture. More importantly, it acted as a shared set of tools in debates between Reformed theologians and their Catholic counterparts. As Richard Muller has argued, this 'scholastic' or 'orthodox' approach was not backward-looking, but concerned with providing a 'right' and 'academic' (in the original sense of the Latin word *scholasticus*) method for efficiently obtaining biblical knowledge. With slight revisions from Renaissance manuals on logic and rhetoric this fundamentally 'Aristotelian' system underpinned the foundations of the great expansion of Protestant systematic theology in the seventeenth century.[89] As the evidence of many of the *theses theologicae* surviving from Beza's period as rector of the Academy shows, syllogistic reasoning remained a central component of the disputations given by students.[90] In this sense, Aristotelian logic was

---

pas, ont vu avec deplaisir vos Animadaversiones contre Aristote.' Kingdon, *Geneva and the Consolidation of the French Protestant Movement*, p. 120: Beza to Ramus, 1 December 1570: 'quod nobis certum ac consitutum sit & in ipsis tradendis Logicis, & in caeteris explicandis disciplinis ab Aristotelis sententia ne tantillum quidem deflectere'.

[87]   *RCP*, vol. 3, p. 26; Lewis, 'The Genevan Academy', p. 60.

[88]   Charles Borgeaud, 'Cartwright and Melville at the University of Geneva, 1569–1574', *American Historical Review* 5.2 (1899): 284–90, at 288.

[89]   Muller, *After Calvin, passim*.

[90]   Irena Backus, 'L'Enseignement de la Logique à l'Académie de Genève entre 1559 et 1565', *Revue de Théologie et Philosophie*, 111 (1979): 153–63; Pierre Fraenkel, 'De l'Écriture à la Dispute: Le Cas de l'Académie de Genève sous Théodore de Bèze', *Cahiers de la Revue de Théologie et Philosophie* (Lausanne, 1977); Henri Heyer, *Catalogue des Theses de Théologie Soutenues à l'Académie de Genève Pendant les XVIᵉ, XVIIᵉ et XVIIIᵉ Siècles* (Geneva, 1898).

the foundation for the teaching of logic and other related subjects in the Calvinist educational programme at Geneva, and Beza could not allow Ramus to undermine that. By extension, we have to bear in mind when discussing Melville's educational approach that as a Calvinist theologian, trained in this environment, he would never completely throw out the tools of Aristotelian logic in favour of an exclusive devotion to Ramus, particularly when one adds to this the thorough grounding he would have received in Aristotle in his undergraduate studies at St Andrews. The evidence of form and content of disputations under Melville shows that while he incorporated Ramist elements into his teaching (particularly in the exposition of theology), his students incorporated this innovation into a framework that was still predominantly Aristotelian in form.[91]

The last three years of Melville's time at Geneva indicate the growing shift in his intellectual priorities towards matters of divinity, strengthened by his introduction to the leading exponents of English Presbyterianism. It was shortly after the Ramus incident that Thomas Cartwright arrived in Geneva. Cartwright was one of the leaders of the English Puritan movement, and had just been dismissed from his professorial post in Cambridge for his views on church polity. The first mention of Cartwright in Geneva occurred in June 1571, where he agreed to deliver theology lectures on Thursdays and Fridays in the *schola publica*. The recurring plague that afflicted Geneva in this period increased in virulence in the following month, killing the philosophy professor Job Veryat and heavily debilitating François Portus. Cartwright proved invaluable to Beza in keeping tuition afloat at the *schola*.[92] Walter Travers, Cartwright's fellow Puritan leader, also arrived in Geneva at some point in 1571. While Cartwright left Geneva in January of the following year, Travers appears to have stayed in Geneva until 1576.[93] Both these men had a catalysing effect on Melville in his theological instruction, but to what extent is impossible to say. In 1574 Travers published at La Rochelle his treatise on Presbyterian polity, the *Ecclesiasticae Disciplinae … Explicatio*.[94] Melville valued this work highly enough to present it as a gift to Alexander Arbuthnott, the principal of King's College, on his return to Scotland.[95] Melville also offered both men teaching posts at St Mary's College just prior to his accession to the

---

[91]   See below, Chapter 6.

[92]   Borgeaud, 'Cartwright and Melville', pp. 284–90; Pearson, *Thomas Cartwright*, pp. 46–52; Patrick Collinson, *The Elizabethan Puritan Movement* (London, 1982 edn), pp. 110–13, 124.

[93]   Pearson, *Thomas Cartwright*, pp. 50–52; Samuel J. Knox, *Walter Travers: Paragon of Elizabethan Puritanism* (London, 1962), pp. 27, 42.

[94]   Knox, *Walter Travers*, p. 29.

[95]   Durkan and Kirk, p. 270.

principal's chair in 1579, showing again his high regard for their work.[96] It certainly seems more than a coincidence that it was only after meeting these men that Melville began in earnest to seek direct higher training in divinity, as the *Compagnie* records show.

However, perhaps the most profound influence on Melville that convinced him to pursue a career in divinity came not from the teaching staff or colleagues around him, but from the outrage he felt at the massacres in France in August 1572. The wholesale slaughter of Protestants spurred him to devote a considerable portion of his first published work to discussing the events of St Bartholomew's Day. This volume, entitled the *Carmen Mosis* and dedicated to the young King James VI, was published in Basle at some point in 1574.[97] It consisted of a highly ornate poetic paraphrase of the *Song of Moses*, a paraphrase of Job 3, and a series of eight epigrams and short poems on the massacres which capture the horror and revulsion that Melville felt towards the Catholic mob in France, and his outrage at the Valois dynasty that allowed the atrocities to take place. In terms of content and style a number of these epigrams show some influence of Buchanan, but they seem to be far more in touch with the tracts being issued by Melville's Calvinist counterparts in France and Geneva in the same period. Melville also anonymously contributed one of these poems under the initials A.M.S. (*Andreas Melvinus Scotus*) to the *Epicedia Illustri Heroi Caspari Colinio*, a collection of Latin poetry dedicated to the memory of Coligny edited by his friend and colleague François Portus.[98] One curious omission from the material composed by Melville is the lack of an elegiac verse to Ramus, who was gruesomely murdered in the massacres. Melville's silence on the death of the man he had followed around Europe, and whose ideas contributed substantially to

---

[96]   Andrew Melville and others to Thomas Cartwright and Walter Travers (Edinburgh, n.d., 1579), printed in Thomas Fuller, *The Church History of Britain* (3 vols, London, 1837 edn), vol. 3, pp. 126–7.

[97]   *Carmen Mosis, ex Deuteron. cap. xxxii, quod ipse moriens Israeli tradidit ediscendum et cantandum perpetuo, Latina paraphrasi illustratum. Cui addita sunt nonnulla epigrammata, et Iobi cap. iii. Latino carmine redditum. Andrea Melvino Scoto auctore* (Basle, 1574). The exact dating and the securing of an original copy of this text have as yet proved impossible. M'Crie had a copy, and believed that the poem 'Ad Carolum, Tyrannum Galliarum', with references to Charles IX's death on 30 May 1574 from tuberculosis, must have been written and sent back to Basle after Melville left Geneva. However, given the speed at which we know Melville could work, there may have just been time to complete the book; see M'Crie, pp. 26, 40–42, 447–8. M'Crie and Mellon both give a comprehensive account of the book's contents and the editions of the texts referred to here are contained in *Delitiae Poetarum Scotorum*, vol. 2, pp. 108–12, and Mellon, *L'Académie de Sedan*, pp. 156–68.

[98]   Reid, 'Early Polemic by Andrew Melville', 63–82; Paul Chaix and others, *Les Livres Imprimés à Geneve de 1550 à 1600* (Geneva, 1966), p. 78; Émile Legrand, *Bibliographie Hellénique des XVe et XVIe Siècles* (Paris, 1962), p. xvi.

his educational reform plans, is curious. It can perhaps be seen as a further indicator of Melville dutifully following the party line of the Genevan movement that he had come to embrace so wholeheartedly during his time at the Academy, to the exclusion of other intellectual loyalties.

In writing these poems, and addressing them to the young James VI, it may be that Melville was also attempting to advance the Genevan propaganda machine on the international scene, while making a name for himself at the Scottish court. English translations of a range of the French and Genevan tracts were published in London during the 1570s.[99] As the *Memorials* of Richard Bannatyne record, pamphlets and news regarding the massacres did make their way to Scotland and were translated for the local audience.[100] The printer Thomas Bassandyne imported several dozen copies of Melville's book to Edinburgh,[101] which suggests that it would have been available to the Scottish intelligentsia. In a small way Melville would thus have been helping to communicate the plight of the French Calvinist movement to a sympathetic audience in Scotland.

Conclusion

Conclusions on Melville's early education and intellectual development must remain at best cautious. Limited evidence, despite numerous searches for further material, inhibits any further analysis beyond pure speculation. Nevertheless, one thing is clear: Melville had an insatiable and eclectic intellectual appetite from the outset of his academic career. His precocious attempt to learn Greek was the first achievement in a 15-year period that would see him develop a knowledge of biblical languages unrivalled in Scotland. As Melville progressed from Paris to Geneva, his ideas on educational reform crystallised around those of Ramus, but not without some aid from George Buchanan, whose comments on poetry no doubt influenced Melville's own written style. Melville's modest role at Geneva allowed him contact with the best of the reformed intelligentsia, and it seems that some combination of events and people conspired to drive him towards a religious calling after more than a decade of study in the liberal arts. Whether this was due to the influence of Cartwright and Travers, to the outrages of the Bartholomew's Day massacres, or to the cumulative

---

[99] Robert Kingdon, *Myths about the St Bartholomew's Day Massacres, 1572–1576* (Cambridge, Mass., 1998). Numerous English editions of French tracts from the 1570s exist. See, among others: *Discours Marveilleux*, STC10550–551.5; *Furoribus Gallicis*, STC13847; *Gasparis Colinii Castelloni*, STC22248; *Reveille-matin*, STC1464–1464.5.

[100] Bannatyne, *Memorials*, pp. 268–80.

[101] M'Crie, p. 40.

influence of an extended stay in Geneva, is impossible to say with certainty. Regardless, in his time abroad Melville added ardent support of the Presbyterian polity to a commitment to both European humanism in the broadest sense and to Ramist educational reform. He would use these different influences to create a programme with which he would attempt to transform the Scottish university system in the following decade.

CHAPTER 3

The First Foray into Reform: Melville and the 'Ancient' Universities, 1574–84

The General Assembly that met in Edinburgh in October 1583 had a deeply intellectual flavour to it, with much of its business devoted to the issue of the Protestant reform of the Scottish universities, and the doctrine to be taught within them. Although Robert Pont was elected moderator, he was to be advised on the agenda of business 'for the riper resolutione of matters' by a committee that included Melville and several others interested in educational reform, notably James Lawson (who had been involved in early proposals relating to the foundation of Edinburgh University, which opened its doors in that same month), Principal Thomas Smeaton of Glasgow University and his colleague Peter Blackburn, and the St Andrews regent Nicol Dalgleish. One of the first pieces of assembly business was to 'sight and consider the forme of the new erectioun of the colledge of Aberdeen' which its principal Alexander Arbuthnott had devised with Melville, and which the assembly now gave 'their approbatione thereunto'; another was to organise a commission to the University of St Andrews in March of the following year to ensure that the Protestant 'New Foundation' of the university enacted in 1579 was being upheld, and the staff of King's College were also to appear before this visitation to ensure they were fit to carry out its re-foundation.[1] This discussion of educational reform turned to matters of content when this same group of advisors, along with the provost of St Salvator's James Martine, and the principal of St Leonard's James Wilkie, produced a summary of Latin propositions from the works of Aristotle that were 'erronious, false, and aganis the Religioun, and condemnit be the commoun vote of the haill Kirk'. They urged the assembly to be vigilant for any other similar points arising from Aristotle's works, as 'oft tymes the zouth being curious and of insolent spirits, drinkes in erronious and damnable opiniouns, and … mantaines thair godles and profane opinions obstainately in disputatioun and vtherwayes, to the great slander of the Word of God, and offence of the simple and vnlearnit'.[2]

---

[1] *BUK*, vol. 2, pp. 626–9.

[2] *BUK*, vol. 2, pp. 638–41.

These propositions clearly aimed to guard against an uncritical reading of Aristotle, and to point out areas where his teaching was manifestly opposed to scriptural precepts. However, they have often been taken as evidence, along with the other discussions relating to the universities in this assembly, that by 1583 Melville had engineered a level of control over higher education so complete that the old foundations of higher education in Scotland had been overturned in favour of a radical new settlement, complete with a rejection of traditional Aristotelian teaching. In reality the progress of 'Melvillian' reform at the universities in the decade preceding 1583 had been far more protracted and contingent, and far less successful. While Melville did succeed in carrying out a Protestant re-foundation of the University of Glasgow between 1574 and 1580, plans for similar reforms implemented at St Andrews in 1579 and those discussed by the assembly for King's College largely failed to take root, and the reform programme at Glasgow almost collapsed in upon itself following Melville's departure. The failure of all three reform programmes stemmed to some degree from the association of Melville and his supporters at Aberdeen and Glasgow with radical Presbyterianism, an affiliation which would prove decisive in undoing any possibility of the universities' ideological unification under a single 'Melvillian' programme.

Melville and Glasgow University, 1574–80

Melville returned to Scotland in late July 1574, and at the General Assembly in Edinburgh on 7 August, armed with a recommendation from Theodore Beza and Jean Pinault, was rapidly assimilated into the business of the Kirk.[3] Perhaps due to Melville's influence, this assembly had a particular focus on education,[4] and with John Douglas having died earlier in the year, the commissioners from the Fife Synod attempted to secure Melville for St Mary's. Melville refused this offer and instead followed the 'earnest dealing' of James Boyd, Archbishop of Glasgow, and Andrew Hay, Rector

---

[3]   Borgeaud, 'Cartwright and Melville', 288.

[4]   M'Crie, pp. 26, 40–42, 446–7; *BUK*, vol. 1, pp. 305–6, 309–12. A considerable number of the acts and commissions in the assembly related to education. Commission was given to Robert Graham and John Robertson to plant kirks in Caithness and Sutherland, and particular attention was paid to the need to reform local schools and cathedral and collegiate kirks. In a list of articles presented to the regent on 10 August, the offices of doctor and minister were recognised as the only two legitimate teaching roles in the Kirk. The regent was also entreated to provide stipends for those currently teaching at universities so that 'uther learned men may have occasion to seik places in colledge'. Melville's first assignment for the assembly was part of this educational drive, sitting on a commission with George Buchanan, Peter Young and James Lawson that reviewed a Latin verse paraphrase of Job by Patrick Adamson.

and Dean of the Faculty of Arts at Glasgow and commissioner for the west, to serve as principal of Glasgow.[5] After a short visit to the university, Melville accepted the post and took up residence there in November.[6]

Before his arrival at Glasgow another significant episode in Melville's life took place. The assembly had completed its business by 11 August, and around 20 August Melville arrived at his family home at Baldovy, where he had his first meeting with his nephew James, son of Andrew's elder brother Richard. James, as his *Autobiography and Diary* attests, was immediately spellbound by the intellectual prowess and personality of his uncle. He had recently completed his MA at St Andrews, and after a few days of discussion between Andrew and his father they agreed that James would be 'resigned ower' to Andrew as 'sone and servant'.[7] Andrew also benefited from this arrangement in having a kinsman to take a post alongside him at Glasgow. To that end, for three months Andrew took James through an intellectual regime that reflected in miniature the course that would eventually be offered at Glasgow. Andrew vastly improved James' Latin using the psalms that Buchanan had taught him with in the early 1560s, supported by excerpts from Virgil, Horace, Terence, Caesar and Cicero. He also introduced James to the emerging concepts of critical historical analysis using Bodin's *Method of History*, the rudiments of Greek using passages from Matthew and Romans, and gave him a very basic introduction to Hebrew.[8]

Having given James a crash course in 'godly' humanism, the Melvilles set out from Baldovy in October. Following a two-day visit to Buchanan and a brief audience with James VI at Stirling, they arrived at Glasgow.[9] Melville found a destitute foundation on his arrival, held together by the lone figure of Peter Blackburn, a St Andrews graduate and conservative Aristotelian who had been appointed as a regent between the end of 1573 and April 1574.[10] Relegating Blackburn to the status of college *oeconomus*, and taking on himself most of the burden of teaching, Melville began to develop a unique reformed curriculum for Glasgow.

The work of James Kirk in reconstructing the early history of Glasgow under Melville strongly suggests that humanism and Ramism were the

[5]   M'Crie, p. 29; Calderwood, vol. 3, pp. 329–30.

[6]   M'Crie, p. 30; *JMAD,* pp. 47–8.

[7]   *JMAD,* pp. 36–8.

[8]   *JMAD,* pp. 46–7; Durkan and Kirk, p. 275.

[9]   M'Crie, p. 30; *JMAD,* p. 48.

[10]   Blackburn is on record at St Andrews as a university procurator in 1573. Acta Rectorum, p. 80; Durkan and Kirk, p. 254, and n. 271.

central components of his teaching platform.[11] Greek and Latin were to be taught to the first years through a variety of Greek and Roman authors, including Homer, Hesiod, Pythagoras, Isocrates, Pindar, Virgil and Horace. The *Dialecticae* of Ramus and the *Rhetorica* of Talon were the textbooks of choice for developing good argumentative skills. However, the works of Aristotle were still to be used for the tuition of philosophy, and by 1576 these were being taught solely from the original Greek. Moral philosophy comprised the *Ethics* and *On Virtue*, supplemented by Cicero's *De Officiis* and a selection of Plato's dialogues. Plato was also used to complement Aristotle's *Physics*, *On the World* and *On Heaven* in natural philosophy. Among other 'new' humanist subjects introduced at Glasgow, mathematical tuition was given using Euclid and the *Geometriae*, another work by Ramus. Melville also taught history in the form of sacred chronology, supplementing Bodin with works on chronology by Johannes Sleidan and Philip Melanchthon. Central to this whole enterprise was the teaching of biblical languages, and Hebrew, Syriac and Chaldaic were introduced to students 'with the practice thairof' using the Psalms and songs of Solomon and David, Ezra and the Epistle to the Galatians.[12]

The re-foundation of the college on 13 July 1577, known as the *Nova Erectio*, enshrined the 'Melvillian' reforms in law.[13] A streamlined foundation consisting of a principal, three regents, an *oeconomus*, four poor students and servants was to be supported by the annexation of the parish of Govan to the foundation, adding 24 chalders of victual to the college patrimony.[14] The description of the role of the principal, who was to 'open up the mysteries of faith' using biblical languages and theological instruction, is clearly intended to fit the experience of Melville and the concept of 'doctor' of the church laid down in the *Second Book of Discipline*, the blueprint of a Presbyterian polity for the Kirk developed by the Assembly in 1577/8 to succeed the original reformed settlement outlined in the *First Book of Discipline* of 1560.[15] The programme of each regent having a teaching speciality that developed in the first three years of Melville's principalship was formally ratified, with the first regent teaching rhetoric and Greek, and the second arithmetic, geometry and moral philosophy. The third and senior regent would act as deputy principal and was to teach physics, astronomy and sacred chronology.[16] By 1576, these

---

[11]   Durkan and Kirk, pp. 275–85, 430–48; *JMAD*, pp. 48–50; *Munimenta*, vol. 2, pp. 42–54.

[12]   *JMAD*, p. 49.

[13]   Durkan and Kirk, pp. 283–8.

[14]   Mackie, *University of Glasgow,* p. 67.

[15]   *Second Book*, ed. Kirk, pp. 187–90.

[16]   Durkan and Kirk, p. 444.

staff were all in place. Blaise Laurie, who had come from St Mary's, taught the first years, while James was promoted to second regent, and Peter Blackburn taught the third-year course. Melville took up exclusively the provision of theology and biblical languages, either as part of this course, or perhaps for postgraduates.[17]

The college that emerged from the *Nova Erectio* was one that, on paper at least, mirrored the latest trends in European scholarly development. The minimal evidence that we have for the events at Glasgow in the 1570s suggests that Melville's experiment in educational reform was an unqualified success, and that he did indeed use the works of Ramus alongside other teaching texts. However, our understanding of the curriculum is based solely on the testimony of James Melville written thirty years after the event, the statutes for teaching laid out in the *Nova Erectio* and the statutes that were promulgated for the university shortly after Melville left the college in 1581 or 1582. Although there are no teaching records or contemporary eyewitnesses beyond James Melville to confirm or deny how successful Melville's programme was in practice, it is true that Melville effectively had a free rein at Glasgow and so likely implemented his educational programme with impunity.

The idea that Glasgow was the beginning of a 'radical reform' of the Scottish universities under Melville that was anti-Episcopal certainly needs to be tempered, if surviving evidence relating to the securing of college patrimony in the 1570s and 1580s is anything to go by. The role of James Boyd, Archbishop of Glasgow,[18] has been underplayed in the account of the college's reformation, and it seems a plausible hypothesis that the process of intellectual reform between 1574 and 1581 at Glasgow was supported by financial and practical assistance afforded to Melville by Boyd, the Privy Council and other royal supporters, including Patrick Adamson, Melville's future nemesis in St Andrews.

Boyd was appointed first Protestant archbishop of Glasgow in November 1573,[19] and had studied at a Scottish university in the 1550s and in France in the 1560s. At some point during this period, according to Boyd's son, Boyd and Melville became acquainted.[20] Prior to his elevation to the archbishopric, Boyd held no ministry and lived what appears to have been a life of stoic retirement as a noble gentleman on his Ayrshire

[17]   Mackie, *University of Glasgow*, p. 69.

[18]   Durkan and Kirk, p. 443.

[19]   *Fasti Ecclesiae Scoticanae Medii Aevi Ad Annum 1638*, ed. D.E.R. Watt and A.L. Murray (Edinburgh, 2003), p. 195.

[20]   Robert Wodrow, *Selections from Wodrow's Biographical Collections: Divines of the North-East of Scotland*, ed. R. Lippe (Aberdeen, 1890), pp. 205–6, 208, 210.

estate.[21] Although he appears to have been elevated to the archbishopric simply so his extended kin could drain episcopal revenue, it is clear that he devoted time and effort to improving the fortunes and material stability of the university. From his accession until his death in 1581, Boyd had considerable influence with the Privy Council. His uncle and patron, Robert, fifth Lord Boyd, had a distinguished career as a Protestant reforming noble in the 1550s and 1560s, and his support of the Earl of Morton saw him rewarded with the lands and barony of Grogar and various other escheats. It is likely through him that his nephew was made archbishop.[22] Archbishop Boyd was himself present at both the critical Parliament of Stirling on 15 July 1573 when Morton took control of the king, and at the Privy Council meetings of March 1579 which began a collective attack against the Hamilton family.[23]

The patrimony of Glasgow University had never been firmly established owing to the premature death of its founder, William Turnbull.[24] Small grants of prebendaries, chantries and chaplainries added in the century following the college's inception did little to change this situation. The earliest college rental, dating to 1575, shows an income based largely on annual rents and the vicarage of Colmonell (annexed in 1558) that came to a paltry £100 12s. 4d., while the *Nova Erectio* states that the revenue of the college from the old rentals amounted to no more than £300.[25] There is evidence that Melville and Boyd worked together on several fronts to remedy this situation. On 3 June 1575, following protests by Melville and Peter Blackburn to the Privy Council, the 1573 grant of all annual-rents and chaplainries within the bounds of Glasgow were ratified to the college after disputes with a number of the burgesses over them.[26] This was reinforced by an act of inhibition from the council on 12 December preventing chaplains and possessors of the properties from setting them in any kind of tack, or extended lease.[27] The council were further prevailed upon on 3 February 1576 by Melville and Blackburn to compel David Wemyss to pay them an annual rent of £4 on a house in Rottenrow as heritors to the rights of the vicars choral of Glasgow.[28] Finally, following the *Nova Erectio*, numerous letters of ratification protecting the rights of

---

[21]   Wodrow, *Biographical Collections*, p. 206.

[22]   George R. Hewitt, *Scotland under Morton, 1572–1580* (Edinburgh, 1982) pp. 35–6, n. 13. The first reference is 15 December (*RPC*, vol. 2, p. 313).

[23]   Hewitt, *Scotland under Morton*, pp. 60, 64–5.

[24]   Durkan and Kirk, pp. 21–2; *Munimenta*, vol. 2, p. 21.

[25]   Durkan and Kirk, p. 443.

[26]   *Munimenta*, vol. 1, pp. 94–5.

[27]   *Munimenta*, vol. 1, pp. 96–8. A list of the holders is given.

[28]   *Munimenta*, vol. 1, pp. 98–100.

the masters in their lands were granted in favour of the college, including a letter confirming the exemption of the university from taxation and taking it under the king's protection.[29] These numerous requests for finance from the Privy Council must have been supported and shepherded through with the assistance of Boyd.

Boyd also provided some direct financial remedy for the college. On 26 July 1576, he gave consent to a grant to establish a bursary in philosophy drawn from an annual gift of a chalder of oatmeal from the mill of Partick.[30] On 28 May 1581 he further increased the revenue of the college by granting it the whole of the customs of the Tron, estimated at a value of £20. Although it seems that the college initially had legal difficulty in obtaining these customs, they were valuable enough to be included in the 1587 parliamentary charter of confirmation of the college's property.[31]

The most important financial boon to the college, however, that of the 24 chalders of victual of Govan which was to provide the financial underpinning of the new foundation, came through the dealings of Patrick Adamson. The parsonage had been offered to Melville in 1575 by Morton when it had fallen vacant, supposedly to incline Melville towards his ecclesiastical policy. Melville's refusal to accept the benefice led to it lying vacant until 1577, a situation even Melville's colleagues at Glasgow were critical of.[32] At this stage Adamson, who had been in St Andrews and Paris at the same time as Melville, was minister of Paisley. James Melville tells us that Andrew 'delt ernestlie with the Regent him selff, and be all moyen, namlie, of [i.e., through] the said Mr Patrick', and it was through Adamson that the brokering of a deal to annex Govan to the college was completed, a grant which doubled, and perhaps even quadrupled, the cash value of the college rent book.[33] Thus it seems clear that Adamson, future proponent of Episcopacy and bitter antagonist of Melville, was an ally Melville worked with to develop the foundation of the college.[34]

---

[29]   For example, 1 November 1577, 7 June and 16 December 1578, and 10 March 1579. *Munimenta*, vol. 1, pp. 114–19, 126–30. A letter to the council asking for help with funding issues is recorded in *RPC*, vol. 3, pp. 274–5.

[30]   *Munimenta*, vol. 1, pp. 100–102.

[31]   *Munimenta*, vol. 1, pp. 132–6, 141–3, 150; Mackie, *University of Glasgow*, pp. 85–6. The grant was confirmed by the Lords of Council in June and December of the same year. A suspension had to be issued in 1585 and a decree of confirmation obtained in 1586 against Gavin Hamilton of Hill, Allan Herbertson and Matthew Boyd, burgesses of Glasgow, for their interest in the customs. The later rental of c.1600 shows the customs as being leased for 20s, though the college may have received some additional unmarked payment in compensation for this.

[32]   Hewitt, *Scotland under Morton*, p. 107.

[33]   *JMAD*, pp. 53–4.

[34]   MacDonald, 'Best of Enemies', pp. 260–6.

Some support for Melville's work at Glasgow came from the General Assembly. On 6 August 1575 it acknowledged that funding had to be found not only for schools within Scotland but also for ministers to attend universities and Protestant seminaries abroad. Glasgow was a particular focus, as it was 'but newlie erected, and hathe not suche provision as other universities'.[35] However, the assembly could not provide finance, but merely attempt to exhort and persuade the royal government to do so. That support for the college was provided by the Royal Council, who were persuaded to give it by Boyd and Adamson. The distinct gap between March 1582 and January 1586 in the council records of any further funding for Glasgow suggests that this support ended with the Morton regime and the death of Boyd.[36]

Reform Before the 'New Foundation': St Andrews, 1574–79

While Melville undertook reform at Glasgow, the five-year period between his return to Scotland and the 'New Foundation' of St Andrews in 1579 saw controversy and further attempts at reform there, which he likely influenced. Previous accounts of the university's history have concluded that the visitation led by Morton in April 1574 was a singular exercise with no lasting impact on the university, which passed unheeded by the staff.[37] However, unpublished evidence suggests the visitation was not meant to be one-off, but rather the beginning of an ongoing process of improvement at the university, with considerable intervention by government in its affairs and staffing.[38] At the same time, the General Assembly took a greater role in the process than is apparent for the reform of Glasgow.

One of the central reasons that St Andrews caused considerable concern for the government after 1574 was the lack of trustworthy staff there. With the death of John Douglas on 31 July 1574,[39] the university lost its rector and chancellor. As principal of St Mary's for over twenty years, Douglas was also the last surviving link to the humanist reform movement that had briefly flourished in St Andrews in the late 1550s. It would be another two years before the university had a new chancellor in the form of Patrick

---

[35]   Calderwood, vol. 3, p. 352.

[36]   *Munimenta*, vol. 1, pp. 135–6, 141–2. The last act in 1582 is a confirmation of the small customs of the Tron, the next in 1586 a royal grant ratifying the Tron customs to the college.

[37]   Cant, pp. 57–8.

[38]   NAS, PA10/1. This bundle was discovered by James Kirk, judging from letters enclosed with copies of transcripts of the texts belonging to Professor James Cameron. I am grateful to both Professor Cameron and Dr Robert Smart for making these available to me.

[39]   M'Crie, p. 29.

Adamson, and the staff who were left to manage in the interim were a less than inspiring group. Robert Hamilton, whose ministry and family allegiances had been so controversial in the early 1570s, had been elected rector just prior to the death of Douglas, on 17 March 1574.[40] Following Douglas' death, it would have been expected that Hamilton as second master of St Mary's would ascend automatically to the role of principal. However, there were clearly doubts over his suitability, as he appears to have only been elected to the role on 10 January of the following year.[41] That Hamilton was not the first choice of the masters is also clear from the attempts to persuade Melville at the August General Assembly to enter the post over Hamilton's head.

Grievances and a struggle for power between Hamilton and John Rutherford triggered the next visitation of the university in 1576, co-ordinated between the General Assembly and the Privy Council. On 24 April, the assembly gave commission to James Lawson, Robert Pont, Alexander Arbuthnott, William Christeson, John Row and John Erskine, the Laird of Dun, to visit St Andrews and to report their findings at the next assembly.[42] Nothing was reported in the October meeting, and the business of the 1577 assemblies was largely taken up with the formulation of the *Second Book of Discipline*.[43] However, a visitation was indeed carried out at St Andrews on 8 May 1576 by Lord Glamis, although the records only survive in the National Archives of Scotland. Glamis was accompanied by all the commissioners named by the General Assembly except for Erskine of Dun, along with Sir James Balfour of Pittendreich, William Lundie, James Haliburton (the Provost of Dundee), David Carnegie and Patrick Adamson.[44]

The main reason for the visitation was a dispute between Hamilton and Rutherford over tampering with the rectoral election in the month prior to the General Assembly's commission. On 12 April 1576, the bare bones of a dispute were recorded in the Acta Rectorum.[45] In the presence of a group of royal counsellors (*in coenobio regiis consiliariis*) including Robert Pitcairn, James Balfour of Pittendreich and James Meldrum (a member of the College of Justice), the electors chosen from the four nations had elected John Rutherford rector, a decision which Robert Hamilton refused to ratify

---

[40]   *Acta*, pp. ccxlviii.

[41]   UYSM110/15/10, presentation of Archibald Hamilton to the 2nd master or licentiate's position, 17 January 1575. Robert Hamilton is recorded as being elected to the principal's place on 10 January.

[42]   Calderwood, vol. 3, p. 362; *BUK*, vol. 1, p. 360.

[43]   *BUK*, vol. 1, pp. 383–98; *Second Book*, ed. Kirk, pp. 48–57.

[44]   NAS PA10/1/6.

[45]   Acta Rectorum, pp. 90–91.

following the election on 1 March (*quem Robertus Hamilton pronunciare distulerat primo martii ultimi*). The presence of royal councillors and administrators at what should have been a routine election suggests that all was not right, and that Hamilton had real grievance with his removal from the office of rector.

It seems likely that the problem was a bias of the electors towards Rutherford. Two of the four electors were regents from St Salvator's, one of whom was Rutherford's son. It appears that the other two, John Caldcleuch of St Mary's and Patrick Auchinleck of St Leonard's, were in some way bribed by Rutherford to acquiesce in his promotion. This is confirmed by a series of statutes passed shortly after that the whole university were ordered to hear, relating to the voting rights of those involved in elections. Entitled *contra ambitum* by a later hand ('against corruption'), they stated that anyone attempting to canvass votes or pledges for the office of rector would be removed from consideration, and that only men suitably deserving of the post should apply for it. Ministers or ecclesiastical persons who were used to having a vote in previous times were no longer allowed to take part in elections unless they were full members of the university, and similarly no one was to be allowed a vote in future unless they had received their bachelor's degree and were active in the university community.

The statutes are obscure on specifics,[46] but they do suggest that Rutherford, who often bent rules to suit his own purposes, had attempted to consolidate a hold over the university. It seems conceivable that the members of the university who also served on the kirk session and General Assembly would have reported this to their fellow ministers, triggering the intervention in university business by the commission.

While this may be a possible motivation for the visitation in 1576, many of the statutes and memoranda laid down by the commission were more concerned with building on those laid down by Morton in 1574, and making a number of them more binding.[47] The statutes of 1574 standardising the length of the arts degree, laying down the decree that all regents in philosophy were to teach two full courses upon completing their degree, and ordering the removal of wives and children from the college were reiterated. Moreover, the 1574 statute ordering all staff and

---

[46]   Particularly in their exact dating. They are dated to 8 March, but the introductory text accompanying them apparently dates to 28 April and specifically mentions the archbishop of St Andrews, as the chancellor of the university, being present when the statutes were read out. This is not possible, as Adamson is recorded in the visitation statutes of 8 May as simply being the regent's chaplain, and if he had been promoted before this he would have been given his full title and precedence in the visitation.

[47]   The text of the 1574 visitation is recorded in *Evidence*, pp. 187–9. The 1576 visitation statutes are recorded in NAS PA10/1/2, 4, and 6.

students to be diligent in attending their duties was given teeth in the 1576 visitation, with the principal masters of every college being ordered to pay 40s. for missing one lecture, £4 for two, and £6 per lecture after that. If they missed more than six lectures they would be deprived of their stipend for the year and eventually face removal from office.

More striking in the 1576 visitation was the involvement of the General Assembly in the process. Considerable controversy had arisen in the reformed church over whether it was proper to offer a doctorate in theology, due to the association of normal higher degrees with the Catholic Church, and in the 1574 visitation the order of proceeding for the theology degree was held over. In the 1576 visitation this issue was given over to the jurisdiction of the General Assembly, while the degrees 'to be usit be thame that ar techeris within the universitie' was to be discussed with Morton and the council. The 1574 statute of thrice-yearly visitation to the colleges by the rector and his assessors and the dean of arts was seen to be overambitious, and in its place a cooperative group of 'the visitoris appointit be the Generall Assemblie to visie the kirkis adjacent to the citie of St Andreuis', together with men appointed by the royal government and the rector would make an annual visitation each October. More importantly, until the archbishopric was filled, the role of chancellor was to be supplied by the commissioners from the General Assembly and the regent, though how this would work in practice is unclear.

Although there is no specific mention of any of the developments at Glasgow under Melville in the 1576 visitation, statutes on curricular reform bear his influence. The 1574 visitation had ordered every principal to read a 'publict Latin lesson of Theologie' in their own college every week, and the masters of St Salvator's and St Leonard's were to offer weekly lectures in Greek, Hebrew, rhetoric and mathematics. An account of St Leonard's handed in to the 1576 visitation by James Wilkie shows that he at least had taken this statute seriously. He was teaching Hebrews from a Latin text each Friday, and in church on Saturday and Sunday was reading 'the prayeris and techis the prophet Ezechiel in Ingliche', though no reference was made to Greek or Hebrew. Alongside these public lectures,[48] the masters were now to choose 'ane certane compendium conteining the summe of dialectik quhilk salbe observit in all the collegis and nane othir techit'. Alongside this they were to teach Aristotle and Cicero's *De Officiis* and a selection of his speeches for 'practising and exercising the youtheid in the concepts' of logic and rhetoric. They were also to teach the *Ethics*,

---

[48] That the lectures were to continue rather than be substituted by teaching from the compendiums is clear from the Privy Council records of 12 July 1576, where Morton was still attempting to install William Welwood expressly as one of the staff who would carry out some of the 'public lecturis in liberall sciences' enacted by the 1574 visitation. *RPC*, vol. 2, pp. 542–3.

Economics and *Politics* in moral philosophy, and a 'compendium of the physik', but whether in the original Greek or Latin is unclear, alongside Sacrobosco's *De Sphaera* for teaching 'Arithmetik and Cosmographie'. If the masters could not agree compendia of these texts among themselves, the regent would have them drawn up and sent to them. Considering the texts laid down by the 1576 visitation were among those used by Melville at Glasgow, it seems likely the commissioners had his work at Glasgow in mind and would perhaps have called on him to produce such compendia. Moreover, the fact that the commission was advocating 'compendiums' suggests in itself an awareness of the simplified teaching approach favoured by Ramism.

While the statutes set down by the visitors built on the Morton visitation and encouraged the involvement of the General Assembly, they also provided the staff of St Mary's with an outlet for grievances against their principal, Robert Hamilton. By the end of the 1570s St Mary's in particular was in need of reform. A letter of James Lawson to Morton shows that James Bruce, a regent in the college, was apparently bereft of his stipend, and had been for over two and a half years. Moreover, Hamilton was refusing to give him an adequate chamber in which to live, although one of the chambers that should be used for regents was lying empty.[49] Another document, a collection of general grievances against Hamilton, is remarkably scathing of his handling of the college.[50]

The majority of these complaints were financial in nature, rather than relating to standards of education. Hamilton had taken it upon himself to enter students without consulting the other masters, and the electing of bursars to the foundation by all the masters had ceased. Thus there was no indication of who was supported by the foundation and who was to pay their own board, affecting the college accounts. Hamilton did not share control of the compt books with the other principal masters and they had no idea of the state of the college finances. Miscellaneous funds from various altarages and feuing of college lands were to be accounted for by Hamilton, and added to the college wealth. The masters were to be paid their proper fees from the college patrimony, and the fees raised from 'propynes and gainis' (small fees given up by the students) recorded in Douglas' time were to be restored. Hamilton had also placed someone in

---

[49]   NAS PA10/1/5.

[50]   Balcarres Papers, vol. 7, fos 203 r–v. The document, entitled 'Thir ar the heidis quhairene we complaine and quhilkis we desyr to be amendit and ordor put to in our college', makes repeated reference to 'Bischop Dowglass of guid memorie' and a reference in the ninth complaint to a 'M. Archbald' holding the benefits of an altarage probably refers to Archibald Hamilton, who held the bursary of St John the Evangelist and the chaplainry of St Anthony in the parish church of the Holy Trinity. Hamilton had left by November 1576, suggesting that this document dates prior to then.

the 'west lugin in the east burn venid (wynd)' that lay adjacent to the college, but the masters were unaware of who he was, had seen no rental paid to the college for it, and asked that it be leased out properly. Other criticisms show that the college property had become dilapidated under Hamilton, despite student numbers being at an all-time high.[51] The common books of the college library were scattered with no register or place kept for them, nor was there a secure chest for the college documents. The college itself had not been repaired since before Douglas' death, prompting them to entreat the repair of the windows and other structures from the college expenses.

Another complaint against Hamilton was his choice of candidate for provision to the post of third master of the college. On 26 December 1575 William Welwood, whose father was parliamentary commissioner for St Andrews and thus likely favourable to the Morton regime, was presented to the third master's place in St Mary's.[52] However, a list of the 'founded persons' put forward as part of the 1576 visitation and written not earlier than 1575 states that the place of third master was vacant,[53] while a presentation to the place of third master from 2 April 1575 states Alexander Hamilton had been presented to the post by Robert Hamilton.[54] The Privy Council began the process of legally forcing Hamilton and the other principal masters to accept their ruling in favour of Welwood on 12 July 1576, after both parties had given their evidences into Lord Glamis at the commission meetings.[55] Hamilton and William Skene returned to protest before the Privy Council in October of the same year stating that only the members nominated on the foundation had right of presentation to the post, and thus the entrance was null and void. The Privy Council refused to accept this explanation, having examined the suitability of Welwood as a candidate. They ordered that he be immediately accepted

[51]   See St Andrews matriculations, 1560–78, Appendix. Student numbers were at record and stable levels in the later 1570s, with recorded numbers of entrants averaging at around 55 in each year. Assuming that even just one third of students were staying on and completing the full three-and-a-half-year MA course, there would be around 100 students at the university in any year.

[52]   The office had lain vacant in 1575 (NAS PA10/1/3). There is a possibility that Morton had intended to have Welwood take up this position from April 1574, as the 1574 visitation had decreed that the third master should teach mathematics four times a week, suggesting that Morton had been aware of Welwood before his entrance to the post and that he knew of his mathematical skills.

[53]   NAS PA10/1/3.

[54]   UYSM110/15/12. Alexander was raised from the place of Orator.

[55]   RPC, vol. 2, pp. 542–3. 'At ane certane day bipast befoir Johnne lord Glammis Chancellare, quhom unto my lord Regentis grace gaif commissioun, to heir the ressounis and allegationis of bayth the saidis partiis.'

into office, although this would not prejudge the rights of Hamilton and the other masters to elect according to the foundation in future.[56]

Despite this ruling, Hamilton still refused to accept Welwood's appointment. On 15 August 1578 Andrew Wilson, advocate and son-in-law of Patrick Adamson, put forward a complaint against Welwood, citing his continual absence from the college as grounds for his removal. Welwood appealed to the new university rector, James Wilkie, who upheld his appeal.[57] However, when Wilkie attempted to enter the college to designate a room to Welwood, Hamilton barred the gates. Wilkie referred the matter to a committee led by the chancellor, Patrick Adamson, along with the new provost of St Salvator's, James Martine, and Patrick Auchinleck. This group again found in favour of Welwood, and marched to the college gates and demanded entrance. Hamilton finally obeyed, and the rector and the committee entered, and had the lock on the college gate removed to prevent Hamilton from barring it again.[58]

Although Hamilton remained in place until the enactment of the 'New Foundation' in 1579, it is clear that the 1576 visitation was part of a process that had attempted to deal with him and with the standard of education within the university. It is strange that the visitation records are not mentioned in the published account of the reform of the university, and the proceedings of the government in 1579 appear to ignore them completely. However, they do show that the government and General Assembly were trying, prior to Melville's arrival, to reform St Andrews along 'godly' lines, and the curricular reform put forward does bear his influence.

The visitation records of 1576 provide a welcome snapshot of the fortunes of the university in a period when its administrative records are, on the whole, quite poor. They particularly add to the picture of disagreement and self-interest that surrounds Robert Hamilton, and show how little he lived up to the standards set by his predecessor. It comes as no surprise then that on 8 November 1579, as part of the 'New Foundation and Erection of the three colleges in the University of St Andrews' passed in the parliament at Edinburgh, Hamilton and the other masters of the college were ordered to remove themselves from office 'without dilay', so that St Mary's might be shut until new qualified masters chosen by the government could enter.[59] While the parliament set down in detail how it expected the university to operate following this reformation, and while

[56] *RPC*, vol. 2, pp. 561–3.

[57] Balcarres Papers, vol. 7, fo. 148v.

[58] Linda J. Dunbar, *Reforming the Scottish Church: John Winram (c. 1492–1582) and the Example of Fife* (Aldershot, 2002), pp. 161–2.

[59] *Evidence*, p. 184.

these reforms do bear Melville's intellectual imprint, it is far less obvious how the reform programme was implemented at a university-wide level.

The path to reform itself though is clear enough from the legislative records. In July 1578 a commission made up of Patrick Adamson, James Boyd Archbishop of Glasgow, David Cunningham Bishop of Aberdeen, Robert Earl of Lennox, Robert Earl of Buchan, Andrew Melville and Peter Young was appointed to visit and consider the universities of Scotland, and given far-reaching power to reform any irregularities or lingering Catholicism that they might find. They were to:

> vesy and considder the fundatiouns and erectionis of the universiteis and collegis within this realme; with full power to thame to reform sic thingis as soundis to superstioun, ydolatrie and papistrie, and to displace sic as ar unqualefiit and unmeit to discharge thair office in the saidis universiteis, and to plant sic qualefiit and worthie personis thairintill as thai sall find gude and sufficient for the educatioun of the youth and conform to the commoun weill of this realme ...[60]

Specific powers were given to the commissioners for Aberdeen, who were to meet there in November and submit a report to the Privy Council by 1 January 1579.[61] However, this commission failed to hand in any reform plans to the Privy Council and the General Assembly, apparently frustrated with this lack of progress, made a double supplication to the king in July 1579 that young students be banned from attending 'Parise, or other universiteis or touns professing Papistrie' and that St Andrews be reformed. On 8 August the Privy Council took this matter under consideration, and ordered the original 1578 commission be reinstated and augmented specifically for reforming St Andrews with the addition of Robert, commendator of Dunfermline, George Buchanan, James Haliburton provost of Dundee and Thomas Smeaton, minister of Paisley.[62]

The plan they drew up was certainly scathing in its criticism of the current situation at St Andrews, and aimed to be far-reaching in its reform.[63] Not only were the old foundations and the standard of teaching offered by them incompatible with those required by a 'godly' realm, but parents sending their children to university were 'frustrat of thair expectatioun' that a sound education would be provided. St Mary's was to be the centrepiece of the reform programme, as a school devoted wholly to theology. Five

---

[60]   *RPC*, vol. 3, pp. 199–200; *RPS* 1578/7/5.

[61]   Donaldson, 'Aberdeen University and the Reformation', 142.

[62]   *RPC*, vol. 3, pp. 199–200. Only between four and six of these men were required to meet to form the commission.

[63]   *Evidence*, pp. 183–6.

masters were to offer a four-year course in the Old and New Testament and the commonplaces, with a solid training in the biblical languages. The first master would offer a six-month course in basic Hebrew learned through the reading of David, Solomon and Job, followed by a further six months' tuition in Syriac and Chaldaic through the use of Daniel, Ezra, the Psalm Paraphrases and the New Testament. Second year and half of third year was to offer a course in Mosaic Law interpreted from the Hebrew and tuition in the chronology and history of the Old Testament. The final year-and-a-half of the course would offer interpretation of the writings of the various prophets 'greit and small'. Overarching all this, the fourth and fifth lecturer would teach the Greek New Testament and the common places throughout the course. In addition to a total of three lessons per day, a battery of examinations would enable the students to become 'perfite theologians', including daily repetition of the class material, weekly public disputations and monthly declamations to ensure memorisation and logical exposition of the texts. At the end of each of the three stages of the course, exams would be set by the lecturers to take place on 10 September. Eight bursars in theology were to be attached to the foundation, and were to be rigorously assessed before entrance.

If St Mary's was to become an advanced postgraduate theological school, St Leonard's and St Salvator's were to be the arts colleges that would feed into it. A principal and four masters or regents were to be attached to each college, with their own specialisation rather than teaching a general course. The course prescribed was also the same for each college. The regent of the first year would teach the basics of Greek grammar and offer practice first in Latin prose composition, and then after six months in Greek. The basics of 'Inventioun, dispositioun, and elocutioun' would be taught to second years in the 'schortest, easiest, and most accurate' way, but although this phrase sounds distinctly Ramist no explicit mention is made of his works. The third regent would teach Aristotle's *Organon*, *Ethics* and *Politics* in Greek and Cicero's *De Officiis*, and the fourth natural philosophy from a selection of Aristotle's *Physics* and Sacrobosco's *De Sphaera*. Practical examination was also a central tenet of the arts reforms, with an hour of prose composition prescribed daily for each arts class, and monthly public declamations by each student in Greek and Latin, with the students being competitively ranked so that 'emulation may be sterit up amangis the saidis scollaris'. This was topped off with a weekly lesson for each class on Sundays in Greek, with Luke being read to first years, Acts to the second, and Romans and Hebrews to the older groups.

The choice of curriculum directly follows on from that outlined in the 1576 visitation and was markedly similar to Melville's programme at Glasgow, while the emphasis on practical exercise is clearly Ramist in its outlook. The strict demarcation of the colleges into separate centres for arts and theology also, at a stroke, ended almost two centuries of teaching both subjects within faculties that spread across the university's federal organisation. However, despite these radical elements, much of the structural reform seems to favour the governmental viewpoint. If Melville was the central reforming influence behind the 'New Foundation', one has to wonder how he reacted to the number of bishops involved in the reform commission, not least Adamson and Boyd, who by 1579 he was regularly chastising in the General Assembly. The role of the bishop as chancellor in the affairs of the university was considerably revitalised by the 'New Foundation'. He was to have a central role in the election of staff to both the arts and theology faculties, in conjunction with the rector, the respective deans of faculty and the other masters. The 'wounted obedience' due to the chancellor and the other key officers was to be 'restorit' and the privileges and rights of each office were to be sought out from the university records before March 1580. Moreover, the vacancy of bursaries was to be far more closely monitored by the government and presentation to them was to come under the discretion of the king. Full inventories of the colleges' goods and rentals were to be presented to the Privy Council, and the king was also to enact a full visitation of the university in October 1583, giving the staff four years to embed the reformed curriculum. While this was clearly a bold new era intellectually for the university, it was to conduct its business under a very watchful royal eye.

One also has to wonder how extensive the royal involvement in this process was, and whether or not Morton or even the young James VI had some direct control over it. It seems conceivable that the precocious boy-scholar would take considerable interest, and perhaps an active role, in the reform of the universities, particularly with the twin figures of Morton and Buchanan presiding over him. This would perhaps be an ideal project for the young king to cut his teeth on. If this is the case, it would explain the direct and personal tone of the 'Instructions of James VI' on 14 January 1580, signed by the king, that attempted to provide practical orders for the implementation of the November reform plans.[64] This apparently followed an unrecorded document of 13 December that had reiterated the order to remove Hamilton and his cohorts from St Mary's. There had evidently been protests that the reform programme be put off until the new academic year beginning in October 1580, but the royal response was that 'na fruit' could be had from deferring. An example of the regal tone used throughout this document can be seen in this excerpt, which states that any dissenter would be seen as 'a direct hinderance of the said reformatioun, and a resisting and denying of the auctoritie of Us and our Parliament; out of quhilk errour they mon be put, gif they be our subjectis'.

---

[64]   *JMAD*, p. 76.

How this reform plan was to work in practice was obviously not thought out in full, particularly regarding the senior staffing of the arts colleges. The principal of St Salvator's was to become a professor of medicine, while the principal of St Leonard's was to offer lectures in Plato, each reading four times a week. What texts they were to follow is not specified. Most controversially, the posts in law and mathematics held by William Welwood and Homer Blair following the death of William Skene in St Mary's, were to be transferred to the foundation of St Salvator's and paid for from the college income. Welwood and Blair were to act as public lecturers, offering four weekly lectures at a time and with an audience appointed by the rector and the other masters of the university. The relegation of the principals of St Leonard's and St Salvator's to strict arts tuition and the removal of the law and mathematics professor to the latter college clearly indicates some attempt to accommodate existing staff in the face of the priority of creating a top-level theological college. The regents who would be displaced from these colleges as surplus to the new requirements were to be offered bursaries in theology 'gif they will accept the same'. The existing theology bursars were to use the stipends of the two vacant master posts at St Mary's to fund their studies under the new staff, though when this would begin with the college shut was again left unsaid.

A common table was to be kept for each college, and in order to facilitate collegiate living among staff and students a uniform set of graded bursar fees was to be implemented across all the colleges. James Wilkie, Principal of St Leonard's, was to be allowed to continue teaching the theology lessons he mentioned in the 1576 visitation, and provision was made to annex the wealthy priory of Portmoak to the college. At St Mary's, the second master John Robertson had apparently been named in the document of 13 December as suitably qualified to stay and teach. Only he and the porter were to be allowed to remain in the college, while Robert Hamilton, who 'hes obeyit na thing, bot spendit sa lang tyme in neidles delayis', was to remove himself immediately. St Salvator's was also to obey the reformation without question. However, it is clear that the process would hamstring the university for most of the year. No new bursars in philosophy were to be received until the Michaelmas term of 1580, and while St Mary's was shut the regents desirous of becoming bursars in theology were to be examined and checked for suitability. It would be almost another year before the college would reopen and the Melvilles would begin teaching, with considerable opposition, in St Andrews.

Conservative Backlash: The Failure of Reform at King's College and Glasgow, 1579–84

When Melville and his nephew James moved to St Andrews at the end of 1580, the former must have had high hopes for the dissemination of his educational reform programme across Scotland. Melville believed that St Mary's under his guidance would become the leading Protestant seminary in the country,[65] and at Glasgow he had left two of his most trusted allies to carry on the programme of reform he had initiated. Another of Andrew's nephews, Patrick Melville, succeeded to the place of second master, while Thomas Smeaton was presented under the privy seal to the principalship in November 1581.[66] Smeaton was unique among Melville's friends as an ex-Jesuit who only converted to Protestantism in 1572, several years after he and Melville had first met in Paris.[67] Smeaton's past life made him well aware of the sophistication of the Jesuit educational programme and the threat it posed, and like Melville was as a result ardently anti-Catholic. His sole surviving published work, an 'Orthodox Defence' (*Orthodoxa Responsio*) published in 1579, was a response to the polemical tract *De Confusione Calvinianae Sectae apud Scotos* (1577) written by the apostate and ex-St Mary's regent Archibald Hamilton.[68] Smeaton also favoured Melville's educational programme, and was clearly groomed by the latter to continue his legacy at Glasgow. It was under Smeaton that a number of statutes were promulgated in 1581 that favoured the teaching of Ramist works and reiterated the structural reforms of the *Nova Erectio*.[69]

Over the course of the 1570s Melville had also enlisted the services of another lieutenant at the remaining pre-reformation university, King's College. Alexander Arbuthnott, who had been appointed as the first Protestant principal of the university on 3 July 1569 following the purge of Catholic staff by the Earl of Moray, shared Melville's interests in Continental humanism and university reform. Arbuthnott had studied civil law at Bourges and was widely respected for the breadth of his learning,

---

[65]   *Evidence*, p. 184; *BUK*, vol. 2, pp. 466, 471; *JMAD*, pp. 82–83.

[66]   *JMAD*, p. 84.

[67]   For Smeaton's biography, see Henry M.B. Reid, *The Divinity Principals in the University of Glasgow 1545–1654* (Glasgow, 1917), pp. 83–105, and John Durkan, 'Smeaton, Thomas (1536–1583)', *ODNB* [25757, accessed 29 July 2009].

[68]   Thomas Smeaton, *Ad virulentem Archibaldi Hamiltonii apostatae dialogum, de confusione Calvinianae sectae apud Scotos impie conscriptum, orthodoxa responsio* (Edinburgh, 1579).

[69]   Durkan and Kirk, pp. 277, 370–1; *Munimenta*, vol. 2, pp. 42–54. The statutes believed to be promulgated shortly after Melville's departure in 1580, though likely drafted by him owing to the quality of the Latin, show Ramist works were to be used by the teaching staff.

and when Melville returned to Scotland in 1574 the two had become fast friends. According to James Melville, after the 1575 General Assembly he and his uncle had travelled to Angus with Arbuthnott to discuss Melville's plans for reform, and at this meeting the putative ideas for the *Nova Erectio* of Glasgow were laid down, along with a similar plan for Aberdeen which Arbuthnott was to enact.[70]

With these allies in place, the stage was set for Melville to reform all of Scotland's universities and create an intellectual programme that met the aims of a 'godly' and Presbyterian-minded society. However, within four years of Melville's arrival at St Mary's any prospect of such a unified and cohesive settlement lay in tatters. In the same way that radical ecclesiastical politics would undermine Melville's effectiveness in St Andrews and incur the wrath of James VI and the Privy Council,[71] increasing governmental displeasure at the involvement of the universities in temporal and spiritual politics led to the programme of reform being severely compromised at Glasgow and almost entirely abandoned at King's College. These two universities would uphold some curricular elements of Melville's reform programme in the aftermath of the early 1580s, but any chance that the universities would become as ideologically and intellectually linked as Melville had perhaps hoped was well and truly gone.

The cause of this failure, as it would be at St Mary's, was the turmoil caused by the manoeuvrings of several factions at court for control of the young James VI, beginning with the rise to power of Esmé Stewart, James' French cousin. Stewart, who held the hereditary title of Lord d'Aubigny, arrived in Scotland on 8 September 1579, and his close relationship with James and his meteoric rise to power, which included his elevation to the Dukedom of Lennox, made him a natural focus for the Kirk's fears over Catholic recusancy. Supported by another of the young king's favourites, James Stewart (made Earl of Arran in April 1581), Lennox consolidated his power with the removal and execution of the Regent Morton in May 1580 on a charge of collusion in the murder of Henry Lord Darnley, Mary Stewart's husband and James VI's father, in 1567.[72]

Despite the fact that Lennox converted to Protestantism and that the king and his household signed a confession of faith known as the King's or Negative Confession denouncing Catholicism in 1581, the Kirk remained suspicious of what it believed was an administration quietly open to a rapprochement with Rome. Compounding this suspicion was an increasing ideological divide between the Kirk and the royal government. While the

---

[70] Stevenson, *King's College*, pp. 25–30.

[71] See below, Chapter 4.

[72] Donaldson, *James V– James VII*, pp. 171–3; Hewitt, *Scotland under Morton*, pp. 188–207; MacDonald, *Jacobean Kirk*, pp. 18–20.

crown remained committed to the inclusion of bishops within the Kirk as a method for enforcing the royal will in church affairs, and to a direct role for the king himself within the Kirk as its temporal head, over the course of the later 1570s growing support had emerged within the ranks of the General Assembly for a more democratic form of governance via a series of overlapping church courts and councils. These ranged from the parochial kirk session (a group of ministers and lay elders chosen by the congregation to enforce moral discipline in the parish), to presbyteries (the ministers of a group of adjacent parishes which acted as the 'appelate court' for the kirk sessions and dealt with ministerial oversight), regional synods (made up of representatives of a number of presbyteries), and finally to the national General Assembly. This presbyterian polity was articulated at length in the *Second Book of Discipline*, and the ideology at the heart of this vision, known as the 'Two Kingdoms' theory, was the espousal of the sovereignty of Christ over the Kirk and the exclusion of temporal rule from church affairs, thus making the king unable to claim headship or superiority over the church, although (as James VI was constantly reminded) as a subject of the spiritual kingdom he was subject to the criticism and censure of the ministers. By extension, bishops, who had been seen by many of the early Scottish reformers as hopelessly corrupt and were described as 'dumb dogges' and 'belly-gods' for their impiety, greed and avarice, were also equally out of place in this church structure.[73]

While Melville has often been credited as the driving force behind Presbyterianism in Scotland, recent research has clearly shown that he was no more than an active member of a wider faction within the Kirk supportive of this shift, and that this group may have been no more than a vocal minority among the greater body of the ministry who were more moderate and flexible in their outlook towards polity.[74] However, the battle over ecclesiastical politics between the crown and the vocal adherents of Presbyterianism that unfolded in the 1580s had a direct impact on Melville's programme of educational reform, and this turmoil manifested in very different ways at each university. In Glasgow, radical protest by a group of Presbyterian ministers and scholars led by Smeaton against the ecclesiastical policies of the Lennox regime, carried out with the blessing and support of Melville, almost undid the successes that had been achieved in reforming the college. The trigger for this unrest was the elevation in Autumn 1581 of Robert Montgomery to the archbishopric of Glasgow by the Lennox regime. Montgomery, minister of Stirling, was nominated by the crown to the vacant archbishopric, and in exchange for an annual

---

[73]   For a fuller discussion of these issues, see Donaldson, *James V–James VII*, pp. 148–50, 197–211; *Second Book*, ed. Kirk, *passim*.

[74]   MacDonald, *Jacobean Kirk*, *passim*.

salary of £1,000 agreed to lease the temporalities of the see to the Duke of Lennox. The chapter responsible for his confirmation, which included Smeaton, the rector of the university Andrew Hay, and the dean of the faculty of arts Andrew Polwarth, refused to accept the nomination, and despite the royal government ordering that Montgomery be accepted this did not stop him from being subjected to an extensive prosecution, led by Andrew Melville, as to the quality of his ministry in the General Assembly of October 1581.[75]

The detailed inquest into Montgomery's doctrine revealed another central issue with his suitability as a minister – his support of the royal supremacy in the church. Despite a bizarre criticism that he had argued from the pulpit that women were circumcised 'in the foir skin of their foirheid', the rest of the allegations against him attacked him for describing church polity and discipline as indifferent 'trifles of policie', for claiming from the pulpit that Presbyterian ministers were seditious, and for contending that Presbyterian interpretations of scripture were overly literal and precise, or else unsubstantiated, on matters of church organisation. After a lengthy discussion taking several days, the assembly ended by ordering the presbytery of Stirling to undertake a detailed examination of Montgomery's life and conversation and to report their findings to the synod of Lothian, who had full power to enact any measures they felt necessary against him. In the meantime, Montgomery was to remain in the ministry of Stirling and cease any attempts to obtain the elevation to Glasgow, under pain of excommunication.[76]

Following the decree of the assembly, on 21 November 1581 the Stirling presbytery began an extended process of trial and examination against Montgomery which mirrored the criticisms raised earlier against him. Besides allegations of regular intemperate outbursts brought on 'eftir meikill drink' and continued absenteeism, the presbytery also found 'that his doctrein is nocht formall nor sensablle to the commone pepill, and that his jestur in pulpet is nocht decent at sum tymis'. On 13 March 1582 the presbytery suspended him from his ministry and excommunicated him.[77] In retaliation, the Privy Council summoned the chapter of Glasgow for their refusal to accept Montgomery's nomination, and on 12 April declared that this constituted a failure by the chapter to present a candidate under the terms of the Leith concordat. The right of presentation now

---

[75] RPC, vol. 3, pp. 474–6; BUK, vol. 2, pp. 524–5, 528–9, 533–4, 538, 541–7.

[76] BUK, vol. 2, pp. 524–5, 528–9, 533–4, 538, 541–7.

[77] Stirling Presbytery Records 1581–1587, ed. James Kirk (Edinburgh, 1981), pp. 13–38. A summons to try Montgomery had been raised on 26 September, following a letter of Montgomery's given to the Presbytery on 12 September 1581 advising them of his absence; see pp. 6–10.

fell to the crown which duly recognised Montgomery, and forbade any further dissension.[78] Undeterred, on 24 April 1582 the General Assembly convened in St Andrews, with Andrew Melville as moderator, and its central business was upholding the action taken against Montgomery by the Stirling presbytery, despite letters of horning raised by the royal government threatening any assembly members who took action in this matter. The escalating tensions of the situation were momentarily defused when Montgomery agreed to accept the authority of the General Assembly and promised not to make any further attempt to obtain the archbishopric on pain of excommunication, but final judgement on the matter was held over until the next assembly.[79]

Meanwhile, events in Glasgow were no less filled with crisis and confrontation, and a flashpoint was reached on 22 April. Montgomery had attempted to preach in the city, but a mob was apparently raised at the instigation of Thomas Smeaton, the regents Peter Blackburn and Blaise Laurie, and the other members of the Glasgow chapter. This mob:

> to the nowmer of fouretie personis, all bodin in feir of weir, with jakkis, stelibonettis, hagbuttis, pistolettis … come and enterit be leddirs in the revestrie of the Hie Kirk of Glasgow, and detenit the same be force of armes the space of sex houres or thairby, of mynd to have attemptit sum uther heich interpryse, to the troubling of the gude and quiet estate of the cuntrie.[80]

The 'heich interpryse' was nothing more menacing than barring Montgomery from entry while Smeaton subjected him to a lengthy sermon on simony.[81] However, the royal government were sufficiently worried to order Smeaton and his accomplices to compear before the Privy Council on 10 September for their part in this student 'riot'.[82]

This episode clearly suggests radical resistance at Glasgow by an effectively mobilised group of students, all of whom were ideologically committed to Presbyterianism. However, the justification for their behaviour, given as part of grievances prepared by the General Assembly for the king at a crisis meeting on 27 June following the events of the riot and a dispute over the expulsion of Robert Durie from his ministerial charge in Edinburgh for sedition, suggests that they were reacting to several acts of violence visited upon them by supporters of Montgomery. The Glasgow provost John Stewart of Minto and his baillies had apparently forcibly

---

[78]   *RPC*, vol. 3, pp. 474–6; *BUK*, vol. 2, pp. 571–5.

[79]   *BUK*, vol. 2, pp. 557–66, 569.

[80]   *RPC*, vol. 3, pp. 489–91.

[81]   Durkan and Kirk, pp. 335–6.

[82]   *RPC*, vol. 3, pp. 489–91.

removed John Howieson, the moderator of the Glasgow presbytery, and placed him in the tollbooth for discussing the Montgomery case, and had also expelled the city minister David Wemyss for refusing to give up his pulpit for the Archbishop.[83] They also argued that Minto and the Council had not only violently assaulted the students but had thoroughly disrupted the university, as the 'Ministers, Masters of Colledgis, and scholers of Glasgow ... were, be letters of horning, compellit to leave thair flockes and schooles destitute, and sensyne, from tyme to tyme, and place to place, have bein delayit and continued'.[84]

There were two very different versions of events circulating in relation to this episode, but although the behaviour of the members of the college had caused considerable consternation to the royal government, political events at court postponed any further action against them. William Ruthven, the first earl of Gowrie, disturbed by the pro-French and pro-Catholic leanings of the Lennox and Arran regime and worried by the considerable amounts of royal debt he had become personally liable for during his time as treasurer in their administration, seized the king on 23 August 1582 in the coup d'etát known as the 'Ruthven Raid'.[85] Supported by a coalition of Protestant and pro-English lords including the earls of Angus and Mar, Lord Lindsay of the Byres, and the Master of Glamis, the radical presbyterian ministers also supported the actions of this faction.[86] During their ten-month rule the raiders granted a number of concessions to the Kirk including tighter controls on bishops and formal approval of kirk sessions and synods, although they stopped short of ratifying the *Second Book of Discipline*. Despite having the backing of hard-line Protestants within the country, the regime failed to get the English backing it hoped would consolidate its position and were threatened by a coalition led by the earls of Huntly, Crawford, Argyll and Rothes who conspired to bring about the king's release. James VI escaped from the Ruthven Lords in June 1583, and James Stewart, Earl of Arran quickly resumed control of the country. The new administration condemned the actions of the Ruthven Lords as treason in December 1583, by which point most of the lords were

---

[83]   Durkan and Kirk, p. 336.

[84]   *BUK*, vol. 2, pp. 583.

[85]   Donaldson, *James V–James VII*, pp. 178–9 ; Dawson, *Scotland Re-formed*, pp. 310–12; George R. Hewitt, 'Ruthven Raiders (act. 1581–1585)', *ODNB* [69938, accessed 31 July 2009]; Sharon Adams, 'Ruthven, William, fourth Lord Ruthven and first earl of Gowrie (c.1543–1584)', *ODNB* [24375, accessed 31 July 2009].

[86]   *BUK*, vol. 2, pp. 594–6. James Melville was certainly supportive, believing the seizure brought a 'grait releive to the kirk and common-wealth'; *JMAD*, pp. 133–4.

either in ward or in exile. Gowrie was arrested early in 1584 and executed on 2 May.[87]

During the ascendancy of the Raiders the local balance of power in Glasgow shifted in favour of the Kirk, and the Laird of Minto and his supporters were tried before the General Assembly, admitted their complicity in the attack on Howieson, and were referred to the Glasgow Presbytery for punishment.[88] There also appears to have been an attempt to further augment the staff at the college with another opponent of Montgomery, as Patrick Sharp, who was master of the grammar school and had taken part in the 1582 riot, resigned his commission 'be advise of the maisteris of the Vniuersitie and wtheris', presumably to take up a post as regent.[89]

The royal government was clearly aggrieved by the move to elevate Sharp to the college, as in April 1583 they ordered the General Assembly to recognise the king's rights as 'patron and erecter of the Colledge of Glasgow' and not to make any alteration to the staff of the college.[90] However, following the removal of the Ruthven faction events at the college soon took a turn for the worse, beginning with the sudden and premature death of Smeaton on 13 December 1583.[91] A successor to Smeaton was not appointed until January 1586, and in the intervening period the government did its best to eradicate Presbyterian dissidents within the college. With the return of Arran to ascendancy over the royal administration, a corresponding shift in ecclesiastical policy took place, culminating in the 'Black Acts' of May 1584 which reaffirmed the royal supremacy, proscribed presbyteries, and restored the power and jurisdiction of the Episcopal hierarchy in Scotland.[92]

As part of this process, Robert Montgomery had his diocesan jurisdiction and prerogatives restored by royal letters in the June immediately following the 'Black Acts'. On 8 July these letters were publicly read and accepted by the council and 'ane reasonable number of the commounalitie' in Glasgow, at which time the Provost and baillies removed the minister David Wemyss from the pulpit in favour of the Archbishop.[93] The four regents

---

[87]   Donaldson, *James V–James VII*, p. 180; Maurice Lee, *John Maitland of Thirlestane and the Foundation of Stewart Despotism in Scotland* (Princeton, 1959), pp. 46–7. Mar and Glamis fled to Ireland, while Angus was warded in the Highlands.

[88]   *BUK*, vol. 2, pp. 597–600.

[89]   *Extracts from the Records of the Burgh of Glasgow A.D. 1573–1642*, ed. J.D. Marwick (Glasgow, 1876), p. 99.

[90]   *BUK*, vol. 2, p. 620.

[91]   John Durkan, 'Smeaton, Thomas (1536–1583)'.

[92]   Dawson, *Scotland Re-formed*, pp. 312–14; MacDonald, *Jacobean Kirk*, pp. 26–9.

[93]   *Extracts from the Records of the Burgh of Glasgow*, pp. 108–9.

of the college refused to attend Montgomery's public preaching, arguing
it would be wrong to listen owing to his excommunication, and they
were summoned before the royal council for contempt at the beginning of
August. All four were ordered into ward, with two being held in the castle
of Glasgow and two in St Andrews castle. The college was closed, 'and
the scholars commaunded to goe home, till new Masters were provided'.[94]
The rector Andrew Hay and the dean of arts Andrew Polwarth were also
removed: they had been summoned to appear before the Privy Council on
unspecified charges in the preceding May, and while Hay had appeared and
was subsequently warded north of the Tay, Polwarth fled to England.[95]

The college appears to have opened again, at least in some reduced
capacity, at some point in late 1584, as graduation numbers make clear that
there was no major loss of continuity in teaching.[96] Who taught is not clear,
but it seems that perhaps Patrick Sharp changed his attitude towards the
Presbyterian faction sufficiently to make him suitable to continue teaching.
He was confirmed as the new principal in January 1586, and although
he had been present at the student riot in 1582 and spent considerable
time in his first year as principal with Andrew Melville when the latter
returned from exile, he would prove intellectually and religiously to be
far more amenable to royal policy. Under him, the advances in curriculum
instituted by Melville, and the evidence of radical Presbyterianism among
the student populace, appear to have dissipated, as the town council and
royal government began to exert ever greater control over the college.[97]

With Glasgow shut down, further punitive action for the Presbyterian
support of the Ruthven Raid was taken, perhaps unexpectedly, against
King's College. David Stevenson's comprehensive assessment of the
fragmentary evidence for this period of the university's history shows
that James VI actively discouraged the process of reform there following
his escape from the Ruthven lords.[98] Official sanction for reforming
King's College had been granted in the Parliament of July 1578 when
commissioners were appointed to visit it as part of a wider review of all
three universities.[99] However, the only evidence that any work had been

---

[94] Calderwood, vol. 8, pp. 271–2. This information was included in a text drafted by
the Presbyterian ministers in exile at Newcastle on 10 August 1584; see Calderwood, vol. 4,
pp. 150–7.

[95] With Melville and the other Presbyterian exiles; see below, Chapter 4. Durkan and
Kirk, p. 337; *RPC*, vol. 3, pp. 631–2, 662–3.

[96] *Munimenta*, vol. 3, pp. 4–5. 18 graduates are recorded for 1583, 15 for 1584 and
1585 respectively, but only 6 for 1586 and 9 for 1587, suggesting there had been some
disruption to the number of entrants in 1583/4.

[97] Durkan and Kirk, p. 338. See below, Chapters 7–8.

[98] Stevenson, *King's College*, pp. 30–35.

[99] *RPS*, 1578/7/5 [accessed 20 August 2009].

undertaken was a parliamentary Act of 29 November 1581 granting power to the parliamentary management committee known as the lords of the articles to review outstanding articles from both the current session and the parliament of November 1579, which also noted an article for the reformation of the college of Aberdeen, an article advocating the erection of a college in Orkney and a general act of reform for the universities.[100] This shows that some form of reform plan for Aberdeen had been placed before the Council, and commissioners were appointed to take the programme further. The next evidence of progress, however, occurred while James was under the ward of the Ruthvens, when a further commission was appointed between the General Assembly and the Royal Council in October and November 1582, led by the Earl Marischal.[101]

The commissioners from both the General Assembly and the royal government met in Aberdeen on 12 March 1583, and it was at this meeting that a reform plan was put together that either established or developed what we now know as the *Nova Fundatio*, the abortive re-foundation of the college that clearly shows the influence of Melville's educational reform programme and which now survives only in a copy dating from the late eighteenth century.[102] It is likely this *Nova Fundatio* which was spoken of promisingly in the April General Assembly where 'it was found travels had been taken therein, and ane order set doune which is in the Principalls hands'.[103] The same assembly also ordained James Lawson, Andrew Melville, Nicol Dalgleish and Robert Pont to review the proceedings of the said Commissioners and the text of the planned re-foundation, so that the Earl Marsichal 'may travel for the Kings Majesties confirmatione thereof'. The same men were to convene a separate meeting in St Andrews on 5 September to examine the staff of King's to see 'that they be sufficient and qualified, conforme to the new erection'.[104]

Things changed rapidly in the summer. With the control of the Ruthven faction weakening in the second quarter of 1583, James VI wrote to David Cunningham, Bishop of Aberdeen on 25 May ordering him to stop the Assembly's planned reform and 'to observe and keep the heads of your foundation, and in no way to hurt the funds', and also to forbid Arbuthnott from leaving to take up a proposed ministerial post at St Andrews, as doing so would not only have weakened teaching provision at King's but have materially strengthened the number of supporters Melville had in

100   *RPS*, 1581/10/28 [accessed 30 March 2010].
101   *BUK*, vol. 2, pp. 593–4; *RSS*, vol. 8, no. 2254, pp. 389–90.
102   Stevenson, *King's College*, pp. 30–40, 149–66.
103   *BUK*, vol. 2, p. 614.
104   *BUK*, vol. 2, pp. 624–5.

St Andrews.[105] The aggression of the royal government has convincingly been explained as stemming from fear over the potential radicalisation of education at King's,[106] and in the wake of the events at Glasgow in the preceding year and the Ruthven Raid it is understandable why.

Royal displeasure, however, was no impediment to the General Assembly. At its meeting in October 1583 it was noted that the staff at Aberdeen who were to be summoned in September remained untried, so a new commission consisting of the Rector, Andrew Melville, Thomas Buchanan, Robert Wilkie of St Leonard's and James Martine of St Salvator's, was formed to undertake this. To assuage fears that the college would descend into absenteeism and chaos if all the staff were summoned at once, the sub-principal and two regents were ordered to present themselves on 6 March 1584, and the remaining two regents on the last day of April. Peter Blackburn, then minister of Aberdeen, was also to give the staff plenty of advance warning so no excuse could be made for non-attendance. More importantly, the putative *Nova Fundatio* was discussed at the assembly, and with Thomas Smeaton, Andrew Melville, Nicol Dalgleish and James Martine having read over it and agreed with its contents, 'the whole Assemblie giveth their approbatione therto'.[107]

Despite obtaining the approval and consent of the Kirk, the mounting pressure from the royal government to drop reform plans at Aberdeen gained significant ground when Alexander Arbuthnott died suddenly on 10 October 1583.[108] Without support on the ground in Aberdeen, and with the flight of Melville and his supporters into exile early in the following year, the reform programme at Aberdeen was quietly suppressed. In February 1584 Walter Stewart was appointed as principal[109] and, like Patrick Sharp at Glasgow, would prove to be inert in matters of constitutional reform and passive to the royal will.

The only surviving evidence from the March 1583 commission, a document ratified by James VI in August 1584, gives a highly obscure account of the events of the preceding year, and may well have been retroactively tampered with.[110] Noting that there had been a 'langsum delay' in taking any account of the college revenues since Alexander Arbuthnott had entered the college in 1569, and also noting that in 1583

---

[105]   *BUK*, vol. 2, p. 634.

[106]   Stevenson, *King's College*, pp. 32–4.

[107]   *BUK*, vol. 2, pp. 627, 629.

[108]   James Kirk, 'Arbuthnot, Alexander (1538–1583)', *ODNB* [605, accessed 20 Aug 2009].

[109]   *RSS*, vol. 8, 1857, p. 312.

[110]   *RSS*, vol. 8, 2254, pp. 389–90. This reading owes everything to David Stevenson's ingenious interpretation of events.

there had been talk of him moving to St Andrews, the royal government had established the commission 'to sie and considder that the fundatioun of the said college wer conformabill in all respectis' to the 'New Foundation' at St Andrews, and to check 'the admissioun of bursaris and specialie for ordour taking anent the distributioun of the rentis thairof'. The commissioners had indeed met at Aberdeen, but once they had received a full account of the revenues they had 'hard, futit, concludit and subscryvit the samn', and apart from checking that teaching was broadly comparable with that at other universities had left. Seeing the commission had been granted chiefly to ensure the college was financially solvent, the king now publicly ratified the accounts so that no one could pretend 'ony ignorance thairof or esteem thameselffis onywyise prejudgit throw the generalitie of the said college contenit in the said commissioun'. This menacing phrase appears to be a veiled criticism of those pushing for educational reform as advocated by the March 1583 commission, and the ratification is most conspicuous for its complete lack of any mention of constitutional innovation or revision. Given the events of the previous three years and the evident links between religious radicalism and the putative Melvillian reform programme, it was clear that by early 1584 the government were in no mood to entertain anything that might ideologically advance support for radical Presbyterianism, and were willing to resort to altering the governmental record of events in line with this policy.

With the death of the leading proponent of reform at Aberdeen, a royal placeman in control, and an embargo on any further developments, the curricular experiment at Aberdeen soon fizzled out. In August 1584 a parliamentary commission was appointed consisting of James Stewart, Earl of Arran, John Maitland of Thirlestane, Alexander Hay of Easter Kennet, and the bishops of St Andrews and Aberdeen to visit King's at the supplication of the masters, who had 'conceived a form of erection in the college of Aberdeen and union of the old rentals with the new' that they wished approved.[111] Whether this was a revision of the *Nova Fundatio* or merely an attempt to consolidate properly the patrimony of the college on the back of the 1583 commission, the commission is noticeable for its complete lack of men who had been involved with the Melvillian educational experiment.

This parliamentary commission made no further reports, however, and only two other attempts at reform were made in Aberdeen prior to the re-foundation of the College under Bishop Patrick Forbes of Corse in 1617. The first was in April 1593, when the general assembly attempted to establish a new commission led by the Earl Marischal and Andrew Melville to visit King's College and to reform any abuses that they

---

[111]   *RPS*, 1584/5/92 [accessed 20 August 2009].

encountered, but no proceedings were recorded.[112] The next took place in November 1597, when Parliament passed an Act ratifying and approving 'the new foundation of his majesty's college of old Aberdeen to be revised by his highness's commissioners' John Lindsay of Balcarres, the Lord of Session James Elphinstone of Barnton, and David Cunningham, Bishop of Aberdeen.[113] Elphinstone was apparently a kinsman of the original founder of the college, Bishop William Elphinstone, and he succeeded Balcarres as secretary in 1598. Given Balcarres' extensive role in stifling dissent at St Andrews in the later 1590s and his sustained attack on Melville and his supporters,[114] it does not seem unreasonable to assume that Elphinstone would take a similar tack to protect the reputation of his family in relation to King's College.

These tantalising suppositions aside, the brief flashes of reform in the 1590s gave way to a period of inertia and stagnation at King's that lasted almost twenty years.[115] The complete and total victory of the royal will over reform at Aberdeen shows that just as royal support had been carefully integrated into the reform programme at St Andrews, the absence of similar support at Aberdeen had led to swift royal reaction as soon as James VI was in a position to do so.

It is little wonder that Melville mourned the deaths of Arbuthnott and Smeaton so profoundly, as seen in his epitaph to both men:

> Scarcely, alas, scarcely had we mourned taken Arbuthnott … but death seizes another [Smeaton], and one funeral is made more bitter by another, and a greater man dies with his great light extinguished. Arbuthnott, the North Star, caused the darkness to flee from the night, but you, the Glaswegian star, were shining at mid-day.[116]

He had not only lost two dear friends and allies, but the two lieutenants he had assumed would consolidate his intellectual programme in the west and north-east were now dead, and the opportunity to link fully his work at St Mary's with reforms at both King's and Glasgow was over.

---

[112]   BUK, vol. 3, p. 811.

[113]   RPS, 1597/11/70 [accessed 30 March 2010].

[114]   See below pp. 160–172.

[115]   Stevenson, King's College, p. 39.

[116]   Reid, The Divinity Principals, p. 102: 'Vix heu, vix raptum deflevimus Arbuthnetum,/ Vix heu justa datis solvimus inferiis,/ Et premit altera mors, et funere funus acerbat,/ Et magno extincto lumine majus obit./ Ille quidem Arctoa tenebras de nocte fugabat,/ Fulgebas medio Glasgua stella die.'

Conclusion

In theory the 'Melvillian' reform of the universities was a central priority for the Scottish Kirk in the 1570s and 1580s, as demonstrated most clearly by the evidence of the October 1583 assembly minutes. In practice the process of implementing reform was far more contingent on both the individual staff at each university and on local and national politics. The actions of the Ruthven Raiders and the resulting political fallout from the king's escape had a massive impact on the progress of reform at all three universities. This episode had the most direct and arresting affect on Aberdeen, where attempts to bring in sweeping constitutional reform under the *Nova Fundatio* were vigorously opposed by a re-invigorated government staunchly opposed to any action associated with Melville's ideological radicalism. It would be almost four decades before true progress in reform at King's was achieved under the modernising Bishop Patrick Forbes of Corse, although along very different lines than those envisaged by Melville.[117] Glasgow University was resuscitated and restored to some level of distinction by Melville during his six years there, and in many ways his own boast later in his life that he had brought 'the matters of Rome, Jerusalem, Greece and Athens into the Glaswegian desert' (*qui Romam et Solymam et Grais in Glascua Athenas/Tesqua ... tuli*) was well founded.[118] However, it does seem that he had more help from the civil and episcopal authorities in doing this than has been previously recognised, and the same issues of radicalism that plagued reform at Aberdeen almost brought the university back to the state of collapse it had faced before Melville's arrival during the brief principalship of Thomas Smeaton. The civil government continued to maintain a clear involvement in St Andrews throughout the 1570s, although the staff there must take most of the credit in completing the process of re-orienting the university towards a Protestant settlement that had been started in the immediate aftermath of the reformation. Although there were still apparent traces of Catholicism in the early 1570s, St Andrews had clearly broken by then with its traditional past and had done so with minimal disruption. That spirit of slow and moderate reform was entrenched among the masters of the university, and would lead to explosive results in the decade after they were confronted with the much more ambitious and far-reaching reform plan of 1579.

---

[117]   Stevenson, *King's College*, pp. 61–93.

[118]   Melville, 'Prosopopeia Apologetica' (c.1608), in Edinburgh University Library DC6.45, pp. 22–3.

CHAPTER 4

Reform and Reaction at St Andrews, 1579–88

This chapter charts the response of the principal masters and regents of St Andrews to the 'New Foundation' and to the arrival of Andrew Melville amongst them. By early 1588, it was clear to a visitation of the university that the 'Melvillian' reform programme had largely failed to make an impact. As an anonymous writer made clear in a 'memorial' given to the commission:

> It is mast difficill in this confused tyme (quhen all folkis ar loukand to the weltering of the warld), to effectuat ony gude commoun werk, although men wer nevir sa weill willit; and speciallie quhair ye ar not certainly instructit, and hes na greit hope of thankes for your travell ... do sumquhat, for God's sake, that others be your exemple may imitate your trade, for schamis cause, althogh schame workis not mekle this fatall yeir 1588.[1]

The reasons for the failure at St Andrews of the intellectual programme that had been adopted apparently wholeheartedly at Glasgow are many. Conservatism, familial interest and a lack of clarity over the roles of each college following the 'New Foundation' played their part at St Salvator's, which under its provost James Martine emerged as a bastion of resistance towards Melville's ideas and which enjoyed the patronage and support of the crown. Conversely, Melville's radical Presbyterianism and continual altercations with the royal government over church politics led to his continued (and often forced) absence from St Andrews and impeded the progress of the reform programme at St Mary's, a situation greatly exacerbated by Melville's personal feud with Archbishop Patrick Adamson. However, by 1588 a measure of progress and stability had been achieved in the areas of curriculum and teaching, particularly at St Leonard's. Although we know far too little about the adoption of the 'New Foundation' there in practical terms, teaching evidence for the college in this decade shows that the masters did engage with the intellectual components of Melville's programme, and particularly with the works of Ramus, although in a decidedly less enthusiastic fashion than Melville had hoped.

---

[1]   *Evidence*, p. 193.

St Salvator's, James Martine and the 'New Foundation'

At 11 a.m. on 29 August 1577, John Rutherford, 'extenuat in his bodie and decayit in the strenthe thairoff', stepped down from the office of provost of St Salvator's. By the time-honoured means of an oath and the placing of a ring upon his finger, Rutherford elected in his place James Martine, second master and parson of Kemback.[2] Martine would hold the provostry of the college for an astounding 43 years,[3] but his first decade as provost was riven by infighting among the masters and accusations of corruption and nepotism that culminated in massive uproar at the 1588 visitation.

Martine was born between 1540 and 1543, and entered St Salvator's between 1557 and 1561.[4] Rutherford apparently took great personal interest in Martine, and upon his graduation gave him a post as a regent specialising in mathematics.[5] Rutherford, who had studied under the great scholastic Nicolas de Grouchy and had been tutor to Montaigne, also held minor distinction as a logician in his own right. His *Commentariorum de Arte Disserendi Libri Quatuor*, published in 1557 and again in 1577 at Edinburgh, was a commentary on Aristotle's logic, written in what Alexander Broadie has described as 'Ciceronian Latin with a liberal sprinkling of Greek'.[6] Rutherford dispensed with the late-scholastic discussions of terms and exponibles that his predecessor John Mair and his students had spent much of their time on, but was vehemently supportive of Aristotle in the formulation and division of logic and rhetoric. Rutherford's known library, and comments in his work, suggest that he gave Ramus and his works short shrift.[7] He probably passed this viewpoint on to Martine, who had no education outside the college to give him cause to question

---

[2] UYSS110/G10.3, AH2.

[3] UYSL156, fos 254–7; Walter Macfarlane, *Genealogical Collections Concerning Families in Scotland*, ed. J.T. Clark (2 vols, Edinburgh, 1900), vol. 2, p. 190.

[4] *Early Records*, p. 268; UYSL156, fos 254–57. The university records tell us that Martine entered St Salvator's College in 1561, but Robert Barron, Martine's biographer, states that he entered the college in 1557. Considering the fragmentary nature of the graduation and matriculation records for the early 1560s, it may be that there has been some confusion in recording intrants and graduates. A 1557 entrance date would certainly make sense, putting Martine in his early teens.

[5] UYSL156, fo. 255: 'Unde statim post adeptam Lauream Magistratem, ab eo in professorem numerum cooptatus est.'

[6] Alexander Broadie, 'Philosophy in Renaissance Scotland: Loss and Gain', in MacQueen, *Humanism in Renaissance Scotland*, pp. 75–96, at pp. 84–5; Alexander Broadie, *The Circle of John Mair* (Oxford, 1985), pp. 1–6, 264–6; John Durkan, 'John Rutherford and Montaigne: an Early Influence?', in *Bibliotheque d'Humanisme et Renaissance* 41 (1979): 115–22.

[7] Rutherford's library included numerous editions of Aristotle and works by Ramus' opponent Jakob Schegk, and in his *De Arte Disserendi* he described Ramus and his followers

it. Martine went to study in France at some point in the later 1560s,[8] but Rutherford called him back before he had a chance to spend any real time there and on 29 July 1570 he was elected as third master and parson of Dunino.[9] Events conspired to push Martine further up the professorial ladder while he was still young and inexperienced. Following the death of David Guild in September 1574 he was promoted to second master,[10] and within three years was elevated to provost.

The masters at the college in the 1570s were a group of nepotistic and self-interested individuals. Prior to Martine's appointment in 1570, the college staff had been made up of John Rutherford, William Ramsay and David Guild. Guild was highly conservative and had been part of the pre-reformation college,[11] and Ramsay had been involved just prior to his death with the controversy surrounding the second master of St Mary's and minister of the town, Robert Hamilton.[12] They were joined by Homer Blair, Ramsay's maternal nephew who became professor of mathematics in the college following the 'New Foundation' but was at this stage a regent, having graduated in 1566.[13] Ramsay had been using a theological bursary set up by John Mair and William Manderston in the 1530s to supplement his income as rector of Kemback, and this was given over to his nephew.[14] Thomas Brown became third master in February 1576 on the death of David Guild, and was promoted to second master at some point in late 1577, when John Rutherford Junior, the son of the old provost and beneficiary of a wide range of college patrimony from his father,[15] took up Brown's old post.

Judging from evidence within the college records of how this group of masters conducted themselves in the years on either side of 1579, one would

---

as 'professors of lying', guilty of 'shameless philosophy and empty loquacity'. Durkan, 'John Rutherford and Montaigne', 119–20.

[8]   Barron records that Martine 'in Galliam proficisci decrevit, ad uberiorem ingenii cultum capessendum, moresque elegantius formandos'. Baron gives a name for where Martine is studying, but it is illegible.

[9]   UYSS110/H1–2, AE16. He was confirmed in the post by James VI on 30 November 1570 (*RSS*, vol. 6, 1026, pp. 190–1).

[10]   UYSS150/2, fo. 150r; UYSS110/G4. Thomas Brown was promoted to the position of third master, and both men were witnesses to a tack set on the teinds of Cults on 21 January 1575.

[11]   Guild and William Cranston had both opposed the entrance of John Rutherford as dean of arts on 4 November 1557 due to his being unordained. *Acta*, pp. lxiii–lxvii, ccxxxiii, 409–11.

[12]   See Chapter 1.

[13]   *Early Records*, pp. 160, 271. Blair entered the college in 1564.

[14]   UYSS150/2, fo. 154v; UYSS110/AE4.

[15]   See, among other examples, UYSS110/G3–4; *RSS*, vol. 7, 1218, p. 182 (14 October 1577).

almost think that no 'New Foundation' had been ordered for St Salvator's. There is no evidence of changes of title or profession, or anything that suggests reform was embraced by the college or that the masters had made any attempt to improve their teaching or their curriculum. Instead, what we find is the continuing spectre of lax standards of discipline among students and petty jealousies and disputes among staff. Financial management and control of college revenues remained the priority for Martine and the other masters, a particular source of tension within the college that would fester throughout the 1580s.

These issues were in evidence before Martine assumed the provostry of the college, with John Rutherford involved in a range of irregular financial dealings relating to the annexed parish of Cults that supported the stipend of the provost.[16] On 13 and 14 February 1575–6, following the death of David Guild, Rutherford, Martine and the new third master Thomas Brown were granted letters of horning to compel the town commissary William Skene to allow them to confirm the testaments of their colleagues when they died, without outside reference.[17] Martine used this privilege when he became provost to confirm William Ramsay's testament of 1570.[18] While this may have simply been an attempt to ensure that masters had executors in place to settle their affairs, it does seem macabre that this privilege would be so contested.

John Rutherford died at some point between 26 September and 13 December 1577,[19] leaving Martine in complete control. In the five years following Rutherford's death there were several attempts made by the new provost to consolidate control of college finances and the provision of prebendaries and college positions to himself, in the face of growing opposition from new and more vocal staff. On 14 July 1579 Thomas Brown died, and on 3 September 1579 Rutherford Junior was admitted to the second master's place.[20] The most senior regent in the college was David Monypenny, who had graduated as a bachelor in 1573 and as master in 1575, and who should have been first in line for the position. However, Martine opposed his entrance, forcing Monypenny to petition the Privy Council for the position, and on 12 August 1579 a royal order compelled Martine to accept him immediately.[21] Monypenny came from a local

---

[16]   UYSS110/G3–4.

[17]   UYSS110AD2–3; UYSS150/2, fos 154v–155r.

[18]   UYSS150/2, fo. 154v.

[19]   According to references within UYSS110/G3, AP1.

[20]   UYSS150/2, fo. 155v; UYSS110/H3.

[21]   UYSS110/C4.4. A reference to the 'removing of Mr Johne Ker' from one of the master's positions suggests that Martine had filled the position with this man, and there is a reference to a John Kerr graduating from the college in 1568. There is no mention of Kerr in

family that lived in nearby Pitmillie, so there may have been some form of local tension between the two men. The appointment of Monypenny at the behest of the civil authority would introduce a master critical of James Martine unafraid to speak his mind, and who would be a staunch ally of Melville.

This dispute was followed on 1 December 1579 by Martine's unsuccessful attempts to intrude a member of his extended kin, Magnus Arthur, into a regent position. This arbitrary inclusion was manifestly against the newly-implemented tenets of election laid down by the 'New Foundation' and Arthur was described as woefully unqualified by the other masters, who successfully petitioned the Privy Council to have him removed.[22] However, in 1582, the principal masters and regents authorised the intromission of all the 'commonrentis' of the college to James Martine, providing that he 'furneis the kitchene and hall' and 'sustene honorabilly and sufficientlie the haill fundatt personis within the said college in meale and drink' each year from Michaelmas until the vacation on 1 September.[23] In July of the same year another document was drawn up, allocating the control and presentation of six of the college bursaries to the principal masters. On the pretext that previously the masters had been 'extraordinarlie requeistit and sollistit to committ and ressave ma bursaris than is prescrived in this foundatioun' and that presentation to bursaries had caused great 'stryfe and contentioun' between the principal masters, the right of presentation was to be divided among them from Michaelmas 1583 or whenever the bursaries became vacant. Three were to be given to James Martine, two to John Rutherford Junior and one to David Monypenny.[24] However, by 1585 Martine had also managed to place his brothers David and William in another two prebends within the college,[25] so whether this process of consolidation was a genuine attempt by Martine to streamline the college patrimony or to gain better control of the college finance is open to debate.

---

the muniment records before or after this decree beyond this, but there is a cryptic reference in the 1588 visitation records in the Balcarres Papers made by William Cranston suggesting that Kerr had been briefly admitted to the position at some point in the preceding decade.

[22]   *RPC*, vol. 3, pp. 243–4.

[23]   UYSS110/AH4. The document may be a forgery, as the masters complain to the 1588 commission that it was made without their consent.

[24]   UYSS400/1.

[25]   UYSS110/O1–3; Macfarlane, *Genealogical Collections*, p. 191; Balcarres Papers, vol. 7, fo. 133v. An assignment of an annual rent of 20 merks to the prebends of the college by Robert Bruce of Pitlethie and his spouse in July and August 1585 records the Martines as two of eight prebendaries, while Macfarlane records William Martine receiving his prebendary from Thomas, Master of Cassillis in December 1579 upon the demission of James Winchester. A complaint of the masters on 16 April 1588 was that David Martine had been a bursar for 'xii yeiris'.

Complicating this situation, Martine had strong ties to the local kingroup that supported Episcopacy and the authority of the king in ecclesiastical matters. Martine's eulogist, Robert Barron, stated that one of Martine's greatest qualities was his loyalty to the royal government and to moderation in religious polity:

> Anyone who began to be the least familiar with him knew … he set a singular example in being favourable to his king and in requiring obedience from everybody. He always followed moderate advice, [and] he was the most zealous for ecclesiastical peace. As a consequence, he was especially dear to his prince.[26]

Martine's family were closely aligned through marriage with the Arthur family, who were in turn connected to the family of Archbishop Patrick Adamson. One of the only pieces of General Assembly business that Martine was part of was a commission chosen to go with Adamson and the Earl Marischal to northern Scotland to hunt out suspected Catholics.[27] When Adamson was ordered to take up twice-weekly lectures in theology following the removal of Melville from teaching in 1586, he was ordered to do so not in St Mary's but in St Salvator's.[28]

Martine also had a good relationship with the king, or at least the royal government, in the early 1580s. An undated document of early 1580 shows one of the few references to the 'New Foundation' in the St Salvator's muniments, where James confirmed the right of Martine as provost to the rents and duties of Cults which he had 'in tymes bypast befoir the new order takin'.[29] Martine secured the gift of the prebendary of Balhousie to his illegitimate nephew William Martine from the Earl of Cassillis on 11 December 1579, and the Privy Council supported his attempts to recover payment of the prebendary in July 1583 when payment was not forthcoming from its tenant, Colin Eviot.[30] The king also offered financial support and patronage to Martine, for on 13 July 1583 James, understanding that Martine was 'burdenit not only with the bringing up of the yowth within the said college … bot also of the preaching of the evangel at the kirk of the Cultis oulklie distant frome our said citie

---

[26]   UYSL156, fo. 256: 'Sciunt enim, quicunque cum eo paulo familiarius coeperunt … in rege suo solendo et obsequium et apud omnes conciliando singulare exemplum fuit. Moderata consilia semper secutus est, et pacis ecclesiasticae studiosissimus erat. Unde principi suo in primis charus extitit.'

[27]   Calderwood, vol. 3, p. 599; *BUK*, vol. 2, p. 570.

[28]   M'Crie, pp. 428–9.

[29]   UYSS110/C4.5.

[30]   UYSS110/J21–24.

sewin mylis', ordered an annual grant of £200 to be given to him from the exchequer. This was an extraordinary amount that was almost double his annual income from the parish of Cults,[31] although it seems unlikely that Martine ever received it as further grants for the same amount were made to him in the 1590s. It does show, however, that in contrast to the radical Presbyterian Melville in St Mary's, the royal government and the archbishop appeared to have a friend and colleague in St Salvator's who was amenable to them, and who was rewarded as a result.

Shortly after the visitation of April 1588, Martine was sent two documents by the commission. The first was a copy of a missive to the Lords of Council and James VI listing a series of damning complaints against him, ranging from his refusal to allow the 'tenour of the said reformatioun' of the college to helping himself to a large portion of the college patrimony.[32] The second, a decree from the royal chancellor John Maitland of Thirlestane, described Martine as being 'negligent in his office in the rewlling and governance of the said college' and ordered his immediate removal.[33] The range of abuses that had led to this deprivation included Martine's behaviour towards his colleagues, but also his involvement in family politics in the burgh. Moreover, accounts of Martine and his fellow staff given in as part of the deprivation hearing show just how far from upholding the ideals of the 'New Foundation' they were.

The hostility of the other masters of the college towards Martine had become increasingly worse throughout the 1580s. In 1585, David Monypenny was appointed to the position of second master following the resignation of John Rutherford Junior. The regent William Cranston, nephew of the Catholic recusant who had held the post of provost prior to Rutherford senior, was appointed as third master.[34] These men, elevated to new roles of authority, did not agree with the level of control that Martine had achieved over the college. On 18 and 19 March 1587 Monypenny, Cranston, Welwood and Blair, with the other regents of the college, complained to the rector James Wilkie that Martine had assumed control of the college rents and did not make them privy to their administration. After consultation with the masters Wilkie ordered that Alexander Clepan be made *oeconomus* of the college. David Monypenny was made comptroller of the rents, and was to consult with Clepan over the status of the accounts and provide regular reports to the other masters.[35] Martine refused point blank to accept the ordinance as lawful. The dispute came

[31]   UYSS110/C4.6–7.
[32]   Balcarres Papers, vol. 7, fos 148r/v.
[33]   Balcarres Papers, vol. 7, fo. 132v.
[34]   UYSS110/C4.8, AE18.
[35]   Balcarres Papers, vol. 7, fo. 100r.

before Adamson who appears to have agreed with Wilkie, as Martine then went to the Privy Council and secured the approval of James VI for his intromission with the rents. The king declared that Martine had 'sustenit honourablie the haill foundat personis' during his period of intromission and that any process upheld against him by the university staff should cease immediately. There was thus an increasing division between the provost and masters of the college that had nothing to do with educational standards and everything to do with money.

The next issue was again monetary, this time relating to the addition of extraordinary professors to the college patrimony. As we have seen, the 'New Foundation' had proposed that the professors of mathematics and law, who from April 1574 had held the positions of third and fourth master in St Mary's, were to be moved to St Salvator's.[36] They were both to act as public lecturers, and were each to receive £100 and a chalder of oats from St Salvator's to pay their board and expenses.[37] This drain on finance angered the masters from the outset, and a supplication for more funds was presented to the Privy Council in 1583, with the additional comment that Welwood was failing to carry out his duties as mathematician. In March 1587 Welwood transferred to the lawyer's post following the demission of John Arthur, Martine's cousin, and Homer Blair took up Welwood's post as mathematician.[38] Martine would thus have been doubly aggrieved at having to support Welwood, who was depriving a member of his family and holding a position unwanted by the rest of the college.

These issues were exacerbated by the fact that Welwood was a member of a burgh family resolutely opposed to Martine's. The feud between the kingroups made up of the Smith, Welwood and Geddie families on the one hand, and the Martines and Arthurs on the other, has been extensively documented by John Cairns.[39] The Welwoods were merchants and burgesses, and supporters of Melville and the Presbyterian faction in St Andrews. Welwood wrote a number of verses in his printed works in praise of Melville, and Melville repaid the compliment in the preface to Welwood's 1582 work outlining a process for extracting water from coal shafts.[40] Welwood had also been warded in St Andrews Castle in December

---

[36]   See above, Chapter 3.

[37]   *Evidence*, pp. 184–6.

[38]   UYSS200/1–2; UYSS110/AH6. Arthur had taken the stipend from the post following the death of William Skene on 2 September 1582 but appears not to have taught.

[39]   Cairns, 'Academic Feud'.

[40]   See Melville's prefatory verse to William Welwood, *Guilielmi Velvod de aqua in altum per fistulas plumbeas facile exprimenda apologia demonstrativa* (Edinburgh, 1582).

1584, following the flight of Melville and the Presbyterian ministers to England.[41]

The dissension between the masters and Martine came to an explosive head before the 1588 visitation. The Balcarres Papers contain over twenty unpublished folios of detailed accusations and counter-accusations between the factions that show, even when allowance is made for exaggeration, that educational standards and behaviour were far from what the 'New Foundation' envisaged. When the visitation commenced on 16 April 1588, William Cranston was first to present a list of 'heidis' criticising Martine. Again, finance was the central issue. Martine had sold off much of the college victual gathered in 1576 and 1577 to various parties with no account made to the college. He had received over 300 merks from various sources for the college upkeep but had kept it for himself. The masters were also furious that Martine had set the valuable lands of Forteviot in tack to Alexander Bonar, after a lengthy legal battle had been undertaken in the late 1570s to regain them.[42] He had received a bursar called James Boyd into the college without consent in 1585 and had sold two other bursaries, one to George Gledstanes and another to Andrew Guthrie for his son. Martine had then divided the profit between himself and his brother Allan, whom he had arranged with Alexander Bonar would also receive a pension of 20 merks out of the lands of Forteviot. He had presented his brother David in 1577, when the latter was 'ane litill boy', to two bursaries of theology worth a total of 60 merks each and he had bought James Winchester's liferent of the prebendary of St Michael and given it to his other brother William. Indeed, Martine was charged with having attempted literally to sell the roof off the college: before he would allow Cranston to ascend to a master's position he wanted written agreement to set a croft owned by the college near St Andrews Castle in feu to his brother Allan, which had traditionally been set to the Jack family in exchange for pointing and mending the slates.[43]

The masters followed Cranston with a condemnation of Martine's behaviour. Martine was delated for allowing his cousin to take the stipend of the lawyer and not teach. Martine did not teach at all, and the masters could not get students to attend lectures as he did not discipline the students on a Saturday as he was supposed to. This resulted in the students wandering outside the college, attacking the porter when he tried to stop

---

[41]   Cairns, 'Academic Feud', 258–60.

[42]   The church of Forteviot in Perthshire had been attached to the college in 1495 as a prebend providing a chorister for the college choir. Although this gift had lapsed over the course of the sixteenth century, Martine successfully reclaimed it in legal proceedings over the course of 1578–9, bringing an annual rent of 300 merks to the college. Cant, *The College of St Salvator*, pp. 28–30, 170; UYSS110/E2, E4.6, E4.9–10.

[43]   Balcarres Papers, vol. 7, fos 133r/v.

them, and only speaking 'most filthie and ungodlie Scottis'. Worse still, David Martine had slandered William Cranston, attacked him with a knife and attempted to remove him from the common hall with his friends. In addition to the financial misdemeanours specified by Cranston, Martine had also intromitted the crop of 1585 and from May until September of the following year had left the college devoid of enough money to pay for adequate victual.[44] Finally, the college itself was in a poor state of repair and the library and evidences entirely scattered, an accusation to some extent borne out by a paltry list of books belonging to the college that was put forward as the library inventory.[45]

Martine was given a night to read over the articles and respond to each charge before the commission. His responses were hardly inspiring. With regard to the allegation of non-teaching, he complained that the profession of medicine that he had been allocated in the 'New Foundation' had never been 'professit in this universitie at ony tyme befor' and that he had been promised that when the reforms came into effect he would not be 'burdenit' with teaching it. Despite this, he had taught 'sum warkes of Galene, Serveill and Hippocrates' and the time lost before the commission was the longest he had been away from teaching. Martine stated that John Arthur had been lawfully provided to the position of lawyer and that he had been compelled regularly to make residence and teach. He further claimed that Cranston had started the fight with his brother and that he had referred them both to the rector for further adjudication.

In terms of finance, Martine conceded that the masters should hear a weekly compt of the college accounts, and that they should have adequate storage for the college books and evidence. However, he strenuously denied any wrong-doing in the administration of the rents, and alleged that David Monypenny and the other masters had approved a compt he made to them on 2 January 1588. He refused to take responsibility for the setting of Forteviot in tack to Alexander Bonar, for he was only 'head of the chapter' that agreed the tack at the time. However, Martine admitted that his brother Allan had been given a 20 merk pension from the parsonage. On the subject of his brother David, all he would say was that 'according to the law of natur he using all lawfull meanis is bound to prefer him to uthers not preiudging the rentall of the colledge', and had provided him as a student who 'travells as worthelie and diligentlie as ony uther professour'.[46]

---

[44] Balcarres Papers, vol. 7, fos 135r–136v.

[45] Balcarres Papers, vol. 7, fo. 101r. Durkan, 'The Early Library of St Salvator's', *The Bibliotheck* 3 (1962): 97–100.

[46] Balcarres Papers, vol. 7, fos 139r–142v.

Martine then launched into a slew of counter-charges, stating that the 'desolat estait' of the college was down to his colleagues. Where the masters were supposed to engage students in teaching and declamation for six or seven hours a day, the masters taught for half an hour or less. Martine's account, though obviously exaggerated, seems too specific to be completely false.[47] Martine was hypocritically furious that the masters had circumvented the usual process of appeal before the rector and chancellor and now 'troublit' the king and his council, presumably because he did not wish attention to be drawn too closely to the workings of the college. Eight of the twelve attacks made by Martine turned on the reputation of Cranston and the fact that his uncle had made off with large amounts of the college property.

However, it was in Martine's suggestions for remedying the situation that the real problems he had with the current state of the college came to light:

> forsamekill as all the forsaid enormities misorderis decay of doctrin and discipline within the said college hes preceadit of the breaking of the maist ancient and luvabill foundatioune therof (for sen the lait act of reformatioune we haiv nather kepit the said act nor the said auld fundatioune bot everie man hes takin so mekill of the ane and so mekill of the uther as schewit best to his awin forme) heirfor I maist humelie beseiche your Lordis that the first maist ancient fundatioune, sa far as it may stand with Godis word, be rescrivit and reestablischit to the auld integritie with all the haill liberties and privilegis thairof.[48]

Martine felt that his rights as 'ordinary magistrate' of the college were completely compromised by the 'New Foundation', and desired all the privileges and rights of the old foundation be restored to him. Martine wanted to return to teaching theology, which he felt was his traditional right as provost of the college, and not to be burdened with the unheard-of novelty of medicine. Moreover, Martine completely condemned the 'Melvillian' process of professorial specialisation as 'sen this new ordour was embracit thair nevir passit from this universitie sa guid philosopheris as of befoir ffor sa lang as the auld forme was kepit and observit our

---

[47]   The text reads: 'Thay uss na maner of disciplin in correcting and punisching. Thay waige in the toune resorting to commoune tavernis and keitchpillis. Thay mak thair disciplis companyeonis and familiaris with thame. Thay attend not to conduct upoune the play dayis their disciplis to the feildis and agane to the college nather will thay their disciplis chalmeris at morning and evening. Thay do not resort to the commoune prayeris of the colledge nather upone preaching dayis in the oulk will thay convein into the yett of the colledge to go to the kirk togidder with thair disciplis.'

[48]   Balcarres Papers, vol. 7, fos 143r–144r.

scolleris excellit all uther nationnis in philosophie'. Martine blamed the demise of regenting for this decay, and the students' lack of grounding in the basics of logic stopped them from becoming 'guid and perfect physicianis'. Martine clearly had some vested interest in removing the public professors of law and mathematics because of their drain on college revenues. However, he believed that Welwood did not have enough students to justify his existence and that Blair's teaching of 'the spheir' and other basic arithmetic could be carried out by 'everie regent'. The failure of the two to live *collegialiter* particularly galled Martine. That Martine was not entirely cynical and self-interested is clear from his desire that women visitors be entirely banned from the college, and that, 'becauss the college is burdenit with expenssis in buying herbs and kaill in the toune', three vacant yards within the college be reclaimed as communal gardens.[49]

The other masters provided a final rebuttal against Martine,[50] and William Welwood denied the legitimacy of the complaints against him since he was not technically part of the old foundation,[51] but the commission had had enough. Drawing a line under what they saw as an unprofitable and circular squabble, they summarised the complaints and responses given to them regarding the state of funding and teaching at the college, and made a note to 'avise with the council' regarding the 'lang articles in writ' they had received.[52]

Despite the massive split between the staff, and their failure to adopt the 1579 reforms, it appears that some of the tenets of the 'New Foundation' did make it through to practice. This shift was was most notable in terms of the basic Greek tuition which appears to have finally been incorporated into the college course, though when in the decade preceding 1588 is unfortunately unclear. The masters as a whole had refused to abandon fully the practice of regenting, and William Cranston was reduced to teaching grammar to a small group made up of the college patron John, fifth Earl of Cassillis and others, wanting a class 'be ressoun of the pest'. Despite this, Homer Blair taught 'the Arithmetique of Ramus' for an hour on Mondays, Tuesdays and Fridays, and David Monypenny taught the *Physics* from the original Greek at his appointed hours. Despite the criticisms made against David Martine, he apparently taught the first years the basic precepts of Greek and Latin using excerpts of Isocrates, Aristotle and Homer, and the basics of logic using Porphyry. No mention is made of Ramus' *Dialecticae*, although another regent, Robert Wemyss, taught the second class using Talon's *Rhetorica* and some orations of Cicero, again showing that some

49   Balcarres Papers, vol. 7, fos 144r–145v.
50   Balcarres Papers, vol. 7, fos 146r/v.
51   Balcarres Papers, vol. 7, fos 150r–152r.
52   *Evidence*, p. 194.

of the texts used by Melville at Glasgow had filtered through to the colleges at St Andrews.[53]

The process rumbled on against Martine, for further testimony was submitted by Homer Blair to the Lords. However, excluding the two documents that called for Martine's deprivation, no other evidence survives to indicate he was removed for any length of time. It seems that the initial flare-up was resolved without resorting to drastic action. What, then, are we to make of this confused and extensive episode? Was Martine really a corrupt embezzler intent on impeding reform, or victim of an overambitious academic *coup*? The evidence is contradictory, but it does seem to suggest that Martine was a man out of time in some senses. Trained by a school of men who were raised in the conservative atmosphere of pre-reformation St Andrews and who were perfectly happy to exploit college revenues for familial gain, Martine saw nothing wrong with his nepotistic attitude to prebendaries. It is this aspect of college life that the other masters of St Salvator's seemed most resentful about – Martine had better control and access to the college revenue then they did, and it does seem that Martine was on occasion genuinely trying to consolidate the college's finances. Perhaps his biggest disadvantage was the lack of a broader European education that would have made him happier to engage with 'Melvillian' reform, as it is clear that part of the dissension was caused by the greater willingness of the other masters to move with the intellectual tides sweeping the university. However, Martine resented the confusion reform had brought to the educational programme he had trained under and what it had done to the standard of discipline in the college, and clearly desired a return to the established patterns of teaching he was familiar with. It would be several decades before Martine achieved his wish, but in the meantime it was far from likely that reform would unfold under his supervision.

The Melvilles and the Impact of Religious Dissent on St Mary's

In some ways, however, St Salvator's was far more successful as a practical provider of education than St Mary's in the 1580s. At the behest of the royal government, Melville and his nephew James moved to the college in December 1580, which had been closed since the 'New Foundation' was enacted in the preceding year.[54] The next eight years would see the college closed more often than it was open, and its finances and organisation badly managed. That Melville's handling of St Mary's was so poor compared to

---

[53] *Evidence*, p. 194.

[54] See above, p. 95.

his time at Glasgow is down to his continual conflict with Patrick Adamson and James VI. This conflict saw Melville warded or banished for much of the 1580s, leaving the burden of responsibility for the college solely on the inexperienced James Melville.

On their arrival in St Andrews, the two Melvilles quickly assimilated into the local life of the church, with James preaching to the local parish on Sunday afternoons and Andrew, surprisingly, working with Patrick Adamson to preach the morning service. James' account of their first year in St Andrews noted that no one was more welcoming to them than Adamson, 'wha resorted to our lessones, and keiped verie familiar frindschipe with Mr Andro, promising what could ly in him for the weill of that wark'.[55] The Melvilles were also part of the administration of university business, for both were recorded as assessors for the nation of Angus in 1580.[56] However, their first year was one of turmoil and upheaval, which began as soon as they arrived. It also saw the development of tensions between Andrew and Adamson that had huge impact on St Mary's in the following years.

One immediate issue for Melville was his relations with other staff, foremost among these being the restitution demanded by Robert Hamilton as ex-principal of the college. Despite Hamilton being commanded to confine himself to the ministry of St Andrews, and to remove himself immediately in the visitation of January 1580, he still pursued Melville for financial compensation he felt was owed him at his removal.[57] Hamilton died on 16 April 1581, but Thomas Buchanan, minister of Ceres, married Hamilton's widow and morbidly pursued the claim for himself. The process was eventually settled by allocating a glebe of the college to Hamilton's widow for her lifetime, some time before 1591.[58] Another staffing issue was what should be done with Robert Caldcleuch, a regent in the college under Hamilton. Despite James Melville's anecdotal evidence that Caldcleuch had threatened to 'hough', or hamstring, the new principal on his takeover of the college, he was content to take a diminished place as a bursar on the new foundation.[59]

Melville also had considerable difficulties with the town council, then ruled by the oligarchic Learmonth family. Following Hamilton's death, the parish ministry remained vacant.[60] The Melvilles were desirous that

[55]   *JMAD*, p. 85; MacDonald, 'Best of Enemies', pp. 267–71.

[56]   Acta Rectorum, pp. 100–101.

[57]   *Evidence*, p. 190; *JMAD*, pp. 122–3.

[58]   M'Crie, pp. 77–8. No reference exists in the muniments to state which glebe this was, however.

[59]   *JMAD*, p. 123.

[60]   *StAKSR*, pp. 481, 488. The statute was put forward that the first business of the session on Wednesdays would be to organise who would 'mak the sermonis in this parroche kirk the nixt Fryday Sonday and Weddinsday thaireftir'. M'Crie, p. 86; *StAKSR*, p. lxvii.

Thomas Smeaton of Glasgow University or Alexander Arbuthnott of King's College be moved to the post, not only for their ministerial skills but also for their value in helping with teaching within St Mary's.[61] Melville suggested in the pulpit that the position was being kept vacant by the collusion of James Learmonth of Dairsie, the town provost, and the commendator of St Andrews priory, Robert Stewart, both of whom he claimed were pocketing the ministerial stipend. Melville directed his sermon at the 'rewlars' of the town in general, which may explain the hugely unpopular response that it received, with James Melville noting that for some time after the sermon the whole 'Town, University and all malcontents' were against Melville and his supporters, and 'ther was na thing bot affixing of placarts upon the Collage yet, bosting with batoning, burning and chassing out of the town'.[62]

Learmonth was chastised by the presbytery for walking out of Melville's sermon, and Melville used another sermon to attack his kinsman James Learmonth of Balcomie for putting up a placard insulting him. The Learmonths and Stewart were called before the General Assembly, where they were condemned and ordered to public repentance.[63] Despite these incidents, a permanent minister was not found for the parish until John Rutherford Junior accepted the post in July 1584.[64] The Melvilles had in the meantime alienated themselves from the burgh oligarchy, and drawn a clear boundary between the standard of behaviour in the town and their own zealous expectations.

Nothing in the university muniments reveals the extent of Melville's teaching in his early years at St Mary's or how successful it was, and James Melville provides only the most tantalising of glimpses. Apart from the initial confrontations with staff and town members, Melville apparently settled down to teach between 1582 and 1584 with a pared-down staff consisting of his nephew and the old professor John Robertson. James Melville took on the role of first master and taught the rudiments of Hebrew grammar, and Robertson taught students the precepts of the New Testament, supervised by Andrew who must have supplied the additional tuition required in Greek, Chaldaic and Syriac. Andrew also supplied the teaching of the theological common places that spanned the entire length of the divinity course.[65] No mention is made of the teaching of the history of the Old Testament, the exposition of Mosaic Law, or the exegesis of the prophets that was supposed to comprise the last two years

---

[61]   Stevenson, *King's College*, p. 32.

[62]   *JMAD*, p. 125.

[63]   *JMAD*, pp. 126–7.

[64]   *StAKSR*, p. lxvii.

[65]   *JMAD*, p. 84.

of tuition. However, Melville's well-known interest in sacred chronology and Old Testament history suggests he would have provided at least a basic grounding in these subjects.[66] Despite having his nephew on hand, it must have felt for Melville in this initial period as if he had returned to the difficult situation of teaching that presented itself in his first four years at Glasgow.

Melville's involvment in church business in his early years at St Mary's clearly took time out of his teaching, as is demonstrated in a letter by one of his students, Stephen Powle. Powle (c.1553–1630) was the youngest son of the English chancery clerk Thomas Powle, and took his BA and MA at Oxford between 1564 and 1572. He briefly entered into a career in law between 1574 and 1579, before engaging on a three-year tour of the Continent including time in Geneva, Basel, Strasbourg, Speyer, Heidelberg and Paris. By April 1583 he had come to St Andrews, where he spent six months studying under Melville. His later career saw him rise to the post of deputy clerk of the crown in chancery and receiving a knighthood from James VI and I on 8 July 1604.[67] Powle sent a letter to Melville on 30 April 1583, while the latter was attending General Assembly business in Edinburgh, that shows how keenly his absence was felt in St Andrews:

> I have heard that you, most distinguished Melville, have been hampered with more serious business,[68] or (to speak more accurately), weighed down by enemies, as though by waves; I thought it wasn't my business to offend your ears with an empty din of words, or to disturb your studies and more serious endeavours with my trifles, that is, my salutations. But as soon as I heard that you had been freed from those troubles ... how could I not do other than congratulate you, and rejoice myself! And for that reason behold my letters, both witnesses of my present disposition, and also hostages to the future; and earnest pleas that you fly back to us (at the most opportune time that you are able) ... How avidly will your Powle embrace you, your presence thrill him, your humorous conversations and your very holy discussions restore his mind, and console his soul ... I am compelled to take the part of Penelope that I may call you, Ulysses, now long detained not by the Trojan War but by debate in Edinburgh, back to your Ithaca.[69]

---

[66]   Reid, 'Andrew Melville, Sacred Chronology', 1–21.

[67]   P.R.N. Carter, 'Powle, Sir Stephen (c.1553–1630)', *ODNB* [56051, accessed 20 June 2008].

[68]   Presumably the trial against Archbishop Montgomery. See above, Chapter 3.

[69]   Stephen Powle to Andrew Melville, St Andrews 30 April 1583 (Bodleian Library, Oxford, MS Tanner 168 fo. 203v): 'Cum negotiis magis seriis te impeditum, vel (ut verius dicam) adversariorum quasi fluctibus oppressum audivi, ornatissime Melvine, mearum esse partium putavi non inani verborum strepitu suas aures offendere, vel studia et conatus graviores nugis meis, id est, salutationibus, interturbare. At vero quam primum istis molestiis te liberatum fuisse ... non potui non, quin et tibi gratularer, et mihi ipsi gauderem! Earumque

Powle's tone is clearly one of great reverence and affection for his teacher. However, it suggests that Melville had been absent for most of his time at the college, and the entreaty for Melville's return home was perhaps due to the fact that Powle knew he only had a limited time in St Andrews and wished to make the most of it by actually studying under Melville.

While Melville was missed at St Mary's, his involvement in church politics in the early 1580s not only kept him away for lengthy spells but also led to political retaliation against him, with serious repercussions for the college. On 30 May 1582, just after the clash between the General Assembly and the crown over the elevation of Montgomery to the archbishopric of Glasgow had reached fever pitch,[70] the Edinburgh ministers James Lawson and John Durie were charged to compear before the Royal Council at Dalkeith, following sermons preached against Lennox and his administration. Durie was forced to remove himself from Edinburgh on 2 June.[71] His expulsion and the continuing controversy regarding Montgomery prompted an extraordinary General Assembly on 27 June in Edinburgh, which Melville led. He opened it with an outburst that would no doubt have angered the royal government inveighing 'against the bloodie guillie [knife] of absolute authoritie, whereby men intended to pull the crown off Christ's head, and to wring the scepter out of his hand' and suggesting that a conspiracy to restore Mary to the throne was under way.[72] After heated debate amongst the ministers, Durie agreed to remove himself from the city.[73] The ministers, meanwhile, accused the king in a series of complaints of trying to erect a 'new Popedome' by confounding the 'two jurisdictions' of the civil and ecclesiastical spheres.[74]

Following the Ruthven Raid and the king's captivity in 1582-3,[75] one of James VI's greatest supporters was Patrick Adamson. Throughout the ascendancy of the Ruthven Lords, Adamson had hidden 'lyk a tod [toad] in his hole' inside the episcopal palace at St Andrews, pleading ill health.[76] When the king managed to free himself, Adamson immediately resumed preaching in St Andrews, defending the memory of Lennox, who had

---

ob causam, en literas meas, et praesentis testes voluntatis meae, et etiam obsides futurae, ac ut ad nos quam ritissime poteris advoles hortatores ... Penelopis personam cogor induere, ut te Ulyssem non Troiano bello sed Edinburgensi disceptatione, iam diu detentum, at Ithacam tuam revocem.'

[70] See above, pp. 96–101.
[71] Calderwood, vol. 3, pp. 620–1.
[72] Calderwood, vol. 3, p. 622.
[73] Calderwood, vol. 3, pp. 623–5.
[74] Calderwood, vol. 3, pp. 628–31.
[75] See above, pp. 100–101.
[76] *JMAD*, pp. 137–8.

died in Paris on 26 May.[77] The Presbyterian party in the Kirk had been closely allied with the Ruthven Lords, and the political support around Melville and his fellow ministers unravelled in the ensuing winter as a result. Adamson played a central role in this. In December 1583 he went to London with certification from James VI to discuss a potential scheme of conformity for the Scottish and English churches that supported Episcopacy and the royal supremacy in ecclesiastical governance. Adamson also wrote a series of 'Articles to the French Kirk at London' which were passed to Geneva and other churches on the Continent discrediting Melville and his faction as troublemakers, to which Melville sent out an impassioned rebuttal.[78] Although Adamson made a complete disgrace of himself, begging the French ambassadors for money and clothes and behaving poorly in company, he was able to gather evidence for building a sustained polemical case against the supporters of Presbyterianism.[79]

Melville was himself courting unorthodoxy at the same time. For an unknown reason, in January 1584 he provided a letter of commendation to the sectarian Robert Brown, and the families that had arrived with him from Flanders. Brown advocated separation from all churches where excommunication was not used against unrepentant offenders, described having witnesses at baptisms as a 'simplie evill' practice, and held other heterodox opinions. He and his companions had a tense appearance before the Edinburgh Kirk Session on 14 January, but yet were allowed to remain at the Canongate, where Brown continued circulating his controversial views in pamphlet form.[80] Why Melville would choose to support Brown is unclear. It may be that they had met while Melville was on the Continent, or they may have shared similar views on excommunication, on which Melville believed the church had full jurisdiction.[81]

On Saturday 8 February 1584 Melville was summoned to appear before the Privy Council, within two days, for preaching treason in a sermon on Daniel 4. Despite the lack of time to prepare, Melville appeared before the council as requested, armed with a written rebuttal of the charges[82] and a testimonial of the masters and regents of the university who had heard his preaching.[83] Melville's 'declinature' began by refuting the legality of the trial before the Privy Council, and complained that the accusation

[77]   David Moysie, *Memoirs of the Affairs of Scotland, 1577–1603* (Edinburgh, 1830), p. 45.

[78]   Mullan, *Episcopacy in Scotland*, p. 56; *JMAD*, pp. 141, 148–64.

[79]   MacDonald, *Jacobean Kirk*, p. 25.

[80]   Calderwood, vol. 4, p. 1.

[81]   Melville to Beza, NLS Wodrow Folio 42, fos 11 r/v; M'Crie, pp. 71–2.

[82]   M'Crie, pp. 91–101.

[83]   M'Crie, note X; Calderwood, vol. 3, pp. 304–6.

made against him came from William Stewart, an agent of Robert Stewart Bishop of Caithness who sought revenge against Melville for his criticism of Stewart's failure to fill the St Andrews parish.[84] In terms of doctrine, however, Melville's defence was incendiary. Discussing the example of Daniel offering the history of the tyrant king Nebuchadnezzar to his son Balthazar, Melville argued that ministers should always offer up similar examples to their own kings, but in an aside stated that if today 'a minister would rehearse in the court the exemple that fell out in King James the Thrid's dayes, who was abused by the flatterie of his courteours, he sould be said to vaig frome his text, and perchance accused of treasoun'. Melville was also alleged to have implied Mary was the figure of Nebuchadnezzar, who was banished for 14 years and was supposed to rise again, though he denied ever saying this. However, he did portray Nebuchadnezzar as a king ungrateful to God, pointing out that 'whether it be by electioun, successioun, or other ordinar middess that kings are advanced it is God that makes kings; which all is easilie forgett by them'. Melville followed this with the examples of David and Solomon, and Joas, 'in his tender age made king', who were also punished by God for their lack of faith. The tone of Melville's declinature, like his sermon, was one of haughty unrepentance, exacerbated by his harangue of the council when he slammed down his Hebrew Bible on their bench and proclaimed 'there is my instructions and warrant. Lett see which of you can judge theron, or controll me therin.'[85]

Following heated discussions between Melville and the council, he was ordered into ward on 18 February.[86] When Melville found out that he was to be held in Blackness, 'a foule hole' kept by supporters loyal to the anti-Presbyterian royal chancellor, James Stewart Earl of Arran, he decided to flee to England. After dinner and consultation with his fellow ministers at James Lawson's house, Melville set sail with his brother Roger and within a day had landed at Berwick. There he wrote to both Stephen Powle and the pastor of the foreigner's church in London, Jean Castoll, to announce his intention to come to England, and to ask for a place to stay.[87]

---

[84]   Calderwood, vol. 4, pp. 2–10. As a minister being accused of incorrect doctrine, Melville argued he should be tried before the General Assembly. As a preacher in St Andrews, he should be tried by the local ministers. As a doctor of the church, he should be tried first by the university court of the rector and his assessors, with at least two witnesses to stand by the accusation.

[85]   *JMAD*, pp. 141–3.

[86]   Calderwood, vol. 4, p. 12. M'Crie, p. 427.

[87]   Calderwood, vol. 4, p. 12. *JMAD*, p. 144; Andrew Melville to Jean Castoll, Berwick, 23 February 1584 (British Library, Cott. Cal. D IX); Andrew Melville to Stephen Powle, Berwick, 25 February 1584, Stephen Powle to Andrew Melville, 1 March 1584 (Oxford, Bodleian Library (Copy) MS Tanner 168, fo. 204v).

With Melville's flight, the supervision of the college fell in the first of a series of delegations to his nephew James. Returning to St Andrews, James packed up Andrew's books to save them from seizure. Following a heavy sickness, he set about providing tuition in March and April as best he could, continuing his regular teaching in Greek and Hebrew while taking up his uncle's lessons in the common-places. James also continued the practice of making students give a sample exegesis of a chapter of the Bible at the dinner table.[88]

James was supported in his endeavours by several of the other masters and students of the university, who, feeling sympathy for him, attended his lessons and provided some assistance. The 1588 account of the college states that James Melville had been helped by two of the other bursars in theology. James Robertson, who became minister at Dundee, entered the college at Martinmas 1583, and John Caldcleuch, as an extant bursar and previous master under the Hamilton regime, also took some part in the teaching duties of the college. Melville was also supported by Robert Bruce and Robert Durie.[89] Bruce had graduated from St Salvator's in 1572, and following a period in Louvain and France studying law, secured leave from his father to attend the theology course at St Mary's in 1583. Bruce was made a bursar on the foundation at some point before 1585,[90] and James encouraged him in private exercise to expound the whole of Romans and Hebrews. Bruce was so impressive he provided a sermon at one of the Sunday morning services in the town, which 'a multitude of the best peiple of the town' heard.[91]

However, there were serious underlying issues at the college beyond teaching provision. The account of 1584 in James' *Autobiography* makes no mention of the second master John Robertson, or what he was doing. Immediately after Melville's removal, Adamson moved quickly to consolidate his hold over St Andrews. On his recommendation, Robertson was presented to the college as principal with full jurisdiction to admit bursars and poor scholars and administer the rents and income of the college.[92] It seems odd that James would continue to teach in this situation, suggesting that Robertson did not immediately take up the post.

While no evidence of major upheaval is recorded in the Acta Rectorum, statutes promulgated in the faculty of Arts in March 1584 and likely

---

[88] *JMAD*, pp. 145–6.

[89] Thomas Buchanan also appeared to have supported James, named by Melville as a 'dear friend' and his name is given in the list of assessors for 1583/4 with James, though Andrew was by this point absent. Acta Rectorum, p. 103.

[90] Balcarres Papers, vol. 7, fo. 238r. Durie is one of six bursars recorded for 1585.

[91] *Evidence*, p. 193; *JMAD*, pp. 146–8, 218.

[92] M'Crie, p. 124.

supported by Adamson upheld a number of the traditional features of the arts course that had been in existence before the 'New Foundation', particularly defending the traditional practices of disputation, along with restating the prerogatives of the chancellor in relation to awarding the MA degree.[93] Although the twin trial of *temptamen* and *examen* had atrophied over the course of the sixteenth century, a programme approximating this practice appears to have been envisaged by Adamson and the members of the arts faculty where final year students would undergo the now traditional single public disputation (known as *vicos* or 'vikis' in the vernacular) at the end of June each year, followed by a private ordinary exam before the masters on the 'black stone' (*nigri lapidis*) a month later, where those who successfully completed both were to be awarded their degree on 20 August. The public disputations would continue in a defence by the graduating class of a series of published *theses philosophicae*, in evidence at St Andrews from the early 1600s and earlier elsewhere, and would form a core part of the exam process throughout the seventeenth century.

Those entering their third year were to undertake a public disputation between 10 and 20 October each year, and an interesting addition to this programme for younger students offers another tantalising piece of evidence regarding the evolution of the arts programme at St Andrews. A group described as *Graeci* and *rhetores* (presumably the second year students) were to be examined at the same time as the bachelors gave their disputations before giving a public declamation of their own before the whole assembled university at the beginning of November. This suggests that by early 1584 the first years were indeed devoting more time to rhetoric alongside the traditional study of logic, and were also gaining knowledge of basic Greek. The remaining statutes were common-sense ones regarding the supervision and timing of examinations and the issue of student fees. It is clear from this brief list that while Melville was outwith the university attempts were made to provide a range of statutes that, although acknowledging some advances and modernisation in arts teaching, maintained as traditional a course structure as the 'New Foundation' would allow.

In April, David Auchmoutie, who was *oeconomus* for the years prior to 1584[94] and controlled the uptaking and distribution of all the rents, resigned his office. James Melville suggests that the impetus for Auchmoutie's actions came from Adamson, whom he had 'intelligence and collusion' with, and perhaps Auchmoutie did not want to be at a college associated with the Melvilles in such a tense political climate. Auchmoutie had collected the 'best and surest part and payment of the

---

[93]   *Acta*, pp. 455–6.

[94]   *Evidence*, p. 193.

college leiving', presumably the rents of the parish of Tannadyce,[95] but had chosen to resign when the harvest was at its lowest and 'all things war at the deirest'. The prospect of attempting to administer the college rents and the student programme of exercise and disputation was more than James could bear, knowing that the students would leave if sufficient board was not available. However, James discharged Auchmoutie, and enlisted the aid of his wife and Robert Bruce to carry out his duties.[96]

As part of the royal government's continued support for an erastian and Episcopal church, in May 1584 Parliament passed the 'Black Acts' (as they were labelled by Presbyterian chroniclers for the threat they posed to Scottish conciliar church government), stating that the crown had supreme authority over both temporal and spiritual spheres. The acts also reasserted the rights and privileges of bishops in the ecclesiastical hierarchy, and prohibited ecclesiastical assemblies at all levels without royal sanction. With them a 'bull' was given to Adamson restoring him to the jurisdiction and privileges he expected as an archbishop. Included with these were rights to enact visitations of the university and implement reforms as he saw fit.[97] Simultaneously, the college finances had reached such dire states that James was compelled to travel to the annexed benefices in Angus and the Mearns to take up what he could of the rents. On his return his uncle Roger warned him that Adamson was coming with a commission of magistrates to seize him, and convinced him to flee to Dundee. That same night Adamson and the magistrates of the town searched the college and James' home, and finding letters from Andrew hoped to seize him for collusion with an outlaw. Following a tense and difficult overnight journey by boat, Melville arrived in Berwick to meet his uncle, James Lawson, and a number of other exiled Presbyterian ministers. He was joined by James Robertson and John Caldcleuch.[98]

In England, the Melvilles occupied themselves by visiting the universities of Oxford and Cambridge between 4 and 19 July 1584 for a conference with the leading English Puritans. They networked with academics and theologians there, and in London at conferences in November 1584 and February 1585.[99] The conferences passed a number of resolutions that furthered the development of a Presbyterian polity for England, with the Scottish ministers providing considerable input. With support from

---

[95]   The compt for 1585 shows that Tannadyce was worth £255 18s in money, with an undisclosed lease in victual.

[96]   *JMAD*, p. 165.

[97]   Mullan, *Episcopacy in Scotland*, p. 57; *JMAD*, pp. 194–6; Calderwood, vol. 4, p. 143; *RPS*, 1584/5/1-26 [accessed 1 April 2010].

[98]   *JMAD*, pp. 166–71, 218.

[99]   *JMAD*, pp. 218–19.

Henry Walsingham, the Secretary of State, and with a number of ministers joining Melville in May and June 1584, the possibility was entertained that Melville and his compatriots would settle in London.[100] Brief attempts were made to set up a foreigner's church for the exiles, though this was prevented by diplomatic pressure from the Master of Gray, the Scottish ambassador.

A polemic battle between Adamson and the Melvilles continued unabated, despite two nations separating them. In January 1585 Adamson published his *Declaration of his Majesty's Intention and Meaning Toward the Lait Actis of Parliament*, a tract defending the king's actions in Parliament, and outlining the Episcopal church governed by the supreme royal power that Adamson envisaged. This was followed a month later by a two-fold response from the Melvilles, in the form of an *Answere to the Declaration of Certan Intentions Sett Out in the Kings Name* penned by Andrew, and a metaphorical dialogue by James on the subject entitled *Zelator, Temporizar, and Palomon*.[101]

This situation continued until November 1585, when the exiled Ruthven Lords returned to Scotland, with Andrew in tow. James returned home by December, having received confirmation it was safe to do so on 6 November, and went immediately to St Mary's while his uncle remained at Glasgow. Again, the process of trying to resurrect the college and its finances fell to him. James' *Autobiography*, and an unpublished and previously unseen account of the college living for 1585–86, outline how he attempted to restore the dilapidated rents and to balance the finances for the period of closure. They show how detrimental the absence of the Melvilles and their supporters had been to the college.[102] While the masters had been in exile, the ministers serving at the majority of the kirks annexed to the college had illegally obtained letters freeing them from the obligation to pay rent. James spent the first part of December at the Parliament in Linlithgow, obtaining an act that the rents of the benefices be restored to the masters and waiting for letters of restitution and repossession. In February James again had to wait on the Privy Council at Stirling to provide a formal charter suspending the ministers' assignations, and obtaining letters notifying tenants that they should resume payment to the college masters.[103] The college had fallen into a severe state of disrepair

---

[100]   Gordon Donaldson, 'Scottish Presbyterian Exiles in England, 1584–8', *Scottish Church History Society Records* 14 (1960–62): 67–80, at 75–6.

[101]   Calderwood, vol. 4, pp. 20–108; for a fuller discussion of the polemic in this period, see Mason, 'George Buchanan, James VI, and the Presbyterians', pp. 187–214.

[102]   Balcarres Papers, vol. 7, fos 238–240v. The same account also shows that James Melville had returned home by 5 December, much earlier than previous estimates of 27 December. Donaldson, 'Presbyterian Exiles', p. 77; *JMAD*, p. 245.

[103]   Balcarres Papers, vol. 7, fos 236r, 238v; *APS*, III, 295, no. 24.

during 1585, and just under £40 was spent by James in replacing much of the roofing, a number of the college windows and parts of the college dykes.[104]

James did well to keep the college together through a highly fraught period, and in the new year things began to improve. The plague that had killed almost 400 in St Andrews in the winter of 1585 started to abate, allowing students to return.[105]

In March 1586 Andrew finally returned to St Andrews after four months at Glasgow, getting acquainted with the new principal, Patrick Sharp. The return of Melville into territory that Adamson now had control over must have been difficult, and two documents written by Adamson and Melville, likely dating from this period, reflect this.[106] The work by Adamson, entitled *Some Erroneous Assertions ... by Andrew Melville, professing a new and unheard-of Theology, in his lectures concerning Episcopacy* collects together some alleged remarks made by Melville in his public sermons over the nature of a bishop outlined in 1 Timothy, while Melville's *Archiepiscopal Blossoms* is a series of short criticisms levelled at Adamson. The works show the two men diametrically opposed over church governance, with Adamson defending the legitimacy of Episcopacy using the Bible and church fathers including Gregory Nanzanius, fifth-century Bishop of Constantinople. After attacking Melville's view of polity, Adamson also accused him of a number of heresies. Melville had allegedly called Augustine and Epiphanius heretics for condemning Arius' belief in the parity of all ministers, and Adamson charged him with believing in prayers for the souls of the dead. Adamson also called him a 'Cabbalist' and 'Thalmudist', who believed that God acted as a scriptural 'doctor' and catechist to Adam when he was created. Melville's response consisted only of bullet points attacking Adamson's views on Episcopacy, but did accuse the archbishop of having no respect or interest in the biblical languages.[107] A poem of Melville's from this period, the sarcastically-titled 'Victory-Song of Patrick Adamson' (*Epinikion Patricii Adamsoni*), also captures the palpable loathing he now held for his old colleague:

---

[104]   Balcarres Papers, vol. 7, fos 236v–237r.

[105]   *JMAD*, p. 245.

[106]   Patrick Adamson, *Assertiones quaedam, ex aliis eiusmodi innumeris erroneae, per Andream Melvinam, novam et inauditam Theologiam profitentem, in suis praelectionibus de Episcopatu, pro certis et indubitatis in medium allatae, ac palam affirmatae, in Scholis Theologicis fani Andreae, Regni Scotiae metropoleos*, in Adamson, *Opera*, ed. T. Wilson (1620). This may have circulated in pamphlet form in the 1580s, but the first surviving copy is in the 1620 edition of Adamson's works by Wilson; Andrew Melville, *Floretum Archiepiscopale*, NLS Wodrow Folio 42, fos 47r/v. This appears never to have been published, but may have circulated in manuscript form.

[107]   Melville, *Floretum Archiepiscopale*.

That man [Adamson] with little holiness, both little learned, and with little skill in speaking, ... a bishop, a blockhead, a court attendant ... a sacrilegious man who, for sacrilegious bronze, consumes, drinks, eats up and devours what would support a hundred widows, two hundred colleagues, three hundred orphans.[108]

Melville barely had time to settle in again at St Mary's before this feud caused his removal once more. On 26 April 1586 James Melville preached the opening sermon at the Fife Synod, at his uncle's recommendation, on Romans 12:3–8.[109] He attacked Adamson, who was present, for overthrowing the liberty of the church and called for his removal. The synod placed Adamson on trial, and despite complaints that he would not accept Lord Lindsay and the Melvilles as judges, they were allowed to stay on the panel. The synod excommunicated him and had the sentence read against him by Andrew Hunter, minister of Carnbee. Adamson retaliated with an excommunication of his own against the Melvilles and appealed to the king, the Privy Council and Parliament for arbitration of the issue.

Even Thomas M'Crie admits that the action of excommunication headed by the Melvilles was 'precipitant and irregular', and that the synod did not have jurisdiction to implement it.[110] Moreover, the choice of the Melvilles not to recuse themselves obviously removed any objectivity from the proceedings. The enmity between Adamson and Melville had grown so serious that the former believed a rumour that on the Sunday after the excommunication, when he decided to preach publicly despite the synod's decision, a group of men led by Melville and the Laird of Lundie were coming to hang him. Adamson was so terrified on hearing this rumour that he fled to the belfry of the church and the town baillies had to coax him down.[111] James Melville states he was ill in bed when this happened,[112] and it seems highly unlikely that his uncle would condone such an action, but Adamson's biographer records that the archbishop saw this as a real threat.[113]

On 10 May the General Assembly nullified the sentence of excommunication against Adamson, when he agreed to demit his authority

---

[108]   Thomas Wilson (ed.), *Viri clarissimi A. Melvini Musae et P. Adamsoni vita et palinodia et celsae commissionis cue delagatae potestatis regiae in causis ecclesiasticis brevis & aperta descriptio* (Netherlands, 1620), p. 5: 'Sanctulus ille, doctulusque,/ Et disertulus ... Episcopus, Baro, Comes ... Et de sacrilego profanus aere/ Pitissat, bibit, exedit, voratque,/ Quod centum viduas alat, ducentos/ Symmystas alat, orphanos trecentos.'

[109]   *JMAD*, p. 245.

[110]   M'Crie, p. 126.

[111]   M'Crie, pp. 127–8; Calderwood, vol. 3, pp. 499–503.

[112]   *JMAD*, p. 201.

[113]   *Vita Patricii Adamsoni*, in *Opera*, ed. Wilson, p. 6.

over the synod and to accept censure from the assembly. While it seems odd that Adamson would agree to such strictures, the king had called the assembly and had also spoken privately with the ministers who chose the moderator, suggesting he reached a private agreement with them in order to resolve the dispute quickly.[114]

Melville was perceived by the king to have been the leading force behind the excommunication and was not allowed to escape punishment. On 26 May, for the 'dissention and diversitie' caused by the schism between him and Adamson that had caused the cessation of theology tuition at St Andrews 'thir two years bygane', Melville was to be warded north of the Tay, on the pretext that he was to hunt out Jesuits and recusants in the north. In the meantime, his place at St Mary's was to remain vacant, and James was to continue teaching 'as he will answer to God'. In Melville's place, Adamson was to teach theology in St Salvator's each Tuesday and Thursday beginning Tuesday 1 June, in Latin, which the whole university were to attend.[115]

Once again the supervision of the college fell to James Melville, who returned to 'that lang interrupted and almost ruyned wark'. The summer passed with James teaching what he could alongside Adamson.[116] Andrew appears to have instructed James to ascend to the place of third master, or perhaps the students still at St Mary's by this point had advanced beyond basic grammar, for James began to teach biblical history, with geography and sacred chronology, highlighting key textual points in Latin and Greek as they went along. James also lectured on 1 Timothy, and obviously had a copy of Adamson's 'Assertions', as he taught 'insisting on the contraverted questionnes, bringing in all the Bischopes reasones, and refuting them, and establissing the treuthe to my uttermaist'.

In June and July, however, James was forced to forego teaching for the rest of the summer as he worked to return his uncle to the college. The chief falconer at Falkland, John Irving, held a tack from St Mary's of the kirk of Conveth that was due for renewal. Irving had notified James VI of this, and the king wrote to James 'twyse or thryse' to come to Falkland on 22 May with all haste to discuss the conditions of Andrew's return.[117] However, each times James journeyed down, at great expense, he found only Irving waiting for him, eager to discuss his tack. James apparently promised to take the matter under consideration, and sent a delegation of the dean of arts and a professor from each college to the king, asking him

114   Calderwood, vol. 3, p. 881; M'Crie, p. 128.

115   M'Crie, pp. 428–9. *JMAD*, p. 249. The act of council does not specify that Adamson preach in Latin nor that the university attend, but James records this.

116   *JMAD*, p. 249.

117   Balcarres Papers, vol. 7, fo. 236r.

to reinstate Andrew. Once Irving's claim had been acknowledged the king became strangely attentive to the plight of the Melvilles, and James was sent to Andrew in Angus to seek assurance of his good behaviour and to get his pledge to leave the archbishop in peace. James accompanied Andrew to a meeting with the king on 3 July, who was given leave to return to St Mary's on 15 August, though according to James' later account he did not do so until September. Irving's tack was renewed, and in exchange the king promised to 'better the college twyse sa mikle', which translated into a confirmatory grant of prebendaries and smallholdings before Parliament on 31 January 1587.[118]

Andrew was thus allowed to resume his duties, and the college finances were moderately improved. However, the business with Irving had been hard on James and the college. The process of travelling back and forth between Falkland and Angus cost James £5 18s. 18d., a fraction of the costs the college incurred in these years of disorder. Following the dispute with the ministers and tenants in the preceding year, the rents of 1586 were not collected in. By January 1587 the college was in extensive financial difficulty, and James was delegated by the other masters to intromit them as best he could. James spent ten days that month in the parish of Tyningham negotiating the rents due to the college from the tenants, agreeing with them that they would deliver them to Edinburgh on 20 January. When they failed to do so, James had to visit Edinburgh again on 28 January to collect them. At the same time he witnessed the annexation of the prebendaries from James VI to the college and had the necessary legal documentation drawn up, and also answered a summons for the ongoing legal contest being waged by the family of Robert Hamilton for the back rent due to the late principal on his expulsion. James returned home on 7 February, but in April was on the move again, this time heading to Conveth and Tannadyce to receive rents for the Candlemas term. On 14 and 20 August James went with Richard Ainslie, one of the college bursars, to get money from all the parishes in Angus and the Mearns for the Lammas term, but despite travelling the rents were still not completely in by 20 October.[119]

The cost of all this was extensive. The compt of the rents for 1585 show that the college received 14 chalders and 8 bolls in victual which were quickly consumed among the staff and six bursars, and £865 16s. in money. The legal actions between December 1585 and July 1586 had cost £51, and those of the next year a total of £107 3s. 4d. The repairs of

---

[118] *Evidence*, p. 193; Balcarres Papers, vol. 7, fo. 236r.; *JMAD*, pp. 250–1; *RPS*, 1587/7/110 [accessed 1 April 2010].

[119] William Morris, another bursar, had also been over to collect rent from one of the towns but ended up in debt when his horse fell ill and he was forced to spend eight days there at a cost of 40s.

the college and the costs of maintaining basic staff in 1585 had cost £67 2s. 8d., with staff costs of £27 2s. 8d. coming out of James Melville's own pocket until the rents for 1586 could be fully taken up, while repairs in 1586 had cost £46 3s. 2d. £149 4s. 8d. remained unpaid from the ministers in the parishes annexed to the college, and other legal actions including the pursuit of David Auchmoutie for his withholding of the 'great yard' of the college in 1585 came to £108 13s. 10d. The fees paid out to the masters, who had been so long without stipend, totalled £410 5s. 11d. The total cost of all this and a small additional debt from a previous compt was £866 9s. 8d., and if this compt provides a record for all the college income for the period between 1584 and 1587 then this would mean the college was in debt by 13s. 8d.[120] All in all, the college had weathered the political dissension of the Melvillian exile and return – but only just, and only thanks to James Melville.

Andrew returned to teaching and, for a brief moment during 1587, student life appears to have had some semblance of normality. The college successfully completed its compt under the new *oeconomus* John Caldcleuch, who appears to have been promoted from his position as bursar during Melville's exile. The rent and victual Caldcleuch took in supported the masters and five bursars, and although the college ended up overspent for the year by £46 16s. 4d., the additional money had been spent buying new linen, napkins and dishes for the college.[121] Adamson was out of favour once more in St Andrews by the beginning of the year, having been charged with calling the attendees of his sermons 'goats' hiding in the flock of true Christians. Despite claiming that Melville had some collusion in this name-calling and that he had heard an unorthodox sermon preached by his enemy on Christmas Day regarding the birth of Christ, Adamson still found himself isolated and out of favour.[122]

The highpoint of the year was the entertaining of the king (at a cost of £10 to the college)[123] when he arrived with the French poet Guillaume Du Bartas at the end of June. The king and Du Bartas listened to a series of lectures by Melville, and a declamation between him and Adamson regarding Episcopacy and the nature of royal authority. Melville circumvented the king's injunction that no disrespect be given to the archbishop by refuting arguments on Episcopacy solely from Catholic authors. Though this was daring, Du Bartas and the king both admitted that Melville had a

---

120   Balcarres Papers, vol. 7, fos 236r–239v.

121   Balcarres Papers, vol. 7, fos 241 r/v.

122   *StAPR*, pp. 12–13. Adamson described himself as 'disagreeing and dissassenting fra the neoteriks that hes writting of the birthe of Christ quhome Mr Androw Melvine followis'.

123   Balcarres Papers, vol. 7, fos 241 r/v.

considerable store of knowledge, and delivered his lecture with 'far more spirit and courage' than Adamson.[124]

In October 1586 James was appointed to the ministry of Kilrenny and Anstruther, leaving the college he had worked hard to maintain. James finally left for the parish with his family at Whitsunday 1587,[125] and was followed by James Robertson, leaving Andrew, John Robertson and John Caldcleuch to teach. Despite the fact that the college had reached a form of equilibrium by 1587, the 1588 visitation shows starkly how little had been achieved by the end of the first decade of the 'New Foundation'. The report of the visitation commission for 16 April acknowledges that a full rental for the college was not available owing to the issues with David Auchmoutie, but also states that on the departure of the Melvilles in 1584 Learmonth of Dairsie had taken the charter box of evidence relating to the college and had later restored it to John Robertson, without a detailed inventory. On the tumult of the college since the entry of the Melvilles in 1580 the commissioners simply stated 'the troublis and pest stayed the haill wark quhill May 1586'.[126]

Teaching was not meeting the standards required by the 'New Foundation', primarily because there were only three masters instead of the five who were supposed to be allocated to the college. John Caldcleuch had taken up the teaching of Hebrew, and John Robertson continued his teaching for an hour on Mondays, Tuesdays and Thursdays in the New Testament. Melville taught a lesson from the Psalms in Hebrew each day from five until six a.m., and the common-places from ten to eleven a.m. on Monday, Wednesday and Friday. The masters took turns on alternate Sundays to offer lectures in English from Hebrews or 'sum uther pairte' of scripture. There was an addition to the staff, however, for Patrick Melville, Andrew's other nephew, had joined the college from his post at Glasgow at some point in 1587. As he was yet to give 'specimen doctrine', he only taught for an hour at five a.m. every day from Ecclesiastes. Moreover, eight bursars were in the college as the tenor of the 'New Foundation' dictated, and each Saturday they took turns to preach in English, and public declamations were held between ten and twelve a.m.. Those living *collegialiter* also expounded a verse of scripture with ensuing discussion at dinner each day, showing that despite the paucity of teaching students were getting a chance to preach and explore biblical textual issues that would prepare them for the ministry.[127]

---

[124] M'Crie, pp. 132–4.

[125] *JMAD*, p. 257.

[126] *Evidence*, p. 193.

[127] *Evidence*, pp. 193–4.

A compt was to be given to the commission in early May to see if the rents would allow for the full complement of masters required by the foundation, but when the commissioners returned they were disappointed. No compt was presented because the discharges given to Auchmoutie while Andrew was in exile were held to be invalid and so the compt was deemed incorrect. Worse still, no register of the college evidence or of the college library had been prepared. The excuse given, used for the whole visitation, was because of 'Mr Androis truble, and that thay skantlie understuid the contentis of thair awne evidentis'. They were ordered to prepare inventories and present them to the Clerk Register by the end of the month. With that the visitation commissioners left the college, in the same state of flux it had been in for the better part of a decade.[128] The 1588 visitation showed that the college was still feeling the impact of Melville's exile even two years later, with continuing irregularities in finance and administration. That the college had kept going at all was down to the tenacity and hard work of the inexperienced James Melville, and it is clear that for a completely different set of reasons to those at St Salvator's the 'New Foundation' had failed to take root at St Mary's.

St Leonards – the Enigmatic Case Study of Success?

Fragmentary evidence surviving for St Leonard's suggests that under the rector James Wilkie the college was moderately successful prior to 1588 in balancing college administration with reform. The masters there had adopted elements of the programme outlined in the 'New Foundation', but not the full range of teaching. Extensive Greek and Latin tuition was offered, and the college finances and lands seem to have been in relatively good shape in the late 1570s and 1580s, bolstered by a range of considerable grants of property made to the college by James VI and John Winram. On 26 March 1577 James VI gifted St Leonard's with the lands of Monydie Roger in the Perthshire parish of Auchterhome,[129] and on 28 November 1581 the priory of Portmoak was annexed to the college, providing two new bursaries.[130] Following the death of John Winram on 18 September 1582,[131] the full rents and belongings of the priory passed to the masters. They formally entered into possession of it in the following

---

[128]   *Evidence*, p. 195.
[129]   UYSL110/I1–6.
[130]   UYSL110/H1.
[131]   UYSL110/H3.

October, taking a detailed inventory of what was a very richly furnished house.[132]

Despite the lack of evidence for the college, St Leonard's offers us the first real insight into the initial impact of the 'New Foundation' on teaching in the arts colleges. Notes from the lectures on dialectic given by John Malcolm, a regent in the college between 1584 and 1586, are the earliest surviving evidence for teaching in the 'Melvillian' period. If they are representative of the views of the arts masters then the idea that Ramism was wholly embraced at the university at the expense of Aristotle has to be reassessed. James Melville recorded that Malcolm was one of the regents in the college who reacted strongly against Melville for his critical reassessment of Aristotle in theology teaching:

> [The regents,] wha heiring, in Mr Androe's ordinar publict lessones of Theologie, thair Aristotle ... mightelie confuted, handling the heids anent God, Providence, Creation, &c., maid a strange steir in the Universitie, and cryed, 'Great Diana of the Ephesians', thair bread-winner, thair honour, thair estimation, all was gean, giff Aristotle sould be sa owirharled in the heiring of thair schollars; and sa dressit publict orationes against Mr Androe's doctrine. But Mr Andro insisted mightelie against tham in his ordinar lessones ... with sic force of treuthe, evidence of reasone, and spirituall eloquence, that he dashit tham, and in end convicted tham sa in conscience, that the cheiff Coryphoes amangs tham becam grait students of Theologie, and speciall professed frinds of Mr Andro ...[133]

It is true that Malcolm later became a minister at Perth, and that he and Melville remained good friends,[134] but his lecture notes reveal a more nuanced picture than that painted by James Melville. Provocatively entitled 'Dialectic taught according to the wisdom of Aristotle, not the "opinion' of Ramus" (*DIANETICA Ad Aristotelis Scientiam non ad Rami Opinionem Continuatam*),[135] what Malcolm offers in his lectures is a summary exposition of the central tenets of Aristotelian logic, but with reference to specifically Ramist terms and couched in a completely Ramist framework. It begins with the most general statement possible about philosophy and logic, that philosophy is the love of wisdom (*amor sapientiae*) divided into 'analytic' (formal) logic and 'dialectic' (informal or rhetorical) branches, maintaining the traditional distinction between the two sciences that Ramus had removed. Yet Malcolm also notably splits his lectures into two halves,

---

[132]   UYSL110/H2.

[133]   *JMAD*, pp. 123–4.

[134]   Melville provided a liminary verse for Malcolm's only known published work, his *Commentarium Acta Apostolorum* (Middleburg, 1615).

[135]   St Andrews University, MSBC59.

the first dealing with 'invention' or the finding of topics for argument, and the second dealing with 'disposition' or construction of argument, echoing the Ramist organisation of logic into 'invention' and 'judgement'.[136] He then proceeds via dichotomy and increasing specialisation to go through every component of logical argument.

However, here the boundary between Ramus and Aristotle becomes blurred. The section on 'invention' discusses genus and species and the four causes, but in discussing the ways that topics for an argument can be 'invented' Malcolm offers an all-inclusive outline showing how Aristotle's ten categories can be used for this purpose, as well as a discussion of how it can be done using the Ramist topics of distribution, opposition, similitude, comparison, conjugation, notation, and human and divine testimony.[137] Further to this, Malcolm's text is replete with examples drawn from classical literature, a hallmark of the Ramist method. Malcolm's list of authors makes for impressive and eclectic reading: he includes extensive quotations from Cicero's orations, from Ausonius, Ovid, Martial, Plautus, Horace, Juvenal and Persius, and even single quotes from Buchanan's tenth psalm and from the Epistle to the Romans.

The second half of the work, on 'disposition', completely breaks with the tone and style of the first, offering a short but very traditional account of the four types of basic logical argument – syllogism, enthymeme, induction and example – along with an account of the main parts of the syllogism.[138] The final section, a very detailed discussion outlining the three classes of 'figura' that can be applied to syllogisms, their medieval names (Barbara, Celarent, Darii, Ferio and so on) and the rules for conversion between them, is slightly bewildering in terms of the classical and more general nature of the earlier part of the work.[139]

The slightly schizophrenic nature of these notes is perhaps explained by the suggestion that Melville's arrival in St Andrews prompted a voguish fashion in the students for Ramism, which Malcolm felt he had to pander to in order to engage them. He seems to suggest this in his introduction to the work, where he notes that even though he is teaching using the Ramist method, the focus on Aristotle's logic will be unpopular:

> I seem to be about to teach something not at all pleasing perhaps to the heathens [following] Ramus, and to those who have been sworn to his sect (let envy be absent from the word) ... I am going to reveal them as a new school of falsified 'philosophy' (this is what they call it), because they either have not

[136] MSBC59, fos 2r–2v.
[137] MSBC59, fos 3r–10r.
[138] MSBC59, fos 10r–15r.
[139] MSBC59, fos 15r–22r.

understood [philosophy], or they have passed it by while it was in operation, or they have been unwilling to enter upon the right footpath while it was open to them ... What [Ramism] is, and why it does not shrink from the light, and flee the censures of philosophers, this is my short reckoning. The first point is that it is entirely in agreement with the mind of Aristotle. The second is that I could smell that the university's quite absurd, pernicious opinion, which is dangerous to youth entering upon the philosophical course, had filled up the minds of many. And naturally I am unwilling to say that the dialectical opinion of Ramus' narrow system should be given priority, but that it should be reconciled with Aristotle's, [which is] broad, useful and necessary. Thus I predicted it would happen that the brilliant opinion of the noble philosophy of the Peripatetic (pardon my saying so) was beginning to stink, and was not being retained in its own place (because the conversations of depraved people have often been a hindrance to things well arranged, and to good men) and the *frivolous wisdom* of Ramus, praised beyond measure by people ignorant of Aristotelian precision in argument, would obliterate it. For they say that the very delightful loftiness of philosophical disputations should be neglected, and abstruse investigations, and everything should be judged by reference to plebeian and common praxis.[140]

Malcolm's comments say something very important about how the new ideas associated with the 'Melvillian' reform plan were received in St Andrews. Rather than suggesting that he and his cohorts were blindly bound to a conservative or reductive mode of teaching, Malcolm is clearly familiar with the work of Ramus but simply sees no intellectual merit in it, and is disapproving of the interest that students and other masters appear to take in it. In many ways, he shares the concerns of the St Salvator's provost James Martine – namely, that the focus in Ramism on practical application and method ('praxis') at the expense of more in-depth philosophical training left students intellectually impoverished and lacking the ability to hold nuanced debate. These lectures clearly show

---

[140]   MSBC59, fos 1r–1v: 'tametsi Rami gentilibus forte, eiusque sectae coniuratis (absit verbo invidia) rem non ad modum gratam facturus videar ... qui novam interpolatae philosophiae scholam (sic sunt locuturi) aperiam, quam illi vel non agnoverunt, vel agintam [agentem?] praeterierunt, vel patentem recto tramite inire noluerunt ... Quid vero sit, cur lucem non reformidet, neque philosophorum censuram defugiat, haec nostra compendiaria ratio. Primum est, quia ad Aristotelis mentem est continuata: Deinde, quia subolfecerim perabsurdam hanc opinionem Reipublicae Literariae perniciosam, quia iuventuti stadium philosophicum ineunti periculosam, multorum animos opplevisse; Illam scilicet stricti iuris Rami dialecticam nolim dicere praeponendam, sed cum Aristotelis fusa, utili, et necessaria esse componendam: Hinc augurabar fore ut praeclara illa nobilis Perapatetici philosophiae, ne dicam obolesceret, sed non suo haberetur loco, pravorum enim hominum sermones rebus bene constitutis, virisque bonis saepe obfuerunt) et Rami κενοσοφια ab ignavis Aristotelicae subtalitatis supra modum laudata subolesceret: Eam dicunt illi negligendam esse ream multo iucundissimam philosophicarum disputationum sublimitatem, et abstrusas disquisitiones, omniaque ad plebeiam, et proletariam praxin referenda.'

that the adoption of new intellectual modes at St Andrews was far from easy or free from critical scrutiny.

If Malcolm's notes show that Ramism was making headway among students in the early 1580s, the visitation account of the college for 1588 paints a slightly different picture, although it was on the whole far more positive than that of the other colleges.[141] The college had 'ressavit the Reformatioune of 1579' in terms of teaching, but had not followed the financial terms laid down for dividing stipends and assigning rent to the staff. Wilkie had taken on board the proposals to create four specialised regents for teaching, but no mention is made of the texts of Ramus. Malcolm taught Greek to the first years, and William March taught the basics of logic and rhetoric using Cicero, Porphyry, Demosthenes and Aristotle's *Categories*. Alexander Lindsay taught the third class using the *Organon* and *Ethics* of Aristotle, and Andrew Duncan provided tuition in physics and mathematics using *De Sphaera* and the *Physics*.

The college had also enlarged slightly beyond the scope outlined in 1579, adding Daniel Wilkie to the staff as a regent offering remedial Latin grammar for new entrants, and the college supported 15 bursars on the rents of the college. It was also well run in terms of discipline and finance. The college was 'eque with thair rent' despite having a total of 18 live-in students, and a compt was held daily, monthly, quarterly and yearly, and meticulously written up. The only real issue that the college had with students was that the 'banquetting, reatousnes of clething and libertie' granted at BA examinations should be removed (providing the masters got their graduation fee of 'tria nobilia'). They also could not agree a set fee for boarders as required by the Act of Parliament, for they charged £22 per quarter whereas St Salvator's only charged £18.

It is thus clear, on limited evidence, that the college was well organised and had quietly continued about its business during the 1580s while its counterparts were troubled by internal and external strife. However, the evidence also suggests that the initial fad for Ramism that had likely arrived with Melville had quietly died down and a more traditional curriculum had prevailed, at least in St Leonard's. Malcolm's lecture notes show clearly that the staff were fully capable of intelligent and critical judgement when it came to modern philosophical teaching, and as specialists in arts had more reservations about the merits of the Ramist method than the theologically-oriented Melville.

---

[141]   *Evidence*, p. 195.

Conclusion

The years 1579–88 were ones of disruption and dislocation for the University of St Andrews. The vagueness of the direction given by the royal council for the implementation of the 'New Foundation' left huge gaps in the administrative settlement of the university which the masters of St Salvator's, a self-interested and volatile group at the best of times, could easily exploit. The conservative and nepotistic Martine and his colleagues were entrenched in their own way of handling the college's intellectual and financial business, and the attempts to shoehorn a new constitutional settlement onto them, particularly in the addition of two new masters to the rents (and in the case of William Welwood, one of whom Martine must have personally detested as a rival on many different levels) left the college more divided and unreformed than at any other time in its history. Conversely, Melville's religious radicalism and clashes with the government had a material impact on his ability to carry out his duties as principal of St Mary's. His continued absence from the college meant that the programme of 'Melvillian' reform was found wanting where it was arguably needed most, and it was largely down to the hard work and tenacity of his nephew (and to a large dose of simple good fortune if the college accounts are any indicator) that the college continued in any form in the 1580s. It seems ironic that the greatest success in the first decade of 'Melvillian' reform at St Andrews was at St Leonard's, where moderate changes to an already stable foundation seems to have yielded considerable results, although we know too little about the process there to draw this conclusion with certainty. What is clear from the teaching evidence at the college is that in intellectual terms the wider scope of Melville's reform programme, particularly his endorsement of Ramism, met with polite bemusement at best and critical disdain at worst. However, masters like John Malcolm were at least willing to engage with the tenets of Ramism in order to appease students keen to try out the latest trends in Continental learning, however vacuous they themselves thought these tenets were. While Melville would go on to consolidate his hold over the university in the 1590s, the mixed response across the university to the 'New Foundation' makes it clear that by any standard of judgement the programme of reform he had hoped to implement at St Andrews had fallen drastically short by the end of its first decade in operation. Whether he was able to reverse its fortunes when he assumed the rectorate of the university in the following decade remains to be seen.

CHAPTER 5

The Rise and Fall of 'Melvillian' St Andrews, 1588–97

The visitation of 1588 revealed the limited impact of educational reform at St Andrews, but following this there was a marked rise in Melville's fortunes, both at court and in St Andrews. This included his assumption in 1590 of the role of rector of the university. However, the second half of the 1590s saw Melville fall from grace as rapidly as he had ascended. The royal commission that visited the university in the summer of 1597 not only deprived Melville of the rectorate, but also severely curtailed his freedom of movement and his involvement in ecclesiastical politics, and attempted to bring the administration of the university entirely under royal control. The commision's actions were part of a wider attempt by the royal government to arrest the momentum of the Presbyterian party in Kirk affairs, which James VI believed had sponsored a riot in Edinburgh against him on 17 December 1596. The lead commissioner and chancellor of the university, John Lindsay of Menmuir, also had a personal grudge against the St Andrews Presbytery for his humiliation in the pulpit by one of their ministers late in the preceding year. However, the proceedings of the royal commission were not entirely arbitrary or politically motivated. On the contrary, draft proposals for the overhaul of the university's administration show that it clearly aimed to make St Andrews a public institution, free from the ancient privileges awarded to it by the Catholic Church and answerable to government for its conduct. Moreover, accusations denouncing Melville's performance as rector, though perhaps influenced by political factors, appear to have had some real foundation if the gaps in university record-keeping and administration during his tenure are anything to go by.

Politics and Teaching at St Andrews, 1588–96

In the aftermath of the events off the English coast in the summer of 1588, and amidst a growing fear of encroaching Catholic and Jesuit influence in Scottish affairs, the king and Kirk enjoyed a period of uneasy co-operation. James VI accepted a growing level of support and advice from the Kirk in state matters, and also showed some willingness to deal with the recusant earls of Huntly, Erroll and Angus, who were seen as the most pressing Catholic threat to the country. When Huntly was found to be carrying out secret negotiations with King Philip of Spain in 1589 he was warded in Edinburgh castle and, following a rumour on his release that he and Errol were planning to take an army into southern Scotland, he surrendered without a fight to a military force led by James VI at the Brig o' Dee near Aberdeen. In the following year when James sailed to Denmark to meet his bride Princess Anne, he left the country in the hands of a coalition of ministers and Privy Council members, with a prominent position in government given to the Presbyterian minister Robert Bruce. On his return he ratified a range of anti-Catholic legislation and supportive measures for the Kirk that gained him a standing ovation at the General Assembly in August 1591, and in 1592 Parliament passed the 'Golden Act' that legally recognised the Presbyterian church government.

A further conspiracy led by the Catholic earls, known as the 'Affair of the Spanish Blanks', came to light early in 1593. Despite some reluctance to persecute the earls, James bowed to pressure from both Parliament and Kirk and took a military force against them to the north-east in autumn 1594.[1] It is a telling indicator of how close the Presbyterian party and the king had become that Melville and a number of other ministers accompanied him, and it was due to Melville's rather merciless stance against the earls in council meetings that the king slighted Huntly and Errol's castles at Strathbogie and Slains.[2] By the beginning of the following year the earls had left the country, along with the king's chief political rival Francis Stewart fifth Earl of Bothwell. Relations between the government and the Kirk grew to such an extent that the presbyteries worked with local government to organise local militias who were to assemble in the event of a Catholic invasion. By the beginning of 1596 there was even discussion of a new system of ecclesiastical funding that would give the Kirk political representation. The 'constant platt', devised by the king's secretary John Lindsay of Menmuir, advocated the creation of 51 parliamentary representatives drawn from the presbyteries. These representatives would replace the surviving bishops, abbots and other ecclesiastical commendators as they died out, and would result in far tighter control by the Kirk over existing church lands.[3]

The growing relationship between king and Kirk in the early 1590s mirrors in many ways the complex one between the king and Melville.

---

[1]   MacDonald, *Jacobean Kirk*, pp. 39–59; Donaldson, *James V–James VII*, pp. 186–96; Ruth Grant, 'The Brig o' Dee Affair, the Sixth Earl of Huntly and the Politics of the Counter-Reformation', in *The Reign of James VI*, pp. 93–109.

[2]   *JMAD*, pp. 318–19; Calderwood, vol. 5, p. 357.

[3]   MacDonald, *Jacobean Kirk*, pp. 62–3.

Following the heated events of the preceding decade a measure of rapprochement developed between the two men. Anecdotal evidence of their meetings, captured by James Melville and David Calderwood, shows that Melville enjoyed a great deal of liberty with James VI, taking an active role in several council meetings and exhorting him to deal with the threat posed by Catholic recusancy.[4] Melville's growing friendship with the king is reflected in the fact that he wrote two lengthy poems for court events in this period. The 'Small Garland' (*Stephaniskion*) was recited before Queen Anne at her coronation in May 1590, and the 'Birth of the Scoto-Brittanic Prince' (*Principis Scoti-Britannorum Natalia*) was written to celebrate the birth of Prince Henry in 1594. Both poems were full of praise for the Stewart line and extolled the importance of a king to a well-ordered society, and were so well liked by James VI that he ordered their immediate publication.[5]

As Melville grew in favour at court, he consolidated his place in St Andrews, particularly in St Mary's. Melville was appointed rector of the university in March 1590 following the death of James Wilkie, and he would hold this post unchallenged for seven years.[6] Melville also continued to hold his post as principal of St Mary's. The combined authority of both roles gave him a free hand in dictating policy and staffing at the college, which he used to secure the appointment of John Johnston in 1593.[7] Johnston was initially opposed as second master by John Caldcleuch,[8] who continued to be difficult and argumentative towards Melville. Caldcleuch was incensed at the intrusion of Johnston, and one of the few papers surviving for St Mary's in this period records his list of grievances at this turn of events, given in before the Privy Council. However, Caldcleuch was not only unsuccessful in his petition, but was removed from his post for disrupting the college and attempting to appeal unlawfully to the civil government above the decision of Melville and his assessors.[9]

It is easy to see why Melville would be keen to employ Johnston, as they shared much in common. Johnston was originally educated at King's College, Aberdeen and, like Melville, had studied in several institutions on the Continent. Unlike Melville, his studies led him not to France but to reformed centres in Switzerland and the Palatinate including Rostock, Helmstedt and Heidelberg. Johnston and his fellow Aberdeen alumnus,

---

[4] Calderwood, vol. 5, pp. 288–9, 330–1; *JMAD*, pp. 313, 318–20.

[5] Williamson and McGinnis, pp. 31–2, 276–87; *JMAD*, p.279.

[6] Acta Rectorum, p. 109; M'Crie, pp. 153–4.

[7] Johnston first appears on the presbytery on 19 April 1593. *StAPR*, p. 125.

[8] Caldcleuch was still a member of the college staff as late as 19 October 1592, as he was still part of the presbytery in his capacity as a master of St Mary's. *StAPR*, p. 110.

[9] *JMAD*, p. 314; Balcarres Papers, vol. 7, fos 263r–265v.

Robert Howie, also shared Melville's distinction of being the first to print a work by George Buchanan. Melville had shepherded Buchanan's *History* through the press in the early 1580s, while Johnston and Howie prepared the first two editions of his *De Sphaera* in 1586 and 1587 at Herborn from manuscripts in their possession.[10]

Johnston also shared Melville's interest in Ramism, if his early published works are any indicator. While Johnston published a very traditional set of *theses physiologicae* on Aristotle's *Physics* during his regency at Heidelberg in the later 1580s, he also wrote a pamphlet in response to criticisms of Ramus by his former colleague at Helmstedt, Owen Günther. In 1589, in consultation with Johannes Piscator, he also produced an introductory manual for the study of theology. This manual apparently used the Ramist 'method' in its organisation and featured various 'tabulae' that logically expounded the main heads of doctrine.[11] Unfortunately, neither of these works has survived and their contents are only known from scattered references in Johnston's correspondence. However, they do suggest that Johnston, like his elder colleague Melville, engaged with the works of Ramus during his Continental education.

In early 1592 the Zurich linguist and scholar Casper Waser visited St Andrews, which caused a considerable stir among both the town and gown community. Born in 1565, Waser had matriculated at Heidelberg on 1 May 1585 and at Basel in November 1586, and it was at the former that he likely made the acquaintance of Johnston. The pair met again in London between December 1591 and March 1592, where Johnston had been forced to stop on his journey home due to serious illness. Waser was visiting Britain as tutor to the young German noble J.P. Hainzel von Degerstein, and in the first half of 1592 the two travelled to Scotland, eventually getting as far north as Aberdeen. Waser and his young charge paid a visit to St Andrews between 12 and 17 May, and made the acquaintance of Melville and the ministers and councilmen of the city, who continued to correspond with Waser after his return home.[12] A batch of letters sent to him in February 1594 gives a number of insights into academic life at St Andrews, particularly at St Mary's, and the list of correspondents is itself revealing.[13] A letter to Waser from David Monypenny, the dean of arts and second master of St Salvator's, shows he was spending considerable time with his colleagues at St Mary's. He had clearly become a good friend

10   Cameron, *Letters*, pp. xvii, xx, xxv–xxvi.

11   Cameron, *Letters*, pp. xxix–xxxii, 35–6, 52.

12   Cameron, *Letters*, pp. xxxv, lvii, lxviii, 92, 304–5.

13   Cameron, *Letters*, pp. 90–93 (Johnston to Waser, 19 February 1594), 360 (Cassilis to Waser, 12 February), 361–2 (Monypenny to Waser, 13 February).

to Melville, whom he describes as his *magnificus rector*.[14] The alliance of Monypenny with the 'Melvillian' faction in the university suggests that he supported Presbyterianism, or that the underlying tensions between him and James Martine were still unresolved and Monypenny saw this alliance as another opportunity to undermine him. Another of the correspondents was John Kennedy, the young fifth Earl of Cassilis. Cassilis, who was born in 1574/5,[15] had succeeded to the title at an early age and was served heir to his father in 1588. He matriculated in St Salvator's at some point in the late 1580s, and was enrolled as a divinity student by the time of Waser's visit in early 1592, for he is described in another letter to Waser as having lived in St Mary's for 'another year' (*apud nos in Collegio Theologico alterum annum vivit*). Cassilis, as hereditary presenter to many of the bursaries and prebendaries of St Salvator's, would have been another valuable ally for Melville. His letter to Waser shows a young man who was extremely devout and deeply interested in theology.

One of the only fragments alluding to the actual content of teaching in this period is found in a letter by Johnston to Waser, though it may be a throwaway comment. There is nothing concrete to show that Hebrew, Chaldaic and Syriac were being taught to the students in the early 1590s, but Johnston notes in a terse comment that Waser's *Institutio Linguae Syrae ex Optimis Scriptionibus*, published at Leyden in 1594, had been 'seen and tried out' at the college (*Grammatica tua Syra nobis visa est et probata*).[16] Whether this means it was actually being used as part of a teaching programme in near Eastern languages at the college, or was merely browsed through by staff, is unknown. However, it is worth noting that advanced biblical languages were clearly under discussion at St Mary's, even if there is no way to prove they were fully taught beyond the fact that provision for their tuition was included in the 'New Foundation'.

Perhaps heeding the warnings of the visitation commission to maintain better records, divinity students began to be formally recorded after 1588 in a register separate from the matriculation roll found in the Acta Rectorum.[17] Although those recorded do not represent the entire divinity student body,[18] it is clear that new entrants to the college between 1588

---

[14]   However, this was also a standard title used in many German academies and universities. I am grateful to Professor Howard Hotson for this observation.

[15]   Alan R. MacDonald, 'Kennedy, John, fifth Earl of Cassillis (1574/5–1615)', *ODNB* [15377, accessed 14 March 2008]. Cameron cites Cassilis as being born in 1567: *Letters*, p. 93.

[16]   Cameron, *Letters*, pp. 90, 93.

[17]   UYUY152/2. Although known as 'Howie's Book' because it features many entries by Howie from his period as principal, the title is misleading, as the register was started long before his arrival at the university.

[18]   See comments on the student register in the 1597 visitation, discussed below, p. 166.

and 1596[19] must have been few in number, fluctuating between a low of three entrants per year (in 1594) and a high of 14 (in 1588). A tentative analysis based on recurring names in the register suggests that while approximately 40 per cent of this group stayed for just one year, around 50 per cent stayed for two, three or four years, with just under 10 per cent staying on for five or six years. While this suggests that many students were merely gaining some practical theological 'polish' following their MAs, a significant percentage were staying on for the equivalent of an extended period of divinity study.

Melville and the other masters of theology were also heavily involved in the St Andrews Presbytery, the 'appellate court' and jurisdictional superior to the local kirk session.[20] The presbytery was a particular concern of St Mary's and the local ministers, as statutes in 1586 and 1590 confirmed that regents in philosophy could not sit on it, but only those holding the ecclesiastical offices of 'pastor' or 'doctor'.[21] Melville was moderator of the presbytery between October 1593 and April 1594 and on at least one other occasion, and there are numerous references to his acting as a commissioner and visitor for presbytery business.[22] By far the most important function of the presbytery in relation to the university was in trying the doctrine and preaching of divinity students and ministers in the weekly 'exercise'. This could take the form of either a public disputation or lecture before the town congregation or an assembly of students, or a private session before the presbytery where a text would be subjected to systematic exposition and discussion. In the case of the latter one minister or student was proposed as 'maker' or chief speaker on the text, while a second would 'add' further points on its broader themes without the detailed exegesis. The person chosen to 'add' became the 'maker' in the following week.[23] This programme can be seen in action in the example of the divinity student Nathaniel Harlaw. On 15 April 1590, Harlaw was given eight days to prepare a sermon on John 3 which he would give at 2 p.m. 'in the New Colledge scholis'. Two weeks later he was given the same length of time to prepare for a further public trial of 'the heads of catechisme'. Having passed this, Harlaw was then ordered on 21 May 'to studie to Calvinis cathechisme and to give ane compt of the questionis and answeris

---

[19]   See Appendix, Table 3.

[20]   *StAPR*, pp. iv–vi.

[21]   *StAPR*, pp. ix–x, 45.

[22]   *StAPR*, pp. xxiv–xxv, 41 (26 March 1590, visitation to Abdie to examine Nans Murit for witchcraft), 47 (30 April, visitation to Auchtermoonzie), 52 (18 June, trial of religious faith of Master of Angus), 57 (3 September, mediation of feud between Laird of Craighall and the 'guidman of Callinch'), 68 (15 October, visit to Laird of Forret).

[23]   *StAPR*, pp. xii–xiv; Kirk, 'Melvillian Movement', pp. 374–8.

thairof being, and for him places of scripture and ressonis to conferm the said answeris', to be tried on 1 August. Harlaw was clearly successful, for he was appointed to the ministry at Ormiston in the following year. Similarly, Robert Yule was recommended to the parishioners at Largo after being found to be 'indewit with guid qualeteis' in February 1592, and the presbytery minutes record a number of other students who underwent the same process.[24] Divinity students who were sufficiently skilled were also occasionally allowed to participate in the practical work of the church. On 7 March 1594 licence was given to any of the theology students who had been on the 'exercise' to help Andrew Moncrieff dispense the sacrament to his parish at communion.[25]

Outwith St Mary's, Melville's influence in church and town affairs also grew considerably. By 1591 his erstwhile enemy Patrick Adamson had fallen completely from royal favour, owing to the massive debts he had incurred in England, and his continued changeability towards church politics.[26] Disgraced and penniless, Adamson turned to Melville, and despite the great chasm that had developed between them, Melville offered him financial aid. This support did not come without cost, however, for Adamson was forced to recant his support for Episcopacy in a written 'Refutation' (*Palinodia*), which was circulated widely in both Scots and Latin to other Presbyterian communities across Europe.[27] Adamson died on 10 February 1592, and by then Melville had taken considerable steps to ensure that a large body of Presbyterian supporters were in place in the local church. It was through his 'cairfull procurement' at the General Assembly and the St Andrews Kirk Session that the radical minister David Black, one of Melville's fellow exiles from the mid-1580s, was appointed minister of St Andrews in 1590. In 1593, owing to an increasingly heavy workload, Robert Wallace was nominated to join Black as a further charge to the city, and the parish was divided between the two men. Both men were powerful public speakers as well as strict disciplinarians, and between them enforced a range of fines and humiliating punishments for immoral behaviour and failure to keep the Sabbath.[28]

---

[24]   *StAPR*, pp. 43, 47, 48, 50 (John Wemyss and Nathaniel Harlaw), 56 (trial and censure of ministers), 68–9 (Robert Buchanan), 93, 95, 98 (Robert Yule), 113–14, 118 (John Dykes, Gilbert Ramsay), 131–2 (Alexander Forsyth), 133 (John Kinnear). For further examples of case studies relating to the education of ministers in Fife, see McCallum, *Reforming the Scottish Parish*, pp. 134–51, esp. pp. 145–51.

[25]   *StAPR*, p. 156.

[26]   *StAPR*, p. 82.

[27]   MacDonald, 'Best of Enemies', pp. 273–5; Mullan, *Episcopacy in Scotland*, pp. 71–3.

[28]   James K. Cameron, 'Black, David (c.1546–1603)', *ODNB* [70046, accessed 14 March 2008].

Accompanying this growth in discipline was a noticeable increase in the involvement of Melville and his colleagues in the kirk session. Before 1590, only James Wilkie, James Martine and John Robertson had represented the university as elders, but after Melville replaced John Robertson on the eldership in January 1591 this rapidly changed. In the next election in November 1593, the kirk session practically doubled in size, as did university representation on the eldership.[29] Melville and Robert Wilkie of St Leonard's were joined by John Johnston from St Mary's, with Homer Blair replacing a conspicuously absent Martine, along with the St Leonard's regent William March and the St Salvator's regent James Ross. In the following year the session was split into two separate bodies, one for the south parish under Robert Wallace and one for the north under David Black. The university representatives were joined at this stage by William Welwood and Homer Blair, the two masters most poorly treated by Martine in the 1580s. These two separate bodies of elders were also now to be organised into groups to regularly 'oversie the maners and conversatioun of the pepill', a process repeated in the elections in October of the following year.[30] This showed a paramount focus on discipline in the city, spearheaded by Melville and his colleagues at the university.

On a number of occasions Melville's involvement in town politics had a direct impact on St Mary's. In the summer of 1591[31] a riot broke out between the townspeople and St Mary's that saw the gate of the college being torn off and a threat made to burn the entire building down. The spark for the riot was accidental enough. John Caldcleuch had been practising archery in the college garden with a number of theology students when he accidentally missed the target and shot the arrow down the passageway leading onto the street, where he wounded an elderly maltman in the neck. Upon hearing this a number of the townspeople, who already disliked Melville because of his harangues in the pulpit over their moral conduct and drinking, allied with Learmonth of Dairsie. After smashing the gate they made straight for the principal's chamber where he was firmly ensconced, and attempted to smash the door in with wooden beams while Melville hurled rebukes at them. It was only through the mediations

---

[29]   From 16 elders and 11 deacons in 1591 to 39 and 20 respectively in 1593. *StAKSR*, pp. 694–5, 760–1.

[30]   *StAKSR*, pp. 788–92, 802–4.

[31]   James Melville ascribes this event to the summer of 1592, but a reference in the presbytery records to 'the tumult quhilk wes aganis the New Colledge' on 24 June 1591 shows it was in the preceding year. *StAPR*, p. 80. A full account of this episode and the names of those involved is given in *RPC*, vol. 4, pp. 639–41, where the entry (dated 23 June 1591) states the event took place on 4 June, and this date is confirmed in the burgh court records (I am grateful to Dr Elizabeth Ewan for this latter reference). See also *RPC*, vol. 4, p. 661, where the band of good behaviour and decrees are reaffirmed.

of David Black, Robert Wilkie, and the other masters of the university that the disorder was calmed. While James VI wanted the prosecution of the townspeople involved upon hearing of the disorder, the event was dealt with quietly by taking bonds of assurance that such an action would not happen again.[32] It is clear though that the attack was less to do with the conduct of the members of the college, than with Melville's turbulent relationship with the leading men in the town.

A similar episode in 1593, this time involving Melville and the Presbyterian faction of the town in the provost elections, further confirms that Melville's interference in local affairs was a major source of friction. At the annual election in Michaelmas 1593, the Presbyterian supporter Captain William Murray was narrowly elected to the post by the craft guilds and tradesmen of the city, ousting Learmonth from what in effect had been a hereditary office. Learmonth was so enraged by this assault on his power that he sanctioned a series of night attacks on some of the citizens, in one case abducting a man's daughter. He then brought together a band of armed men and took them to harass the town, at which point Melville, decked out in a corslet and armed with a 'whait speare' (a sign of his rectorial office), convened an assembly of masters of the university to oppose him. With the aid of John Lindsay, Sir George Douglas and a number of other local men, the group took to arms to defend the town. Although the election was disputed before the Convention of Estates in the following November, Murray was upheld as provost.[33] Melville was clearly a rector and university man who was far more active in the political affairs of the city than any of his predecessors, and carried considerable sway.

Elsewhere in the university, the masters at the other colleges appear to have accepted Melville's growing favour without complaint, and to have carried on with little disruption to their business. The record for entrants to St Salvator's for the period 1588–96[34] is only partially complete, but the years 1589–91 and 1593, which appear relatively representative, show student numbers remained steady at about two thirds of those of St Leonard's, climbing as high as 24 entrants in 1589 before dipping to ten in the following year, and then levelling out to an average of around 15 students. Politics at the college continued to overlap with those in the town, and the college was rocked in the aftermath of the 1588 visitation by an escalation of the feud between the Martine and Welwood families.

---

[32]   *JMAD*, pp. 307–9.

[33]   *JMAD*, pp. 313–14; Cameron, *Letters*, p. 92, n. 17.

[34]   See Appendix, Table 1. This is ignoring 1588, which appears to have been a particularly poor year all around, and the years 1594–96, for which no specific college data is available.

A central player in this escalation was none other than Patrick Adamson. At some point between 18 December 1588 and 9 March 1589, following an earlier confrontation, William Welwood was ambushed and stabbed by Henry Hamilton, one of the archbishop's retainers. Welwood was taken to his mother's house, but a posse led by Hamilton, Adamson's brother-in-law James Arthur and a baillie of the town attempted to gain entry. They were met by John Welwood, William's brother, and several of his Geddie and Smith kinsmen, and in their attempt to apprehend Hamilton James Arthur was stabbed to death.[35]

James Melville states that Adamson had ordered the attack on Welwood as revenge against the Presbyterian faction in the town, and this may well be true. Hamilton and the Arthurs involved certainly had close affiliations of business and service with Adamson, but that Adamson chose to target Welwood and not the Melvilles casts doubt on this explanation. The proximity in time to the quarrel between Welwood and Martine, however, particularly given the fact that it was still unresolved at the time of the attack, suggests that it may have been Martine influencing the archbishop through his Arthur kinsmen to order the assault.[36]

The arbitration process that followed the murder between 9 and 24 March was swift and exacting. James Smith, John Welwood and John Geddie, as ring-leaders in the quarrel, were to be banished from Scotland on pain of 5,000 merks each, and a number of their kinsmen banished from St Andrews. The sentence was supported by the king and a commission to oversee its execution was set up by act of Privy Council on 3 April, and carried out on or before 3 May 1589. While this sequence of events did not remove Welwood from his office in St Salvator's, removing three of his merchant kinsmen from their base of operations would have crippled his family's ability to raise income, and appears to have forced him to halt further public opposition to Martine.[37]

The arbitration did temporarily settle the Welwood–Arthur feud, along with the conflicts in the college. Following these events Martine and his family quietly continued to consolidate their hold over finance and posts in St Salvator's. In February 1590, David Martine was promoted from a regenting post to the place of third master following the resignation of William Cranston.[38] Why Cranston chose to resign is unclear, but with two Martines as his colleagues it is clear why David Monypenny may have felt isolated in the college and turned to support from masters in the other colleges.

---

[35]   Cairns, 'Academic Feud', 260–1.

[36]   *JMAD*, pp. 273–4; Cairns, 'Academic Feud', 261.

[37]   Cairns, 'Academic Feud', 262–3.

[38]   UYSS110/AE18. Martine, 'unus regentium', was elected on 25 February 1590.

The consolidation of the college rents and patrimony in this period was also supported by royal aid. In winter 1590–91 James VI ordered that Martine's stipend be augmented, this time with 8 bolls wheat, 16 bolls beer, 24 bolls meal, and 32 bolls oats instead of the £200 cash that had been offered previously in 1587.[39] On 5 July 1592, an Act of Parliament was passed confirming the annexation of all the old chaplainries and prebendaries to the college that had been part of the pre-reformation college patrimony.[40]

Events had also taken a seemingly victorious turn for Martine and his family against the Welwoods in 1589/90. By 1591, however, Martine was engaged in a process of reconciliation with Welwood and the mathematician Homer Blair regarding their stipends, a problem unresolved from 1588. In November 1591 it was agreed that Blair and Welwood be paid their stipend of £100 and a chalder of oats each, and Welwood gave written acknowledgement that he had been paid.[41] On 19 February 1592, Blair was reconfirmed in his holding of the Manderston theology bursary by James Martine, David Monypenny and David Martine as part of his fee, along with various other small holdings and lands.[42]

Although Martine's softening in attitude towards these men is partially explained by the fact that he required the support of all the college masters in continuing legal actions regarding the annexed parish of Forteviot, where various claimants were attempting to sue for the rents,[43] the main reason Martine would have been interested in improving relations with Welwood was the rising favour of the Presbyterian faction in local and national politics, which obviously had an adverse impact on his family's standing in the town. The growing favour of the Presbyterians saw the return of the banished Welwood kinsmen by Act of Parliament on 8 June 1594, providing they agreed to stand trial or make restitution for the murder of James Arthur.[44] Between October 1595 and September 1596 a process of reconciliation led by a neutral commission of presbytery members and local men made considerable progress, as James Smith and John Welwood appeared before the kirk session on 3 September to declare mutual amity.[45] Although he could have sat on the presbytery proceedings as nominal minister of Cults, Martine conspicuously stayed out of the reconciliation process. Overall, it is clear that, while Melville, Welwood

---

39   UYSS110/C4.12.

40   UYSS110/C4.14, E4.22, E5.

41   UYSS110/AH13–14.

42   UYSS110/AH9–12.

43   UYSS110/E3, E4.23; UYSS110/G10.5–10.24.

44   *RPS* 1594/4/79 [accessed 1 July 2010].

45   *StAPR*, pp. 172–5, 178.

and their supporters enjoyed royal support and local power, the provost of St Salvator's was aware there was little he could do to influence town or university politics, and he chose accordingly to let events play out as they would in the hope that favour would eventually fall from Melville's party – which it did, suddenly and swiftly, at the end of 1596.

Arts Tuition in the 1580s and Early 1590s: The St Leonard's College Orator's Book

While the politics of the masters of St Mary's and St Salvator's are relatively easy to reconstruct in the 1590s, as in the preceding decade nothing of substance survives to tell us about events at St Leonard's. The barest munimentary evidence shows that the remnants of the priory lands attached to the college were still being sold off by their titular commendator, Ludovic Stewart the second Duke of Lennox, well into the 1590s, but this was clearly not having a major impact on the college. It had by far the largest number of matriculated students of any of the three colleges in the period, with recorded figures staying firmly above 20 entrants per year and rising as high as 36 in 1590.[46] However, St Leonard's offers us the first detailed insight into teaching at St Andrews in the 'Melvillian' era, and the college appears from this evidence to have had a far more developed and consistent teaching programme than its counterparts. The College Orator's Book is a large collection of essays and poetry by St Leonard's students from the first half of the 1590s, recited by students in the third and fourth year of their MA degree. These students took turns as a group on Saturday mornings to read an essay on a subject of their choosing in a public assembly of the college. After the reading the *lector*'s essay was transcribed into the book, with a note of who would take the role in the following week, which moved in rotation through the senior students.

The first 440 pages of the Orator's Book cover a period beginning at an undetermined start date in 1589, and ending with an oration given on 18 June 1595. However, appended to the end of the document are two Latin orations given in the exact same format as the others in the book dating from 1560/61.[47] These two orations were part of the collection of manuscripts taken from the university by the historian and former Principal of St Mary's, John Lee, when he took up a post at Edinburgh University. These papers have only been returned to the university in a piecemeal

---

46   See Appendix, Table 1.

47   UYSL320, pp. 440–4.

fashion following the auction of his estate.[48] We have no further evidence of provenance for these orations, or whether they were part of a much larger collection of student essays from the earlier period. If this is the case, however, it would suggest that this practice, and the style and content of the orations, remained completely unchanged despite the various reforms of the university in the thirty years following 1560. More importantly, if the content of these orations and their sources is indicative of intellectual culture at the university in the early 1560s, it suggests that, at St Leonard's at least, drilling students in the use of classical texts and in the production of elegant Latin was well entrenched far earlier than we have presumed. This has considerable implications for the idea that Melville made the biggest advances in bringing the 'new learning' of Renaissance humanism to St Andrews via the 'New Foundation'. It suggests, in fact, that St Leonard's was possibly teaching along these lines well before his arrival, and before any of the reforms considered for St Andrews after 1560.

However, there is nothing else to corroborate or disprove this thesis. The only other set of lecture notes to survive from this period, those dictated from courses under the St Leonard's regent John Echline at some point between 1592 and 1603,[49] merely provide a basic introduction to logic. The first half of the text offers a brief outline of Porphyry's *Isagoge*,[50] while the second part comprises very summary notes on a number of books selected from the *Organon*.[51] These latter notes share many of the traditional features found in John Malcolm's notes, including an exposition of the main kinds of syllogism and of the various modes of proposition,[52] but make no reference to the original Greek of the texts. This may simply mean that the younger students, who although barely into their teens would likely have at least intermediate Latin from their time at grammar school, were expected to grasp the rudimentary elements of logic in a language they were comfortable with before studying Aristotle's works in their original language. However, this is pure conjecture, and Echline's

---

[48]   F. Macdonald, 'Lee, John (1779–1859)', *ODNB* [16296, accessed 25 Feb 2008]; St Andrews University Library, Lee sale catalogue.

[49]   Robert N. Smart, 'Draft Biographical Register of Students at the University of St Andrews, 1579–1747' (n.p.). Echline matriculated 1586/87, and received his MA in 1590. He was a regent by 9 December 1592 and had left by 7 November 1605.

[50]   University of St Andrews MS36226, *Capitula quaedam eorum quae a Porphyrio imbecillitati non parum utilia*, pp. 1–23.

[51]   St Andrews University, MS36226, pp. 23–34 (De Interpretatione chapters 1–10), 35–43 (Prior Analytics), 45–64, 73–81 (Compendium of Books 1 and 2 'of Demonstration', presumably Posterior Analytics), 83–9 (Topics, Book 1, chs 1–12).

[52]   MS36226, pp. 40–43, where the syllogisms are listed by the traditional figural names of Barbara, Celarent, Darii and Ferio.

notes ultimately do not help to clarify our understanding of teaching as it is evidenced from the Orator's Book.

These tantalising suggestions aside, the bulk of the Orator's Book shows that, by the early 1590s at least, the college was trying to drum the ability to declaim successfully into its students. These candidates were expected to produce orations in Latin and Greek, on a range of classically inspired themes and from a variety of authors. A paraphrase of the Horatian trope on 'Why death ought not to be feared' is the subject of numerous orations and of an extended Latin poem.[53] Other titles include the surprisingly contentious 'Why no republic or *civitas* can be governed by a king, emperor or magistrate',[54] and 'Why virtue [and, in another example, charity] is to be preferred to all possessions',[55] giving an idea of the classical and republican flavour of the texts the students were immersed in. Still others simply sing the praises of poetry, rhetoric or jurisprudence.[56] A few of the texts also discuss rudimentary aspects of philosophy, including a defence of the supremacy of Aristotle and a discussion of why 'essence is not individual'.[57] Perhaps with a mind to the potential ministerial careers of many of these students, some orations also expound on solid Christian themes and draw on biblical content. These include one on free will, two praising Christ for his constancy on the cross and as the source of all truth and glory, and an extended poem on Genesis.[58]

The texts themselves are highly formulaic, as the contents of an example oration by William Boswell on 'Why death ought not to be feared' from

---

[53]   UYSL320, pp. 10–12 [William Boswell, 1589/90]; pp. 177–83: 'Carmen Quod Mortem Non Esse Timendam' [James Willocks, 12 May 1592]; p. 292: 'Mori Non Miserum Esse' [John Barron, 8 December 1593].

[54]   UYSL320, pp. 316–18: 'Nulla Republica aut Civitas sive Rege Imperatore, aut Magistratu Aliquo Gubernari Possit' [William Penman, 10 February 1594].

[55]   UYSL320, pp. 258–9: 'Virtus est Praeferenda Omnibusque Quibuscumque Possessionibus' [William Penman, 5 May 1593]; pp. 260–3: 'Contendit Charitatem Ab Omnibus Esse Amplexandam' [George Chalmers, 12 May 1593].

[56]   UYSL320, p. 184: 'Quod Iustitia Prudentiae Dignitatis Palmam Longe Praeripeat, Oratio' [Adam Davidson, 21 May 1592], pp. 191–5: 'De Exercitiis in Re Poetica et Oratoria Hebdomadariis perennies Classes atque Ordines Instituendis Oratio' [David Lindsay, 1592], pp. 227–9: 'De Eloquentiae Laudibus Deo Duce Agemus' [John Barron, 3 February 1593].

[57]   UYSL320, p. 274, 'Individua Non Differunt Essentia' [David Porteous, 9 July 1593]; p. 299: 'Quisquis Aristoelis Vult Profligare Labores Noscat in Assuetis Verba Volare Volis' [John Douglas, 4 January 1593/4].

[58]   UYSL320, pp. 365–9: 'Deo Duce de Fortitudine et Constantia Christiana in Cruce Referendo Deo Duce Agemus' [John Barron, 7 December 1594]; pp. 394–5: 'Omnem Gloria Immoderato Laudis Appetitum Perire, Veramque Gloriam in Solo Jesu Christo Fundari Deo Duce Docebimus'; pp. 399–407, 'Carmen' on Genesis; pp. 107–9: 'In Nullo Homine Esse Liberum Arbitrium Deo Auspice Docebimus' [Archibald Dunmure, 1590].

1589/90[59] will suffice to show. Many of the senior students gave three or even four orations in the final two years of their degree, giving them multiple chances to prepare and deliver a polished oration. Boswell presented a further two orations in the course of his degree, one in Latin and one in Greek in 1590.[60] Like many an undergraduate essay, Boswell's text suffers from considerable errors in syntax and structure, as well as repetitiveness, but on the whole is relatively sound. In the first section of his text, he attempts rhetorically to beg the pardon of his audience for his lack of skill and for mistakes occasioned by fear of the heavy task upon his shoulders. He turns to an unlikely mix of quotes from Virgil, Ovid, Horace, Ennius and Cicero and a paraphrase of some quotations of Christ's teachings from the New Testament to support his main contention, showing the fusion of Christian and classical learning these students were exposed to.

He then goes on to offer examples of men who have faced death valiantly and who have earned eternal merit as a result, including Lucius Brutus 'who was killed in liberating his nation' (*non solus Lucium Brutium, qui in liberanda patria est interfectus*), the two Scipios, and Marcus Marcellus among others, before offering some closing remarks around the saying that death makes equals of all people, from paupers to kings (*nam omnibus mors aequa est ut est vetus Carmen, pauperibus reges ... aequat*). Boswell's example shows that students were clearly being trained in giving short speeches that followed formulaic patterns and that used a number of rhetorical devices to support their points, including quotations and illustrative examples.

While these orations give some sense of the tuition being given to students, they also suggest two noticeable gaps in the curriculum. Firstly, although two orations exhort the audience on the benefits of learning both Greek and Latin, and a number of orations use the odd Greek word, less than 5 per cent of the texts are actually in Greek. The orations that are in Greek only appear sporadically in the overall body of texts, as a cluster of four orations in 1590, a single oration by Patrick Ramsay in November 1594, and a further three in 1595.[61] This suggests that only a handful of students in the period covered by the Orator's Book actually progressed with Greek far enough to be proficient beyond a very basic level. In many ways this should not come as a surprise, as students had far more scope to engage with Latin as the main language of study and discourse at both the university and during their earlier grammar school education. The small

---

[59]   UYSL320, pp. 10–12.

[60]   Smart, 'Draft Biographical Register'.

[61]   UYSL320, pp. 48–55 [1590], 361–4 [1594], 407–15 [1595]. The latter group of three are, however, split into two in March and one in June, with no further texts recorded in the intervening period.

number of orations may thus simply indicate that Greek was the preserve of students who displayed sufficient linguistic aptitude to take it further, or had perhaps learned the language on their own or elsewhere.[62]

Secondly, none of the texts make mention of Ramus or his works, or show any structural bias towards Ramism. There are two orations that have titles discussing the benefits of 'conjoining philosophy with eloquence' which obviously echo the main objective of Ramus' work. However, on closer inspection these discuss more generally the role of oratory in combining rhetorical excellence with poetic flair, rather than debating the merits of Ramist ideology.[63] As a result, although it is clear from these texts that humanist Latin and thorough grounding in the classics was one of the priorities for teachers in St Leonard's, the alleged priority of Melville to inculcate the Ramist 'method' in students is not as apparent in the evidence for St Leonard's as it is in the later evidence for St Mary's.

On the other hand, the very existence of such a well-regulated and well-recorded exercise, and the fact that so many students had multiple chances to deliver speeches, also shows a level of organisation and consistency in the senior degree programme at St Leonard's that is not in evidence at any of the other colleges, or indeed at the other Scottish universities, in this period. This may well be an accident of survival, and nothing more. However, the fact that such a monumental volume exists only for St Leonard's perhaps reflects the fact that they had achieved a far superior level of educational provision and administration than their counterparts at St Andrews and elsewhere.

The Crisis of 1596 and the Visitation of 1597

Despite the increase in co-operation between the king and Kirk throughout the early 1590s, the spectre of Catholicism in Scottish affairs over the course of 1596 rapidly undid this relationship. The Octavians, a group of eight officials appointed in early 1596 to supervise the king's parlous finances, were suspected of Catholic sympathies,[64] and there was great insecurity over the influence that this group of men wielded. This was exacerbated by the king's continued refusal to forfeit the wives of the exiled Catholic earls from their hereditary property. When Huntly and Erroll

---

[62]   A useful comparison is the state of Greek studies at Oxford at the turn of the seventeenth century. Mordechai Feingold, 'The Humanities', in Tyacke (ed.), *Seventeenth-Century Oxford*, pp. 256–61.

[63]   UYSL320, p. 231.

[64]   MacDonald, *Jacobean Kirk*, p. 61; *JMAD*, p. 330; Donaldson, *James V–James VII*, p. 217, n. 14.

returned to Scotland in the latter half of the year, a commission of General Assembly delegates, led by Melville, went to Falkland in September to exhort the king to deal with them. It was during this visit that Melville grabbed the king by the sleeve and, in what Alan MacDonald has rightly described as the 'language of crisis and confrontation', harangued him as 'God's sillie vassall' and announced 'thair is twa kings and twa kingdoms ... Thair is Chryst Jesus the king ... whase subject King James the Saxt is, and of whase kingdome [is] nocht a king, nor a lord, nor a heid, bot a member'.[65] This was the most extreme and shocking speech that Melville had made regarding royal authority since the mid-1580s, and the force of it emphasises how tense the situation between the Kirk and the royal government had become. This meeting also represented a break in the relationship between James VI and Melville, with their air of mutual respect vanishing after this.

The confrontation reached a critical point in November, when David Black was summoned to appear before the Privy Council for preaching a treasonous sermon denouncing all kings as 'the devillis childrene' and attacking both James and Queen Anne for their lack of commitment to the Kirk. On 9 December Black was found guilty of sedition and was ordered into ward north of the Tay, and the king ordered the commissioners of the General Assembly who had come to Edinburgh in support of Black, including Melville, to leave the city.[66] The ministers of Edinburgh were left to continue pleading the case with the Privy Council, and on 17 December a delegation led by Lords Lindsay and Forbes, and the ministers Robert Bruce and William Watson, approached the Tolbooth to appeal to the king and the Lords of Session. In their train were a large number of burgesses, nobles and lairds who had been roused in a sermon by Walter Balcanquhal earlier that morning to join the delegation. James VI remained locked within the Tolbooth and refused to come out, and when the lead delegates returned to the crowd outside a rumour was sparked of an armed Catholic plot, resulting in an angry call for arms. Although the town provost Alexander Hume calmed the situation, the king felt seriously threatened and condemned the ministers, who in turn blamed the rapid escalation of events on James' refusal to heed their exhortations. The king and Privy Council removed themselves to Linlithgow, where the episode was given a much more treasonous complexion when Lord Hamilton appeared with an alleged letter from Bruce and Balcanquhal. This letter apparently stated they would pledge Hamilton their support to become king if he supported their actions, in effect suggesting the men had tried to engineer a clerical *coup*. Edinburgh Council, fearful of losing the power and prestige

[65] MacDonald, *Jacobean Kirk*, pp. 63–5; *JMAD*, pp. 369–71.
[66] MacDonald, *Jacobean Kirk*, p. 68.

associated with its role as the centre of royal administration, offered an unequivocal apology and substantial financial remuneration to the king for the muddled events of this 'riot', and the Edinburgh ministers fled the city after their arrest was ordered.[67]

James VI followed this order in the opening months of 1597 with swift and decisive action. On 6 January he banned all ecclesiastical courts, other than the kirk session, from meeting in Edinburgh. In February 1597, he ordered a meeting of ecclesiastical representatives at Perth to discuss a series of articles on church polity that would curb the jurisdiction of the Kirk over secular authority, which also confirmed the king's right, established in the 'Golden Act' of 1592, to dictate the time and place of the General Assembly. The king ordered and attended an assembly at Dundee in May, where the legality of the Perth meeting was approved, the Catholic earls were absolved from further prosecution, and the commission of the General Assembly was changed from a small group of ministers acting as representatives of the wider Presbyterian interest into a regulated body that would act as the 'judicial committee' and liaise with the crown in church matters.[68]

Against the backdrop of growing royal involvement in the Kirk, a specific issue with the behaviour of the ministry at St Andrews had considerable impact on the affairs of the university. In November 1596 the second minister in St Andrews, Robert Wallace, had condemned the royal secretary John Lindsay of Balcarres, also known as Lord Menmuir, for arbitrarily dealing with the trial of David Black and with accepting bribes to do so. Lindsay had played a central role in government since the early 1580s as a leading privy councillor and parliamentarian, and until this point had enjoyed a good relationship with the Kirk; in the summer of 1596 he had drawn up a draft proposal (known as the 'constant platt') to provide a fairer system of funding for all of Scotland's parishes from the revenues of the former bishoprics, and to provide each presbytery with a representative in Parliament.[69] He was thus a highly influential figure in both court and ecclesiastical politics, and by targeting Lindsay Wallace was leaving himself open to the opprobrium of a powerful enemy. Lindsay sent a letter to Wallace at the end of January 1597 seeking an apology, to which he received an insulting response from the minister. Lindsay dispatched his agents John Wemyss and David Lindsay to the presbytery to intercede on his behalf, and directed letters to his old friend Melville to secure him

---

[67]   MacDonald, *Jacobean Kirk*, pp. 68–73; Julian Goodare, 'The Attempted Scottish *Coup* of 1596', in Goodare and MacDonald (eds), *Sixteenth-Century Scotland*, pp. 311–36.

[68]   MacDonald, *Jacobean Kirk*, pp. 74–82.

[69]   Alan R. MacDonald, 'Lindsay, John, of Balcarres, Lord Menmuir (1552–1598)', *ODNB* [16705, accessed 8 June 2010].

justice.[70] Melville offered assurances in a letter of 21 February that he would be willing 'to do all guid affiris to yor Grace's contentement',[71] but the response of the presbytery five days later was cool to say the least. They stated that 'according to the canon of the apostil 1 Timothy 5.19 they could noth receawe ane accusatioun aganis ane elder without tuo or thrie witnesis', and that they would not proceed until they had such testimony.[72]

Despite attempts by John Johnston to intervene and placate Lindsay, the confrontations between Lindsay's representatives and the presbytery grew ever more heated. James VI also interceded on Lindsay's behalf, and issued letters of horning to force the witnesses to the sermon to compear before the presbytery.[73] At the same time, a letter to Lindsay on 4 March shows increasing ambivalence on the part of his agents towards Melville, who noted 'albeit he gave us ane verie guid countenance and apperit to mein verie weill to your Lord yet cald we find him nawayis myndit to satisfie ... that no inconvenienc we culd allege culd be able to pervert the wordis of the Scripture'.[74] At this meeting Melville also added rather disingenuously that he had only one vote and had little power in the presbytery, although Lindsay's agents knew full well that Melville had far more authority than he was willing to admit.

Things reached a head at the next presbytery meeting on 10 March, to which David Lindsay and John Wemyss had taken a party of witnesses who had heard Wallace's sermon. The presbytery only accepted the commissary clerk Robert Maule and John Arnot as representative witnesses, and denied them as 'apostolic' on the basis that 'thair compeirance wes to give obedience to his majesties letteris' and not to assist in the accusation out of good conscience. The meeting broke up in disarray:

> quhairupon efter ane verie hote ressouning we callit in upone our notar and taik instrumentis in his hand baith of thair refusall to give us anser in writ and of thair generall anser to our replyis qullk perturbit thaim verie mekill and movat Mr Andro Melvil to fall out in verie greit railling against us eftir this.[75]

Lindsay attempted to present a further bill of supplication before the presbytery, but nothing further has been recorded. This episode seems to have further fuelled the anger and suspicion of both Lindsay and James

---

[70]   Balcarres Papers, vol. 7, fos 56r–62r.

[71]   Balcarres Papers, vol. 8, fos 64r/v.

[72]   StAPR, pp. 215–16.

[73]   Balcarres Papers, vol. 8, fos 86r–87r.

[74]   Balcarres Papers, vol. 8, fos 75r/v.

[75]   Balcarres Papers, vol. 8, fos 79r/v.

VI towards the presbytery,[76] and Lindsay's personal humiliation at the hands of men he regarded as friends in the presbytery, coupled with the king's intense personal suspicion of the radical nature of the ministers at St Andrews, would make for a powerful combination that affected the severity of the visitation in the following summer.

The royal visitation convened at St Andrews on 7 July 1597 and continued without a break for five days, summoning the masters of the university to appear on 8 July.[77] This visitation has always been explained as a thinly-veiled attack on Melville and St Andrews as a stronghold of Presbyterianism, and much of the evidence and actions recorded by it certainly fits this interpretation. The visitation commission was large by normal standards, including 13 men in addition to the king. The suggestion that it was targeted at humbling Melville is borne out by some of the names of the sederunt. In addition to John Lindsay, Learmonth of Dairsie and his kinsman Learmonth of Balcomie were appointed to the commission, no doubt keen to get revenge on Melville for his condemnatory attitude towards them and their humiliation in the 1593 provost's election. Also on the commission was George Gledstanes, who had been transferred into St Andrews as a minister just prior to the visitation following the suspension of Robert Wallace. Wallace's right to stay in office by a directive of the presbytery had been summarily overturned by the new church establishment, and the entrance of George Gledstanes into St Andrews was a further act of the royal will. Gledstanes, a staunch royal supporter, would from 1597 onwards act as a check on Melville in St Andrews, but played only a minor role in this visitation.

One of the first acts of the commission was to establish a ruling council for the university, made up of Lindsay as chancellor, George Young as Conservator of Privileges, David Carnegy of Culluthie, and the ministers David Lindsay, Robert Rollock and Thomas Buchanan, all of whom except Buchanan were on the visitation commission. The commission banned all teaching staff not holding a pastoral post from taking part in any 'Sessiounis, Presbetereis, Generall or Synodall Assemblies'. Instead of any master from the university being able to attend these sessions a commission of three was to be chosen to represent the university, from which only one could attend the General Assembly at any time. Moreover, theology students and masters were banned from attending the presbyterial

---

[76]   Lindsay's last recorded letter of 15 March to Wemyss records ominously 'ye sall witt the king is informit that the presbiteri preatches against al qlk was don in the last general assemblie ... quherby his majestie is determined to put ordor to them'. Balcarres Papers, vol. 8, fos 73r/v.

[77]   For what follows on this visitation, see *Evidence*, pp. 196–8; Balcarres Papers, vol. 8, fos 26v, 51r–64v; *JMAD*, pp. 417–19.

'exercise' in St Andrews, presumably to stop young students from being involved in its very politically and ideologically charged atmosphere.

While there is some evidence that the other colleges were ordered to collect material together to present to the commission, the proceedings make no mention of St Leonard's. They also make only fleeting reference to St Salvator's, stating that the regents now taught according to the 'New Foundation' and that Martine still taught medicine, despite his earlier complaints that it was not in line with his traditional duties as provost. The college had still failed to organise its evidence and financial controls better, and was instructed to improve this situation. However, the two public professors, William Welwood and Homer Blair, were discussed in detail, with Welwood singled out particularly. On 9 July, the visitors found Welwood guilty of not teaching four times a week as ordered by the 'New Foundation', and he was also charged with 'the neglect of making and keeping of a register of his auditouris, and not leving *collegialiter*', charges Martine had brought against him a decade previously. A further, more serious conclusion was reached, when it was found 'that the Professioun of the Lawes is na wayes necessar at this tyme in the Universitie, and that Maister Williame Walwood, Professor thairof, had transgressit this Fundatioun, and the Act of Parliament maid thairanent', and was ordered to be deprived immediately. The removal of one of Melville's central allies in St Salvator's, who was also a particular thorn in the side of the royalist Provost Martine, must have been at least partially influenced by the political situation within the town. This is especially true when one considers that by removing Welwood the visitation was effectively terminating law tuition in Scotland, without offering a suitable alternative or replacement. Such a drastic action would indicate that the commission was more concerned with quashing Presbyterian supporters than worrying about the more detailed issues of Scottish educational provision.

Further to this, the bulk of the visitation focussed exclusively on Melville's conduct in the university, firstly in managing St Mary's. The letters summoning the masters of the university ordered Melville and the other two masters of St Mary's to appear a day before the other colleges, showing that their behaviour was top of the list of things to deal with. The visitation offered a range of sustained criticisms against the form and content of theology teaching, and against the masters themselves, and it is unclear to what extent these criticisms were entirely justified. One of the main issues was that 'doctors' of the church and the masters of St Mary's attended synods and general assemblies to the detriment of teaching. As a result the quality of teaching was 'arbitrary', in the sense that it was done when the masters felt like it. The masters admitted that there were only three as opposed to the five teaching staff projected in the 'New Foundation', but protested that the commission's complaint that 'the text of the auld and new testament [was] not teachit nor the least part therof in xii years' was complete nonsense, as was the accusation that the 'repetitions, examinatiouns and disputations' used to test students were no longer in effect. However, while the masters did state that there was a theology course being taught daily by Patrick Melville and John Johnston, and that Andrew also passed through the common-places of theology in a four-year cycle, they did not provide evidence that a four-year programme approximating an actual divinity degree was in effect, which is what the commission appear to have wanted to hear.

The perennial issues of finance and administration at St Mary's resurfaced before the commission, and the admissions of the masters on this account are fairly damning, considering the stern reprimands of the visitation in the preceding decade. While the masters stated that they lived *collegialiter* in accordance with the foundation, they admitted that the register of divinity students did not take full account of all those studying in the college, though to what extent is unknown. The students also kept the vacation 'langer nor the moneth of September', which was supposed to be the beginning of term. Melville also admitted on 10 July that he was unable to produce either a register of tacks on the college, or that he kept a breakdown of the college finances, and instead of taking just the allotted £100 and 3 chalders established for the principal in the 'New Foundation' and the £100 and single chalder due to both Patrick Melville and John Johnston as junior masters, Melville was drawing off a further two chalders for each of them. This was presumably due to the effects of high inflation over the preceding two decades on the real value of their allocated stipends, but how Melville was collecting it from the rents was not specified. Bursaries were another bone of contention, as although the 'New Foundation' prescribed eight bursars to be appointed to the foundation, Melville and his colleagues were maintaining 11 from the college rents. Assurances were made that these bursars were regularly checked for their suitability and were not allowed to hold a place longer than four years. However, a particular criticism, most likely voiced by the king himself, was that vacant bursaries were not advertised for his presentation to worthy candidates.

Melville's handling of the rectorate was the central issue of the commission. After two days of examination, he was found to 'have not performit the office of a Rector', given a vote of no confidence, and removed from the post. Ironically, one of the main charges laid against him was that neither in administration of the university nor its finances did he conform 'to the reformit Fundation and Act of Parliament' which he in all likelihood devised. However, from the surviving evidence of Melville's rectorate there was more to his removal than simple political considerations. A single, telling entry in the Acta Rectorum is all that accounts for the period from

the beginning of Melville's time as rector in March 1590 until the end of
the rectorate of his replacement Robert Wilkie in March 1608:

> For the whole period of the magistracy of these men nothing was inserted
> in this book, on account, I believe, of their modesty, because they thought
> nothing had been done by them that was worthy of setting down in writing.
> Yet it is beyond controversy that they had carried out a very many most worthy
> deeds, and each man had done so both with honour and the greatest praise, but
> without any pretence of show.[78]

This was clearly written by an ally of both men, and may well be true, for
it is clear that in the 1592 dispute with John Caldcleuch recourse was had
to Melville as rector. Nevertheless, it is equally telling that no other records
of student discipline or of legal dispute were recorded under Melville or
Wilkie. It also seems more than a coincidence that for three of the seven years
of Melville's rectorate there are no detailed records for the matriculations
of students into their respective colleges, although overall student numbers
are noted.[79] This was another significant duty that Melville was supposed
to carry out, and failed to do, suggesting that while he may have been an
inspirational intellectual and teacher he in no way wished to take on the
general administration and welfare of the university.

Before judging him too harshly, we should note that Melville did state
that he never officially accepted the role of rector, and indeed there is no
formal election noted for him. His curiously terse statement found in the
printed records of the visitation that he took up the office 'bot conditionallie,
that he sould find the concurrence of the Universitie to the execution
thairof' and a similar statement about taking up the role of principal of St
Mary's is borne out in a further comment recorded by him in the unprinted
'faultes and causes of deprivation' taken down by the commission. He
stated that he 'acknawledgis nether the fundatioun nor reformation nor
the offices of rectorie nor provestry except in setting of taks, but noth
in government'. It is unclear what he meant by this, but it suggests that
he only accepted partial responsibility for the role of rector, perhaps as a
figurehead for administration of university finances, and never intended to
take on the wider responsibilities of the role. This certainly fits with what
James Melville records of his attitude to the deposition, namely that 'he
wald have gladlie bein quyt' of the office 'for that it importeth a mixture

---

[78]   Acta Rectorum, p. 109: 'Toto tempore nihil de eorum magistrate huic libro insertum
est credo propter modestiam quia putarunt a se nihil gest[ur]um esse quod esset literarum
monumentis dignum quum tamen extra controversiam plurima dignissima gesta fuerint enim
uterque et honore quam etiam maxima cum laude sed sine ostentatione gesserunt.'

[79]   See Appendix, Table 1.

of the Civill Magistracie, with the Ministerie Ecclesiastic, war nocht from yeir to yeir the haill Universitie haid burdenit him thairwithe'.[80] This still does not explain why he reacted against the charge that he did not do the full duties of the principal of St Mary's, but does perhaps explain that in his own conscience, and knowing how involved with ecclesiastical politics he was, he never intended to take on the full scope of duties involved in both roles.

Despite these overtly political actions, there is a range of evidence that supports a more civic-minded interpretation of events at the university in 1597. The king had taken steps to establish a new commission to pursue some course of reform at St Andrews in the summer prior to the events of late 1596, showing that the visitation was not just a sudden and politically-motivated attack.[81] Other actions of the visitation suggest this was a commission primarily concerned with improving the administration of St Andrews. In terms of theology teaching, they were not simply critical of Melville and the other masters, but tried to provide them with support and to regularise teaching further. Each of the masters was to have a further two chalders of victual added to their stipend, recognising Melville's own actions in taking up extra victual for their support. The newly established council was to elect a fourth master for the college, with the consent of the other masters, providing that his fee did not come out of their income. The four were to teach a full four-year course until a fifth master could be appointed, and this course was to comprise Melville teaching the common places of theology and law and history of the Bible, the second master teaching the New Testament, and the third and fourth masters teaching a selection of books from the Old Testament. All this was to be done 'without derogatioun' of the 1579 foundation, which suggests that although the interim teaching plan made no mention of biblical languages the masters were expected to continue teaching them, until a fifth master could be appointed.

New strictures on book-keeping and staff were the most notable changes made by the commission. For one thing, the commission appeared to be focussed on revitalising the importance and authority of the role of rector, whose arbitration in university disputes and administrations was to be augmented and rejuvenated following its slump in fortunes under Melville. Firstly, they intended to institute a rule whereby the rector could only hold the post for a maximum of three years, suggesting that they wanted to see the role being effectively transferred between university staff and not allowed to languish. The printed statutes note 'ane Advocate, ane Agent, and a wryter for the haill Universitie', and each of these men

---

[80]   *JMAD*, p. 418.

[81]   Balcarres Papers, vol. 7, fo. 51r.

were to be part of a support network around the rector. The advocate, also referred to as a 'procurator fiscal' for the university, was to act on behalf of the rector as an accuser in all disciplinary matters where a master was deemed to have transgressed the foundation or been non-resident and taught less than eight times in the year. There was also an additional clause that the offices of 'Lawer and Mathematicien' be deprived after any absence of longer than a fortnight, likely aimed at Welwood's continued non-residence and Blair's prolonged absence through ill-health. The agent or 'beadle' was to act as a messenger and notifier in disciplinary cases, making sure that masters were provided with summonses similar to those given out by sheriff's messengers in civil trials. Any decisions made by the advocate and rector in proceedings would be supported by the Lords of Session with letters decretal, and deprivation enacted where necessary. The chancellor would provide support to the rector in special cases, but was not to have any greater role in administering discipline than this. The 'writer', a student who was to be sworn in formally in the presence of the other masters, was to ensure that not only the rector's acts of discipline were recorded but also that the university registers were kept up to date, and copies lodged with the local commissary court. Moreover, in response to the criticisms that the rigours of examination were not kept within the colleges, the roles of deans of faculty for both arts and divinity were laid down again. The deans were to ensure that examinations, disputations and teaching hours were kept, that registers of students in both faculties were properly administered, and that degrees were only administered to worthy students.

It having been established that there was no clear understanding of the rentals due to each college and of the tacks set on the college properties, it was decided that far tighter controls were to be imposed on finance. A central role in this process was given to the chancellor. An *oeconomus* was to be selected for each college and elected with his consent, who would give a daily account and an annual end of year account to the masters of their finances, and copies of these were to be delivered to the chancellor for his attention. If there was any surplus rental at the end of the year, the chancellor was to receive a third of it so that he could appoint bursars to the relevant college. The colleges were to receive the remainder to spend as they saw fit, and if the rents could bear it 'ane musician and player upon instrumentis' was also to be provided for each of the arts colleges. No tacks on college properties were to be set without the chancellor's consent, and if they had to be set they were only to be paid in oat meal and not in other fixed quantities of victual or money, presumably to get the best return by avoiding the effects of inflation on agreements fixed in cash. The continual problem of paying ministers in the parishes annexed to the colleges was to be solved by allocating the glebes and vicarages of each church to the relevant parish minister, thus removing unnecessary tacks and other financial agreements. Any existing tacks were to be reviewed to ensure that income due to the colleges was coming in and could be applied effectively.

Most startling in these statutes, however, was the recommendation that all staff be bound by financial interest to promoting the welfare of the college. Each principal was to find caution with a 'landed gentilman' for the huge sum of 2000 merks upon their entry to the office, which would be forfeit if they transgressed the foundation in any way. A similar sum was appointed to be found for each of the regents. The *oeconomus* for each college was to find caution for a year's worth of their college's rent which would be forfeit if there were anything lacking from their rentals. These financial strictures were something completely novel at the university, and like the regulation of legal procedure this appears to have been another attempt to make university staff accountable to government by one of the most effective means available.

Although there is no evidence that these latter proposals were fully enacted, it is clear that the actual meeting of the visitation in July was not intended to be the end of supervision by the commission. Ongoing examinations into the university appear to have continued, at least for St Salvator's. Ten days after the official visitation ended, James Martine wrote up an account of all the known prebendaries, altarages and chaplainries attached to the college and who held their right of presentation, while Homer Blair compiled a list of the college writs and evidences. These lists were sent to John Lindsay for his perusal, suggesting that his newly revitalised authority as chancellor was to be followed up with immediate effect.[82] On 19 July, a series of complaints was given in by St Mary's over the interference of the royal government in the allocation of stipends to ministers, following on from the injunction that all vicarages and glebes would be given to the local parish ministers. This again suggests that the council established in 1597 was meant to continue as an arbiter in the management of the university.[83]

A series of documents, drawn up by Lindsay in October of the same year, shows he aimed to systematise the procedures and operation of the university on a far greater scale than even the visitation records indicate. He submitted a list of almost forty questions to the university masters, trying to get further information on some of the issues of procedure raised by the visitation. These included a range of questions checking that Melville and his colleagues were maintaining their teaching and seeking clarification of electoral procedures and the roles of the various staff. Lindsay also

---

[82]   Balcarres Papers, vol. 7, fos 79r–99v.

[83]   Balcarres Papers, vol. 7, fos 226r–230v, 233r–235v.

asked for a detailed breakdown of the expenditure and economy of the university, including a request for information on the diet of the masters and students, how much bread and ale would be required to support the average member of staff, how many portions of beef could be expected from a carcass based on current consumption rates in the college, and whether servants also had their board supplied in the same manner as the masters and regents.

These detailed enquiries were actually part of a wider plan by Lindsay, reminiscent on a smaller scale of his attempts to rationalise the stipends of ministers with the 'constant platt', to provide an overarching structure of fees and board for the various foundationers. Two copies of this plan, entitled 'The reckoning of the sustentatioune of the foundit persones in the university', show he had seriously tried to work out calculations for providing board for all the members of the university from a planned centralised fund.[84] No further records survive to indicate what the wider significance of this reckoning was or whether the disparate documents given in to Lindsay in late 1597 constitute another 'mini-visitation' of the university, or evidence of the actual exercise of power by the university council. The fact that in the following month both St Salvator's and St Leonard's produced rentals for the chancellor suggests that they had some inkling of the intent of the scheme, though they presumably would have found it a highly disagreeable concept to stomach.[85] What these documents collectively show, however, is that government was no longer content to leave St Andrews alone between what had been previously sporadic visitations and high-level statute reforms. After the 1597 visitation, the influence of royal power at the university would grow in much the same way as it did in many other aspects of Scottish society, and Melville's influence in both the university and the wider ecclesiastical situation in Scotland would become increasingly marginalised. While Melville would react positively to this situation by greatly developing the provision of theological education at St Andrews over the following decade, any chance he had of establishing full control over the university was well and truly over.

Conclusion

It is clear that the religious and political affiliations of Melville and his cohorts played a large part in their growth in favour with the king in the early 1590s, and equally in their heavy-handed marginalisation at the end

---

84   Balcarres Papers, vol. 7, fos 68r–76v.
85   Balcarres Papers, vol. 7, fos 121r–131r.

of the decade. It is also clear that Melville's ability to influence university politics also rose and fell in correlation with this, and that the other masters of the university accepted the political reality and were happy to treat him as a superior until it was no longer expedient to do so. In the same way, many of the actions and recommendations put forward by the visitation council in 1597 were politically motivated, and less to do with Melville's fitness or otherwise as rector. Yet underlying this, the themes seen in the decades since 1560 continued to shape politics and events at the university in the 1590s. In terms of teaching, consistently high standards of education in Latin, and to a lesser extent Greek, were visible in St Leonard's, which was unaffected by the vicissitudes of political disruption and may well reflect a tradition there going back far further than has been previously believed. James Martine continued to augment the patrimony held by his family within St Salvator's during this decade, but with a more cautious eye on William Welwood while the star of the Episcopal party in St Andrews was on the wane. Finally, the influence of the civil government in the university continued to grow, and the natural development of the trend seen under the various regents during the minority of James VI was carried on by the king himself, with additional impetus provided by the threat he felt from the Presbyterian party at St Andrews. The turn of the century would see a radical shift back towards royal and Episcopal priorities at the university, and Melville's final decade there would be a difficult one as he tried to adjust to a university with an agenda very different from his own.

CHAPTER 6

The Rise of 'the Moderates' in St Andrews, 1597–1606

At St Andrews the decade after 1597 offers a strange contradiction in terms of sources. Not only does the evidence of reforming commissions and visitations dry up, but so too do the unprinted sources in the Balcarres Papers and the university muniments, while the narratives of David Calderwood and James Melville also cease to be interested in university affairs. There is thus a large gap in sources between the visitation of 1599 and Melville's eventual removal from St Andrews in 1606, except for some references to his behaviour and conduct in the St Andrews Presbytery. On the other hand, the period between 1595 and 1603 is the first time that we see actual teaching sources in abundance for the university, especially for divinity. What emerges from both sets of sources is the marginalisation of Melville and his colleagues in St Mary's by the royal government and its supporters at the university. Detailed accounts of the colleges prepared between the 1597 and 1599 visitations suggest that there was a growing air of stability across the university following the turmoil of the 1580s and 1590s. Melville, deprived of a voice in national church politics, seems to have focussed his efforts upon the education of local ministers and students, and on providing them with the tools to combat unorthodox doctrinal viewpoints, particulary those of Catholicism. A survey of the sources that survive for teaching at St Mary's reflects what one would perhaps expect given Melville's intellectual background – namely tuition that blended a Ramist approach to biblical exposition and exegesis with Calvinist and Presbyterian theological commonplaces. However, from a comparison with the sources that survive for arts teaching after 1597 it seems possible to detect a divergence in teaching between the colleges, with St Salvator's and St Leonard's staunchly defending the use of Aristotelian and other traditional texts above all others, including those by Ramus. Together, these sources suggest that the period of ideological ferment at St Andrews was over and, despite Melville still being in residence, a new age of royally-controlled moderation was already being ushered in.

University Affairs and Politics after 1597

In the aftermath of the 1597 visitation, James VI continued his attempts to exercise royal control over Kirk proceedings, and a growing majority of ministers seemed to support this action. The king continued to dictate when and where the General Assembly should meet, and there was no dissent when he ordered just one assembly in 1601 and then prorogued the next meeting until July 1604. The extent to which royal power was unopposed is clear from the appointment in 1600 of David Lindsay, Peter Blackburn and George Gledstanes as bishops of Ross, Aberdeen and Caithness, an action that would have been unheard of five years previously. Melville was unable to rally any opposition to this process, as he was banned by the king from attending the assembly after 1597. Even though Melville and John Johnston appeared at the March 1598 assembly as commissioners for the St Andrews Presbytery they were summarily ordered to leave as unlawful representatives.[1]

We have already seen that in the aftermath of the July 1597 visitation there was a continued correspondence between the university chancellor and royal secretary John Lindsay and the masters of the university.[2] Following this visitation the masters made a concerted effort to improve their record keeping and general administration. After the failure between 1594 and 1597 to record which colleges new students were matriculating into, the new rector Robert Wilkie ensured that this fault was remedied, and the records throw considerable light on the undergraduate student populace towards the end of the 'Melvillian' period.[3] New entrants in arts appear to have notably increased, fluctuating between 11 (1598) and 30 (1599 and 1606) per year for St Salvator's, and 14 (1598) and a high of 49 (1606) for St Leonard's. Over the decade as a whole from 1597 to 1606, there was a total of 488 recorded new students, marking considerable growth on the previous decade when numbers struggled to rise above 400. Except for 1601, when St Leonard's had 41 entrants compared to 16 in St Salvator's, there was an almost even split in the ratio of entrants between the colleges. This was a change to the trend of the previous two decades, when St Leonard's had a marginal numerical superiority over its counterpart. While this may simply be down to chance, it is possible that this reflects a conscious division of students into equal numbers among the two arts colleges, or perhaps more likely that with the resurgence of royal

---

[1]   Donaldson, *Scotland: James V–James VII*, pp. 200–202; MacDonald, Jacobean Kirk, pp. 78–82.

[2]   See above, pp. 160–171.

[3]   See Appendix Tables 1 and 3.

and Episcopal power at the university St Salvator's was again coming into greater favour and thus attracting more students.

Out of this body 274 students are recorded as receiving their MA, or just over 56 per cent. Conversely, just 79 students, or 16 per cent, are recorded as taking their BA. Taken together, this evidence suggests that the BA, which had been extremely popular in the early decades after 1560, had begun to fall into abeyance, with students more likely to undertake the entire course of MA study at the university. Whether this reflects a growing trend of stability at the university, or a growing level of student wealth, is impossible to say, but it is clear that a full degree-level education was a growing priority for Scottish students.

The records kept for divinity students in the same decade show that student numbers at St Mary's had remained largely static, rising from a total of 86 recorded students between 1588 and 1596 to a total of 95 between 1597 and 1606. It is clear that Melville's restriction to teaching in St Mary's after the visitation of 1597 had a positive effect: while numbers fluctuated between five and nine entrants for the years 1596–98, they jumped to 14 in 1599, 15 in 1600 and 17 in 1601. The known origins of the student body at St Mary's between 1588 and 1606 are also of interest, as only 29 students from St Salvator's and 39 from St Leonard's were known to have proceeded to the college. This equals just over 8 per cent of all known matriculated students and just under 14 per cent of MA graduates, which again suggests that students attending St Andrews were primarily interested in receiving a good arts degree, with very few going on to study theology at a higher level. It also meant that the remaining 113 students, or 62 per cent of the overall divinity body, were coming from other Scottish universities or from abroad, showing that Melville's reputation really was attracting a wide student following.

Following the 1597 visitation tensions among the masters at St Salvator's were still noticeable. On 19 January 1597 Martine had refused the presentation of Andrew Monypenny to the prebendary of Muirton by the Earl of Cassilis, 'in respect of his minoritie and hes age as also that the said Mr James haid put and placit ane uther [unspecified] persone alreddie therintill'.[4] Following the death of the third master David Martine in 1595, who was apparently replaced by William Cranston, Martine began to groom another member of his family for a post in the college. A royal letter of 1 March 1599 shows that Cranston had been replaced as holder of the prebendary of Balgonar by George Martine.[5] George Martine was witness as a student of the college in August of that year to the redemption of an annual rent on Markinch, the proceeds from which were to be used

4   UYSS110/J25.
5   UYSS110/K4.7.

'upone the reparatione and reedifeing of some ... decayit and ruinus pairtis' of the college, especially the 'separatione and biggine' of the tenements of the college between the steeple at the east and Butts Wynd at the west.[6] James VI also appointed full control of the chaplainry of St Katharine's to the masters of the college,[7] further showing it was stable and flourishing under the new royal and Episcopal regime.

A visitation was sent to the university by the government in July 1599 for which no other records have come to light save those already published, and which made a number of small operational changes to the university.[8] On the whole, however, it was a continuation and augmentation of the processes established in the 1597 visitation. This was probably why it was referred to as the king's 'second visitation' rather than being seen as an entirely new commission. The biggest change it made was a re-ordering of the university council, with the creation of the Lord Chancellor John Graham, Earl of Montrose as the new chancellor of the university, and a greater role afforded to George Gledstanes, who was appointed vice-chancellor. As the local parish minister and a favourite of James VI appointed in the aftermath of the 'riot' of 1596, Gledstanes' growing importance as a royal spokesman was evident in this appointment. He and Andrew Melville would come to numerous blows over the former's continual interference in the university.

The commission also made new appointments to the university council, with Montrose replacing John Lindsay (who had died in 1598), and Peter Bishop of Dunkeld, John Learmonth of Balcomie and James Nicholson replacing David Carnegie of Culluthie, Robert Rollock and Thomas Buchanan. That the visitation was following up on earlier business rather than making radically new policy is clear from the raft of rather prosaic recommendations it made. These included a note to St Leonard's to elect an *oeconomus*, and an order that a trial be made of the still extremely unwell Homer Blair for his suitability as a master.

It was at this visitation, however, that Melville was formally established as dean of theology, although the post had clearly been under discussion at the 1597 visitation. St Mary's was still an area where the council exercised greater caution and oversight than they did with the other colleges, and a number of statutes were passed to ensure that the college's financial management was reviewed by the council. There was also a minor restructuring of the theology course to reflect the fact that a fourth master had still not been found. Melville was to teach the common-places and history of the Bible as stipulated in the 1597 visitation, while John

6   UYSS110/C4.16.

7   UYSS110/C2.

8   For the proceedings of this visitation, see *Evidence*, p. 199.

Johnston was to teach a quarter of the New Testament each year. Patrick Melville was to teach the entrants in the first year 'the halie languages, with the practice thereof, in some of the practical books', and those who passed basic examinations were to be taught a third of the books of the prophets for the remaining three years of the course. The vice-chancellor, rector, the dean of theology and the other two principals were to be the annual examiners for the theology students.

The government's growing authority is also clear in the statute that asked for a formal divinity degree to be re-established, the form of which would be 'appointed by his majesty'. While official divinity degrees would not be reinstated until 1616,[9] Melville's distaste for any such formal qualification due to its Catholic overtones was clearly being disregarded. From 1600 onwards sporadic MA awards are recorded for a number of St Mary's students, with one award being made in 1600 and one in 1603, and three awards in 1601. Only the 1603 entrant, William Davidson, is recorded as having spent enough time at the college to qualify for a full degree, but it may be that the other students had also been there for a similar length of time.[10] This may be an indicator that some kind of theological degree was awarded to students who desired one before more formal qualifications were established under the principalship of Robert Howie. Again though, the image of stability and increasing royal control is apparent throughout these statutes, and the fact that there is little in the way of dissent or dispute recorded by this visitation suggests that the new status quo was broadly accepted.

Perhaps realising that the complete removal of law tuition in 1597 was a rash action, the commission ordained that the council should 'seek out an sufficient learned person in the laws' who could work as both lawyer in the college and commissary in the town, the name of whom was to be reported to the king by 1 August. Surprisingly, William Welwood was chosen to return to the college and resume his post. However, his later career in St Salvator's until his resignation in 1611, and the fortune of his family, show that Martine and his kin had clearly gained the upper hand in both the college and the town in their ongoing feud. When Melville and Welwood had been removed from their positions of authority in 1597, further moves were made against the Welwood family as a whole. Welwood's brother-in-law, James Smith, was murdered on the Anstruther Road in September 1597, and the blame for the murder was immediately laid upon the Arthurs. Both the presbytery and kirk session were heavily involved in the mediation of the feud, with a prominent role taken by George Gledstanes. However, tensions continued to run high, resulting

---

[9]   Cant, pp. 70, 73.
[10]   See Appendix Table 2.

in the attempted shooting of Welwood's sister, Esther, in the town centre by Arthur kinsmen in September 1598.[11] It was after the feud had been brought to an uneasy settlement in the first half of 1600 that Welwood returned to his post, but under severely limited licence.[12] James VI ordered the formal reappointment of Welwood to the professorship of law in June, but he was allowed to keep only the £100 cash from his salary in 1599 and had to give over the victual portion to the common use of the college as a punishment.[13] Further to this, he was to sign a humiliating bond of good behaviour before Sir Patrick Murray of Wemyss, George Gledstanes, the rector Robert Wilkie and James Nicholson. James VI was keen to see this latter stipulation enforced, as he wrote to Martine and the other masters on 3 November asking them to ensure that Welwood signed the bond, or be refused his stipend.[14] Welwood signed it before Murray, the commissary clerks David Maul and James Mitchelson, and Robert Howie in his capacity as minister of Dundee on 13 January 1601. Welwood reaffirmed this bond on 29 July 1603, and thereafter appears to have quietly gone about his duties in the college.[15]

Melville's final years at St Andrews also show how far he had been marginalised. Unable to contribute at a national level to church politics, Melville put all his energy into extending his educational programme into the presbytery for the benefit of both students and local ministers. It is likely no coincidence that from the beginning of 1598 Melville took a considerably more active role in the exercise, appearing at three different instances in the year to 'make' and 'add' to the text. He is most likely responsible for the return of students to the exercise in November of the same year, despite the royal injunctions of the preceding year prohibiting their attendance. It is also probably no coincidence that a new form of trial, the formal disputation within the presbytery, made its appearance in this year. Unlike the exercise, the disputation appears to have been a more formal and academic exercise than the simple exegesis of a text. Its first recorded instance on 23 March 1598 suggests it was triggered by a General Assembly ordinance earlier that month that had called for a common 'head' or topic in religion to be regularly treated with a public disputation and examination. The disputations were to be 'in forme of short propositionis' taken from 1 Timothy which would be written and presented to the presbytery in the first instance by James Melville. On 30 March the theses were given over by him, and the seriousness attached

[11]   Cairns, 'Academic Feud', 270–6.
[12]   Cairns, 'Academic Feud', 276–7.
[13]   UYSS110/C4.17.
[14]   UYSS110/C4.18.
[15]   UYSS200/4.

to the dispute was clear from the fact that 'all discipleine [was] to seis befoir none' so that all the masters of the university as well as the ministers could attend. Andrew Melville was chosen to be *praeses* over the dispute, while James Melville was to sustain against Robert Wilkie and the assembled ministers of the presbytery who were 'to be in reddines with thair argumentis giff the tym will serve'. Following the initial exercise, the preparation of theses was ordered by Robert Wilkie on 7 April, by George Gledstanes on 22 June, by Andrew Duncan on 28 September, by William Murray on 4 January and by David Lindsay on 5 April.[16]

In November of the following year these piecemeal disputations were replaced by a much larger and more systematic programme of 'commoun heidis of the controversies betuix the Kirk and the papistes'. This programme of 13 separate topics, repeating *verbatim* many of those found in the *theses theologicae*, was likely written by Melville, and he was to provide the disputation on the first head, 'De Scriptura'. The extended notes on the topics attack the theology of the Catholic Church, and the further subdivision of many of the topics into a list of discussion questions does bear a slight Ramist influence, suggesting their authorship by Melville. These heads were each allocated to a different minister in the presbytery, and over the course of the following year one was taken up each month in turn. After 13 November 1600 the programme became irregular, as the next entry for a head was 'De Coena' (defendant unknown) on 17 February 1602 which was then followed by Alexander Forsyth on 'De 5 Falsa Nominatis Sacramentis' on 29 April, William Welwood on 'De Praedestinatione' on 10 June and, finally, John Dykes on 'De Ecclesia' on 28 April 1603.[17] James VI appears to have been highly suspicious of these disputations, for an act delivered to the presbytery on 15 July 1602 shows he believed that 'thai and utheris that ar on the exerceis transgress the actis of the generall assemblie by particuler applicatioun in the exerceis and disavowing of thingis authorized be the assemblie', and he desired 'to hawe sure informatioun of the weritie anent that presbyterie ther behaviour in doctrine and discipline that thei be nocht exponit to sinister calumnyis'. On 26 May 1603, the presbytery decided that the disputations would in future only be held in Latin in St Mary's before the masters and students, so that the 'weak populace' might not get seditious ideas from

---

[16] *StAPR*, pp. 255–7, 339, 349, 353, 362.

[17] *StAPR*, pp. 358–9. Although a note on 26 May 1603 states 'that mair nor half a zeir syne the controwertit heidis wer dewydit and ane appoyntit for ewerie ane of the brether' (363), and one by John Carmichael on *De Conciliis* did go ahead as it was apparently suggested that he had spoken unfavourably about the king in his treatment.

the disputations. However, formal treatment of the heads did sporadically continue in the records.[18]

The presbytery records also reflect the increasing persecution and intolerance of Melville, spearheaded by George Gledstanes. In addition to his work mediating the Arthur–Welwood feud, Gledstanes also frequently deputised on royal diplomatic business, particularly after his appointment as archbishop on 12 October 1604. While he enjoyed the favour of royal privilege, he also incurred the distaste of his fellow presbytery members for his 'courtliness'.[19] A number of clashes between Gledstanes and Melville are recorded, and they show clearly that Gledstanes was gaining the upper hand in the early 1600s. On 24 September 1601 a visitation of the presbytery criticised Gledstanes for 'melling in the action betuix the Universitie and the town of Sanctandrois'. This was a reference to a dispute between the university and the town council over the university's right to elect members to the kirk session eldership, a practice which had fallen into abeyance since the previous decade. This dispute reached the pulpit in May of the following year, when Melville complained loudly that Gledstanes had 'cryit out publictlie against the Universitie as sic quha wald exeme themself be discipline, he having no occasioun except that, laitlie befoir the universitie maid intimatioun to [the Kirk] session of thair privilege'. The matter was prorogued to the wider presbytery, and Gledstanes 'promeist' that he would ensure university representation on the eldership, showing how influential he had become.

Melville's aggressive posture against Gledstanes, however, had backfired. On 8 July Gledstanes accused Melville of making unfavourable comments about him and the other ministers in St Andrews in his sermon of the preceding week on Ephesians 5:11. While Melville protested that this accusation was made with 'licht informatioun', the charge was taken seriously by the Privy Council, who were unfortunately meeting at the same time in St Andrews. Melville was warded within the college by the council, and though he was not held for any length of time the impact of this episode was not lost on him.[20] While Melville was mentioned as a member of a commission on witchcraft on 20 October 1603, the next significant reference in the presbytery records relating to him is that of the following month, where on 24 November he is recorded as being 'speciallie absent' from the presbytery meetings, and apparently had been for some

---

[18]   *StAPR*, pp. 363–4.

[19]   Alan R. MacDonald, 'Gledstanes, George (c.1562–1615)', *ODNB* [10784, accessed 20 June 2008].

[20]   M'Crie, pp. 234–5; *StAPR*, pp. 354, 358, n. 308 and 312; *JMAD*, p. 545; *RPC*, vol. 6, pp. 408–9; Calderwood, vol. 6, p. 157. On the issue of the privileges of the university, see *RStAKS*, pp. xcvii, 806, 831; *StAPR*, pp. 344, 354–6.

time.[21] The final reference to Melville in the records, on 10 January 1605, shows how much he had been placed on the defensive. He is found seeking a deposition from all the other presbytery members regarding the veracity and soundness of his doctrine as a precaution against Gledstanes.[22] It was a huge reversal of fortune for Melville, who just ten years previously had been at the height of his powers in St Andrews and would likely have never expected such a resurgence of Episcopal power.

Teaching at St Mary's under Melville

It is only in the 1590s that we begin to get real evidence of the form and content of divinity teaching at St Mary's under Melville, and what survives shows the Ramist method was indeed used at St Mary's. However, it confirms that this was done more to allow for the pragmatic exposition of biblical texts and dogma as part of a broader education in humanist education than for any implicit notion of inculcating Ramism for its own sake as a radical ideology.

A 'Commentary on the Epistle to the Romans' (*Commentarius in divinam Pauli epistolam ad Romanos*) by Melville is his only surviving set of theology lectures. Copied from Melville's own manuscript in 1601 by the Heidelberg student Daniel Demetrius, this commentary was unknown to Thomas M'Crie, and was published by the Wodrow Society in 1850 with Charles Ferme's *Logical Analysis of the Epistle to the Romans*.[23] While Melville's 'Commentary' is indeed logically and systematically organised, it does not suggest that he slavishly followed a Ramist approach in his biblical exegesis. The text is not actually a detailed commentary, but rather a summary analysis of each of the 16 chapters of Romans, preceded by a short summary of the text (the *argumentum epistolae*).[24]

Melville starts with a very general account of the text before moving on to a specific account of each of the chapters. This might suggest that at a very high level he was following the third rule of the Ramist 'method' of organising material whereby the most general characteristics of a subject

---

[21]   *StAPR*, pp. 375–6, 379.

[22]   *StAPR*, pp. 399–402, 423–7, 446–8.

[23]   Charles Ferme, *A Logical Analysis of the Epistle to the Romans, Translated by William Skae: and a Commentary on the same Epistle by Andrew Melville, in the Original Latin*, ed. W.L. Alexander (Edinburgh, 1850). The *Commentarius* comprises pp. 385–515. The endnote at p. 515 states that Demetrius took down the commentary in July 1606 in 'the space of eight days, having followed the example of Andrew Melville' (*Quem imposuit Daniel Demetrius, octo dierum spatio, exemplar Andr. Melvini secutus*). See also Cameron, 'Andrew Melville in St Andrews', p. 71 and M'Crie, endnote.

[24]   Melville, *Commentarius*, pp. 385–90.

are placed first, before moving on to the less conspicuous and more specific ones. Moreover, the way in which he summarises the argument of the epistle heavily uses dichotomy. Melville begins with perhaps the most general statement he can make, namely that the text, which he sees as 'embracing the whole of Christian doctrine' (*summam Christianismi complexa*), is comprised of a prograph, graph and epigraph (given in the original Greek and in Latin translation as *praescriptio, scriptio* and *postscriptio*) which, as the beginning, middle and end of the text, make up a perfect and sacred whole.[25]

He then goes on to expound logically the contents of each of these sections in dichotomous terms. The preface, the first 17 verses of chapter 1, is divided into two parts, firstly that of Paul announcing his apostolic duty and office toward the Romans, and then announcing his zeal and goodwill towards them. The central text, spanning the end of chapter 1 to chapter 15 verse 14, also contains two parts: a section Melville calls the *doctrina*, which runs to the end of chapter 11 and comprises Paul's exposition of the divine truth of salvation given to the human race by Christ and conferred through his Gospel. The second is an *exhortatio* in chapters 12–15 on the various ways one can lead a Christian life.[26] The final section, the epigraph, includes the second half of chapter 15 and chapter 16 and again contains two sections, the 'apology' (*excusatio*) and 'greeting' (*salutatio*). Each has two parts, the former providing a written greeting to the Romans and an apology for Paul's failure to visit them (*altera libertatis in scribendo, altera dilati adventus*), and the latter providing a 'more human greeting' (*humaniorem voco salutationem*) to those at Rome as well as a 'more religious' one calling for obedience to God that 'finishes the epistle' (*salutatio religiosor ... qua epistolam claudit*).[27]

Melville expands on this outline as he carries out a verse by verse summary of the text. However, he is less apparently Ramist in his approach, preferring to sum up simply the key points of each verse as they come up, with no especial dichotomy or arrangement. The feature that strikes the reader most is instead the focus on critically examining key words and phrases of the original Greek text, and in assessing Paul's literary ability and mastery of the epistle form. Melville adds a short philological section to his summary of chapter 1 where he outlines a series of criticisms (*Elenchoi*) to interpretations by other unspecified authors of words and phrases in the first 17 verses.[28] Melville sees this section as the thematic 'preface' (*exordium epistolae, sive praeloquium*) to the entire book, which

25   Melville, *Commentarius*, p. 385.

26   Melville, *Commentarius*, pp. 386–9.

27   Melville, *Commentarius*, p. 390.

28   Melville, *Commentarius*, pp. 391–406.

may explain why he devotes particular philological attention to it. These include justifying Paul's usage of the word δουλος (*doulos*, 'servant') to describe himself as a servant of Christ and as a bearer of the apostolic duty and office in verse 1, a defence of Paul's syntactical choice in using the verb ελθειν (*elthein*, 'to go, to come') with the participle δεόμενος (*deomenos*, 'being wanted, needed, begged') in verse 10, and an approval of his use of the phrase τουτο δε εστιν ('this is') to soften the harshness of the word στηριχθηναι (*sterikhthenai*, 'to be obliged, or bound, to do something') in verse 11. This interest in the literary and syntactical merit of the Greek used by Paul is continued throughout the text, but is also expanded to include analysis in places of the etymology of Greek words and phrases, including an account of the transmission of various words in the Gospel from Hebrew and Greek texts,[29] and a table of the various Greek forms of the names of Adam and Christ in the exposition of chapter 5, verses 15–19.[30]

There are no major doctrinal controversies in this decidedly Calvinist work, or any instances of truly original theological thought on Melville's part. Like most reformed theologians, Melville believed that Romans was a critically important text for the understanding of salvation, and he is clearly trying to impress the importance of this on his students, along with explaining the concept of justification in predestinarian terms.[31] There are, however, some instances where he is seen to give tacit support to a Presbyterian interpretation of doctrine. His exegesis of chapter 1 verse 15 states that Paul was given his apostolic office both through the authority of the Antioch Presbytery and by divine appointment from God in Acts 9, a viewpoint which Melville had engaged in heated debate over with Patrick Adamson in the 1580s.[32]

Melville's exegesis of chapter 13 and its critical passages over obedience to the temporal magistrate is extremely short and relatively tame considering his known exposure to Calvinist resistance theory and to the works of Buchanan.[33] He does state that there is a critical difference between obeying 'kind and just princes' (*benefici et justi principes*) who serve the public good and rule with the common consent of all, and obeying 'impious and unjust tyranny' (*impiam et injustam tyrranidem*) which is not legitimate and ought not to be obeyed. However, the main thrust of the text is to give a number of reasons why the legitimate magistrate *must* be obeyed and why those who resist the magistrate's authority deserve

---

[29] Melville, *Commentarius*, p. 402.

[30] Melville, *Commentarius*, p. 449.

[31] See, for example, Melville, *Commentarius*, pp. 441–59.

[32] Melville, *Commentarius*, p. 394; see also pp. 131–3.

[33] Melville, *Commentarius*, pp. 496–500.

contempt and punishment. This is hardly the interpretation one would expect from the 'radical exponent of the two kingdoms theory',[34] and delineates the distance between Melville's actual recorded thought and his portrayal in Presbyterian narratives.

Overall, the 'Commentary' fails to provide deep insight into Melville's own theology beyond confirming his Calvinist credentials. However, It is nevertheless a clear and highly effective text as an introductory criticism of Romans. Its focus on Greek syntax and etymology suggests that if this was the standard of lectures offered by Melville, he must have achieved his aim of inculcating a thorough understanding of the New Testament with specific reference to its source language in his students.

To what extent, however, is this approach reflected in the surviving texts of divinity students who studied under him? We are fortunate that seven *theses theologicae*, the pamphlets printed for the formal disputation at the end of the theology course, have survived from Melville's period as principal of St Mary's that provide some answers to this question.[35] Not only are they the earliest surviving evidence of theological teaching at St Andrews, they are also the earliest detailed examples of theology tuition at any Scottish university, all being printed between 1595 and 1602. The *theses theologicae* are unique in the fact that six of the seven defended were done so by individuals, the complete opposite of the process that took place in the arts faculty, which were defended *en masse* by the graduating class.[36] The names of the respondents show that the attestations of James Melville that the school attracted international renown were not without substance. They included Christopher Jansen (Johannides) a Dane, in 1595; Jean Masson, a Frenchman, in 1597; the Scots Patrick Geddie and John Scharp in 1600 (who became minister of Orwell and Professor of Theology at Dauphine and Edinburgh respectively); and Thomas Lundie and Andrew Morton, later ministers at Alyth and Cults, in 1602.[37] While

[34]   Donaldson, *James V– James VII*, pp. 148–50, 168, 197–200, 204–5, 266–7.

[35]   Christopher Jansen, *De praedestinatione, sive de causis salutis et damnationis aeternae disputatio* (Edinburgh, 1595); Jean Masson, *De libero arbitrio theses theologicae* (Edinburgh, 1597); Patrick Geddie, *De iustificatione hominis coram Deo, theses theologicae* (Edinburgh, 1600); John Scharp, *Theses theologicae de peccato* (Edinburgh, 1600); Thomas Lundie, *Utrum episcopus Romanis sit Antichristus necne?* (Edinburgh, 1602); Andrew Morton, *Theses theologicae de sacramentis et missa idololatrica* (Edinburgh, 1602). For detailed bibliographical information on these and all other St Andrews theses before 1747 see Ronald G. Cant, 'The St Andrews University Theses, 1579–1747: A Bibliographical Introduction', *Edinburgh Bibliographical Society Transactions* 2.2 (1941): 105–50, at 143–7, and 'Supplement', ibid. 2.4 (1945): 263–73.

[36]   James F. Kellas Johnstone, 'Notes on the Academic Theses of Scotland', *Records of the Glasgow Bibliographical Society* 8 (1930): 81–98.

[37]   Cant, 'Theses', pp. 114–15. I am grateful to Dr John McCallum for providing me with the name of Patrick Geddie's parish.

the granting of degrees in divinity in this period was largely in abeyance, these theses appear to have been connected with graduation for divinity students in that they marked the formal end of the taught theological course, much in the same way that defence of a thesis at Geneva marked the end of the course with the awarding of a 'testimonial' letter rather than a degree.[38] The fact that three of the six were Scots who went directly into the local ministry backs up the idea that the teaching at St Mary's and these disputations were a key part of their intellectual preparation for service in the Scottish church.

Each of the individual *theses theologicae* rigorously expounds a central topic of Calvinist theology in entirely standard terms. Thus Jansen discussed the doctrine of predestination and the means by which someone was elect or reprobate in 1595, and Masson discussed the nature of free will in 1597. Justification by faith alone and a disputation on the nature, causes and effect of sin were undertaken respectively by Geddie and Scharp in 1600. In 1602 the disputations had a decidedly anti-papal flavour, with Andrew Morton proving why there were only two true sacraments and why the Mass was idolatrous, and Thomas Lundie offering a disputation on whether or not the pope was the Antichrist.

In a sense, the choice of these topics is obvious, and completely expected. Following his formative experience of witnessing the Jesuits in action in Paris in the 1560s, Melville had explicitly stated that his hope for St Mary's on his accession was to create an 'anti-seminary' as rigorous in inculcating Calvinist doctrine in its students as the Jesuit schools were in inculcating Catholicism.[39] Each heading or 'thesis' within these works would have to be defended successfully by the respondent in order to pass the examination, and by having students recite 'true' dogma the masters of St Mary's were giving future ministers the practical skills necessary to defend their religion. This is especially clear from the footnotes and marginal comments at the end of each thesis citing the relevant scriptural passages they draw upon.[40] In addition to marginal references, the end of Lundie's thesis is further bolstered by over twenty quotations from scripture defending it, while at the end of the theses of Morton and Geddie there are lists of 'discussion questions' (*problemata*) to show the respondent's awareness of doctrinal issues that could be raised by others.[41] The topics of these theses are identical to many of the *theses theologicae* defended at Geneva in the same period under Beza, suggesting that Melville was following the content of

---

[38]   Gillian Lewis, 'The Genevan Academy', p. 47 and n. 13; see also Chapter 2.

[39]   *JMAD*, p. 76.

[40]   Jansen and Masson use footnotes; Geddie, Scharp, Lundie and Morton marginal comments. Lundie, pp. 6–7; Morton, p. 10.

[41]   Lundie, pp. 6–8; Morton, p. 11 ; Geddie, p. 11.

theses that he had seen during his period as a regent there.[42] The fact that each of them was defended by a single person also mirrors the Continental practice of individual rather than group disputation.[43]

The thesis on predestination defended by Jansen is the earliest surviving example in the series of seven, and is dated 10 April 1595.[44] Jansen first splits his text into two parts, the first dealing with a general outline of the doctrine.[45] He then outlines the causes of predestination, distinguishing between those who are elect and those who are reprobate, and logically proceeds through first the causes, the means, the purpose and signs of election, undertaking a similar process for condemnation.[46] The second section outlines the 'application' of the doctrine and its three main 'uses' (*applicationem et usum*), which are to remind the elect Christian to give gratitude to God for his salvation, to follow zealously his internal religious calling and to have faith against the devil.[47]

Throughout the work Jansen is at pains to stress the orthodox views of Calvinist doctrine on the subject. The basis of election is either the 'sole efficacy of passive obedience' or the 'suffering and death of Jesus Christ'. The cause of predestination is the 'will or pleasure' of God, because 'scripture suggests to us no other cause beyond this' and it would be 'rash, reckless and impious curiosity' to look for another.[48] Jansen takes specific care to point out that the doctrine of the Pelagians or Semi-Pelagians, 'who outwith God invent the causes of human salvation in humanity itself',

---

[42]   Backus, 'L'Enseignement de la Logique', 153–63; Fraenkel, 'De l'Ecriture à la Dispute'; Henri Heyer, *Catalogue des Theses de Théologie*, pp. 9–27.

[43]   Robert Howie, for example, defended a number of theses on his own while in Basle between 1588 and 1591, and sent copies back to Melville, John Johnston and Robert Rollock. Cameron, *Letters*, pp. xliii–xlvii.

[44]   Jansen's thesis does not have a date printed on the frontispiece, but a hand-written note, in what looks like Melville's hand, states 'Ad 10 diem Aprilis hora et loco solitis.'

[45]   Jansen, thesis 3.

[46]   Jansen, theses 4–31.

[47]   Jansen, thesis 37: 'Usus denique huius doctrinae sunt isti: Primus, ut perpetuo hanc doctrinam, omnem gloriam salutis nostrae unico benignissimo DEO tribuamus, & grati infinitam eius bontatem celebremus'; thesis 38: 'Secundus, ut gratitudinem nostram, per omnem vitam sanctitate & bonis operibus DEO probare, et firmam vocationem nostram efficere studeamus'; thesis 39: 'Tertius usus, ut persuasi de divina erga nos misericordia & amore in Christo firmissimum solatium hinc petamus & hauriamus in omni tentatione nostra, adversus omnia ignita tela diaboli.'

[48]   Jansen, thesis 8 (note brackets refer to marginalia, and are not used by the authors here as a way of listing points): 'Voluntatem sive (a) beneplacitum DEI supremam causam Praedestinationis dicimus: quia (b) Scriptura supra hanc nullam alia[m] causam nobis proponit, & fides simul cum Scriptura in hac unica causa nos acquiescere iubet. Ita ut huius causae (c) causam quaerere, temerariae sit audaciae ac impiae curiositatum'; thesis 20: Fundamentum Electionis & Salutis nostrae est in solo merito & unica efficacia obedientiae passiuae, seu passionis & (a) mortis Iesu Christi.'

are completely false, and follows Paul and Augustine in arguing that God did not first elect people who were worthy, 'but by election he made the worthy'.[49]

A similar process takes place in Scharp's thesis on sin. Sin is dichotomised after a general introduction as being committed either by angels or men (*peccatum est hominum, aut angelorum*),[50] and then as being 'original or actual' (*Estque originale, vel actuale*). Scharp then describes in logical form first the origin, nature, types, causes and effects of both kinds of sin.[51] In terms that could be interchangeably either Ramist or Aristotelian, the 'material' cause for original sin is the disobedience of the divine command by Adam, and the 'formal' cause of original sin takes the form of the payment exacted on every member of the human race afterwards. The causes of original sin are divided into two categories, the 'external' – the temptation of the devil via the serpent, the suspicion and envy of God by Adam, Eve – and the 'internal' cause of free will.[52] The 'effects' of sin are the ability to sense nudity and feel terror before God, exclusion from Eden, mortality and sickness, the feeling of lust, and for Eve the pain of childbirth.[53] 'Actual' sin logically follows, Scharp argues, from original sin, and is when transgressions against divine decree are either internally thought or externally acted out.[54] The work ends by detailing the main types of sin that are found in scripture, and further divides these sins into two categories of a 'lighter' type that will still allow election and a 'heavier' type that will see the condemned spend eternity in hell.[55] Scharp,

---

[49]   Jansen, thesis 16: 'Falsissimum ergo est dogmatum Pelagianorum, tum Semi-pelagianorum, qui extra Deum causas salutis humanae in hominibus ipsis comminiscuntur'; thesis 19: 'Cum Apostolo igitur asserimus DEUM antequam iacerentur fundamenta Mundi nos elegisse ut Sancti essemus, non autem, quia sanctos futuros praevidit tanquam ex operibus nostris. Neque elegit dignos, sed eligendo dignos facit, inquit rectissimè Augustinus lib. 5 ...'.

[50]   Scharp, theses 10, 13.

[51]   Scharp, theses 15–25.

[52]   Scharp, thesis 20: 'Causae vero huius primi peccati aliae externae fuerunt (a) quarum efficiens principalis fuit Diabolus, qui instrumento serpente utens, omenas animae facultates Evae ad defectionem sollicitavit ac tandem abripuit, (b) tum suspicionem invidiae et malignitatis in Deo ... (d) Interna verò causa fuit libera hominis voluntas ...'.

[53]   Scharp, thesis 21: 'Huius peccati poena Adamo & Evae communis, fuit (a) sensus nuditatis & miseri[a]e tam corporis, quàm animae; & (b) consicentiae terror, quo à facie Dei ipsos voce in iudicium vocantos sese absconderunt; denique spiritualis illa (c) censura, summaria nempe excommunicatio, & exclusio è Paradiso ... (d) singularis verò poena Evae molestum viri dominium ... (e) Adamo verò vita aerumnosa & laboriosa inflicta fuit ...'.

[54]   Scharp, thesis 30: 'Peccatum hoc variè distribui potest, estque internum, in motu mentis, voluntatis, aut affectum, vel externum, in gestu, dicto, facto, contra legem Dei.'

[55]   Scharp, thesis 34: 'Ut autem peccata (a) paria non sunt (quemadmodum Stoici voluerunt) sed alia aliis graviora & leviora, ita peccatorum poenè aliae graviores, aliae leviores sunt ...'.

like Jansen, also takes time to refute the views of other 'heretical' groups on original sin, denying not only the Pelagians but also the views of the Anabaptists and of course the Catholic viewpoint, again emphasising the central importance and inherent rightness of Calvinist doctrine.[56]

In this way all the individual theses, to some extent, give their exposition of Calvinist theology couched in a dichotomous framework, and using Ramist terms. Masson's thesis on free will starts with its definition, dichotomises it as being held by both angels and men, and then proceeds to expound logically the four states that comprise the cycle of free will, under the headings of creation, corruption, regeneration and glorification.[57] Thomson's thesis only allows for the two reformed sacraments, baptism and the Lord's Supper, and within each sacrament there are two 'material' actions, the 'external' visible ceremony and the 'internal' action performed by the Holy Spirit. The 'material' of the Lord's Supper is the bread and wine, and the 'form' that which Christ and his disciples followed. There is a double action to the performance of the Eucharist, the first on the half of the minister 'to bless and break and dispense' the sacrament, and the second on the parishioners 'to accept, eat and drink' it.[58] While Geddie's theses on justification are not strictly dichotomous like the others, the terms used to describe the nature of justification are more obviously Ramist. Thus the 'efficient cause' of justification is the Holy Trinity, the 'material cause' is the physical attributes of Christ's death on the cross and the spilling of his blood, the 'effects' of justification include the surety of salvation before God, absolution from sin and eternal life, the 'subjects' of justification are the elect, and the 'adjuncts or properties' of the doctrine are its 'unity, perfection, and immutability'.[59]

---

[56] Scharp, thesis 16: 'ac proinde non sunt audiendi Pelagiani, qui omnes in Adamo peccasse primique illius peccati reatu teneri negant; nec Anabaptistae, qui hoc nixi fundamento pedobaptisimum reiiciunt; denique nec Pontificii, qui peccatum originis non propriè peccatum, sed tantum alienae culpae imputationem absque proprio vitio esse volunt.'

[57] Masson, theses 1, 19–42.

[58] Morton, thesis 4: 'In omni sacramento est duplex material ... una externa & visibilis, nempe elementa cum ritibus sacramentalibus: Altera interna & invisibilis, scilicet Christus cum suis beneficiis'; thesis 6: 'Sacramenta alia sunt Veteris Testamenti, alia Novi ... Novi Testamenti sunt, quae illis veteribus abrogates successere: nempe Baptismatus & Coena Domini'; thesis 12: 'Coenae Sacrae materia externa est panis cibarius, & vinum fructus vitis ... Forma est, quam Christus, Evangelistae, & Apostoli descripserunt, & observarunt'; thesis 13: Circa hanc Sacramenti materiam est duplex action: una ... nempe benedicere, frangere, praebere: alia sumentium: accipere, edere, bibere.'

[59] Geddie, thesis 6: 'Causa efficiens est (a) Deus Pater;' thesis 9: 'Materialem causam unà cum Spiritu sancto disertè in Scripturis loquente ponimus Christi obedientiam usque ad (a) mortem crucis'; thesis 15: 'Effecta sunt, (a) conscientarum coràm Deo placida quies (b) gloriatio fidei, ac certitudo salutis ... (a) libertas Christiana cùm a reatu seu Legis maledictione, tum à corruptione ... ipsa denique (c) aeterna vita'; thesis 16: 'Subiectum

However, one must be careful not to overstate the point; there is no exact layout applied to all these theses, nor is there an exclusively Ramist vocabulary used in the technical intellectual language of the works. There are a mixture of phrases in each that could come from both the range of 'artificial' and 'non-artificial' arguments of Ramus, or from the ten categories of Aristotle, or indeed from the general accrued baggage of intellectual discourse as shaped by both scholastic and humanist logic. Thus, like Melville's commentary on Romans, while there is obvious exposure to the logic of Ramus in these theses, the influence of Ramism at St Mary's clearly did not lead to a complete removal of the modes of thought and language stemming from Aristotelian logic.

The thesis entitled 'Whether or not the Bishop of Rome is the Antichrist?' was one of the last two theses tried under Melville at St Andrews. Although the topic initially seems shocking, it was probably one of the safest theological subjects to expound upon in a rhetorical debate in the religious environment of early-seventeenth century Scotland. This text is interesting primarily because the central consideration of the work is to distinguish why a Catholic or Episcopal form of ecclesiastical polity is corrupt and unacceptable, and to establish the superiority of the Presbyterian to the Episcopalian mode of church government.

The text is split into two sections, the first focussing on problems of meaning regarding the word 'bishop', and the second on the same problem regarding 'Antichrist'. Lundie argues that the office of bishop was founded by the Gospels but may be either 'just' or 'unjust'. A 'just' bishop is Christ himself or a 'bishop' in the Presbyterian sense of an overseer of a single flock who governs the church in assembly with fellow bishops or presbyters.[60] The 'unjust' bishop is 'human' and 'satanic', in the sense that humans through the power of Satan began to set up hierarchies within the church. These hierarchies produced 'a regard for rank of distinction, the higher to the lower, in respect of which a man is said to be called bishop, or archbishop, or metropolitan, or patriarch, or pope'.[61] Lundie uses the term 'hierarchicopolitus' throughout the work to imply an Episcopal office that has been corrupted with worldly concerns. His final justification for

---

proprium seu ordinarium sunt electi hominess adulti'; thesis 17: 'Adiuncta seu proprietates sunt, unitas, perfectio, & immutabilitas.'

[60] Lundie, theses 1–6, esp. thesis 2: 'Episcopatus, de quo nunc agitur, est praefectura Ecclesiastica, non legalis, sed Evangelica. (a) Estque Iustus aut Iniustus'; thesis 6: 'Ordinarius Episcopatus, qui & iustus & divinus ets, ut diximus, relationem habet ad gregem & populum Christianum, id est, ad singularem (a) Ecclesiam, cui praeest.'

[61] Lundie, theses 7–12, esp. thesis 9: 'Satanicus veró Episcopatus, est is in quem humanus Episcopatus, auctore Satana, paulatim corruptus degeneravit: qui suis gradibus distinctus, relationem habet pro distinctionis gradu, superior ad inferiorem, cuius respectu Episcopus dicitur, aut Archiepiscopus, aut Metropolitanus, aut Patriarcha, aut universalis Episcopus.'

viewing the papacy as the Antichrist is that the pope is the agent of Satan who exerts a continual hold on the earth by means of his hereditary office, and who confuses both the temporal and spiritual swords.[62]

There is, as one would expect from the title and from the examples given, a heavy flavour of apocalypticism to this text, a subject Melville was himself fascinated with.[63] In thesis 18, the most detailed concluding section, Lundie provides a list of specific scriptural 'proofs' for attributing the distinguishing features and actions of the Antichrist in Revelation directly to the pope. He uses standard material found in contemporary reformed commentaries on Revelation which would have been commonplace in discussions of the text in St Mary's, but there is one significant addition worth noting. In point 13 of this thesis, Lundie attributes special significance to the corruption of the Catholic Church between the papacies of Sylvester II and Gregory VII (AD 999–1085):

> The Pope of the Romans has Satan as a *co-worker*: and along with the false miracles, and signs and omens which he brags about, each one from Sylvester 2 to Gregory 7 inclusively, with many others afterwards, has been a magician, and a necromancer, and is an adept in the wicked arts and devilish slights of their papacies.[64]

As Howard Hotson has shown, the view that the mid-eleventh century heralded the age of the Antichrist was one that would play a key role in the seventeenth century, when the millenarian movement attempted to project the coming of a final holy war into the future.[65] While this idea is not prevalent in Melville's surviving writings on Revelation, this section shows that Lundie had been made aware during his theological instruction that the popes of the eleventh century also had special significance in the Antichristian mythology among Reformed commentators, from which we can infer that the discussions on eschatological issues in St Mary's were broader than the surviving evidence indicates.

---

[62]   Lundie, theses 13–18, esp. thesis 13: 'Hierarchicopoliticus, qui cum Episcopatu Hierarchico, id est spirituali tyrannide temporalem dominatum invasit ... & coniuncto vel confuso potiùs in persona unius utroque gladio, libidinem & luxum inexplebili avaritia & superba crudelitate cumulavit ...'.

[63]   Reid, 'Andrew Melville, Sacred Chronology', 1–21.

[64]   Geddie, thesis 18.13: 'Papa Rom. Satanam συνεργον habet: (a) & praeter fictitia miracula, & signa & prodigia quae iactat, (b) à Silvestro .2. ad Gregorium .7. inclusive, cum aliis postea multis, quisque fuit magus, & necromantes, & artibus nefariis & praestigiis Diabolicis Pontificatum est adeptus.'

[65]   Howard Hotson, 'The Historiographical Origins of Calvinist Millenarianism', in Bruce Gordon (ed.) *Protestant History and Identity in Sixteenth-Century Europe, volume 2: the Later Reformation* (Aldershot, 1996), pp. 159–80.

The final *theses theologicae*, the class thesis of 1599, shows the public face of theological education at St Andrews. Entitled 'An Academic School on Subjects of Divinity for the Purpose of Seeking and Finding the Truth'[66] and defended on 26 and 27 July, they were overseen and authored by Melville. A note in the presbytery minutes in the preceding week states that Melville would like the assembled ministers to forego the exercise on the following Thursday and Friday to attend the 'publik disputis' at St Mary's, suggesting these were also presented before the members of the university council just after the visitation. Their contents suggest that, despite the condemnatory comments of the 1597 and 1599 visitations on the quality of religious teaching, instruction was orthodox, wide-ranging and rigorously intellectual.

The initial opening 'preparatory questions' (*progymnasmata*) of the text are fascinating. *Progymnasmata* were in origin training texts in rhetoric on a range of matters by the fourth-century Greek Aphthonius. Like their namesakes, they seem to have been made artificially difficult or contradictory to show off the skill of the students in debating. However, despite their slightly contrived nature, they show that debates were held at St Mary's about theological topics ranging from the relevance of Aristotle to theological teaching to the relation of 'sciences' such as logic and rhetoric to the one 'true' science, theology. For example, the first three questions debate whether scripture can be understood using the tools of logic and rhetoric, and conversely whether the importance attached to these arts can be justified from scripture. The second and third questions focus on whether the language used in these arts should in fact come from scripture exclusively rather than classical sources, and whether Hebrew is the exclusive language that should be used for both argumentation and biblical exegesis.[67] Questions 4–8 debate the importance of Aristotle, his works and the usefulness of Aristotelian terminology in theological teaching. These questions show that real intellectual effort was made at St Mary's to assess the importance of these works to theology, and again show that Aristotle had in no way been wholly discarded in favour of Ramism.

---

[66]   *Scholastica diatriba de rebus divinis ad inquirendam et inveniendam veritatem, a candidates S. Theol. Habenda (Deo Volente) ad d. XXVI et XXVII Julii in Scholis Theologicis Acad. Andreanae, Spiritu Sancto Praeside, D. And. Melvino S. Theol. D. et Illius facultatis Decano συζητησιν moderante* (Edinburgh, 1599).

[67]   *Scholastica diatriba, progymnasmata* 1: 'Utrum sacrae Theologiae & scripturae interpretatio sit ad praeceptiones artiu[m] & scientarium, quas homines ingenio & industria excogitàrunt, tanquam ad normam ακριβως exigenda: An ipsae potiùs artes & scientiae ex scriptura disceptandae & disjudicandae veniunt?' *Progymnasmata* 2: 'Utrum ut Grámatica linguae Sanctae ex Scripturis sacris petenda & probanda, ita & Rhetorica & Logica divinae dictionis & sapientiae ex eodem fonte haurienda?' *Progymasmata* 3: Utrum quicquid Graeci de Graeca, Latini de Latina lingua praeceperunt, id omne vel quaerendum in Hebraica vel praecipiendum?'

Question 4 debates whether the categories of Aristotle and of Porphyry should be kept apart from theological terminology, while questions 5 and 6 debate whether Aristotelian doctrines on the prediction of the future can be related to the doctrines of divine prophecy. Question 7 debates whether Aristotle's doctrine of questioning and responding in *Topics* book 8 can be used in theological instruction, while question 8 debates whether the validity of arguments in the *Sophistical Refutations* is acceptable.[68]

The remaining questions focus partially on theology, and partially on some problematic ideas arising from scripture that have a scientific bent to them. These include whether heaven moves and the planets are at rest, or, 'as scripture asserts', that the reverse was true, and whether 'at the beginning and first point of all time' all things were created or only the shapeless matter of the void, along with questions focussing on the order of creation in the Mosaic narration and whether the world is joined together with an inherent natural reason.[69]

The central part of the text, entitled 'brief summaries on matters of divinity' (*Aphorismi de Rebus Divinis*) is a short general exposition of Calvinist theology. It opens with a summary account of what Melville believed theology was, essentially the understandable essence of God given to us both directly by divine will and by the scriptures and biblical authors:

> Holy Scripture is perfect, transparent in itself, [is] itself His intermediary, the supreme judge of all controversies [and] of divine authority. [It is these texts], bound together in the Canonical Books and the Old and New Testaments, written together in Hebrew and Greek letters, which alone are the authentic texts and from which, in Latin or the vernacular, it is impious and close to foolish to consult in debates.[70]

---

[68] *Progymnasmata* 4–8. *Progymnasmata* 4: 'Utrum attributionis sive enuntiationes de Deo rebusq[ue] divinis omnes intra metas Porphyrianorum categorematum, vel Aristotelicarum categoriarum, vel argumentorum Inventionis logicae, ab aliis descriptorum, coerceri aut possint aut debeant?' *Progymnasmata* 5: 'Utrum Paulinae α ωοδ ειξεις ωνε ματιχαι, sint ad analyticum Aristotelicae eruditionis modum necessario vel revocandae vel exigendae?' *Progymnasmata* 6: 'Utrum divinae de rebus futuris praedictiones cum Aristotelica de futuris contingentibus doctrina conveniant necne?' *Progymnasmata* 7: 'Utrum dialectica interrogandi & respondendi ratio ab Arist. 8. top. descripta, ad Theologicas [...] traduci cum fructu & sine detrimento possit?' *Progymnasmata* 8: 'Utrum ... absque Aristotelica Elenchorum doctrina & dissolvi & profligari, vel rectius vel expeditius possint?'

[69] *Progymnasmata*, 12–15, 17–22. *Progymnasmata* 12: 'Cum sanctae literae Solem, Lunam Stellas secundum positum a Deo in natura ordinem moveri passim asserant, Caelum vero nusquam; an Christianus pie & ex fide affirmaverit Caelum moveri; Solem, Lunam, Stellas quiescere?' *Progymnasmata* 15: 'Utrum Temporis initio primoque puncto omnis omnium rerum creaturum, vel saltem visibilium Materia informis creata fuerit necne?'

[70] *Aphorismi* 3: 'Sacra haec scriptura est perfecta, in se perspicua, sui ipsius interpres, s mus omnium controversiarum Iudex, divinae authoritatis, in libris Canonicis & V. &

The text then briefly expounds the concepts of free will, justification by faith and the nature of sin, which mirror the language and material found in the other *theses theologicae*. This is followed by an exposition of the importance of natural law and Mosaic law, while the final part of the text gives a series of short questions for debate, summarising the issues raised from the preceding topics.[71] Controversial religious questions such as 'Is there only one true religion or many?', 'Is all sin prohibited by law?', and 'Should false or "antichristian" religion still be borne in a Christian republic?' begin this section, but soon give way to a series of questions relating to moral imperatives for good governance. These include questions asking whether the death penalty ought to be applied to heretics, whether it is lawful to counter force with force, whether the law of war is legitimate, whether natural law allows personal vengeance, whether marriage is a divine, civil or ecclesiastical law, and whether desertion is a just cause for divorce. There are also three questions relating specifically to witchcraft, debating how witches' bodies transform, and how their powers are enhanced by the devil, and how they should be dealt with by law.[72]

The wide-ranging nature of these topics, which go beyond simple theological issues, may have been Melville's attempt to show the visitation how theological training could inform practical matters of governance and statecraft. Fundamentally though, the class thesis shows the rigorous and systematic grounding in Calvinist doctrine that was being offered to the students at St Mary's, and suggests that allegations by the visitation commission that Melville's teaching was unstructured and 'arbitrary' did not have a strict basis in fact. It also shows that the relevance of Aristotle was still hotly debated at St Mary's, and although Melville clearly taught along Ramist lines he recognised the underlying importance of Aristotelian teaching to university education.

Teaching at St Salvator's and St Leonard's, 1597–1606

It is clear from the range of speeches in the College Orator's Book that by the end of the sixteenth century humanistic study and exposition of classical literature was a central component of arts teaching at St Andrews, at least for St Leonard's. However, the final criteria for the award of an

---

N. T, comprehensa, Hebraicis & Graecis literis conscripta, quarum aeditiones solae sunt authenticae, à quibus ad Latinas vel vernaculas in controversiis provocare stultum iuxtà ac impium est.'

[71] *Aphorismi* 4–34.

[72] See, for example, Q. 4: An omne peccatum lege prohibeatur?'; Q. 6: 'Sive una Religio vera, an multiplex?'; and Q. 7: 'An falsa Religio aut Anitchristiana etiam ferenda in Rep. Christiana?' Questions 18–20 are on witchcraft.

MA degree in both of the arts colleges hinged on student performance in defending a broad range of propositions covering all the subject areas they had been taught, where they would be ranked alongside their classmates in order of merit. This process was completed by late spring of the student's final year,[73] and the practice had developed by the end of the sixteenth century that in the following June or July the graduands would publicly defend a set of class theses, written by their regent. The laureation ceremony was a very public event and attracted a large gathering of masters, local ministers and town dignitaries, and it is likely that the practice of printing these theses as a keepsake of the event originated at St Andrews during Melville's rectorate.[74] The only two sets of arts graduation theses extant from the 'Melvillian' period are those defended at both St Salvator's and St Leonard's in 1603. The St Salvator's theses,[75] supervised by John Petrie, contain three main sections – entitled 'On the Nature of [Academic] Disciplines in General', 'On Universals, Individuals, and Second Notions' and 'On the Nature of Logic' – and three smaller sections of 'selected theses' on logic, ethics and physics. The St Leonard's theses,[76] supervised by Daniel Wilkie, contain two larger sets of theses on logic and physics, and four smaller sets of theses on ethics, arithmetic, geometry and Sacrobosco's *De Sphaera*, with a final set of 'problemata' offering some general questions for discussion.

In addition to these, there also survives a set of *theses physicae* on Aristotle's *On Generation* and *On Corruption* which were defended by Tobias Mierbeck, a Netherlandish student, in 1600.[77] These *theses physicae* are unique in the history of Scottish graduation theses, both by virtue of their exclusive focus on natural philosophy, and by the fact that they were defended by an individual. Mierbeck is recorded as a student at

---

[73] *Acta*, pp. lxxxix–cxvii.

[74] Cant, pp. 65–6; Christine Shepherd, 'Philosophy and Science in the Arts Curriculum of the Scottish Universities in the Seventeenth Century' (unpublished Edinburgh University PhD thesis, 1975), pp. 10–11. The earliest surviving set of graduation theses in Scotland are those defended in 1596 at Edinburgh, which also has a set for most years in the early 1600s.

[75] John Petrie (Praeses), *Theses aliquot philosophicae in publicam disputationem a generosis nonnullis Salvatoriani Gymnasii adolescentibus proponendae, propugnandaeque, Deo bene favente, ad fanum Andreae in scholis theologicis ad diem [15] Iulii* (Edinburgh, 1603).

[76] Daniel Wilkie (Praeses), *Theses philosophicae quaedam, a generosis quibusdam adolescentibus Leonardinis laureâ donandis, in publicam* suzetesin *propositae ... sunt propugnaturi, in scholis theologicis. Academiae Andreapolitanae. Ad 12 Calendas Iulii* (Edinburgh, 1603).

[77] Tobias Mierbeck, *Theses physicae De Generatione et Corruptione quas favente Deo Opt. Max. defendere conabor sub praesidio clarissimi viri D. M. Ioannis Echlini philosophiae professoris in alma Academia Santandreana dignissimi* (Edinburgh, 1600).

St Mary's in the 1599/1600 academic year but is not found elsewhere in the matriculation and graduation rolls, making it likely that he had come to St Andrews for some postgraduate divinity education, having obtained his MA elsewhere.[78] Although the St Salvator's regent John Echline is the *praeses* for the disputation, Mierbeck's theses are specifically dedicated to Andrew Melville, John Johnston and Patrick Melville.[79] It appears that Mierbeck chose to defend them as a demonstration of his academic skills at the end of his time in St Andrews rather than for any specific degree.

The small set of theses extant for the 'Melvillian' period are almost entirely occupied with the exposition of Aristotelian texts and ideas, and they mirror the debates and terminology found in the survey of teaching evidence across the Scottish universities in the seventeenth century by Christine Shepherd, who argued that Scottish academics remained wholly attached to Aristotle and his scholastic commentators in all aspects of the curriculum in the first half of the seventeenth century.[80] The theses on logic centre on defending formal subject-predicate logic and the correct construction and exposition of syllogisms, while those on moral philosophy are primarily drawn from the discussions on goodness and virtue found in the *Ethics*. In terms of natural philosophy, Mierbeck's work is simply a summary of *On Generation and Corruption*, with the occasional reference to *On Sense and Sensation*, and the *Meteorics*. The bulk of the *theses physicae* in the other arts theses are also concerned with the principles, effects and elements involved in the creation and destruction of things. There are no theses on *De Sphaera* in the St Salvator's theses, apparently due to there being not enough time to debate them at the laureation ceremony.[81] Those in St Leonard's practically quote *verbatim* from Sacrobosco in propositions on the nature of the sphere and its technical definition, and in discussions on the Zodiac and solar and lunar eclipses.[82]

---

[78]   Smart, 'Draft Biographical Register'.

[79]   Mierbeck, [*]2[b]: 'Clarissimis Ornatiss. D. Professoribus Sacrosanctae Theologiae in Lycaeo Andreano D. Andreae Melvino, D. Iohanni Ionstono, D. Patricio Melvino, has de generatione & corruptione Theses in debitae observanti[a]e signum lubens meritoque D. D. D. D. defendens.'

[80]   Shepherd, 'Philosophy and Science', *passim*; Christine Shepherd, 'Newtonianism in the Scottish Universities in the Seventeenth Century', in R.H. Campbell and Andrew S. Skinner (eds), *The Origins and Nature of the Scottish Enlightenment* (Edinburgh, 1982), pp. 65–85. There are some exceptions to Shepherd's overall thesis, however – for example, the curriculum recorded in 1641 at King's College shows that Keckermann and Alsted were recommended authors for reading in economics, politics and metaphysics – see 'Collegii regii Aberdonensis leges veteres de novo promulgatae anno 1641', *Fasti Aberdonenses*, pp. 230–1. I am grateful to Professor Howard Hotson for this observation.

[81]   There is a note to this effect on the title page.

[82]   Lynn Thorndike, *The Sphere of Sacrobosco and Its Commentators* (Chicago, 1949), pp. 118–42.

Interestingly, there are no formal theses on metaphysics in these early works, and here there is a distinct break with the later theses, which often feature them. The earliest surviving set of theses at St Andrews after the 'Melvillian' period, from St Salvator's in 1608, also omits a section on metaphysics, and it is only in the surviving theses after 1611 that they begin to reappear, albeit sporadically.[83] This perhaps suggests that Melville, who felt like many reformed theologians that metaphysics was overly speculative and unprofitable, was successful during his time as rector in removing it from the university curriculum. There is also further confirmatory evidence in all three theses of at least partial reading of Aristotle in Greek. Both the St Salvator's and St Leonard's theses have a range of transliterated words excerpted from the original texts,[84] while Mierbeck quotes a number of Greek phrases directly and in one proposition even debates the etymology of a Greek phrase.[85]

That said, the sources used in the St Leonard's and St Salvator's theses show that the limited evidence of progress in linguistic and philosophical study was tempered by a continued adherence to a limited range of older authorities in logic and philosophy outside Aristotle, with very little reference to the works of modern Continental scholars. In addition to Aristotle and Sacrobosco, the only other author cited in the St Leonard's theses is Porphyry on logic.[86] The evidence for the St Salvator's theses is slightly better. In discussing the various range of academic disciplines in the first section, Bodin is cited as the authority on the subject of history, and while Plato's conception of Forms is vehemently denied in the section on universals, it shows nevertheless that he was also being read in St Salvator's.[87] However, the only other authorities cited in these theses were Averroës, Avicenna, Duns Scotus and Thomas Aquinas, reflecting the highly scholastic inheritance in the college.[88]

The difference in sources is marked between these theses and Mierbeck's. In addition to discussing Plato's theories on generation versus Aristotle's, Mierbeck cites the work of a range of 'modern' Aristotelian commentators, including the Italians Gerolamo Cardano (1501–76) and Jacopo Zabarella (1533–89), and the doctors of the school of philosophy that flourished at the

---

[83]   Shepherd, 'Philosophy and Science', pp. 142, 164–5.

[84]   Petrie, 'De disciplinarum natura', theses 3, 5, 20,27, 31, 35; 'De universalibus', thesis 1; Wilkie, 'theses logicae', 1, 17, 18, 19, 21; 'theses ethicae', 3; 'theses physicae', 4, 9.

[85]   Mierbeck, theses 3, 8, 14, 21, 21, 45, 50, Corollarium.

[86]   Wilkie, 'theses logicae', 3.

[87]   Petrie, 'De discipinarum natura', thesis 14; 'De universalibus', thesis 1.

[88]   Petrie, 'Selectiores theses aliquot ex singulis libris logicis', thesis 3; 'Selectiores aliquot ethicae', thesis 4.

University of Coimbra in the late sixteenth and early seventeenth century.[89] All these authors were recognised for integrating traditional commentaries on Aristotle with the critical ideals of Renaissance humanism, including a focus on the original Greek, and were among the first to be critical of the conceptions underlying Aristotelian physics.[90] Mierbeck's theses are the earliest in Scotland by almost a decade to make reference to Zabarella. His reading of such contemporary Continental scholarship shows a divergence from Scottish academics in keeping up with the latest intellectual trends.

There is also a marked difference between the organisation and style of Mierbeck's theses and those of the arts colleges, and they further suggest that Ramism as a teaching method was largely confined to those under the supervision of Melville and his colleagues. There is no evidence of the Ramist 'method' or of dichotomy in the arts colleges theses, save that the first proposition in each section of the St Leonard's theses begins with a general definition of the subject under discussion before moving on to specific issues. Mierbeck's thesis, conversely, seems clearly guided by Ramism. Instead of providing a commentary on the text of *On Generation and Corruption* as it is organised by Aristotle, Mierbeck begins with a highly generalised statement outlining the context of the work in reference to Aristotle's other texts on physics, and then proceeds to move through the contents of the work in increasingly specialised terms. Theses 2 to 12 discuss the basic principles of matter, form and privation underlying Aristotle's generative theory, before moving on in theses 13 to 29 to discuss in turn each of the six factors that can specifically affect matter, including generation and corruption, alteration, growth and decrease, contact, acting and being affected, and mixing. Theses 30 to 45 take this discussion to the level logically following this, treating the four basic underlying elements of cold, heat, wetness and dryness and their relationships with one another, before ending the discussion in the last four theses and summary 'collarium' outlining the 'efficient and common end' of generation and corruption.

This reordering of Aristotle's text, which treats first on the factors affecting matter before proceeding to the principles underlying it, suggests Mierbeck is following the Ramist 'method of prudence' in arranging his text to make the discussion more palatable and straightforward to his listeners. This is further evidenced by the fact that he pauses at regular points to restate what section of the text he is about to discuss,[91] and also uses dichotomy to split a number of his theses.[92] Again, it appears from this evidence that Mierbeck, being taught by Melville and his colleagues

---

[89]   Mierbeck, theses 22, 48–9, Corollarium.
[90]   Shepherd, 'Philosophy and Science', pp. 64, 210–11.
[91]   Mierbeck, theses 2, 14, 30, 47.
[92]   Mierbeck, theses 31, 42, 44, 49.

in St Mary's, was more willing to embrace Ramist ideas than the masters of the arts colleges.

The section of the St Salvator's theses on the 'Nature of Logic' shows that the formal Aristotelian approach to logic continued to be defended in the college against the new ideas brought to St Andrews by Melville, even two decades after his arrival there. Although this section of some twenty theses looks on the surface as innocuous and dry as the rest of the text, it contains a number of pointed criticisms that relate specifically to Ramus and his 'method', though Ramus himself is not mentioned by name. The first two syllogisms of this section defend logic as a discipline in itself and attack an unspecified type of logic that only has a limited usefulness when it is 'brought to bear upon the teaching of other disciplines', which sounds like a description of Ramism by its detractors. The fact that it is curiously referred to here as 'that logic of yours' (*logica ista*) may perhaps be a pointed criticism of Melville and his colleagues who would likely have been present at the graduation ceremony.[93] The third, eighteenth and nineteenth syllogisms in this section state that only the formal syllogism is the true subject of logic. It serves a very specific, and essential, technical function of forming and analysing arguments in the mind so that formally 'true' propositions can then be discerned from false ones. Only the syllogism and the 'proper outcomes' attached to it belong to the discipline of logic, suggesting by default that the less formal method of argumentation developed by Ramus is incompatible with this model.[94] However, the strongest evidence that this section is not just a general defence of the rightness of Aristotelian logic is found in theses 23 to 26, where a sustained attack on specifically Ramist terms is enjoined. Thesis 23 states:

> If anyone thinks that 'Method' or a system can be a logical discipline in itself, he not only overturns the aim of logic of discerning true from false, but in our opinion at any rate he will never deliver an account of a single, adequate and reciprocal end to logic: so ['Method'] is not a suitable [academic] subject. [95]

---

[93]   Petrie, 'De natura logicae', thesis 2: 'Logica ista, sive docens sive in usu posita una eademque manens specie disciplina, in proprium ultimumque finem neque cognitionem subiecti sui propositam habet, neque moralem actionem, neque in externa material operationem ullam, sed tantum certam utilitatem adderendam percipiendis tradendisque Disciplinis aliis.'

[94]   Petrie, 'De natura logicae', thesis 3: 'Illud est Subiectum logicae, cuius explicatio primario in logica suscepta est. Ergo Syllogismus est Subiectum logicae'; thesis 19: 'Tres ergo solos logicae fines proprios agnoscimus: formationem notionis Syllogismi in animo nostro, Constructionem Syllogismi realis beneficio eius notionis formatae, & Discriminationem veri a falso eius constructi Syllogismi beneficio.'

[95]   Petrie, 'De natura logicae', thesis 23: 'Si quis Methodum, sive odinem per se logica disciplinae esse putet, is non solum illum logicae finem veri a falso discernendi eversumit [*sic:*

Theses 24 to 26 take to task the Ramist terms of 'invention' and 'disposition', and the Ramist dichotomy of all logical teaching into two categories. Theses 24 and 25 state that Aristotle only used the term 'invention' to refer to the 'ultimate end of logic of discerning true from false', and the term 'disposition' to refer to the middle term of a syllogism, and that he 'rightly did not acknowledge' any other usage for these terms.[96] Attacking the sublimation of rhetoric into logic under the Ramist method, thesis 26 states that many parts of logic, including 'category, noun, verb, enunciation, and the correct way of questioning and responding', do not fit into the neat Ramist dichotomy under these terms, and so it is 'quite inept' to try to shoehorn them in.[97] While we have to be careful here to attribute criticism of Ramus to these theses when he is not specifically mentioned, it is nevertheless clear that the masters of St Salvator's continued to be vehemently defensive of the authority of Aristotle.

Although there are no further sets of theses to better our understanding, judging from the authors and examples cited above it appears that philosophical teaching in the arts college at St Andrews in this period never turned fully away from Aristotle. In many ways, Mierbeck's theses are the exception that proves the rule. As a student under Melville, his critical engagement with 'modern' Aristotelian commentators and the usage of the Ramist 'method' to structure his work stands in sharp contrast with the approaches and authors adopted by the masters of St Leonard's and St Salvator's, who treated Ramism with thorough scepticism and disdain. Also, the fact that the traditional method of disputation and logical analysis appears to have co-existed alongside the humanist orations in the College Orator's Book can be taken as evidence that two very different but complementary academic styles were incorporated into MA teaching, and this continued throughout the post-reformation period at the university. If this is the case, then we have to revise the simplistic viewpoint that with the advance of humanism in Scottish education, traditional approaches to formal logic were summarily thrown out. If the *theses philosophicae* are anything to go by, logic continued to dominate the arts curriculum right

---

evertit], sed nex is nostra quidem sententia, unum unquam logicae adequatum ac reciprocum finem reddere valebit: immo nec idoneum subiectum.'

[96]   Petrie, 'De natura logicae', thesis 24: 'Omnis Inventio logica proprie ad illum ultimam logicae finem spectat discenendi ver a falso: Merito ergo Arist[otle] non aliam in logica sua ivnentionem agnovit ...'; thesis 25: 'Omnia dispositio logica eorum est, in quibus disponendis naturam ab arte logica iuvari operae pretium est: Merito igitur Aristotle in logica sua non aliam agnovit disospitionem ...'.

[97]   Petrie, 'De natura logicae', thesis 26: 'Pleraeque sunt partes Logicae, quae neque ad inveniendam neque ad disponendum spectant proprie: ut pars de Categ[oria], de Nomine, Verbo, Enuntiatione, ac recta interrogandi ratione, & de recta ratione responendi &c: Inepte igitur admodum in Inventionem & Dispositionem distribuitur Logica.'

through the 'Melvillian' ascendancy, to enjoy renewed life in the more conservative environment of the seventeenth-century university.

Conclusion

While Melville would continue in his role as principal of St Mary's until he was called to Hampton Court in August 1606, the political and intellectual momentum at the university had clearly swung away from him and his party, perhaps as much as a decade before this. The increasing difficulty he had in making his voice heard, even in university affairs and in the local pulpit, reflects the growing intolerance that the king held for radical religious dissidents, and his attitude was represented in St Andrews by Gledstanes. Although the university was clearly developing and expanding in this period, and reaching a level of stability and solvency previously unseen, it was a process that was largely out of Melville's hands. He clearly continued to attract a wide range of students, and obviously provided erudite and accomplished theological education. However, there was clearly a further divergence intellectually in teaching method and content between Melville and his more conservative counterparts in St Salvator's and St Leonard's. They had perhaps absorbed a greater sense of the importance of the classical languages from Melville, particularly in reading Aristotle in the original Greek. Yet they had discarded the rest of his reformed teaching programme, particularly his adherence to Ramus and his methods, which by the turn of the century must have appeared increasingly out of vogue. In his final years at the university, frustrated and isolated, it must have been hard for Melville to believe he had achieved any real measure of the reform programme he had planned two decades earlier.

CHAPTER 7

'Godly' Humanism, Civic Control: Scotland's Protestant Arts Colleges, 1582–c.1606

Between 1574 and 1606, the progress of Melville's intellectual reform programme was less than sweeping across the 'ancient' universities of Scotland. Both King's College and the colleges at St Andrews outwith his direct control largely failed to engage with his innovations, and although he left Glasgow fully reformed in line with his programme, a severe political backlash against the students and masters for their support of radical Presbyterianism in the half decade following his departure seriously hampered the college's ability to function.[1] However, in the last two decades of the sixteenth century new centres of higher education were established across Scotland in locales as far apart as Edinburgh (1583), Fraserburgh (1592) and in New Aberdeen (1593), the burgh adjacent to the village of Old Aberdeen that housed King's College. These institutions owed nothing to the old Catholic Church, and were founded wholly in line with the aims of the local Protestant population, and the magnates and authorities that supported them, to provide a 'godly' education for their children. To what extent did Melville have a role in their foundation and development, and to what extent were they engendered by other factors and parties outwith his control?

There is no simple answer to this question. Firstly, these Protestant 'arts colleges' were founded as part of a much broader academic trend sweeping Europe in the wake of the reformation, albeit one that Melville was familiar with. When Edinburgh, Fraserburgh and Marischal College, Aberdeen (named for its patron and founder, George Keith, fourth Earl Marischal) were established, higher education across the Continent and the British Isles was undergoing exponential growth and change. Out of 137 new universities and higher academies founded between 1500 and 1790, 47 were founded in the half century after 1551 when tensions between rival confessions across Europe were at their height.[2] These new institutions, Protestant and Catholic alike, were all founded in some

---

[1] See above, Chapters 3–6.

[2] Frijhoff, 'Patterns', p. 71.

measure to promote their respective faith among the youths in their localities. While the 16 new Protestant institutions founded in this half century were closely monitored and heavily influenced by their relevant ecclesiastical authorities, it was the state or local magisterial authorities that played the central role in controlling them. Monarchical and magnatial elites were also important in conferring legitimacy on these new Protestant institutions, as with the removal of the papacy as their sponsor so too went their universally recognised status as purveyors of higher education, most notably in the abolition of their right to confer the *licentia ubique docendi* and associated degrees.

These new confessionally-oriented institutions took a bewildering variety of forms, so much so that the most extensive analysis of their proliferation and development deliberately eschews any attempt to group or categorise them.[3] However, in relation to developments in Scotland the example of the Genevan Academy (founded 1558) and the precedent it set for higher education in Calvinist territories is highly significant. Described by one observer as lacking 'any formal, imperial, noble, or even papal privilege',[4] and developing upon the model of Protestant colleges established at Zurich, Berne and Lausanne in the 1520s, the two schools of the academy collectively focussed their curriculum around a broad education in the liberal arts with explicit higher training in divinity. These twin areas were supported by a comprehensive structure of fixed classes and examinations, and overall the programme at the Academy was enriched by a range of professors in endowed chairs in the humanities, and in linguistic and biblical studies. However, a key difference between Geneva and its Catholic counterparts was a conscious lack of any formal degree completing the educational process, with students instead receiving a *testimonium vitae ac doctrinae* relaying their abilities and education to their prospective employer or church at home.[5] As in matters of worship, the traditional symbols and icons of Catholic education were removed at Geneva in favour of a focus on the importance of an individual's own educational experience.

The model of the Genevan Academy was adapted, with some local variation, in a range of Calvinist 'arts colleges' established at Leiden and Helmstedt (both established 1575/6), Orthez (1583), Franeker (1585), Dublin (1592), Uppsala (1595), and in the French Huguenot academies founded or established in place of existing Catholic universities at Nimes

---

    3   Frijhoff, 'Patterns', p. 64.

    4   Notker-Hammerstein, 'Relations with Authority', in Hilde De Ridder-Symoens (ed.), *A History of the University in Europe, volume 2: Universities in Early Modern Europe (1500-1800)* (Cambridge, 1996) , pp. 114-154, at p. 117.

    5   Maag, *Seminary or University?*; Lewis, 'The Genevan Academy'.

(re-founded 1561), Saumur (1596), Montauban (1598), Sedan (1599) and Die (1601).[6] Collectively, these institutions were all controlled by their respective local and ecclesiastical authorities: the Genevan Academy was managed in an uneasy sharing of power between the *Compagnie* of Pastors and the city council, while the Protestant institutes in the Holy Roman Empire and Protestant France were largely answerable to their local Elector or *Duc*, and those in Leiden, Uppsala and elsewhere were governed by their municipal authorities.[7]

All three of Scotland's post-reformation foundations were part of this European-wide group, with Edinburgh and Marischal College founded by the ministers and councillors of their respective towns, and with Marischal and Fraserburgh enjoying the backing and patronage of their local Protestant magnates. The royal government conferred legitimation on all three foundations with letters of authorisation or parliamentary ratification, or both; all three were focussed around a core of arts and theological tuition; and although Fraserburgh would prove to be abortive in the opening decade of the seventeenth century, both Edinburgh and Marischal would later enjoy considerable expansion, as Geneva did, with the addition of specialised professorial chairs in a variety of disciplines.

Melville had extensive experience of the educational paradigm of these Calvinist colleges from his own time on the Continent, and a long chain of historians have, until very recently, supported the view that he was responsible for importing this model into Scotland. This opinion is justified by the fact that many of the components of the curriculum at the new Scottish institutions, along with several of their early staff, owed their intellectual formation to Melville. However, if we scratch the surface of their respective foundations and early histories, we find an altogether more complex picture than one that simply favours Melville as the predominant force behind their creation. At Edinburgh and Marischal, the aims and objectives of the town councils for the colleges in their communities often stood at odds with those of the other parties involved in their creation, whether they were the crown, local magnates, or the Presbyterian intelligentsia. A variance between 'Melvillian' and conservative ideologies can also be seen internally at the institutions themselves, if the fragments of early teaching evidence at Edinburgh can be taken as indicative of the debates taking place within their walls. What emerges from these sources is a complex picture of intellectual life at the early college that does not easily fit a reductive 'pro-' or 'anti-Melvillian' model, and that was clearly in flux in the college's opening decades.

6   Frijhoff, 'Patterns', pp. 85–7.
7   Notker-Hammerstein, 'Relations with Authority', p. 117.

A similar divergence of purpose can also, surprisingly, be seen at work in a sequence of events at Glasgow, the site of Melville's original foray into reform. In the aftermath of the disturbances at the university in the early 1580s, the town council took a number of actions to re-assert control over the college in line with the 'town foundation' they had first suggested in 1573, and did not rest until they had asserted a measure of supervision similar to that exercised by town councils elsewhere. While Glasgow did not become a 'tounis college' after the fashion of Edinburgh or Marischal, events there do suggest that the ideals of locally-controlled higher education were gaining ground in Scottish urban society in the closing years of the sixteenth century, in direct opposition to Melville's programme of reform.

Scotland's First Protestant Arts College: Edinburgh University

The motivations behind the foundation of Edinburgh University, which opened its doors on 10 October 1583,[8] has been the most hotly contested topic in debates on early modern Scottish education. Plans to create a liberal arts college in Edinburgh began in 1558, when Robert Reid, bishop of Orkney, bequeathed in his will the sum of 8000 merks for the creation of three schools – of grammar, arts, and canon and civil law – within a single college in Edinburgh.[9] The vicissitudes of the reformation and the ineptitude of Reid's nephew and chief executor, Abbot Walter of Kinloss, meant that the intended foundation did not materialise, until in the course of 1579 the town council of Edinburgh, in conjunction with a group of Edinburgh ministers headed by James Lawson, a close ally of Melville, put forward the suggestion that 'ane college of theologe' be established on the old site of Trinity College in the north-east of the burgh. Numerous difficulties of financing and siting meant that plans for the college stalled for almost two years, and were resumed only in November 1581, when a council loyal to Esmé Stewart the Duke of Lennox and the king came to power. With commissioners attached to the supplication process including Patrick Adamson and the earl of Arran, Parliament was petitioned to confirm the royal grant to the town in 1567 of the holdings of the old church within the burgh and to secure the funds of Bishop Reid's original bequest.[10] On 14 April 1582, a foundation charter was secured for a *studium generale* from James VI that ratified the grant of 1567 and granted ownership of the

---

[8]   Anderson, Lynch and Phillipson, *University of Edinburgh*, p. 3.

[9]   David B. Horn, 'The Origins of the University of Edinburgh', *University of Edinburgh Journal* 22 (1966): 215–17; Anderson, Lynch and Phillipson, *University of Edinburgh*, p. 6.

[10]   Lynch, 'Edinburgh's "Toun College"', pp. 5–7.

Kirk o' Field site to the college under the discretion of the provost, town council and baillies, with licence to them to annex further benefices for 'the sustentation of the ministry, help for the poor, repair of schools, [and] advancement of letters and knowledge'.[11] Yet again there was a further delay until the college was hastily opened in October 1583, with the first principal Robert Rollock, an ex-regent of St Salvator's, appointed in the month prior.[12]

Interpretations of the early history of the college centre on how far its initial foundation was both developed and controlled by those loyal to the Presbyterian wing of the church and intellectually affiliated with Melville, or by conservatives loyal to the government and interests of the burgh. James Kirk is the most recent in a long line of Edinburgh University historians to argue that the impetus for the college put forward by the ministers in 1579 was carried forward by James Lawson in 1582, and it was Lawson who also ensured the selection of Rollock as principal.[13] However, the work of Michael Lynch, based on his extensive research into the impact of the reformation on the city of Edinburgh,[14] provides a compelling case that the political reality of the college settlement was far more protracted and contingent on burgh politics than a simple insertion of 'Melvillian' values would allow. Lawson was out of favour when the town provost Alexander Clark, who served continually from 1579 until 1584, was successful in securing the foundation charter with the aid of the duke of Lennox and the earl of Arran in April 1582. Moreover, the break following the release of the charter and the resumption of plans for the college seems undoubtedly to stem from the turbulence caused by the Ruthven Raid. During the year that the Raiders were in ascendancy, a new radical town council, allied with the city ministers, attempted to hijack the town plans for the college, only to be thwarted following the king's escape and the regime's collapse in June of the following year. It was this town council that attempted to rush through a settlement for the college in the third quarter of 1583, knowing full well that their year in office would be over by 1 October. The purge of the town council, the largest since the removal of the pro-Catholic council at the hands of the Lords of the Congregation in 1559, meant that the men who initially employed Rollock were not the men he eventually answered to, and the process was completed on 16 October when two of the city's

---

[11]   *Charters, Statutes,and Acts*, pp. 11–12.

[12]   *Select Works of Robert Rollock*, ed. W.M. Gunn (2 vols, Edinburgh, 1849 and 1844), vol 1, p.lxiii–lxiv.

[13]   Kirk, '"Melvillian" Reform', pp. 292–296; Horn, 'The Origins of the University of Edinburgh', 297–305.

[14]   Michael Lynch, *Edinburgh and the Reformation* (Edinburgh, 1981); Anderson, Lynch and Phillipson, *University of Edinburgh*, pp. 3–23; Lynch, 'Edinburgh's "Toun College"', 1–13.

baillies, William Little and Henry Nisbet, supervised the introduction of a conservative curriculum for the university specifically geared to teaching the youth of the city.

When Edinburgh is placed within the context of events at the other universities at the critical juncture of 1583, the explanation of events favouring the royal and local government should come as no surprise. As we have seen, with the failure in the same year of the General Assembly to secure a new foundation at Aberdeen due to governmental pique, the disruption at Glasgow over temporal and ecclesiastical boundaries exacerbated by the radical attitudes of the staff and students, and the hamstringing of reform in St Andrews caused in part by Melville's aggressive involvement in church politics, it is little wonder that Edinburgh's foundation became a political game that was only decisively won by the crown with the escape of the king from the Ruthven Lords.[15]

However, political events are not the only dimension to this debate, and one overlooked issue relating to Edinburgh's early history is whether 'Melvillian' reform made its presence felt intellectually in teaching at the college, particularly under its first principal, Robert Rollock. Rollock had taken his MA at St Andrews between 1574 and 1577 under the regent John Carr, and after graduating taught as a regent in St Salvator's. When the Melvilles transferred to St Andrews in 1580 he combined his own teaching duties with higher studies in divinity and biblical philology at St Mary's.[16] Lynch argued that the relatively short period Rollock spent absorbing divinity teaching from the Melvilles would not have counteracted his much longer period of intellectual fermentation in the staunchly Aristotelian environment of St Salvator's, and although Rollock was a talented theologian, the only definitive evidence that he was anti-Aristotelian was a single reference in his sermon on 1 Corinthians 2 where he attacked scholastic philosophers for having 'turned the gospel of Jesus to Aristotle'.[17]

While it is certainly true that Rollock was likely exposed to a spectrum of intellectual influences in St Andrews during the 1570s and 1580s, there is considerable contemporary anecdotal evidence that Rollock encouraged the use of the Ramist method in early teaching at Edinburgh, and many of Rollock's writings are wholly based on Ramist organisation. A major output of his published oeuvre were logical analyses of scripture, which included commentaries on Ephesians (1590), Daniel (1591), Romans (1594), Thessalonians and Philemon (1598), Colossians (1600), Galatians

---

[15]   See above, Chapters 3 and 4.

[16]   Kirk, '"Melvillian" Reform', pp. 289, 294.

[17]   Lynch, 'Edinburgh's "Toun College"', 8–9.

(1602) and Hebrews (1605).[18] All these commentaries follow the same format, beginning with a general *argumentum* outlining the structure and contexts of the biblical passage under examination at the start of each work. They each then proceed to a chapter by chapter exposition of the text, each chapter opening with a further summary of its contents and then tackling each verse in minute detail. As we have seen already, the treating of material in general terms before proceeding to the more specific is typically Ramist, and these works shared much intellectually and methodologically with Johannes Piscator's partially completed Ramist exposition of the whole of the Old and New Testaments. Indeed, Piscator himself found so much common ground with Rollock's work that in 1601 he prepared a posthumous edition of Rollock's commentaries on Thessalonians and Philemon, with some additional notes and corrections of his own.[19]

Rollock is well known as one of the leading early exponents of covenant theology, and his treatises on systematic theology not only betray a greater debt to Ramism than his logical commentaries, but also reflect the fervent and polemical anti-Roman stance he likely gained from Melville's teaching at St Andrews. Rollock's 'A Treatise of God's Effectual Calling' (*Tractatus De Vocatione Efficaci*), first published in Latin by Robert Waldegrave in 1597 and then in English translation by Henry Holland in 1603, features some of the most explicitly Ramist organisation of any Scottish text of the period.[20] The 'Summary of Theology' attached to the 1597 edition[21] is a highly condensed exposition of Rollock's vision of a reformed systematic theology, and is couched in such a clear and dichotomising logical framework that it could be easily represented in diagrammatical form. The summary begins by first splitting theology into two general heads, one 'of God' and the other 'of the works of God'. After subdividing 'of God' into two divisions (God's nature and his essential attributes, and the Trinity) Rollock then tackles the second head, dividing God's works, decrees and providence into the elements of these aspects which are eternal and outwith time, and those that are executed within time. He then dichotomises those that are executed within time into the creation of all things and the government of all things; subdivides creation into two forms of rational creatures, angels and men; and then under the heading of men proceeds to offer a logical exposition of man's innocence, sin and restoration, Christ's role as mediator in this restoration and the benefits he confers including

---

[18]   Kirk, '"Melvillian" Reform', p. 293; *Select Works of Robert Rollock*, vol. 1, pp. lxxxix–xcv.

[19]   The sub-title of the revised edition reads: 'additae sunt necessariae quaedam notae per Johannem Piscatorem'; *Select Works of Robert Rollock*, vol. 1, p. xciii.

[20]   *Select Works of Robert Rollock*, vol. 1, pp. 29–288.

[21]   *Select Works of Robert Rollock*, vol. 1, pp. 23–8.

election and predestination, and the central blessings that logically follow God's calling man in Christ, including scripture and the covenants of works and grace, love, repentance and faith. Supplementary subjects to this logical framework are the sacraments and the church, which arise from these blessings, and the discipline of the church.

The broader text follows a similar dichotomous branching, beginning in the first chapter with an outline of God's calling the elect to salvation through both the covenant of grace and through faith itself.[22] Chapters 2 to 5 give a summary exposition of the covenants of works and grace and who is included under them.[23] Chapters 6 to 23 outline God's covenant as written in scripture and provide a sustained defence of the primacy of scripture above the established church, the pope and his councils, and Catholic tradition.[24] This section also includes an erudite history of the codification and translation of scripture from the original Hebrew and Greek versions of the Testaments, with a polemical defence of the necessity of vernacular translations in order to allow the people to hear the word. Chapters 24 to 38 look at the characteristics of sin and the blessings conferred on humanity by God's election, and the work concludes with a 'Catechetical Exposition of the Modes of Revelation', an imaginary dialogue of questions and answers that effectively summarises the entire work and reaffirms the understanding of the reader in practical terms.[25]

In addition to the lengthy defence of the primacy of scripture in chapters 6–23, at every stage of the work Rollock regularly pauses to restate his doctrine with an attack against the corresponding Roman Catholic viewpoint, again reflecting the teaching practice in St Mary's. Chapter 5 attacks the Catholic view of the covenants, and chapters 28, 31 and 36 attack the Catholic views of sin, faith and repentance.[26] Rollock's favourite target is the Jesuit and Roman Catholic Apologist Robert Bellarmine (1542–1601), whose most famous 4 volume work *Disputationum Roberti Bellarmini ... de Controversiis Christianae fidei, adversus hujus temporis Haereticos*, is refuted throughout the text, but there are many others Catholic authors attacked by Rollock.[27]

22   *Select Works of Robert Rollock*, vol. 1, pp. 29–33.

23   *Select Works of Robert Rollock*, vol. 1, pp. 33–61.

24   *Select Works of Robert Rollock*, vol. 1, pp. 61–160.

25   *Select Works of Robert Rollock*, vol. 1, pp. 160–273; 274–88.

26   *Select Works of Robert Rollock*, vol. 1, pp. 55–61, 188–94, 212–28, 248–51.

27   Particularly Bellarmine's belief in placing traditions of church above potential deficiencies of scripture, see *Select Works of Robert Rollock*, vol. 1, pp. 96–9, 145 and 151. Rollock's opponents included the anti-Lutheran writers Johannes Eck (Professor of Theology of Ingolstadt and author of *Enchiridion controversiarum*); Albert Pighius (author of *Assertio hierarchiae ecclesiasticae*); Melchior Canus, a Spanish theologian and Professor of Divinity at Salamanca, and ultimately Provincial of Castile; Thomas Stapleton, who became Royal

While this massive piece of work was organised within a Ramist framework, Rollock was equally at home writing highly condensed and effective Ramist summaries, as his 1594 tract *De Aeternae Mentis Divinae Approbatione et Reprobatione* shows.[28] Published on a single sheet of broadside, the text is dichotomised in exactly the same style as the summary of theology attached to the 'Effectual Calling'. Beginning with the statement that God either favours or condemns someone for eternity (*DEUS ab aeterno vel approbat vel improbat aliquid*), it then logically proceeds through the salient features of approbation before moving on to condemnation, and uses the same format to explain both in increasing levels of detail.

It would be remiss, however, to characterise Rollock's entire extant works as Ramist, as this is simply not true, and to try and pigeonhole him as either wholly Ramist or not is oversimplifying matters. While Rollock's densest theological works show organisation around Ramist principles, his broader writings, including his sermons and the lectures that he preached publicly before students in the magistrand's hall at Edinburgh, betray little if anything of a Ramist influence, and are accessible, homely and clearly geared towards a less rarified audience.[29] The considerable attention that has been paid to Rollock's single quotation in his sermon on 1 Corinthians 2,[30] where he criticises Catholic scholastic theology for its dependence on Aristotelian logic, is often used to show Rollock as an anti-Aristotelian and by extension as a Ramist. However, this is missing the implicit anti-Roman connotations of his wider argument:

> [Paul says] 'Na man can see the thingis that ar in God bot the Spreit of God.' ... Now the Apostle heir he meitis the verie pride of the hart of man, that he will conceit of himself, that he be his Spreit will seirche the thingis that is in God ... Suppois thou were ane Monarch, thou art over pert [too bold] to tak on thee to judge of thingis that is spirituall, and spokin spirituallie. This same is the pryde of the Papistis this day. Out will he cum, ane Thomist, ane Scotist, that hes the spreit of ane man onlie, and ane very subtile, or rather ane Sophistical Spreit, ane humane Philosopher, and he will judge of the gospell of Jesus Christ, and turne it over in humane Philosophie. They have turned the gospell of Jesus to Aristotle, all thair writingis ar bot spreitles. Thair is not sa mekle as ane smel of the Spreit of Jesus in them all. Bot O that terrible judgement that abydis sic doctors that are prophane polluters of the gospell of Jesus Christ.

Professor of Divinity at Louvain where he died in 1598; and Peter Canisius, a native of Nimeguen, Jesuit provincial, member of Council of Trent, and author of *Summae doctrinae Christianae*.

[28] *Select Works of Robert Rollock*, vol. 1, pp. 561–6.

[29] *Select Works of Robert Rollock*, vol. 1, pp. 299–449, 457–559; vol. 2, pp. 13–705.

[30] *Select Works of Robert Rollock*, vol.1, pp. 387–8.

While this excerpt clearly advocates that the monarch of the temporal sphere should not take an active role in the spiritual one, it is not an outright condemnation of Aristotle but of the scholastic underpinnings of Catholic theology against the unknowable revelations contained in scripture. Anti-Roman this may be, but this is not a defence of one philosophical system over another, Ramist or otherwise.

The nuances of Rollock's own intellectual outlook aside, the considerable anecdotal and statute evidence relating to early teaching at the university does suggest that Rollock used his position to ensure Ramist texts had a specific role within the curriculum, though not as central a role as has been suggested. Eyewitness acounts of early teaching at the university by one of the first MA graduates John Adamson, Rollock's successor Henry Charteris and the earliest university historian Thomas Craufurd, all provide substantially the same account of teaching as the first set of extant university statutes, the *Disciplina Academiae Edinburgenae* (1628).[31] While it has been suggested that these statutes were drawn up no earlier than 1619,[32] their subtitle (*Prout Observata Sunt Multis Retro Annis*) and a reference to them by Craufurd suggests that their substance had been observed since the college's inception or soon after. The degree programme clearly utilised the works of Ramus, but only as a means by which to inculcate the basic elements of logical disputation in the young entrants before moving on to 'real' logic in the shape of Aristotle.

Students spent most of their first year improving the Latin training they had received in grammar school by translating vernacular passages into Latin and vice versa, and learned basic Greek using Clenard's Greek grammar. Only at the end of the year, around mid-May, were they introduced to logic using the *Dialecticae* of Ramus, at the same time as they were to begin translating Latin themes into Greek, and vice versa. The same focus in the 'Melvillian' curriculum elsewhere on repetition, practice and disputation is evident at Edinburgh, as Greek was to be contextually learned using the grammar in conjunction with regular practice from the New Testament (*cum Grammatica jungitur regularum praxis ex aliqua*

---

[31]   John Adamson, 'Life of Charles Ferme', in Charles Ferme, *A Logical Analysis of the Epistle of Paul to the Romans*, ed. William Skae (Edinburgh, 1850), pp. viii–xx; Henry Charteris, 'Life of Robert Rollock', *Select Works of Robert Rollock*, vol. 1, pp. lvii–lxxxvii; Craufurd, *History of the University of Edinburgh*, pp. 44–6, 57–62; *Charters, Statutes, and Acts*, pp. 54–72.

[32]   Anderson, Lynch and Phillipson, *University of Edinburgh*, pp. 22–4. Craufurd's account of the ratification of the *Disciplinae* suggests they were used from the earliest days of the college's history. Craufurd, *History of the University of Edinburgh*, p. 112: 'This year and the next [1627 and 1628], the whole laws of the Colledge were gathered together, and put in a register. The greatest part of them before this time remained in a schedule in the Principal's hands, and were yearly read (as in the time subsequent) in November, after the examination of the classes.'

portiuncula Novi Testamenti), and by committing the first oration of Isocrates and Phoclides or the first book of Hesiod to memory, which were to be delivered publicly on a Saturday morning before the regent.

The second years would spend the month of October going over what had been learnt in first year prior to a review examination. After the examination, they would be engaged in the production of Greek orations on themes given by the regent, and would be introduced to rhetoric using Talon's *Rhetorica* along with Cassander or something similar, and Apthonius' *Progymnasmata*. Again, the Melvillian focus on practical style and delivery is evident in the fact that students were to focus on speeches and style of delivery in both their logic and rhetoric (*postea oratiunculas conficiunt ad exercitium stili in dialectica et rhetorica*). In January, however, they would advance from Ramus and Talon to more traditional and complex forms of logic. Starting with Porphyry, they would then work their way through the *Categories*, *De Interpretatione*, the *Prior Analytics*, the first, second and eighth books of the *Topics* and the *Sophistical Refutations*. At the end of the year they would study a compendium of arithmetic.

Third year would also start with a review examination, after which students would be taught Hebrew grammar along with the rhetorical and dialectical analysis of a variety of authors. Logical tuition would continue with two books of Aristotle's *Posterior Analytics*, but students would advance to a selection of his *Ethics* and *Physics*, and at the end of the year were provided with a brief overview of human anatomy.

Fourth year would study Aristotle's *On the Heavens*, the regent teaching first the greatest part of the second and fourth book. This would be followed by Sacrobosco's *De Sphaera* with some discussion of planetary theories and constellations and a range of other astronomical texts 'as far as necessary' (*quantum sufficit*), and the three books of Aristotle's *On the Soul*. From the beginning of May students were to rehearse and revise everything they had heard on the course to date, including logic and philosophy, and were to prepare for the public disputation at graduation by rehearsing the theses that would be part of the ceremony.

Overarching all this, the professor of theology would teach the 'method of discussing theology' (*methodum discendi theologiam*), though this may be a later addition to the curriculum rather than something that formally existed in Rollock's time. Besides a weekly reading in Hebrew, teaching would also involve two hours of public tuition on a Tuesday and Thursday, a vernacular exercise for students on a Wednesday, and the defence and disputation of Latin topics on a Friday. Sundays throughout the degree were devoted to the general study of theology at an ever-increasing level of complexity, beginning with catechism in the first and second years and a study of the theological common-places in third and fourth year, but with a focus on areas of religious controversy in the latter (*in maxime necessariis contraversiis exercentur*).

If the evidence in these sources is taken as indicative of the early curriculum at Edinburgh and its application, what do we learn? Firstly, Edinburgh was clearly geared towards a practical and rigorous education. At every stage of study there was considerable time given over to repetition and memorisation of the corpus of material covered in the arts course, especially when one considers that in addition to the exercises noted above every Saturday morning throughout the degree was devoted to at least two hours of public disputation by the students on that year's course material. There was a steady progression in both language training and in developing rhetorical expertise at every level of the course, ultimately with a view to allowing the students to take their place in the world, whether as ministers defending Protestant orthodoxy (as can be seen in the focus on disputing areas of theological controversy), or as administrators, lawyers and civil servants (as can be seen in the focus on defending theses publicly). The emphasis on praxis, memorisation and repetition, and the use of a range of well-chosen authors and examples to aid this, can indeed be construed as Ramist; however, this should not detract from the fact that pragmatism was perhaps an aim that came as much from the needs of the Edinburgh burgesses and local gentry as it did from the works of Ramus. The fact that the works of Ramus and Talon were used as an introduction to logic and rhetoric before the course shifted up a gear intellectually to tackle Aristotle and a range of other authors confirms the view that the use of Ramist texts was not an ideologically-charged manoeuvre on behalf of a 'Melvillian' and Presbyterian teaching staff, but rather an expedient way of teaching logic and rhetoric to young students who for the most part were barely into their teens and fresh from grammar school.

However, while the works of Ramus may have been seen as a necessary means of expediting the educational process, it is clear that not all staff at Edinburgh were comfortable with his reductionist approach, even if it only formed a small part of the actual teaching at the college. A crucial, and hitherto overlooked, component in this discussion is the evidence in the surviving *theses philosophicae* defended at Edinburgh in the first 25 years after its opening. These texts show that even if Rollock himself had been interested in Ramism, the usage of Ramist analysis in preference to Aristotle was not something at all favoured by the other regents in the college, even in the period when Melville was still an active force in Scottish intellectual affairs.

The first published set of theses for Edinburgh is that of 1596, supervised by George Robertson.[33] Craufurd confirms that these were the first ever set published in the history of Edinburgh. Robertson was a graduate of the class of 1588 and the son of a local burgess, and in 1592 he replaced Philip Heslop, who had been appointed to the ministry at Inneresk. There is also a set for 1599 by William Craig,[34] two sets of theses supervised by John Adamson in 1600 and 1604,[35] and two supervised by James Knox for 1601 and 1605. William Craig was a graduate of 1593 and the son of John Craig, minister to the king, who replaced the regent Patrick Sands in October 1597 on Robert Rollock's recommendation and assumed the supervision of the class in their third year. Craig left Scotland in December 1601 for France, to take up a position as professor of divinity in the college at Saumur. In January 1598 Adamson, a graduate of 1597 and the son of Henry Adamson provost of Perth, was elected as regent of the class in their second year as replacement to George Robertson, who left to take a ministerial charge within the city. Adamson resigned after seeing his latter class graduate in 1604 to take up a ministerial position at North Berwick. James Knox was another 1597 graduate chosen to succeed Charles Ferme as regent in winter 1597/8, and resigned after seeing his class of 1605 graduate to take up a position as minister of Kelso.[36] What is interesting to note is that all these regents were products of the Edinburgh degree programme, two of whom (Robertson and Craig) had studied while Rollock was still in charge of the college. Thus the theses that their classes defended at graduation are likely an exact duplication of what they themselves had learned as students.

Every single one of these theses is essentially a commentary on the works of Aristotle, along with varied levels of discussion of Porphyry's *Isagoge* and Sacrobosco's *De Sphaera*. The *theses logicae* in every text

[33]   George Robertson (Praeses), *Theses philosophicae quarum patrocinium suscepere adolescentes laureae candidati easdem propugnaturi ... Edinburgi* (Edinburgh, 1596).

[34]   William Craig (Praeses), *Theses philosophicae, & ex iis illatae conclusiones: quas, auspice et propitio Deo, praeside Guil. Cragio, propugnaturi sunt adolescentes magisterii candidati ... in aede sacra regii collegii* (Edinburgh, 1599).

[35]   John Adamson (Praeses), *Theses philosophicae, quas Dei Opt. Max, ductu & auspiciis, praeside Ioan. Adamsonio ... ex scholis Edinburgi philosophicis hoc 1600. anno emittendi* (Edinburgh, 1600); John Adamson (Praeses), *Theses philosophicae, quas Dei Opt. Max, ductu & auspiciis, praeside Ioan. Adamsonio ... ex Edinburgensi academia hoc 1604 anno cum lurea emittendi* (Edinburgh, 1604).

[36]   James Knox (Praeses), *Theses philosophicae, quas, aupsice & propitio Deo, praeside Ia. Knoxio, propugnabunt adolescentes ad pileum vocandi e scholis Edinburgi philosophicis hac vice emittendi ... in aede sacra regii collegii* (Edinburgh, 1601); James Knox (Praeses), *Theses philosophicae, quas auspice & propitio Deo, praeside Iac. Knoxio, propugnabunt adolescentes magisterii candidati e scholis Edinburgi philosophicis hoc anno 1605 emittendi... in aede sacra regii collegii* (Edinburgh, 1605).

defend the use of the syllogism and the Aristotelian system of deduction of causes from first principles as the best way to understand the world, and they all feature to some extent extended discussions of common Aristotelian debates, such as (in the case of Craig) the concept of first and second notions, or (as in the case of Robertson) the parts of the *Categories* and logical terms. Beyond Aristotle, however, the only other author who regularly crops up in this collection of texts is Ramus, who is consistently denounced by every regent who mentions him.

This condemnation is apparent from the first page of the first set of theses. The prefatory dedication of Robertson's collection condemns the pollution of Aristotelian logic by both Ramism and unspecified interpreters (in all likelihood a veiled reference to scholastic commentaries on Aristotle's texts):

TO THE READER

> While treading the footpath of Philosophy we have surveyed some very pleasant places bedrenched with the dew of nectar, whose cinnamon-like and fragrant scent (or at least we have found it to be so) we now have some inkling of through our keen nostrils, [and which is] neither tasteless to the palate, nor evilly besmeared with the reeking excrement of well-known commentators (*nuncupatorum interpretum*), or tainted with the impure filth of RAMIST teachings. We, who at last have been examined, have taken that journey with fleet swiftness, and we have drawn up that ambrosial liquid by means of the vessel of logical propositions.[37]

For a regent working at an institution apparently committed to Ramism these are strong words indeed, and clearly suggest that Robertson saw no difference between the modern revisions to the teaching of logic and the tortuous complexities of high medieval scholasticism. Both interfered with the purity of Aristotle in the original Greek.

A further direct attack on Ramus is noted in thesis 31 of the *theses logicae*,[38] and this staunch defence of Aristotelian supremacy, delivered hand in hand with a condemnation of Ramism, appears in the majority of

---

[37]   Robertson, p. A1: 'LECTORI: Philosophiae tramitem calcantes, amoeniora quaedam lustravimus loca nectareo rore rorantia, cuius cinnameum odorem odorati, fragrantem etiam, emunctis saltem naribus fore ominati sumus eiusque mellitum saporem, non insipidum palato non illito olenti male nuncupatorum interpretum faece, aut tincto lutulento RAMEAE doctrine coeno: iter istud celeri pernicitate tandem emensi, liquorem illum ambrosium hausimus, ac per thesium alveos derivavimus.'

[38]   Robertson, 'theses logicae' 31: 'In disciplinis contemplativis cernere est principia demonstratiua, affectiones demonstrabiles, subiecta etiam affectionum, quin & animadvertere est nexibus necessitatis ab Arist. I. lib. Post. requisitis ista quam arctissime inter se vinciri.'

the rest of the texts. While William Craig's theses of 1599 make no mention of Ramus, John Adamson echoes Robertson in his 1600 collection. As Robertson attacked the derivative nature of the Ramist system, so too was Adamson keen to point out that a universal method could in no way substitute for the depth and subtlety of a traditional philosophical education:

II. *No one will call himself a good logician thanks to a logical system that has been placed in his bosom, or else stored in his memory.*

1. The primary signifier of Logic is not therefore something [reached] through a system of precepts written by a certain author, but is acquired by the habit and habilitation of a human mind demonstrating the nature of Logic, and showing the signs of someone possessing wisdom.

2. The Ramists cannot be seen to be excused from any blame, who, continually declaring that Logic is a system of piecemeal precepts, are either ignorant of the characteristics of Logic, or pretend to themselves that they know, so that when these 'Logicians' are less able to do the former [ie, the Aristotelian system], they can at least claim possession of the latter.[39]

His other surviving collection from 1604 is only a third of the length of the 1600 theses, running to just seven pages, and features no explicit discussion of Ramus' method. However, the final *theses logicae* does argue that anyone who does not use the components of the syllogism in deductive reasoning are bungling (*insulsum*), stupid (*stolidum*) and blind to Aristotle's light (*caecutiunt ad Aristotelis lucem*).[40]

The final regent of this quartet, James Knox, is equally scathing of Ramus' overt simplification of logic. In his 1601 *theses* he summarises succinctly the central problem facing logicians and academics in relation to

---

Quidquid itaque ranarum instar coaxent Ramaei dantur in scientiis demonstrationes, eaeque quamplures.'

[39] Adamson (1600), 'theses logicae' 2: 'II. *A Systemate Logico, vel in gremio gestato, vel etiam in memoria reposito nemo homo bonus Logicus appellabitur.*

[1]. Non est ergo illa, qua pro systemate conscriptorum à quoquam authore praeceptorum, sed qua pro habitu, & habilitate mentis humanae sumitur, primaria naturam Logicae declarans, & p[os]sidentem scientis titulo insigniens, Logicae significatio.

[2]. Non omni videntur reprehensione vacare Ramaei, qui Logicam esse systema consarcinatarum pręceptionum perpetuò declamitantes, habitum Logicae, vel ignorant, vel nosse se dissimulant, ut cum minus queant ex huius, ex illius saltem posse Logici appellentur.'

[40] Adamson (1604), 'theses logicae' 6.

Ramist teaching, and echoes Adamson's viewpoint of Ramism as stunted and magpie-like:

17. *The transition from one extreme to another is not possible without going through the middle.*

1. There cannot be an immediate transition from ignorance to wisdom.

[...]

4. Exceedingly toilsome and unproductive is that [system] of Ramist wisdom (let the Ramists show their teeth and be burst apart), stitched together by precepts tried only according to the laws [of wisdom, truth and justice].[41]

Knox's attitude is further gleaned in his 1605 theses, only in this later example it is applied more specifically to the issue of the terms that Ramus provided in place of the traditional Aristotelian categories, where he notes that 'the diverse definitions of Logic given by the Peripatetics and Ramists, disagreeing in outward appearance, are given with good reason: but the Ramists have abused these with [their] terminology'.[42]

Thus three out of the four regents openly condemn Ramism, and even Craig makes a concerted effort to defend Aristotle's system as definitive.[43] What are we to make of this? On its own, it would suggest that following the death of Rollock and the removal of his influence within the college, there was an abrupt shift in educational policy from that delineated by the curriculum and statute evidence. This would explain the condemnation seen in the theses, but it still would not explain why Robertson and Craig, both trained within the environs of the college under Rollock, would develop such a contrary attitude to Ramism. There is, however, another possible explanation, particularly when the educational experiment at Edinburgh is viewed in conjunction with the developments under Melville at St Andrews, where there was a strict divergence between the rigid and highly critical adherence to Aristotle among the arts colleges on the one hand, and the use of Ramism in theological teaching in St Mary's. It seems entirely possible that, as at St Andrews, Ramism was used as an introductory tool to facilitate logical thought and expression at the beginning of the degree, and was used

---

[41]   Knox (1601), 'theses logicae' 17: '17. *Ab extremo ad extremum sine medio non datur transitus.* 1. Ab ignorantia ad scientiam transitus non potest esse immediatus. 4. Arduum nimis ac ieiunum est illud Ramaeum Scientiarum σύςκ[εμ]μα, (ringant, rumpantur Ramaei) ex solis praeceptis ad leges [...] examinatis consartinatum.'

[42]   Knox (1605), p. A1: '3.1. Diversas Logice definitiones a Peripateticis & Ramaeis traditas, in speciem concertantes, rite traditas tenemus: sed Ramaei nominibus sunt abusi.'

[43]   Craig, theses 1–4.

as a convenient method by which to explore theology, but was rightly seen by those teaching formal logic and philosophy as no substitute for Aristotle. Further evidence to support this can be seen in the work of Charles Ferme, one of Rollock's first pupils, who was highly conversant in Aristotle but used his training at Edinburgh to produce a *Logical Analysis of the Epistle to the Romans* which mirrored the approach pioneered by his teacher. We also see an openness to using both systems as and when required in Rollock's work, and as noted in Craufurd's account of him as being someone 'of eminent knowledge in the dogmatick philosophie of Aristotle' who 'esteemed much of Ramus his Dialectick'.[44] In the world of late sixteenth-century education, pragmatism and expediency were key, and if Melville had developed a system that incorporated both the nuance of Aristotle and the flexibility of Ramus then we should hardly be surprised that Rollock would use this method at Edinburgh. By extension, when assessing the trends in intellectual outlook and development on offer at Edinburgh in its early years, once we accept that the curriculum offered was not simply reduced to either conservative Aristotelianism or radical Ramism we perhaps get a better sense of the true intellectual ferment in the college in its early years, a ferment replicated elsewhere at exactly the same time.

Godliness in the North-East: Marischal College and the University of Fraserburgh

A little over ten years after the foundation of Edinburgh, another new university was established in New Aberdeen that provided the city with its own Protestant arts college. Marischal College, founded in April 1593 by George Keith, fifth Earl Marischal, was sited less than three miles from King's College in Old Aberdeen, and this proximity has prompted considerable debate – why did Marischal feel the need to create a new institution on the doorstep of such a well-established and ancient university? The foundation has traditionally been explained as an attempt by the Presbyterian earl, frustrated at the lack of reform at King's over the 1580s and early 1590s, to provide an outlet in the north-east for the Reformed brand of European humanism that he himself had come into contact with on the Continent. Like Melville, Marischal had studied in France and Geneva under Beza between 1571 and 1580, and had been excited by the same curriculum that Melville ultimately brought back with him to Scotland.[45] Marischal had led the visitation to King's in November

---

[44]   See note 30, above.

[45]   G.D. Henderson, *The Founding of Marischal College, Aberdeen* (Aberdeen, 1947), pp. 10–15.

1581 and had been the spokeperson for the General Assembly in attempts to have the *Nova Fundatio* ratified by the royal government, and following the failure of the visitations in 1584 and 1592 to achieve any real measure of reform, Marischal may have decided that establishing a college with a new constitution was a more effective use of his energy than pursuing the process of reform at Old Aberdeen.[46]

The foundation charter of the college,[47] ratified at Aberdeen on 2 April 1593, stated that the express aim of the college was 'to do the utmost good to the Church, the Country and the Commonwealth'. Like Edinburgh, Marischal College was concerned with providing the children of the citizens of New Aberdeen with the practical skills necessary for advancement in life, and was to be an institution where they 'might receive a godly and liberal education' that would enable them 'to spread the preaching of God's Word ... to instruct the young, or to administer the government' wherever they were needed.

The curriculum outlined generally in the college constitution, and described in detail in the *Statuta* for the academy drawn up by Principal Gilbert Gray in 1605 and in the *Leges Novae Academiae Aberdonensis* likely produced by one of his successors prior to 1617, clearly drew intellectually on the key tenets of the Continental reformed humanism that the Earl had been exposed to.[48] It also reflected more narrowly the constitutional and curricular mechanisms seen in the Melvillian re-foundations of the ancient universities, particularly the *Nova Fundatio* planned for King's. The new college was to house a principal, three regents and six poor students, and each of the staff members were to have an area of professorial specialisation. The first-year regent was to teach Greek and Latin composition to the students using Clenard's Greek Grammar with a selection of Greek and Roman authors including Isocrates and Demosthenes. The foundation charter also stated that the regent was to introduce entrants to disputation by providing them with 'a short compendium of logical invention and judgement', and both the *Statuta* and *Leges* specifically stated that Ramus' *Dialecticae* was to be used for this purpose.[49] The second-year regent was responsible for ensuring that students continued to develop their written and oral skills in classical languages and for teaching Logic using the *Organon*, together with 'a system of rules of invention and judgement from the best authors of both languages'; the *Statuta* ordered that a series

---

[46]   Stevenson, *King's College*, pp. 30–35; Henderson, *Marischal College*, pp. 22–3.

[47]   *FMA*, I, pp. 60–67.

[48]   Both the *Statuta* and *Leges* are published in Colin A. McLaren, *Aberdeen Students, 1600–1860* (Aberdeen, 2005), pp. 137–67.

[49]   The *Leges* also state that Talon's *Rhetorica* should be taught to the first years, whereas the *Statuta* advocate this should be taught in tandem with Ramus.

of lectures be given on Talon's *Rhetorica* to meet this aim. The senior regent was responsible for teaching moral and natural philosophy to the third years, beginning with selections from the *Ethics* and *Politics* in the original Greek and Cicero's *De Officiis* before moving onto the *Physics* at the end of the year, and also provided an outline of arithmetic and geometry using Ramus' *Arithmeticae* and *Geometriae*. The principal was responsible for teaching biblical languages and general theology, but his remit also included supervising the fourth year, completing tuition of the *Physics* and also providing a 'short explanation of anatomy ... Geography, History, and the outlines of Astronomy'.[50]

The curriculum advocated at Marischal blended the clear adherence to Aristotle seen in higher education elsewhere in Scotland with a more strident commitment to the works of Ramus than any other university foundation of the time. It is thus clear why the foundation of Marischal has traditionally been explained as the act of a Presbyterian and reform-minded magnate, acting under the guidance of Melville and trained in the same European environment. However, a re-examination of the evidence relating to the origins of the foundation, with a special focus on the role of burgh politics in the development of the college, suggests that while the Earl Marischal was clearly the patron and benefactor of the college, far greater credit should be given to the work of the local ministers of the town and the town council in shepherding the foundation through the turmoil of its early development.

In relation to this process, the local context in Aberdeen was everything. The exponential growth of the population of New Aberdeen, increasing by more than 50 per cent between 1575 and 1644, brought with it a sizable population of craftsmen increasingly restive at the control of the town by a small conservative oligarchy of merchant gentry led by the Menzies, who had held the office of provost for the majority of the sixteenth century.[51] By the beginning of the 1590s the guilds had found a leader in John Cheyne, the commissary clerk, who organised a series of public demonstrations and armed gatherings advocating electoral reform and increased representation for the guilds on the council.[52]

---

[50]   The *Leges* drop the requirement to teach anatomy, and add Pliny and Johannes Friege's *Quaestiones Physicae* (Basle, 1579) as set texts.

[51]   Ian Blanchard and others, 'The Economy: Town and Country', in Patricia Dennisoun, David Ditchburn and Michael Lynch (eds), *Aberdeen Before 1800* (East Linton, 2000), pp. 129–58, at pp. 147–8; Michael Lynch and Helen M. Dingwall, 'Elite Society in Town and Country', in *Aberdeen Before 1800*, pp. 181–200, at pp. 187–91; Allan White, 'The Menzies Era: Sixteenth-Century Politics', in *Aberdeen Before 1800*, pp. 224–37.

[52]   Allan White, 'Religion, Politics and Society in Aberdeen, 1543–1593' (University of Edinburgh, unpublished PhD thesis, 1985), pp. 304–45; Aberdeen City Archives, Council Register, vol. 33, part 2 (4 December 1590 to 28 February 1592), pp. 1305–7; Aberdeen

Magnate rivalry for domination in the north-east between the staunchly Protestant Marischal and the pro-Catholic sixth earl of Huntly added a religious dimension to this conflict. The Menzies, who had maintained a stance of 'pragmatic conservatism' towards religion since the onset of the reformation, found themselves increasingly isolated from a population that had come to embrace Protestantism, and in the early 1580s allied themselves with Huntly and used his influence to maintain their hold on power for the remainder of that decade.[53] However, the involvement of Huntly in the Catholic intrigues of 1589 and 1592, when his signature was found on documents implicating him in plots relating to a planned Catholic invasion of Scotland, led to his downfall following a brief rebellion in February 1594. Conversely, Marischal increased his influence following his successful negotiation of the king's marriage to Anne of Denmark in 1589, and with the earl of Atholl replaced Huntly as lieutenant of the north in 1593.[54]

These circumstances were directly connected with the sudden sea-change in the political control of the town on 26 September 1593, when in a landslide victory Cheyne and a number of his associates were elected as provost and baillies of the council.[55] Cheyne's administration, freed from the influence of the Menzies oligarchy, undertook an aggressive overhaul of burgh life, including a firm statutory adherence to Protestantism. The price and quality of bread, beef, ale and other staples was to be more rigorously monitored by the council, new statutes were introduced to improve the speed and fairness of hearings of petitions by the burgh court, and attendance at Sunday sermons and Sabbatarianism more generally were to be enforced.[56] However, the extreme measures enacted by Cheyne's new party appear to have proved less than favourable to everyone, as within a year he had been replaced by another member of his party, John Collison.[57]

The Cheyne faction have been credited as the Presbyterian sympathisers who endorsed and completed Marischal's plans for a 'godly' town college, but this convenient interpretation does not sit well in the context of events

City Archives, Council Register, vol. 34, part 1 (1 October 1591 to 25 September 1593), pp. 295–8, 508; part 2 (2 October 1592 to 25 September 1593), pp. 517–19.

[53]   White, 'Religion, Politics and Society', pp. 311, 317–19.

[54]   Ruth Grant, 'The Brig o' Dee Affair', pp. 93–109; Henderson, *Marischal College*, pp. 74–8.

[55]   Aberdeen City Archive, Council Register 35 (26 September 1593 to September 1594), pp. 1–3.

[56]   Aberdeen City Archive, Council Register 35 (26 September 1593 to September 1594), pp. 3–12, 17–19.

[57]   Aberdeen City Archives, Council Register, Index of volumes I–LXVII (1398–1800), p. 507.

in burgh politics. Firstly, it was while under a Menzies-led town council, with the support of the town ministry, that the majority of the initial administration relating to the college was undertaken. On 2 April 1593 the Earl Marischal signed the foundation charter for the college, witnessed by John Forbes of Pitsligo and James Crichton Younger of Frendraught, the ministers of Aberdeen Peter Blackburn and Robert Howie, and the bishop of Aberdeen David Cunningham.[58] On 21 April the earl handed over the endowed properties to the latter three ministers, and five days later the foundation was approved by the General Assembly.[59] Between 7 and 18 June the ministers involved in signing the foundation elected an *oeconomus* for the college, and had him empowered by the town council to remove unwanted tenants from the Greyfriars' yards and houses which were annexed to the college.[60] In the same month the council bought out the leases held by Patrick and Gilbert Jack on the Greyfriars' buildings on Broad Street in the town to ensure that the college had adequate provision for teaching space.[61]

The Earl Marischal was further active in obtaining confirmation of the college erection before Parliament on 21 July,[62] but the majority of the administrative work was carried out by the council and the three ministers of the town, Cunningham, Blackburn and Howie. All three had intellectual connections with Melville, but in terms of their careers chose to follow a path that supported the king and moderate episcopacy.[63] Cunningham had been a supporter of Melville in Glasgow in the 1570s and had supervised the drafting of the *Second Book of Discipline*, but following his elevation to the bishopric of Aberdeen in 1576 was treated with hostility and censure by the assembly, most notably with a charge of immorality against him in 1586.[64] Blackburn was an ex-regent of St Salvator's and had been the sole member of staff teaching at Glasgow on Melville's arrival there in 1574, but after his appointment as minister to St Nicholas' Kirk in 1582 he also became a strong supporter of the king, and accepted the bishopric of Aberdeen in 1600.[65] Howie was a son of an Aberdeen burgess who

[58] *FMA*, vol. 1, pp. 39–59.

[59] Henderson, *Marischal College*, pp. 87–8; *FMA*, vol 1, pp. 80–4; *BUK*, vol. 3, p. 802.

[60] *Extracts from the Council Register of the Burgh of Aberdeen 1570–1625*, ed. J. Stuart (2 vols, Aberdeen, 1844–8), vol. 2, pp. 79–80; *FMA*, vol. 1, p. 51.

[61] Henderson, *Marischal College*, pp. 86–7.

[62] *FMA*, vol. 1, p. 87.

[63] Henderson, *Marischal College*, pp. 56–63.

[64] *Selections from Wodrow's Biographical Collections*, pp. 57–65.

[65] Durkan and Kirk, p. 254; MacDonald, *Jacobean Kirk*, pp. 71, 94; *Wodrow's Biographical Collections*, pp. 66–79.

had attended Rostock, Herborn and Basel universities, and had travelled on the Continent with his fellow Aberdeen alumni John Johnston.[66] He became first principal of Marischal College, and although in his early career he was a supporter of the Presbyterian party, by the late 1590s he had wholly embraced the royal and Episcopal viewpoint: he was chosen as Melville's successor as principal of St Mary's in 1607 precisely because he supported the royal church settlement and would provide a useful ideological corrective within the city.[67] All three men sought moderation and compromise in spiritual and temporal matters, and were happy to work with the town council without espousing a radical Presbyterian viewpoint or involving themselves in burgh politics.

Despite the radical shift that took place in the make-up of the burgh council in September 1593, both the Menzies and Cheyne-led factions clashed with Marischal over control of the college in the year after its initial ratification. Days before the end of the Menzies regime, on 24 September 1593, a dispute arose between Marischal and the town council over the property that had been endowed to the college. Marischal's charter had annexed the lands of the Dominican, Carmelite and Franciscan friars (otherwise known as the Black, White and Grey Friars) within the city to the college, along with properties in Bervy and Cowy.[68] However, the property of the Greyfriars was technically not his to give, as the rights to it had been granted in a royal act of 1567 to the town council. It appears that an agreement had been reached between the earl and the council that this property would be resigned to him to give over in turn to the college as patron, and a dispute arose on 24 September where a minority of the town council argued that instead they should maintain their perpetual rights as superiors of the lands but donate it directly to the college masters. A compromise was reached when the majority of the council agreed to resign the land, as agreed within the foundation charter, providing that the earl accept a clause that the lands of the Greyfriars

> promisit and granttit be him abefoir [ie, as stated in the April charter] to the said college To Remane th[ere]with annexed thairvnto, according to the fundatioun and Institutioun And the said college nawayis to be translatit furt[h] of this bur[gh]t to ony [o]thr place.[69]

Why this dissension appeared, particularly after the land had been expressly transferred as part of the foundation charter, is unclear. The

---

[66]   See above, pp. 10, 147–8.

[67]   Cameron, *Letters*, pp. 310–11, 316–17, 321–3, 326–7.

[68]   *FMA*, I, pp. 62.

[69]   *FMA*, I, pp. 85–6.

clause inserted suggests that the council were concerned that formally ratifying the transfer of property to the earl would allow him to keep the rents for himself instead of fulfilling his agreement, or that giving the earl full patronage of the college would remove any prestige due to them for their contribution towards the foundation. Regardless, what is clear is that the council under the Menzies regime was just as keen to ensure provision for the college, despite their previous affiliations with the earl of Huntly; and above all, they wanted to ensure that the college, once founded, would remain solely within the control of the town and would be available for its citizenry.

While support for consolidating the college under the aegis of the Earl Marischal had emerged under the Menzies council, tension appears to have arisen once the Cheyne regime was in power. The first piece of information on the development of the college in this period occurs in the financial accounts of the dean of guild where, on 17 December 1593, £9 was paid to raise letters at Edinburgh to suspend charges by the Earl Marischal compelling David Cunningham to present the foundation documents before the Lords of Session, and for counter-letters authorising the bishops to deliver the documents to the town council as having interest. Four days later a further £100 was given to the bishop to allow him to travel to Edinburgh to pursue this business. This action continued into February 1594 when, after miscellaneous expenses to pursue the earl 'in the mater of the college', the town procurator William Oliphant was sent 'be vertew of ane ordinance of counsall ... to persew the actioun of registration of the erectioun of the new college aganis the Erll Merschall.'[70] The legal wrangling over the rights to the registration of the foundation appears to have continued until 20 September 1594, when Robert Howie's first official transaction as principal of the college was to receive the deed of erection from the town council.[71] This act was also one of the last carried out by Cheyne's administration, suggesting that he and his cohorts wished to see the college's foundation secured before being removed from office.

The whole process of foundation and erection, taking over eighteen months from Marischal's original ratification of the college, was thus as protracted and difficult as the opening of the 'tounis college' at Edinburgh. But whereas at Edinburgh the issues and delays had arisen because of two ideologically opposed council factions, in New Aberdeen the issue appears to have been one of differing relationships with the college patron himself. Both the Cheyne and Menzies regimes sought to safeguard the foundation of the college, and both sought to do so in a way that gave the council some

---

[70] 'Extracts from the Accounts of the Burgh of Aberdeen', in *The Miscellany of the Spalding Club*, ed. J. Stuart (5 vols, Aberdeen, 1841–52), vol. 5, pp. 39–181, at pp. 56–7.

[71] *FMA*, vol. 1, p. 89; Henderson, *Marischal College*, p. 88.

measure of control in its administration and credit for its development, regardless of their perceived political and religious affiliations. Why tensions with the earl persisted after the ratification remains a mystery, but it may be that with the complete removal of the Menzies and Huntly from the political landscape in the burgh by the end of 1593 the earl felt less need to maintain involvement in a high-profile public development such as the foundation of a college, and the council were compelled to chase him to complete the process. The fact that there was a commitment from two very different administrations to doing this highlights just how seriously the town took the provision of higher education as a means of improving the lives of their citizens, and how important it was for their own interests to ensure Marischal's project came to fruition.

Outwith his activities developing Marischal College, the earl had also seen to it that Peterhead was erected as a burgh of barony in 1593, and at the same time received a grant from Parliament allowing him an impost of 20d. per 20 bolls weight of goods entering and exiting the port for the space of five years, in order to complete the development of a modern harbour for the town and encourage the local fishing trade.[72] However, the Earl Marischal was not the only Protestant magnate active in the north-east, and in July 1592 Sir Alexander Fraser was granted a *novodamus* of the lands of Philorth by the royal government in order to transform the town of Faithlie into a burgh of barony with the eponymous title of Fraserburgh. In the same charter, Fraser was granted full power 'to build a college or colleges in the said burgh of Fraser, to set up a university ... to raise and endow foundations for their sustenance and provide all privileges necessary'.[73] With this charter, the unlikely university of Fraserburgh was established, and for a short while looked to be a potential competitor to Marischal College in the north-east. The project was advanced enough in December 1597 that Parliament ratified the annexation of revenues from the parishes of Philorth, Tyrie, Crimond and Rathen to pay for teaching staff, and noted that Fraser had begun 'to edify and build up colleges' in the town for that purpose, which comprised a set of buildings with a quadrangular tower in the west end of the town.[74] In the following year the ministry of Philorth fell vacant, and Fraser invited a regent at Edinburgh, Charles Ferme, to take up both the ministry and the office of principal of the newly-founded college.[75] Ferme accepted the former,

---

[72]   *RPS*, 1593/4/68 [accessed 30 March 2010].

[73]   Ian Malley, *The University of Fraserburgh* (Loughborough, 1988), p. 11.

[74]   *RPS*, 1597/11/59 [accessed 30 March 2010]; Malley, *University of Fraserburgh*, pp. 25–9. The tower was still extant, though badly ruined, in the mid-nineteenth century.

[75]   William Alexander, 'Life of Ferme', in Charles Ferme, *A Logical Analysis of the Epistle of Paul to the Romans*, ed. William Skae (Edinburgh, 1850), p. xv; Craufurd,

but waited until the General Assembly approved his holding two offices before finally agreeing to accept the principalship, which they assented to in March 1600.[76]

Beyond this, no evidence survives to tell us what Fraser's motivations were for founding the college, what was taught there by Ferme, or indeed if Ferme taught at all. Wodrow had suggested that the college was designed to act as as alternative establishment for youths from Inverness, Caithness, Moray and Ross who found Aberdeen too far away to attend, and to act more generally as a corrective to recusant Catholicism in the north-east.[77] Ferme was one of the first graduates of Edinburgh University in 1587, and may have replicated the arts course that he had taught as a regent there.[78] Equally, his *Logical Analysis of the Epistle to the Romans* shows that like Rollock and Melville he was influenced by Ramism in his approach to scriptural exposition.[79] The ministers of Crimond, Rathen and Tyrie whose parishes were to provide income to the university were perhaps also to act as regents in the foundation under Ferme, but there is no evidence to suggest that this ever happened.

The university was dealt a death blow when Ferme, who attended the General Assembly convened without royal permission in July 1605 at Aberdeen, was imprisoned until at least 1608. By this time the college had lapsed, if indeed it had ever been truly established. Fraserburgh was far more remote than the eastern burgh of Aberdeen, and although the college had some endowment thanks to the act of 1597, the major source of finance for the development of both the university and the town was the personal capital of Sir Alexander Fraser. By 1613 Fraser had accrued so much debt that he was forced to sell his castle in the burgh and a considerable portion of his lands and the university quietly lapsed, although it was used by the colleges at Aberdeen in the session of 1647–8 as an alternative venue while plague raged in the city.[80] The experiment at Fraserburgh does show, however, how seriously education was taken as a tool for civic improvement in the closing decades of the sixteenth century, and if the foundation had succeeded perhaps other 'arts colleges' would have appeared across Scotland.

University of Edinburgh, p. 42.

[76]   *BUK*, vol. 3, p. 958.

[77]   *Selections from Wodrow's Biographical Collections*, p. 272.

[78]   *Catalogue of Edinburgh University Graduates*, p. 7.

[79]   Ferme, *A Logical Analysis*.

[80]   Malley, *University of Fraserburgh* , pp. 23–4.

The 'Town Foundation' Resurrected? Glasgow and Civic Intervention, 1585–1602

Despite being an 'ancient' university, the trend for greater civic control and involvement in local education was also evident at Glasgow. Following the failed initiative of the 'town foundation' of 1573 and the disturbances of the early 1580s, there were concerted efforts in the last two decades of the sixteenth century to establish supervisory and financial controls over the university that in turn benefited local burgesses and their children.

Beyond his official appointment as principal at the beginning of 1586, nothing survives in either the burgh or university records to give us an indication of Patrick Sharp's relations with the town in the first 15 years of his office. However, towards the end of the 1590s he was involved in a renewed argument between burgh, crown and university over who had jurisdiction over the university and its finances. This argument was triggered in part because Sharp was a less than exemplary administrator, and in part because the burgh council wanted to continue the programme of civic involvement in the university that they had started in the pre-'Melvillian' period with the 'town foundation'. It also reveals that the council-appointed officer who had collected rents for the university in the 1570s was still active, as an entry in the burgh records for 28 February 1601 ordered that the principal and university 'mak thair compt upon the first of Merche as to the first quarter of the yeir' before the council.[81] This was followed by a more serious entry on 11 March:

> In presens of the provost, bailleis, and counsale an deikines, the thried bailleis and certane of the counsale being directit, conforme to ane ordinance of befor, for hering of thair [the university's] comptis, and thair accusatioune in breking of the fundatioune, being convenit with the rector and deyne of faculte to that effect, quha refusit to admit ony assissouris but only the bailleis, thairfor ordanes the bailleis to pas of new agane with the clerk ... to convein with thame and first to heir the greiffis to be gevin in be the commone procuratour, to be accompaneit with the viii of the counsale, being nominat assissouris of befoir ... [for which purpose] Maister Henry Gibsone, clerk, producit the fundatioune buik, togidder with the extract of the fundatioune of the College out of Latine in Scottis thairin contenit.[82]

This entry deserves close scrutiny, as it is clear that for the council there was not simply the issue of financial neglect or mismanagement at stake. The allegation of breach of foundation and production of the town evidence, presumably including a copy of the old town foundation, suggests that the

---

81 *Extracts from the Records of the Burgh of Glasgow*, p. 217.
82 *Extracts from the Records of the Burgh of Glasgow*, pp. 217–18.

council questioned the legality of the Melvillian *Nova Erectio* in relation to their own, despite their knowledge that the former had been ratified by Parliament. Moreover, their insistence that a fuller complement of eight council members be accepted as assessors of the university shows that they still desired that the college be regularly audited by the council and its members, and further suggests that they felt their foundation had some semblance of legal authority.

Over the course of the following month the council repeatedly insisted that the principal, rector and dean of faculty meet with them, and a meeting was agreed on 8 April for the Friday following.[83] While there is no evidence for what was discussed at this meeting it is clear that it did not go well, as the council decided to try another approach by seeking the advice of another council with experience of running a civic college. On 23 May 1601 they appointed James Forret, one of the town baillies, 'to ryde to Edinburgh to advyse and confer with the townes procuratouris and sic vtheris anent the tua fundatiounes of the College, grieffis, and haill proces and comptis thairof', after which they would take whatever advice they received and confer with the king and Privy Council on the issue.[84] Forret was ideally placed for this consultation, as he had other dealings with Edinburgh council as the commissioner for the burghs to France, and in this latter capacity he appears in the Edinburgh minutes on 2 December 1601 after successfully negotiating a reduction in port customs on Scottish exports.[85] On 10 June 1601 Forret was sent to the university to discuss 'the letteres of the College' and must have seen the council in Edinburgh just prior to this, for three days later the Glasgow council convened a meeting with Sharp.[86] Referring to 'the last conclusione done in Edinburgh', they pressed their claim to authority over the university through the 1573 foundation, and Sharp was:

> ather to gif the copey of the new letteres, viz., quhat fundatioune by the townes fundatioune, ather be King or Bischop, onder the privey seale or vtheris, and specially the gift gevin be Quein Mary of the Blakfreris, or ellis be his awin hand wret or subscriptioune, and to reporte quhat he hes to saye or mene thairto aganes the fundatioune.

---

[83]   *Extracts from the Records of the Burgh of Glasgow*, p. 219.

[84]   *Extracts from the Records of the Burgh of Glasgow*, pp. 220–1.

[85]   *Extracts from the Records of the Burgh of Edinburgh, A.D. 1589 to 1603*, ed. M. Wood (Edinburgh, 1927), pp. 296, 314. Forret travelled to France with the diplomatic embassy of Ludovic, Duke of Lennox, which left Scotland on 10 July 1601.

[86]   *Extracts from the Records of the Burgh of Glasgow*, pp. 222–3.

While there are no further references to this episode in the council records, compounded by the fact that the council minutes are wanting from October 1601 to June 1605, a document entitled 'controversies betuix the fundationes of Glasgow college' sheds some light on this rather fraught and obscure period.[87] Comprising an assessment of issues with the university settlement and a series of recommendations for improving it, it begins by directly comparing the terms of the 'town foundation' of 1573 with those of the *Nova Erectio* of 1577 and noting points of dissension. It also suggested that a new foundation be endorsed by the crown of a principal, four regents, 12 poor scholars, a cook and a provisor to replace both previous foundations. While internal evidence shows the 'controversies' were clearly written before 1608,[88] a draft statute stating that the principal should also demit from holding simultaneously the ministry of Govan parish tallies with a similar injunction made in the presbytery records in August 1602, suggesting that it was written either contemporaneously with or just after the events of the 1601 dispute.[89]

It has been argued that this document defended 'the interests of the college rather than the town',[90] as it affirmed the jurisdiction of the principal over 'all the inferiour memberis' of the university, recommended that he be relieved of his ministerial burdens, and planned a large augmentation of the stipends of the teaching staff and of the rights of the chancellor, rector, principal and dean of faculty to admit staff and bursars. However, another reading suggests that it met the interests and aims of the town council far more than it did the university. The 'controversies' and foundations were to be submitted for arbitration by the Privy Council, but the burgh council were only willing to relinquish fully the legality of theirs if 'thair twa priviledgeis concerning presentatioune off bursareis and tryell off comptis ... be reservat' – in other words, as long as the areas that had been of perennial concern to the council were dealt with. Moreover, while it may not in itself be significant that 12 bursars' places – the same number as in the town foundation – were outlined in the recommendations, the fact that eight of these bursaries were to be presented by the town council and four by the crown surely must be. The potential bursars were to be 'parentles haveing na thing for their awin sustentatioune or give thay have parentis that thair povertie be cleirlie notifeit to the admitteris', again suggesting

[87]   Printed in Durkan and Kirk, pp. 423–9. This document was transcribed by James Kirk from the Pollok Maxwell Estate papers.

[88]   The document recommends that a provisor and cook be appointed to the foundation, but after 1608 catering was transferred to an outside party. Durkan and Kirk, pp. 423–4.

[89]   Glasgow City Archives, Presbytery Records, CH2/171/34, p. 133 [30 August 1602].

[90]   Durkan and Kirk, p. 339.

that the council were aiming to provide for the most deserving candidates within the town.[91]

The fact that the 'controversies' recommended a provisor be kept with a role similar to that of the one at work for the council is also significant. The document clearly spelled out his duties, including the collecting of all rents, the auditing of college accounts and the administration of payment to all staff members – thus ratifying the arrangement that had already existed during Melville's tenure as principal of the college where a council-elected officer had taken oversight of the college's finances, and which had been renewed again when James Sharp was appointed to the office on 27 January 1599. The final recommendation of the 'controversies', that the university find funding for a professor of law, was not one borne from idle academic interest either, but can be read as part of a continued commitment to improving the range of civic services and amenities on offer in Glasgow. The council had agreed in December 1596 to send a delegation to the king to convince him to re-house the Edinburgh-based College of Justice in Glasgow;[92] and on 29 November 1599 the king's mediciner Peter Low and his colleague Robert Hamilton were given a letter of gift to examine all medical practitioners within the city and to regularise medical provision there, with those who received licence being obliged to provide free advice to the poor on the first Monday of every month.[93] There is a clear element of civic improvement apparent in these actions, as there is in the justification for the appointment of a lawyer. In Glasgow there were:

> divers judicatoreis, viz., synodall assemblie, presbitrie, sessioune, haldin be ministeris; consistorie be commissaris; burghe and baroune courtis be bailzies; quhais proceidingis aught all to be terminit be the boundis off lawe, the ignorance quhairoff breidis and fosteris mony confusions.[94]

Thus a professor of law would not only be highly desirable for improving the prospects of the university, but would also enrich the practices and administration of the city itself as it developed as a trading and business centre.

If this document does relate to the disputes over university jurisdiction that surfaced in 1601, it certainly suggests that the council had no intention of fully relinquishing control of the university to its staff, and

[91]   Durkan and Kirk, pp. 425–9.

[92]   *Extracts from the Records of the Burgh of Glasgow*, p. 183.

[93]   *Charters and Other Documents Relating to the City of Glasgow AD 1175–1649 Part 1*, ed. J.D. Marwick (Edinburgh, 1897), pp. clxxix–clxxxiii.

[94]   Durkan and Kirk, p. 429.

that the key areas of improvement in relation to burgh life were areas they aimed to gain control over by royal assent. However, if there were further developments along these lines they are now impossible to recover. The Privy Council aimed to settle the disagreements over finance by appointing a commission of visitation on 29 June 1602 that would explicitly 'sicht and considder the fundationis thairof [and] call for a perfyte rental of the revenewis moretefeit thairto', and in addition to testing the qualifications of the masters would make detailed recommendations for the future administration of the university.[95] This commission met in Glasgow on 27 August, and its proceedings support the idea that the 1601 controversy resulted in a victory for the town over the university. Firstly detailed regulations were laid down for rations and meals for the staff and students to ensure there would be no further misappropriation of funds on the pretext of supplying the university with food. These were followed by a striking series of statutes clearly linked to the 'controversies', which suggest that an attempt to reach a compromise had been made by the commission on the basis of their evidence. The establishment of a principal and four regents, in line with the existing situation at the college, was ratified, and augmented fees were provided for the masters, though not at the levels specified in the 'controversies'. The issue of the financial officer was to be resolved by appointing a new administrator who would be sworn in on the authority of the Privy Council, but who would have complete control over the income of the college and its allocation to the ministers. Most importantly, eight bursaries were to be established, four of which were to be presented by the king and the other four by the council, with right of admission by the rector, principal, and dean of arts. This action clearly met the central aim of the council in the 'controversies', especially as it was further ordained that any surplus rents for the year would be spent on more bursaries which would also be presented equally by the king and the council. These acts were given royal assent on 29 August, and the following day the visitation was concluded with the swearing in of William Stirling, a burgess of Glasgow, as the new financial officer of the college before the Privy Council.[96]

The compromising nature of the settlement enacted at Glasgow in 1602, which maintained the autonomy of the college masters largely unimpeded, did not transform Glasgow into a town college on the basis of those flourishing in Edinburgh and in the north-east at the same time. However, it did re-orientate the focus of the university slightly to make it more accountable to civic interests, particularly in the key concessions granted to the council relating to university finance and the provision of

[95]   *RPC*, vol. 6, pp. 408–9.

[96]   *RPC*, vol. 6, pp. 452–6.

bursaries to improve local education. No other records survive to evidence the interactions between the council and the university until the removal of Principal Patrick Sharp in 1614, but the fact that there is no further mention of the council-appointed officer in the extant council minutes (which are wanting between October 1601 and June 1605, August 1613 and December 1616, and September 1617 and September 1623), does suggest that the direct link of financial oversight was not fully maintained. However, the council did continue to present bursaries to students and to provide additional financial assistance wherever possible, and if the advancement of local education in Glasgow was their main aim in promoting civic intervention in the university, then they clearly achieved it.[97]

Conclusion

The new Protestant centres of higher education at Edinburgh, New Aberdeen and Fraserburgh were each created and developed (and in the case of Fraserburgh, shut down) as a result of a unique mix of political intrigue and manoeuvring among crown, church and civic interests that depended entirely upon the local context. Edinburgh went through a number of different iterations in the fevered year prior to its official ratification in line with royal and civic aims and ideology, and if it had been opened in 1582 prior to the exigencies of the Ruthven Raid it is likely that the university would have been much more in keeping with the vision of the local radical ministers for a 'Melvillian' Protestant seminary. At Aberdeen and Fraserburgh, the desire of the local magnate to develop and improve urban and commercial centres in his sphere of influence led directly to the investment that underpinned the foundation of both institutions. However, while Fraserburgh declined very rapidly into a folly that collapsed when the local laird overextended himself, the civic element in New Aberdeen assumed near-exclusive control of Marischal College and turned it to their own aims, cutting across religious and political divides within the town council to do so and clearly causing tensions with the college's benefactor in the process. All three foundations absorbed elements of the 'Melvillian' programme in their curriculum,

---

[97] Bursaries were ordered to be presented to Robert Hamilton on 4 October 1623 and to William Fisher on 2 April 1625, who both appear to have been sons of burgesses. There was also a direct example of support of a poor student beyond bursaries on 17 July 1607: 'Robert Gray, Merchand, is maid burges and frieman of this bruch in favouris of John Bogle, sone to Marcus Bogle, student in the college of Glasgow, for help of his claithis quhen he is maid Master, at Lambes nixt, becaus of his fathiris povertie.' *Extracts from the Records of the Burgh of Glasgow*, pp. 268, 340, 345.

particularly in the clear focus at Marischal and Edinburgh on practical use and application of knowledge and in their engagement with Ramist texts. However, the resulting and apparently competing mix of Ramism and Aristotelianism in early teaching at Edinburgh under Robert Rollock and the first regents suggests that the conflict over the intellectual vision of the university did not simply vanish following its foundation, and that there was considerable ideological ferment within its walls that only settled in the opening years of the seventeenth century. When the account of civic involvement at Glasgow and the attempts there to gear teaching and educational provision to exclusively local interests is added to this picture, it is clear that the Continental trend of establishing Protestant 'arts colleges' under civic oversight was one that enjoyed great vogue in Scotland, even within the older foundations themselves. However, while these new foundations clearly owed something intellectually to Melville's European-inspired reform programme, it was the pressing and pragmatic needs of the local community that played the decisive role in their creation and sustained development.

CHAPTER 8

The Scottish Universities Post-Melville, c. 1606–25

Although it was clear by the turn of the seventeenth century that the 'Melvillian' experiment in educational reform had met with only partial success across the Scottish universities, elements of his intellectual programme had made it in into general teaching and his own work at St Mary's remained geared around the programme that he had developed. However, Melville's political vulnerability in a church increasingly amenable to royal and Episcopal control following the union of the crowns made removal from his high-profile position as principal of the country's only dedicated divinity college simply a matter of time. When in 1606 he was summoned to attend the English court and was subsequently detained indefinitely, George Gledstanes and the range of masters disaffected by Melville during his time at the university, with James Martine prominent among them, moved swiftly to dismantle the remaining traces of his programme. Within five years a complete collapse of the 'New Foundation' of 1579 and a reassertion of all the pre-reformation collegiate foundations and privileges had been achieved, though this was not formally ratified until a revocation of the 'New Foundation' was enacted by Parliament in 1621. Although St Mary's was exempt from this revocation, the remaining staff in the college with connections to Melville were systematically replaced with a group amenable to the royal will, a process which also impacted upon the other colleges.

Freed from the perceived obstacle of Melville's influence, in the following decade the royal government supported attempts to consolidate the financing and oversight of all the universities, culminating most notably in a purge of the staff at Glasgow in 1614 and in the sanctioning of a return to the original foundation at King's College in 1619. However, St Andrews remained the central focus of crown attentions as the university was gradually aligned with the practices and ceremonies at Oxford and Cambridge, reflecting the king's preference that the oldest of the universities and the centre for Scottish theological study should be remodelled as a bastion of orthodoxy. At the same time civic involvement in the provision of local education, seen in the foundation of Edinburgh and Marischal College in the closing decades of the sixteenth century, arguably outstripped royal interests in the universities, with these two foundations enjoying an unparalleled level of investment from local magistrates and benefactors greatly outweighing anything allocated to their older counterparts in the same period.

Finally, while royal and lay interest in the universities contributed to the development of Scottish higher education in very different ways in the final years of the reign of James VI and I, both trends resulted in a stepping away from the aims and methods that Melville had utilised in his reform programme. The extensive range of teaching evidence for this period confirms that the intellectual conservatism and entrenched Aristotelianism visible in earlier sources became fully embedded across the Scottish universities in the years after Melville's removal.

The Consolidation of Control at St Andrews, 1606–11

At the end of August 1606, Andrew Melville arrived in London to attend a meeting at Hampton Court, to which he and several of his Presbyterian colleagues were summoned by the king.[1] The meeting was ostensibly to discuss James VI and I's suspension of the General Assembly in 1604, and his imprisonment and banishment of a group of ministers who had contravened this suspension by holding an assembly without royal consent in Aberdeen in 1605. The first meetings with the king in late September, held before a range of Scottish and English bishops, were soon revealed to be the recalcitrant Melville's last chance to accept the new royal and Episcopal supremacy in the Kirk. When Melville continued to defend the legitimacy of a free General Assembly and of Presbyterianism, the conference soon turned from issues of polity towards his loyalty to the crown. Melville's incendiary behaviour at the conference certainly did not help his case. He berated the king publicly in front of his English councillors, and at one point grabbed the vestments of the Archbishop of Canterbury, Richard Bancroft, and denounced them as 'Romish ragis'. Yet it was an epigram circulating at court that Melville had written, condemning the 'Papist' trappings of the English church service he witnessed in honour of St Michael on 28 September, that provided sufficient grounds to hold him for treason. After initial confinement in the house of the dean of St Paul's, Melville was warded in the Tower of London in April 1607 and his office as principal of St Mary's declared vacant. Four years passed before he was released, and only then on the condition that he did not return home. He opted to accept the invitation of the Protestant Duc de Bouillon to take up a teaching post alongside the Scottish neo-Latinist Arthur Johnstone at the Academy of Sedan in northern France, arriving there in the early summer of 1611. Melville was an active part of the academic community at Sedan,

---

[1] For what follows, see *JMAD*, pp. 653–78; M'Crie, pp. 237–347; MacDonald, *Jacobean Kirk*, pp. 124–5.

and continued writing poetry.[2] However, he never returned to Scotland again. He died in 1622.

With Melville's removal, the growth of crown interest in the university at St Andrews, and the enforcement of the royal prerogative there by those loyal to an episcopal church settlement, reached its apogee. The process of removing the last vestiges of Melville's influence from St Mary's in the year after his imprisonment was a protracted one, and took place against a wider context of disorder and violence at the university. On 28 February 1607 the Privy Council noted that two days earlier students from St Leonard's and St Salvator's had, while attending the burial of the local dignitary Helen Trail, Lady Balcormo, 'invaidit and persewit otheris within the kirkyaird with swordis, battonis, and utheris wapponis, brocht with thame thair for the purpois', and several students had been seriously injured in the ensuing melee. James Martine and Robert Wilkie, as the principals of both colleges, together with their regents and the students involved, were summoned to compear before the Privy Council on 12 March to explain how such a sacrilegious confrontation could have taken place.[3] A further decree on 10 March, noting that the two colleges had 'this lang tyme foisterit privat grudgeis, emulationis, and miscontentment amang thame' which 'now at last … hes burst out in actioun and oppin hostilitie', ordained that they be kept as segregated from one another as possible. During daily exercise St Leonard's students were to go to the St Nicholas fields and St Salvator's to the town links, no masters or regents were to attend church 'bot content thameselffis with thair exercise in thair awne Colledgeis', and the citizens of the town were warned not to aggravate the situation any further by goading students.[4]

Accompanying this decree was the grant of a commission of visitation to Archbishop George Gledstanes to ascertain the causes of the violence.[5] The tenor of this commission showed a clear shift in what the university council, and by extension the crown, thought were the main priorities for governing the university. While it was to carry out the standard issues of assessing staff, restoring order and filling vacant positions, it also noted cryptically that the visitation should ensure there was sufficient 'observatioun and keiping of the first lawis and ordinanceis thairof at the first fundatioun' of the university, with 'punischement of suche as salbe found to haif bene violatteris' of the same. It is unclear whether this 'first fundation' was a reference to the 'New Foundation' of 1579 as the governing constitution of the university, or whether (as seems more

---

2   See the various poems by Melville in Mellon, *L'Académie de Sedan*, pp. 121–209.

3   *RPC*, vol. 7, p. 328.

4   *RPC*, vol. 7, pp. 332–3.

5   *RPC*, vol. 7, pp. 334–5.

likely) this was a tacit announcement that the various components of the university should be governed in accordance with the constitutions that they were first established with, as far as this could be applicable in a Protestant environment.

Another direct aim of the visitation was revealed in a preparatory document circulated prior to its formal declaration. On 9 March, James VI and I dispatched a standardised letter to the privy councillors chosen for the commission to inform them that a visitation of St Andrews was to take place. One key paragraph showed its central intent:

> And whereas We have thought meitt to retayne here Mr. Andrew Melvill, Principall of the New Colledg there, And since that place requyres a resident qualified man to discharge the same, Therefore having made choice of Mr. Robert Howye as a most meitt and sufficient person, both in respect of his lyf and literature, to possess that place: We are to will and requyre yow to see him placed therein ...[6]

For the royal government, Howie was in many ways an obvious choice of successor to Melville, though a choice not without its controversies. Howie had the better part of a decade's experience of study at Continental Calvinist seminaries and had been the inaugural principal of Marischal College, a post which he had held for five years before taking up a ministerial position in Dundee.[7] Although in his early career he had supported Presbyterianism, like the majority of Scottish clergy he was clearly willing to realign his ecclesiastical beliefs in the face of political pressure after the events of 1596/7, and became a strong proponent of royal and Episcopal supremacy. His modified religious beliefs notwithstanding, Howie still courted royal displeasure as an agitator for radical reform of civic administration in Dundee and for better representation of the trade guilds on the burgh council, which resulted in his being banned from taking part in Dundee political life in 1605, and then being translated in the following year to the parish of Keith in Banffshire. Howie took the first opportunity to rehabilitate himself when summoned to Hampton Court to act as one of the crown spokesmen against Melville, an action which no doubt endeared him sufficiently to the king to pave the way for his preferment to Melville's post.[8]

---

[6]   *Original Letters*, vol. 1, pp. 456–7.

[7]   See above pp. 221–4.

[8]   Cameron, *Letters*, pp. xv–xxi, xxiii–xxvii, xliii–xlvii, lxiii–lxxx; James K. Cameron, 'Howie, Robert (d. 1641x7)', *ODNB* [67840, accessed 29 March 2010].

Sufficiently briefed to its purpose, the commission finally met on 16 June in St Andrews.[9] Although no formal record of proceedings for the visitation survives, it evidently discussed the financial state of the university at some length, and the central issue was who should replace Melville.[10] On 23 June it ordered Howie to accept the royal nomination to Melville's vacant post within 15 days, which Howie had refused not on the grounds that he felt uncomfortable replacing the former principal, but that his acceptance would involve his intrusion in precedence above his old travelling companion, John Johnston, who had held the post of second master for more than a decade.[11]

After accepting the position, Howie endured a fraught summer in St Andrews. The staff and students within St Mary's were clearly not disposed to his entrance, and there was doubt in his own mind that he had the full support of the royal government to counter their opposition, as he wrote to the king on 9 August asking for letters of surety that he was 'nocht to be a vicar or deput for ane interim' until Melville was restored to royal favour and released. The resistance to Howie was so great that he even had difficulty securing lodgings for himself in the college. An injunction by the Privy Council of 24 September 1607 noted that while Melville 'for his misbehavioure, dois presentlie remane in prisone', Howie had the right to his rooms and chambers which remained locked. They thus granted commission to Gledstanes to break them open, and remove and inventory all Melville's goods until Melville or a representative came to claim them.[12]

By 28 October matters had reached an interim state of equilibrium in the college, and Gledstanes was proud to report that Howie was installed:

> and that vith such rare lerning as breidis not only contentment to al the Clergie heir, bot also ravisches thame in admiratioun, so the absent his antecessor is not missed, quhyles thay find, in steid of superficiall and feckles inventiones, profitable and substantious theologie.[13]

---

[9] New members were elected to the commission panel on 19 March and the visitation itself was prorogued on 30 April 1607 until 26 May.

[10] We know that it met from a reference in the December 1609 visitation to St Mary's that noted Patrick Melville and the other staff should be paid their full stipend in accordance with the rates agreed at the visitation held in 'St Androis the sextene day of Junii the yeir of God Jai vic and seven yeiris'. UYUY152/2, p. 181.

[11] *RPC*, vol. 7, p. 396; Cameron, *Letters*, lxxii.

[12] Following a royal letter of 6 September discussing the situation. Cameron, *Letters*, lxx–lxxii.

[13] *Original Letters*, vol. 1, pp. 117–19.

However, there were still considerable issues to be resolved within the university, and a second large-scale visitation was granted to Gledstanes which met some time before 17 April 1608. In part the commission dealt with a financial dispute between the laird of Tulliebarne and the Lord Oliphant over the teind sheaves of Forteviot which were annexed to St Salvator's,[14] but Gledstanes reported to the king that the biggest issue was the continued instability of St Mary's. The rents of the college had been so confused 'be the abuse of the preceding Maisteris' that there was insufficient funding to support Howie, and a secondary issue was feuding between Howie and Johnston, as the latter blatantly refused to acknowledge the former's elevation above him. Gledstanes wanted simply to remove Johnston, not only for the friction between him and Howie, but also because he believed Johnston was a seditious reminder to the student body of the regime under Melville. However, his removal proved impossible as 'his great inhabilitie and seiknes hath stayed the executioun thairof', and Johnston continued to hold his post, although he was likely bedridden from shortly after Howie's accession until his death in 1611.[15]

Patrick Melville, the other master at the college, showed a slightly more pragmatic attitude towards events. Although he was one of Melville's nephews, and had studied and taught alongside him at both Glasgow and St Andrews, there is no evidence that Gledstanes or Howie faced any opposition from him as the process of change overtook the college. He would also take an active role in the royal reforms of the university in the following decade, and was one of the first to accept an English-style doctorate in theology when it was introduced in 1616. The issue of finance seemed to have motivated Melville the most, and having wrested control of the college Gledstanes aimed to smooth over this issue by throwing money at the problem. A small-scale internal visitation to the college, undertaken by the university council on 21 December 1609, ordered Gledstanes to take personal supervision of the college *oeconomus* Patrick Orme, ensure that he find caution for providing the expected income to the college, and that he make regular account of its financial status. It also ordered that

---

[14] Gledstanes noted in his justifaction for the commission that 'a great truble and perturbatione sal fall in this cuntrie betwix my Lord of Tilliebarne and his freindis and my Lord Olyphant and his adherentis' over a number of teind sheaves that had fallen to the college. This was resolved on 3 May 1608 when a tack was granted to William Oliphant of Newton of all the teind sheaves of the towns and lands of Kildoning and Pitquhannartie in the parish of Forteviot (Forteviott) [Perthshire] for the space of 19 years, for an unspecified grassum, and considering the utility and profit of the College and its patrimony, and for annual payments of 80 merks for the teind sheaves of Kildoning, and 24 merks for the teind sheaves of Pitquhannartie.

[15] *Original Letters*, vol. 1, pp. 128–31, at p. 130. Calderwood notes that Gledstanes tried to remove Johnston as he was 'unprofitable, pernicious, and his chamber a receptacle to all evill affected persons', thus suggesting the link to sedition. Calderwood, vol. 6, p. 703.

Patrick Melville and the other masters receive their stipend for that year and that Orme hold back a portion of each of the masters' wage to ensure they would have the means to live *collegialiter*.[16]

These actions were to take effect from 1 January 1610, but when it was apparent to another visitation in June that they had not, Gledstanes and the council resorted to simple cash payments to quieten tensions within the college. They ordered the Laird of Balcomie to pay Melville a stipend of £240 from the readiest available income to the college, to pay the cook John Mair his outstanding wage of £260, and to award Howie with £100 and Johnston with a smaller sum of a hundred merks 'in consideratioune of the guid service done' by the two men.[17]

It is difficult to say whether resistance to Howie was sustained beyond the initial period. An admittedly partisan account of his teaching by Calderwood suggests that he was seen as incompetent. When he tried to argue for supremacy of bishops over presbyteries in his early lectures, 'his auditors professed plainlie that they were rather confirmed in their former opinions, nor anie wheate moved', leading to a censure from the presbytery and the offer of a public disputation with David Dalgleish, one of the candidates for the ministry.[18] Howie also supposedly disrupted a visit to St Andrews by the earl of Dunbar and a delegation of English theologians who were there to improve relations between the two churches. In one version of events Howie stood up publicly and denounced the practices of the Kirk, thus torpedoing the talks and embarrassing the king; in another the episode passed without incident.[19] However, the evidence of Howie's wider impact on university life suggests he was accepted largely without issue. His accession did have a minor effect on the number of entrants into the divinity college, which took a considerable dip in 1608, but in 1609 numbers rose again to those of 1607, dipped slightly again in 1610, and then increased considerably in the years following 1611.[20] It is also clear that Howie was personable enough to the broader university community: he was elected deputy rector of the university in March 1608, and was voted into this position annually for a further eight years before being elected rector in 1616.[21]

While Gledstanes and the university council asserted the royal will largely unopposed at St Mary's in the vacuum caused by Melville's departure, their attempts to exert similar levels of interference in staffing

---

[16]   UYUY152/2, pp. 181–2.

[17]   UYSL110/A17.

[18]   Cameron, *Letters*, p. lxxiii; Calderwood, vol. 6, p. 703.

[19]   Calderwood, vol. 6, p. 735.

[20]   See Appendix, Table 3.

[21]   Acta Rectorum, pp. 111–16, 119, 121–3.

at the other colleges met much greater resistance. In part this tension was exacerbated by the level of intervention that James VI and I had come to expect as his prerogative at the universities of Oxford and Cambridge after his assumption of the English throne, a level he now believed should be replicated in St Andrews. The king took a deep and abiding interest in the English universities after his accession. His love of all things intellectual was well known, and he regularly spent August residing at Woodstock, just outside Oxford, at which time he would demand an account of the university's proceedings for the previous year.[22] James also intervened in elections and appointments at both universities at a far greater level than any of his English predecessors. In 1604 alone James sanctioned 17 royal mandates to vacant posts at Oxford and Cambridge, followed by a further four in 1605, 13 in 1606 and 14 in 1607.[23] James was so indiscriminate about issuing nominations under the signet that masters were often faced with the quandary of accepting two rival nominees for the same post, as occurred at Oxford for two lessees at Oriel and All Souls in 1603, and for a fellowship in Magdalen College in 1604. A formal protest from the vice chancellor and several heads of colleges at Cambridge was delivered to the keeper of the signet and the chancellor of the university, Robert Cecil, in July 1607, which complained that the deluge of royal letters allowed unqualified candidates to procure positions against the 'statutes of foundations, oaths of electors and free choice of the fittest'. This led to a reduction of nominations after the 'free-for-all' of the initial years of the reign to a more modest total of three to four per year, which was more in keeping with the average of five or six annual nominations made by Elizabeth in the last decade of her reign. However, on several occasions colleges resisted nominations to the point of almost defying royal prerogative, as occurred in the nominations of new masters for Caius in 1607 and Christ's College in 1609 at Oxford, and in the wardenships of Corpus and All Souls at Oxford in 1614 and 1618.[24]

While St Andrews was clearly willing to accept an increased level of governmental oversight and visitation in the early seventeenth century, and staff in some quarters were no doubt happy to accept the intrusion of Howie in St Mary's, they drew the line at allowing the crown to act as patron in such an untrammelled fashion elsewhere. Ironically, it was James Martine, a long-time supporter of governmental policy at the university,

---

[22]   Kenneth Fincham, 'Oxford and the Early Stuart Polity', in Nicholas Tyacke (ed.), *The History of the University of Oxford, volume 4: Seventeenth-Century Oxford* (Oxford: Clarendon Press, 1997), p. 182.

[23]   Morgan and Brooke, *A History of the University of Cambridge, volume 2*, pp. 413–14.

[24]   Morgan and Brooke, *A History of the University of Cambridge, volume 2*, pp. 406–12; Fincham, 'Oxford and the Early Stuart Polity', pp. 191–8, at p. 193.

who emerged as the main protagonist against crown interference. On 3 August 1609 it came to the Privy Council's attention that, following the resignation of William Wedderburn as a regent in the college, James VI and I had directed letters to Martine ordering that he accept James Scheves as 'able and qualifeit' to fill the place, who was to be accepted following the formality of a trial of his learning. While other members of the election committee were willing to comply, Martine apparently refused on the grounds that he intended 'to intrude a sister sone of his awne in the said place of regencie'. As a result the Lords of Council ordered that Scheves either be accepted or Martine and the other electors appear before the council on 17 August to explain their actions.[25]

Martine and the staff of St Salvator's eventually appeared before the Council on 16 November and resolutely denied accepting the royal directive for several reasons. Firstly, the act of Privy Council of 3 August had been passed in the 'feriot and close tyme of harvest and vacance', when all the members of the university were scattered; secondly, Wedderburn was still active in his post and had not yet resigned, so any attempt to pre-empt this was invalid; and thirdly, even if he had left the post had to be advertised publicly for a month, which it had not. However, the most revealing point of rebuttal shows how little impact the 'New Foundation' had had in St Salvator's and how quickly Martine and the other masters were ready to ignore it as soon as the opportunity arose. They noted that according to the original foundation of the college by Bishop Kennedy, the election of regents to the college pertained to the principal of the college only and that the 'New Foundation' of 1579 'cannot impair the laws and liberties of the ancient foundation of the college, and has never been received or allowed by the provost and masters within the same, but has been protested against by them'. The Council neatly sidestepped the constitutional issues involved in the episode by suspending Scheves' claim on the grounds that the post was not vacant, but it is clear that any pretence to maintaining adherence to the 'New Foundation' had been given up by Martine and his fellows now that its chief protagonist had been thoroughly removed from power.[26]

Martine convinced his colleagues in the other colleges to follow this independent stance. In August of the following year, the king issued another missive ordering the rector and assembled staff of the university to accept Scheves to a post now that Wedderburn was confirmed in his intention to leave the college. A letter directed to the crown shows that a defence of the older constitutional forms of the university was clearly envisaged by the masters over the 'New Foundation', as James' imperious form of election

---

[25]   RPC, vol. 8, pp. 339–40.
[26]   RPC, vol. 8, pp. 375–6.

was 'verie vncouth and strange to ws, nevir being hard nor accustumat of befoir, tending altogether to the everting of our fundationes, quhilk we haue hithertils inviolablie obseruit in electioun of our Maisteris'.[27] This united front appears to have done the trick, for Scheves was never heard of again.

While there was no room for negotiation on interference with staffing, Martine was willing to work with the royal authority to remove as much of the legacy of schism caused by Melville's presence at the university as possible, and worked with the other masters to restore ecclesiastical harmony in the locality. Martine, along with Robert Wilkie, Robert Howie and David Monypenny as the principals of the college and the dean of arts, were all reported by Gledstanes on 10 April 1610 as having accepted a place on the metropolitan high commission for ecclesiastical causes, one of two ecclesiastical courts set up in Scotland on the English model with the power to examine and excommunicate any suspect person, to try the aptitude of any minister and remove him if necessary, and censor any preaching within Scotland.[28] This body largely replaced the General Assembly, which had been suspended indefinitely in the preceding February, and was clearly geared to ensuring the royal supremacy. It was also to try and censor university teaching, and the fact that the masters were willing to take part shows how keen they were to allay the fears of the royal government over suspect doctrine being taught within the colleges.

At the same time, Martine allied with Gledstanes to remove one of Melville's remaining allies within the university, and someone who had been intruded upon the staff of St Salvator's when the 'New Foundation' was implemented. Although William Welwood had been restored to the office of lawyer in the college in 1601, and had continued to teach and to draw his stipend (even on one occasion in 1607 borrowing forty merks from Martine), it is clear that his place in the college was unwelcome.[29] Welwood also faced a sizeable threat from Gledstanes, who along with the rest of the Scottish episcopate, had been gradually restored to much of his pre-reformation prerogatives by 1610. This included the right to appoint judges to the local commissary court, where Welwood would have worked and demonstrated court processes to his students. Gledstanes had shown no support for Welwood's family during their feud with the Arthurs, and he was signatory to a letter of 9 March 1611 that informed Martine and his colleagues that Welwood was to be retired from office, though compensated with the arrears of seven chalders of oats due to

---

27   *Original Letters*, vol. 1, pp. 255–6.
28   *Original Letters*, vol. 1, pp. 242–3; MacDonald, *Jacobean Kirk*, p. 144.
29   UYSS110/C/4/17–18; UYSS200/4–6; Cairns, 'Academic Feud', 276–7.

him from when he was forcibly removed in 1597.[30] That Gledstanes was the chief agent behind this letter is suggested by the fact that his son-in-law, Sir John Wemyss of Craigtoun (whom Gledstanes had appointed as commissary of St Andrews) was suddenly part of the university system. Wemyss had been elected rector on 1 March 1611, and was now 'to goe fordward in teaching the Canoun Law, as ane reddie way to bring out the Presbiterian Discipline fra the heartis of the young ones, and to acquent even the oldest with the auncient Churche Government, quhairof thai ar ignorant'.[31] With Welwood's removal Gledstanes had an opportunity to aggrandise his family, remove the remnants of Melville's cohort in the university, and provide a law teacher who could inculcate a discussion of ecclesiastical law that fostered conformity between the English and Scottish churches. Martine stood to gain the removal of the final obstacle in his way to restoring the old foundation in fact, if not fully in law. On 18 September 1611 Welwood, painfully aware of his isolated situation and of the fact that favour was clearly turning towards restoring the old foundation, quietly resigned from his post and declared himself satisfied as to his payment.[32]

Welwood retired to England, where he lived and worked until at least 1624.[33] The last surviving ardent supporter of Melville, John Johnston, died a little over a month after Welwood's removal on 20 October 1611.[34] With his death, all links to Melville and the defence of the 'New Foundation' were severed, and with it the end of all the experiments of 'Melvillian' re-foundation in Scotland. The next decade would see unprecedented growth and expansion in the universities, but with royal and civic government firmly at the helm.

Crown Intervention in the Universities, Post-Melville

Johnston's death was not only significant as an end to 'Melvillian' involvement in Scottish higher education; it also marked the beginning of a period of growing lay and governmental investment in the universities. In the decade after 1610, the royal government was involved in several disputes at the universities. Firstly, a controversy involving St Andrews and Edinburgh forced the royal government for the first time to set strictures

---

[30]   Cairns, 'Academic Feud', 277–9.

[31]   *Original Letters*, vol. 1, pp. 269–71, at pp. 269–70.

[32]   UYSS200/11–12.

[33]   Cairns, 'Academic Feud', 279–81.

[34]   A council missive was directed to inventory his goods for safekeeping on 21 November 1611. *RPC*, vol. 9, p. 640; also printed in *Original Letters*, vol. 1, p. 439.

on the relationship between them. On 25 July 1611 the masters of St Leonard's appeared before the Council to complain that John Murray, the son of Oliver Murray of Castleton and one of the students at the college, had 'schamefullie, cruellie, and unhonnestlie hurte and woundit' the cook of the college in a violent outburst. Instead of facing punishment at the college, Murray had fled to Edinburgh University where he was received by the Principal, Henry Charteris, and having studied there for over two months was about to be awarded his degree. Fearful of the precedent this would set, St Andrews appealed to the Council who suspended the right of Edinburgh to award a degree to Murray, and James VI and I ordered an enquiry on 15 September as to why Edinburgh had been willing to accept a student without paying sufficient attention to his previous record.[35] However, Edinburgh itself had to launch a supplication for intervention from the Privy Council a little over a month later, as when it became common knowledge among the students that the college was less stringent about upholding standards of discipline they took 'the bauldnes to misknowe the said Principall and Regentis, and to deborde in all kind of uncomelie behaviour and insolencyis'.[36] The Privy Council thus ruled that no university was henceforth to accept any student from elsewhere who had been removed from their studies for violence or lack of discipline.

There was further involvement by the royal government across several of the universities in the early 1610s, some of which was invasive. On 9 December 1613 a large-scale commission of visitation was ordered by the Privy Council for Glasgow, where there were still concerns that the atmosphere under Principal Patrick Sharp was one of stagnation and corruption. The commission was given pointed directions to 'take cognitioun of the literature of the Principall and Regentis of the Colledge, and how by thair travellis, in regaird of the old age of the Principall and utheris many defectis, the same floorischeis in letteris', to ascertain how rents were being used and collected, whether tacks were being set via private agreements that benefited the masters rather than the college, and most seriously 'to try gif the entrie of Regentis and thair admissioun hes bene procured in tyme bypast be brybrie'.[37] No records survive for this commission but what was found at the university clearly substantiated these complaints, and a range of letters by commissioners attached to the

[35]   *RPC*, vol. 9, pp. 229–30, 630.

[36]   *RPC*, vol. 9, p. 272.

[37]   *RPC*, vol. 10, pp. 195–7; *Registrum Magni Sigilli Regum Scotorum: The Register of the Great Seal of Scotland*, ed. J.M. Thomson and others (11 vols, 1882–), vol. 7, 956, pp. 347–8.

visitation describe Sharp in highly unflattering terms.[38] Sharp accepted his forcible resignation on 11 August 1614, some months prior to the arrival in Glasgow on 31 December of a new principal, Robert Boyd, fresh from a teaching position at Saumur. Boyd had been ordered by the king to resign his post in France and to accept the position at Glasgow, an action which clearly shows the growing level of arbitrary power the crown was gaining over higher education.[39] At Old Aberdeen a similar level of involvement was in evidence. A caution of 500 marks was issued by the Privy Council against William Ord, a burgess of the town, for assaulting William Rait and the other masters of King's College, and in 1613 a commission of visitation was also ordered for the university. However, beyond a single entry acknowledging its existence in the Council records no evidence of its discussion or actions has been noted.[40]

The most direct involvement in the universities in the 1610s was at St Andrews, and was tied to bringing the practices and processes of the university into line with those of the English universities, much in the same way that James aimed to bring about ecclesiastical convergence between the two realms in this decade.[41] One development was the creation of a centralised library for the university to allow it to stand alongside the recently constituted Bodleian library at Oxford and the impressive college collections at Cambridge; another was restoring a degree programme in divinity that had sufficient formality and ceremony to reflect the elevated status of divinity graduates. Plans for these developments were shepherded through by Gledstanes from early 1611. He had clearly mentioned the matter of a library to James VI and I, as the university masters wrote to the king in May relating that their 'most prudent chancellor' had informed them of the king's interest in the university and his desire to oversee the foundation of a centralised library, which they could only entreat the king to pursue.[42] A letter of Gledstanes to the king in the following month revealed that the archbishop had continued to develop his plans on both

---

[38]   Robert Wodrow, *Collections upon the Lives of the Reformers and Most Eminent Ministers of the Church of Scotland*, ed. William J. Duncan (2 vols, Glasgow, 1834–5) vol. 2, pp. 115–17. A letter of Sir George Elphinstone of Blythswood, formerly provost of Glasgow, to the future principal on August 15 1614 notes that 'the old man [Sharp] is well satisfyed, and hath given up his place freely, which he behooved to have done otherwise, in respect of his great abuses' (p. 115).

[39]   Durkan and Kirk, p. 416; *Munimenta*, vol. 3, p. 367.

[40]   *RPC*, vol. 8, p. 723; vol. 10, pp. 18, 809.

[41]   Alan R. MacDonald, 'James VI and I, the Church of Scotland, and British Ecclesiastical Convergence', *The History Journal* 48.4 (2005): 885–903; Jenny Wormald, 'The Headaches of Monarchy: Kingship and the Kirk in the Early Seventeenth Century', in Goodare and MacDonald (eds), *Sixteenth-Century Scotland*, pp. 365–94.

[42]   *Original Letters*, vol. 1, pp. 271–2.

fronts, as in addition to reminding the king that he should speak to the archbishop of Canterbury about the plans for the library, he also desired:

> that the forme and ordour of making Bacheliers and Doctours of Divinitie and of the Lawes wer send homeward to me, that I micht once create one or two Doctours, to incite wthers to the fame honour; for we haue appointed both ane Facultie of Theologie and ane Deane therof, namelie, Maifter Robert Howie, quhome we wald wische to haue *Insignia Doctoratus*; and to incourage our ignorant Cleargie to learning ...[43]

This letter shows how serious Gledstanes was about restoring the study of divinity to pre-eminence at St Andrews, and how this should be a prerequisite for any candidates aiming to ascend the Scottish ecclesiastical hierarchy. Although Melville had nominally been appointed to the post of dean of the faculty of theology in the wake of the 1599 visitation, this post had largely been given to him as a face-saving exercise for the restriction of his influence elsewhere within the university, and there is no evidence that the faculty existed *per se* before 1611 beyond the masters of St Mary's. Gledstanes' resurrection of the old faculty, which had lapsed since the reformation but which would ultimately include the principals and other theologians from across the colleges, was a significant step towards restoring one of the major constitutional components of the original pre-reformation university.

In April of the following year Gledstanes finally received from the archbishop of Canterbury an outline of the 'maner of tacking degreies as is useit in the universities in England', which outlined the length of study required for a bachelorship and doctorate in divinity, the process of public preaching and disputation before the university masters that was to take place to satisfy the requirements for the award, and the quality of character candidates were expected to possess.[44] However, it would be five years before these plans would come to some kind of fruition, a year after Gledstanes had died and been replaced by John Spottiswoode, previously the archbishop of Glasgow. In June 1616 the king sent John Young, Dean of Winchester north with a series of reform articles. Young was well-placed to liaise with the university; as son of James VI's former tutor Peter Young and brother to the royal librarian Patrick Young he had important literary connections with the court, and had experience of both Scottish and English university education, having taken his MA at St Andrews in 1606 and his bachelor and doctorate in divinity at Cambridge in 1611 and 1613. His visit to the university in 1616 was one of a number of diplomatic

---

[43]   *Original Letters*, vol. 1, pp. 276–7.

[44]   UYUY152/2, pp. 293–4.

visits to Scotland between 1616 and 1621 on behalf of the king (where his Scottish background gave him added credibility in negotiations), and preceded the king's one and only visit to Scotland after the union of the crowns, in 1617.[45]

Although primarily concerned with the implementation of formal procedures for the divinity degrees at St Andrews, the articles made several significant concessions to a return to the older constitutions that the masters preferred in place of the 'New Foundation'.[46] Recognising the ambiguity that had developed as a result of the proliferation of conflicting foundations, the crown was 'pleased that the auncient Chartour of that Universitie be renewed, confirmed, and enlarged, or (if no such Chartour be) to graunte a new one', so that the issue of the university's constitution would be addressed. The degrees of bachelor and doctor in divinity were expressly reinstated after their hiatus under Melville, and in the same way that candidates in England were expected to dispute publicly before the divinity masters and to give a sermon in public upon the completion of their course, so too were the successful candidates at St Andrews expected to give a sermon in Edinburgh before the assembled lords in St Giles or in the Chapel Royal at Holyrood. This exercise was clearly designed to introduce the next generation of ecclesiastical placemen to the assembled political hierarchy, for it was also noted that only divinity graduates could accept 'eminent places' within the church, and only doctors of divinity could accept bishoprics.

Further evidence that James envisioned St Andrews being refashioned as the pre-eminent Scottish educational centre is evident in the final two statutes of the articles, the first of which ordered that two candidates from every diocese in Scotland were to be funded as divinity scholars at St Mary's. Perhaps also recognising the damage done to the provision of legal education at St Andrews with the continued opposition to William Welwood over the previous few decades, the crown ordained that arts graduates unwilling to enter into the ministry after their studies should be encouraged to head to Edinburgh, 'quahir We wald haf a Reader at least established to teache the Lawis', so that legal tuition could perhaps be undertaken more fittingly in the country's political and administrative centre.[47]

James also implemented plans to develop Oxford and Cambridge in 1617, and the majority of the remaining statutes for St Andrews in

---

[45] Kenneth Fincham, 'Young, John (1585–1654)', *ODNB* [38164, accessed 19 Jan 2010].

[46] For the articles and the royal letter authorising them, see *Original Letters*, vol. 2, pp. 805–9.

[47] Cairns, 'Academic Feud', 279; Acta Rectorum, p. 176.

that year aimed to bring practice there into line with the two English institutions, and to enhance the ceremonial pomp of the university. One expressly stated that all rites for the creation of doctors were to follow those used in England 'and other privileged places in forreyne nationis, or ... as gryte conformitie unto them as the estate of the Countrie may beare', and regular prayers in thanksgiving to the royal family were to follow a similar pattern to those used in the Church of England. Another advocated that 'some longer tyme' be allocated to study in arts before entrance to divinity, presumably a period of seven years to match the official prerequisite length of study in England. Holidays were to be granted for Christmas, Easter, Ascension Day and Whitsunday, with the masters of St Mary's leading the university in services of prayer on each day. There was also to be an annual opening and closing ceremony of thanksgiving to the benefactors of the university, and a further holiday on 5 November with Latin prayer '*in laudem Regis*, with solemne thanksgiving for all hys [the king's] deliveries at other tymes'.[48]

There is no evidence of the detailed discussion that these statutes must have provoked, but a single note attached to them shows that it was again James Martine, along with his fellow principal at St Leonard's, Peter Bruce, who initially refused to accept the articles 'unless the university [body] was first consulted'.[49] It is likely that these two men, although acknowledging that the new statutes allowed tacitly for a return to their old college foundations and thus to their traditional roles as specialists in theology, were unwilling to sanction a plan that manifestly positioned their colleges beneath St Mary's in precedence. However, the promise of a sufficient reward in status appears to have been enough to win them over. On 29 July Martine and Bruce, along with Robert Howie and Patrick Melville, John Strang minister of Errol, Theodore Hay minister of Peebles and David Barclay minister of St Andrews, were provided with doctorates in a service conducted by John Young. The controversy surrounding this ceremony was evident in Calderwood's statement that this 'noveltie was brought in amongst us without advise or consent of the kirk', and in the fact that three other candidates – John Carmichael, David Mearns and John Dykes – refused to accept the degree when offered.[50]

Within the following month, it was clear that the recommendations for the re-formulation of divinity teaching were on their way to being

---

[48]   *Original Letters*, vol. 2, pp. 805–9.

[49]   *Original Letters*, vol. 2, p. 806. The note reads: 'Articuli quidam sequentes oblate sunt Academiae a Doctore Joanne Junio, qui rogavit, ut ab Academia reciperentur, et ut iis subscriberent Primarii Collegiorum Magistri; quod facere recusarunt D. Jacobus Martinus et D. Petrus Brusius nis prius consulta Academia.'

[50]   Calderwood, vol. 7, p. 222; vol. 8, p. 95.

accepted. A letter to John Murray, thanking him for a £10 contribution towards the cost of new books for the university library, saw Howie, Bruce, Barclay and James Blair, a regent in St Mary's, designate themselves as doctors of divinity.[51] Directions passed to John Earl of Montrose, the king's commissioner at the General Assembly convened at Aberdeen in August 1616 to push through articles of conformity between the Scottish and English churches, noted the desire to implement the programme of sponsoring students from each diocese to come to St Andrews, although the crown now advocated that designated students within the province of Glasgow (the dioceses of Glasgow, Galloway, Argyll and the Isles) could attend the university in the west for study up to bachelor level.[52] Collectively, this growing rapprochement with the royal will in relation to divinity education in Scotland mirrored in microcosm the larger acceptance of royal prerogative in the Kirk in the later 1610s. It also shows that in all but formal constitutional terms, the 'Melvillian' vision of theological education at the university had been replaced within a decade of his departure.

The Age of Expansion: the Universities and Investment, 1603–25

While the crown clearly took considerable interest in reforming St Andrews after Melville's removal, it interfered to a far lesser extent in developments at the other pre-reformation universities. Moreover, it only legislated on the new arts colleges at Edinburgh and Aberdeen when one of them directly came into contact with one of the older foundations, as Edinburgh did with St Andrews in 1611. The main reason that Marischal and Edinburgh do not figure largely in the discussion of Privy Council measures and parliamentary acts is that the supervision of these two institutions by their respective town councils, a role implicit in their foundations and early development, continued largely unabated in the early seventeenth century. Both councils regularly hired and replaced regents and other staff when necessary, provided funding for repairs and minor expenditure, and regularly visited the colleges to take account of their finances and standards of teaching. This civic control of the 'toun colleges' clearly demarcated them in terms of governance from their 'ancient' counterparts, and in many ways made them more like the Protestant 'arts academies' that figured so largely in the Continental education of many of the Scottish intelligentsia.

---

[51]   *Original Letters*, vol. 2, pp. 489–90.
[52]   *Original Letters*, vol. 2, p. 483.

Another dividing line between the two groups in the early seventeenth century soon becomes apparent if we approach them in terms of new investment they received. In the years between 1603 and 1625 King's College received, as far as can be found, no additions to the portfolio of existing funding attached to its foundation. At St Andrews in the same period, excluding funds provided by the royal family for books and for roofing the partially completed library building in 1617/18, lay gifts and endowments totalled less than £5,600.[53] At Glasgow new funding was even harder to come by, with gifts from Archbishop Spottiswoode and from lay patrons totalling less than £1,200.[54] Conversely, Edinburgh received a massive injection of funding from a variety of sponsors in and around the town that picked up pace as the century progressed. Between 1598 and 1625 alone, over £18,000 of new investment was generated at the university by civic gift. At Marischal College a similar amount was endowed over the same period, with almost £15,000 of funding received. What were these gifts, and why were they being provided to the new colleges in such numbers?

At Edinburgh, the majority of this funding was provided by the town council. In 1607, the kirk session provided a gift of £8,100 pounds to the college, with the town contributing the annual fees raised by the rental of the town mortcloths towards this.[55] Between 1615 and 1618 the town spent over £9,000 on the construction of 'ane commoune schoole and librarie in thair colledge in the kirkfield', in part funded by a gift of 3,000 marks delivered to the council by Lord Scott of Buccleuch.[56] The council also paid over £140 for a steady trickle of books to the newly endowed library between 1615 and 1625.[57]

While these endowments account for a little under 70 per cent of total college investment, the remainder was provided from over 20 small bequests and legacies by local citizens and benefactors. Ranging in size from 100 merks to £1,000, the conditions and purposes attached to these gifts reveal something of the motivations that underlay their foundation.

---

[53] James B. Salmond and George H. Bushnell, *Henderson's Benefaction: a Tercentenary Acknowledgment of the University's Debt to Alexander Henderson* (St Andrews, 1942), pp. 37–46, at pp. 40 and 45; *RPS* 1617/5/48 [accessed 16 February 2010]. This assumes that the total value of books donated by lay patrons at the founding of the library totalled less than £100.

[54] *Munimenta*, vol. 1, pp. 188–9, 192–3, 197–9, 200–202, 204–5; *Deeds Instituting Bursaries, Scholarships, and other Foundations, in the College and University of Glasgow* (Glasgow, 1850), pp. 8–25.

[55] *Extracts from the Records of the Burgh of Edinburgh, A.D. 1604 to 1626*, ed. M. Wood (Edinburgh, 1931), pp. 44–5, 48–9.

[56] *Edinburgh Burgh Records 1604–1626*, pp. 135, 138.

[57] *Edinburgh Burgh Records 1604–1626*, pp. 128, 248, 290–1.

Four of the grants were established as lump sums that were to be invested by the council in order to provide an annuity for the granter, with the lump sum to pass to the college upon their decease, showing the interaction of practical provision with a desire to contribute to the local community. Six of the legacies were to be split equally with other civic projects, or were conditionally granted should another project fail to achieve completion. When the merchant burgess William Mauld granted a gift of 2,000 merks to create a textiles workhouse for support of the poor in 1617, he stipulated that if the enterprise was not achieved within seven years, half the sum was to be given to the college for the support of the professors and the other half to support a pauper in the hospital.[58] On 23 August 1620 the bequest of William Rig granted 1,250 merks to be split between the workhouse project and the fund for a divinity professor,[59] and the lump sum of 1,000 merks that Charles Shearer, 'indweller in Dort' provided to fund an annuity for the support of his family in Edinburgh was to be divided equally at the last survivor's decease between the college and the hospital in Trinity College.[60] The 1619 legacy of the merchant William Justice was to provide a hundred marks to the Greyfriars church fund, and a hundred to the college,[61] and both Issobel Broun and James Ainslie stipulated that their gifts be split between funding a professorship in divinity and adding funds to the support of the local hospital.[62] Interestingly, eight of the gifts made some or all their provision to supporting the establishment and maintenance of a divinity professor, a position formally created when this role was separated from the responsibilities allocated to the college principal in 1620. This shows how important a priority it was to the local citizenry that higher education in the city paid sufficient attention to 'godly' concerns. While no single overarching purpose is apparent in this eclectic range of gifts, civic patriotism, and the potential for improving the local community as a result of investing in education, is certainly the inherent theme in their provision.

As in the case of Edinburgh, Aberdeen town council paid for considerable investment within the new university. On 30 August 1609 they granted £100 for repairing a house within the college grounds to act as a library for the college, a project to which they paid a further £100 on 20 April 1614.[63] On 8 April 1612 the council authorised the erection of a loft in the old kirk of the town so that the students might have their own space

---

58   *Edinburgh Burgh Records 1604–1626*, p. 170–1.

59   *Edinburgh Burgh Records 1604–1626*, p. 210; Dalzel, vol. 2, p. 75.

60   *Edinburgh Burgh Records 1604–1626*, p. 101.

61   *Edinburgh Burgh Records 1604–1626*, p. 192; Dalzel, vol. 2, p. 72.

62   *Edinburgh Burgh Records 1604–1626*, pp. 246, 248; Dalzel, vol. 2, p. 77, 80.

63   *FMA*, vol. 1, pp. 112, 205–6.

during church service, and on 28 August 1616 directed masons to carry out minor repairs to the back wall within the college bounds.[64] The council agreed to a plan put forward on 11 June 1623 by William Guild, an ex-student of Marischal and minister of King-Edward in the presbytery of Turriff, to transform the 'foirhous' at the front of Greyfriars into a proper entrance to the college, which incorporated a stationer's shop. They also sponsored a short-lived experiment in February 1620 where an annual stipend was granted to the grammar school master David Wedderburn to teach a weekly lesson in Latin grammar, composition and rhetoric in alternate weeks at the college, an arrangement which lasted until the duties of the two posts made this untenable in 1624.[65]

As at Edinburgh, a range of lay and civic gifts were granted to Marischal in the early seventeenth century, but there is a major difference in terms of size between the gifts granted to the two colleges. While the grants made in the former rarely constituted more than a few hundred marks in value, only three of the eight benefactions made to the college between 1606 and 1624 totalled £100 or less, with two totalling 1,000 merks, two 4,000 merks and two 6,000 merks. These gifts were all supplied by ex-students who went into an academic or ministerial career beyond the confines of New Aberdeen. Duncan Liddell (1561–1613), an Aberdonian who studied medicine, mathematics and astronomy across the Continent under luminaries including Tycho Brahe,[66] ordained in July 1612 that the lands of Pitmedden just outside Aberdeen be mortified to enable six bursars in arts and mathematics, and in December 1613 this was enlarged with a further grant of 6,000 merks to provide for a permanent professor of mathematics.[67] James Cargill, another student who excelled in the study and practice of medicine on the Continent in the 1590s at Basle and at Montbelliard, bequeathed 4,000 merks in 1614 for the support of four poor scholars at Marischal, who were each to receive the interest of one quarter of the endowment to fund their course.[68] At his death in 1611 the St Mary's professor and King's graduate John Johnston left the sum of 1,000 merks to mortify a four-year studentship for a divinity scholar at Marischal, to be administered by the local ministry and teaching staff

---

[64]   FMA, vol. 1, p. 120; *Extracts from the Council Register of the Burgh of Aberdeen*, vol. 2, p. 346.

[65]   FMA, vol. 1, p. 185.

[66]   A.G. Molland, 'Duncan Liddell (1561–1613): An Early Benefactor of Marischal College Library', *Aberdeen University Review* 51 (1986): 485–99.

[67]   FMA, vol. 1, pp. 120–39.

[68]   James K. Cameron, 'Some Aberdeen Students on the Continent in the Late Sixteenth and Early Seventeenth Centuries', in Paul Dukes (ed.), *The Universities of Aberdeen and Europe: The First Three Centuries* (Aberdeen, 1995), pp. 57–78; FMA, vol.1, pp. 149–53.

with presentation by the lairds of Caskieben and Crimond.[69] Yet another well-travelled Aberdonian, Patrick Copland, provided the final gift in this series of major endowments. Copland studied at the Aberdeen grammar school and at Marischal, and in 1612 joined the East India Company as a preacher in its naval fleet before settling with his family in the Summer Isles in Bermuda, where he strove to provide 'godly' education to the local populace until his death in 1651.[70] Copland mortified a total of 6,000 merks in three separate benefactions between January 1617 and February 1628 for the purpose of providing a 'reader in Divinity' skilled in the biblical languages who would be chosen by the provost and baillies of the town.

There are two reasons that may have motivated these benefactions, and both reveal something of the nature and quality of education at Marischal. Cargill, Liddell and Johnston had all studied extensively on the Continent, and were recognised as talented and heavyweight academics in their fields. The staff at Marischal in the first half of the seventeenth century mirrored these men: the principals of the college from Robert Howie until Patrick Dun in 1640 had all studied abroad, and each published a range of literary works, something that contemporary principals at other universities often neglected to do once receiving tenure.[71] The staff at Marischal also stuck rigorously to one facet of the 'Melvillian' programme of study that other universities had not, that of each professor having a specialised area of study rather than leading a class through the full MA course. This provision was adopted shortly after the college's foundation and was still in place in 1623.[72] The fact that Cargill, Liddell and Johnston all specialised in teaching aspects of their respective fields seems to have encouraged them to provide funds to develop teaching in their subjects at a college in their home town, where they knew professorial teaching was encouraged.

The other more pragmatic motive that connects these bursaries was simple advancement of families in and around the burgh, especially those of the benefactors. Duncan Liddell specified that his bursaries were to be given to the offspring of his brother's and sisters' children, but if they were not of an age to attend then they were to be specifically employed for 'honest poore mens sounes burgesses of new Ab[er]d[een]'.[73] James Cargill

---

[69]   FMA, vol. 1, pp. 113–17.

[70]   Shona Maclean Vance, 'Copland, Patrick (c.1572–c.1651)', ODNB [66917, accessed 24 March 2010].

[71]   For a list of these works, see FMA, vol. 2, pp. 27–8.

[72]   Henderson, Marischal College, p. 35; Lachrymae Academiae Marischallanae sub obitum moecenatis & fundatoris sui munificentissimi: nobilissimi et illustrissimi Georgii, comitis Marischalli (Aberdeen, 1623).

[73]   FMA, vol. 1, p. 125.

specified that the 500 merks mortified to the grammar school could be moved to Marischal for the use of his 'puire freynds' if there were none at the school, likely referring to poor family members or friends of his kin.[74] This desire to maintain bursars who would come from the town was heeded, unsurprisingly, by the town council and its executors. The first three recipients of Johnston's divinity bursary were all connected with the educational elite in the town and surrounding area, with his nephew John Sanders taking the bursary in 3 July 1616, another kinsman William Johnston on 22 May 1621, and then Alexander Wedderburn on 29 January 1623, brother to the master of the grammar school and to a regent in the college.[75] Moreover, the first Liddel and Cargill bursaries went to the sons of seven local ministers and 15 burgesses who were all employed in highly oligarchic and protected professions as merchants, advocates and craftsmen.[76] As in the case of Edinburgh, it is clear that the wave of investment at Marischal aimed to provide for and promote the interests of the local citizenry above all others, with a particular focus in Aberdeen on advancement of a purely nepotistic kind.

This investment stands in marked contrast to royal gifts across the universities between 1607 and 1625, when the crown gave surprisingly little beyond confirming and ratifying the existing properties of the 'ancient' universities, and those the new colleges received from lay benefactors. On 11 August 1607 James VI and I confirmed all gifts and grants provided to St Andrews from the foundation of the university and reconfirmed the privileges of the rector and conservator to act in all legal actions relating to recovery of university debts.[77] In 1612 the crown reconfirmed the privileges and gifts annexed to St Leonard's college, [78] and also confirmed all the holdings that Edinburgh had accrued since its foundation. Following the royal visit to Scotland in 1617, when James visited the universities of St Andrews and Glasgow and received a delegation of university masters from Edinburgh at Stirling,[79] he enacted a further two charters of confirmation, both dating to 28 June 1617, which ratified all grants ever made to the

---

[74]   *FMA*, vol. 1, p. 150.

[75]   *FMA*, vol. 1, p. 117.

[76]   McLaren, *Aberdeen Students, 1600–1860*, p. 26.

[77]   *RPS*, 1607/3/35 [accessed 16 February 2010].

[78]   *RPS*, 1612/10/45 [accessed 16 February 2010].

[79]   These visits produced a flurry of royal panegyric among the university masters, collected together and published in several volumes, including: Edinburgh University, Νοστωδία *In Jacobi regis in Scotiam reditum* (Edinburgh, 1617); St Andrews University, Χαριστήρια *in adventum Jacobi primi* (Edinburgh, 1617); J. Adamson (ed.), Τὰ τῶν μουσῶν εἰσόδια. *Planctus et vota musarum* (Edinburgh, 1617); J. Adamson, (ed.), Τὰ τῶν μουσῶν εἰσόδια, *The muses welcome* (Edinburgh, 1617).

colleges in Aberdeen.[80] All these grants merely confirmed the existing foundations of landed resources the universities had gradually acquired, and this evidence suggests that the crown was actually stepping away from financing the universities in the early seventeenth century.

There were two notable exceptions to this rule. The first of these was the allocation of funding and books granted to St Andrews to complete the library project started by George Gledstanes in 1611. When this project was established the library had been given 46 books from George Abbot, the Archbishop of Canterbury, along with a gift of 23 books from the family of Peter Young, the king's former tutor and now diplomat, and a small number of additional volumes gifted by various courtiers. In the following year the royal family augmented these gifts with a large grant of 228 books, valued at £267 15s 10d. At the time of the king's visit to Scotland in 1617 the library to house these books had still only been partially completed, and a benefaction of £1,000 was granted by the king to roof the library and allow it to be brought into use. Although the library was not completed by this act, it did contribute significantly to advancing its development until it was finally completed with a further benefaction from Alexander Henderson in 1642.[81]

On 28 June 1617, at the same time as grants were made confirming the lands held by the colleges in Aberdeen, the king made a new and major grant of the kirks, parsonages and vicarages of Kilbride and Renfrew, along with a number of small additional prebendaries, to the impoverished college at Glasgow.[82] As we have seen, one of the major reasons that the college had thrived in the short-term after the *Nova Erectio* of 1577 was due to the royal annexation of the parish of Govan to the foundation, a gift which had brought an additional 24 chalders of victual to the college rental and possibly doubled, or even quadrupled, its annual income.[83] The gift of Kilbride and Renfrew, which also comprised around 24 chalders, would thus have nearly doubled its income again.

Why did James single out these two universities for such extensive gifts? Two reasons immediately spring to mind. James, with an eye for ceremony and ancient tradition, would have naturally inclined himself towards investment in the 'traditional' university foundations, particularly if there was a chance to enhance them to match the status of their English counterparts. This certainly seems the case in St Andrews, where James' financial gift in 1617 was meant to support the administrative and ceremonial interventions of the preceding year. In the case of Glasgow,

---

[80] *RPS*, 1617/5/72; 73 [accessed 16 February 2010].

[81] Salmond and Bushnell, *Henderson's Benefaction*, pp. 37–46, at pp. 40 and 45.

[82] *RPS* 1617/5/48 [accessed 16 February 2010].

[83] See above, Chapter 3.

the grant was for a more prosaic, though not unimportant purpose, of keeping the university financially solvent as it grappled with the ongoing crisis of funding it had faced since its foundation. James must have seen first-hand the state that Glasgow was in when he visited in 1617, and may have simply decided that it needed help where the others did not to retain financial solvency. What does emerge from these two instances is that when the royal government did intervene financially in the universities after the union of the crowns, it did so with an eye to upholding the older and more conservative foundations, and was content to leave the newer ones to develop along paths dictated by local interests.

Intellectual Developments at the Universities, Post-Melville

The sources demonstrating intellectual life at the Scottish universities in the half century after the reformation are admittedly small in number, and provide an oblique understanding at best of the major intellectual debates taking place within their walls. However, following a marginal increase in the number of extant sources in the decades on either side of 1600, in the last two decades of the reign of James VI and I the range of surviving teaching evidence expands considerably, and we find for the first time sufficient material to discern concrete patterns and trends in the curriculum being taught across the universities. What emerges from these sources is confirmation that Aristotle remained the central authority at the heart of the university curriculum, along with limited evidence that he was studied in the original Greek as Melville had intended. However, the broader experimental spirit of Melville's curriculum, and particularly his attempts to engage with authors such as Ramus, had clearly withered on the vine by the early 1610s.

Although no teaching evidence survives for Glasgow until the 1640s, at St Andrews eight separate sets of *theses philosophicae* survive for the period from 1608 to 1625, all by different regents. Interestingly, no further sets of *theses theologicae* were produced at St Andrews or elsewhere beyond the small batch supervised by Melville between 1596 and 1602, which in itself suggests that other masters frowned upon the practice of producing theses for divinity. At Edinburgh, adding to the six sets of theses extant between 1596 and 1605 discussed in Chapter 5, we find an impressive 16 theses surviving between 1607 and 1625, with a complete run of theses for the graduating class for every year from 1612 onwards.[84] Between 1610 and 1624 the same four regents – James Reid, William King, Andrew Young and James Fairley – each took their class through the degree programme,

---

[84]   There are theses missing for the years 1608, 1609 and 1611.

and each produced between three and four sets of theses. Three sets of theses survive for Marischal College by Andrew Aidie and James Sibbald for the period 1616–25,[85] and four for King's College by Alexander Lunan, William and John Forbes, and William Lesley, defended successively between 1622 and 1625. The daily grind of note-taking and dictation is also recorded for the first time in a handful of extant student notebooks on a range of subjects. A 1602–3 notebook for Marischal College is filled with notes on Greek and Latin grammar, while an anonymous notebook dictated under the regent Patrick Dun at Marischal College in 1611, and another belonging to John Elphinstone, Lord Balmerino dictated under David Leech at King's in 1612/13 focus predominantly on logic.[86] Notebooks belonging to the Edinburgh students Alexander Henryson under James Reid (1613/14) and George Livingstone under William King (1619/20), and the notebook of John Moir at Marischal College (1619/20), are chiefly concerned with ethics and physics.[87]

These texts show that in every area of the arts curriculum Aristotle continued to be the central fount of knowledge to a near monolithic extent. All the theses on logic and philosophy centre on expounding problems arising directly from his corpus of texts, with Porphyry's 'Introduction' and Sacrobosco's *De Sphaera* being the only other primary texts regularly discussed. The liberal sprinkling of quotation from Aristotle in the original Greek in these texts, ranging from a few words to several lines, shows that the aim of incorporating Greek into undergraduate teaching was finally meeting with some success in the early seventeenth century. This fact is also attested by the detailed notes on Greek terms and Latin synonyms in the anonymous notebook at Marischal in 1602/03, and by a brief outline of the progress of the entrant class of 1604 at King's that showed several of the students memorising whole orations by Isocrates and parts of the catechism in Greek.[88] Although these sources still do not provide evidence that Scottish students uniformly learnt Greek to the same level of proficiency as Latin, they do show that one of Melville's aims for the broader university curriculum was being met.

The trend of condemnation of Ramism apparent at St Andrews and Edinburgh in the closing decades of the sixteenth century reached its

---

[85]   Aidie produced a set of theses in 1616; Sibbald in 1623 and again in 1625.

[86]   AUL MS 116 (1602–03); AUL MS 113 (Dun); EUL MS La. III.155 (Elphinstone and Balmerino).

[87]   EUL Dc.10.37 (Henryson and Reid); NLS Advocates MS 5.2.3 (Livingstone and King); AUL MS150 (Moir).

[88]   AUL MS 116, inscribed with the names Thomas Forbes, John Forbes and Thomas Johnston; AUL MS K 225/2, 'Nomina eorum qui aliquam graecae linguae praxin memoriae commiserunt' [1604]; McLaren, *Aberdeen Students 1600–1860*, pp. 7–9 and 179–80, at n. 18 and 22.

zenith in the early seventeenth, particularly in the theses at St Andrews in the half-decade after Melville's removal. Given that these theses were performed publicly before George Gledstanes and the assembled university, this was perhaps another outlet for showing that the most controversial component of the 'Melvillian' curriculum was well and truly dead, and for reminding anyone still pursuing such an unprofitable course to desist immediately. These criticisms first appear in general terms in the 1608 theses of the St Salvator's regent William Wedderburn, who notes that only Aristotle had 'brought the logical art wholly under the power of a just method with admirable skill' and whose *Organon*, freeing logicians from 'problems in other respects inexplicable', was deeply envied by a range of unnamed scholars who instead insisted on 'thrusting in some fragments of logical precepts for logic' which did not deserve to be labelled as such.[89] A similar oblique attack is in evidence in the 1611 theses for St Leonard's by John Strang, who declared that logic was restricted to 'exceedingly thin purposes' by those who saw it relating solely to method and a restricted form of syllogism.[90]

What sounds like a general dissatisfaction with non-Aristotelian logic is couched in far more vocal and strident terms in the next pair of surviving texts by Alexander Henderson (St Salvator's, 1611) and James Wemyss (St Leonard's, 1612). In Henderson's collections of theses, flamboyantly entitled 'The exercise of philosophers on logical, ethical, physical and spherical matters' (*Gymnasma philosophicum de rebus logicis, ethicis, physicis et sphaericis*) he makes it clear in one of the *theses logicae* that the specific terms of formal logic only have full validity when marshalled in syllogisms, and that the reduction and indiscriminate mixing of Aristotelian terminology in 'definitions of others, whether from Ramus or more recent authors, evilly mixing together common and particular parts with different [parts], bring together nothing at all'.[91] Wemyss

---

[89] Wedderburn, 'theses logicae', 30: 2. 'Philosopho igitur ut, par est, gratia sit, qui Artem Logicam primus admirabili plane artificio in justam Methodum redegit, nobisque ea exhibuit Organa, quae nodos, alioqui inenodabiles, explicare queant. 3. Hanc autem quo Aristoteli gloriam invident, logicarum prӕceptionum fragmenta quӕdam pro Logica obtrudentes, nӕ illi de Logico merentur male.'

[90] Strang, 'theses logicae', 3: 3. 'Nimis angustis finibus natura[m] Logicae concudunt, qui aut Syllogismum aut Methodum [aut si his etiam addere placet definitionem & divisionem] Logicae subjectum adaequatum autumant.'

[91] Henderson, 'theses logicae', 5.1. 'Non sunt ergo realia entia cum notionalibus in Logicam tangquam in Satyram, promiscuè congerenda. 2. Causa Causatum, Similia Dissimilia, & quae sunt proprietates, differentiae aut species entis, non magis ad Logicam spectant, quam entia Logica ad Rhetoricam. 3. Definiri ergo in Logica non possunt, nisi ut argumenta sunt, vel intelligendi instrumenta, id est, cum respectu ad syllogismum, & in tertia Logicae parte. 4. Omnes ergo eorum definitiones, sive à Ramo, sive recentioribus, ex parte communi & propria heterogeneis male sartae, necquicquam coeunt.'

criticises Ramist terminology in several of his theses, noting that Ramists 'err remarkably' in suggesting that 'being' and 'non-being' (*ens* and *nonens*) are equally the subject of logic, when 'non-being' is traditionally a speculative area reserved to natural philosophy or metaphysics rather than logic.[92] In a thesis following this outlining the idea that substance arises from the fusion of form imparting itself to matter, Wemyss also states that he is absolutely against the Ramists and the German physicist Rudolph Goclenius for thinking the complete opposite, that matter and form only meet in accidental properties alone.[93]

The last reference to Ramist logic seen in the theses in the period up to 1625 is found in Andrew Aidie's Marischal College theses of 1616, where he notes in a single line that he 'does not think that Ramus erred in calling Logic an art', an idea that many of the regents would have found uncontroversial given the level of importance they collectively attached to logical disputation. After this, all references to Ramus cease for the remainder of the reign of James VI and I. Ramist texts would make a re-appearance at the Scottish universities in the curriculum laid down by the Covenanters in the 1640s (not least because in doing so they felt that they were restoring the components of a thoroughly Presbyterian education as laid down by Melville), and a number of regents in the same period, including the future archbishop James Sharp, included discussion of Ramist texts in their lectures. However, as Lynch points out, by the middle of the seventeenth century the radicalism associated with Ramism had lost much of its strength, and his views on logic and philosophy were seen, along with those of Melanchthon, Keckermann and several others, as merely one of a number of interpretations of the Aristotelian system that did not have to be dogmatically followed.[94] With the disappearance of Ramism from view in the latter part of the 1610s, it is thus fair to say that the turbulent flirtation with the Ramist method that had entered the Scottish university system more than forty years earlier with Melville had finally been removed by an increasingly conservative intellectual elite keen to expunge all traces of his programme.

This conservatism is mirrored in the range of secondary authors on Aristotle cited in these theses, all of whom have been described as 'Aristotelian', 'neo-Aristotelian' and 'scholastic' in their intellectual

---

[92] Wemyss, 'theses logicae' 15.6: 'Quàm insigniter errant Ramistate, qui Logicae subjectum esse aiunt ex aequo Ens & Nonens, quis hinc non liquidò videbit?'

[93] Wemyss, 'theses logicae' 18.1: 'Quum ergo substantia sit vel material, quae una numero est in omnibus, Scal. Exerc. 9 quaeque secundum se non est hoc aliquid: vel forma, secundum quam dicitur Τόδε τι: vel ex utrisque quiddam compositum. Arist. 2. de Anim. Cap. I. textu 2. & 35. adversus Ramistas & Rudolphum Goclenium eorum patronum in solis accidentibus veram reperiri contrarietatem, praecisè tuemur.'

[94] Anderson, Lynch and Phillipson, *University of Edinburgh*, pp. 22–4.

outlook. Medieval authorities on Aristotle – Avicenna, Averröes, Duns Scotus and Thomas Aquinas – are one main branch of authors regularly cited, showing the continuity of medieval logic within the Scottish university environment. However, a fairly broad range of 'modern' Aristotelians are also in evidence throughout the texts. Authors cited a handful of times include the Portuguese Jesuit, Pedro da Fonseca (1528–99), who was schooled as a Thomist and produced an internationally acclaimed critical edition and tradition of Aristotle's *Metaphysics*; the Dominican and Cardinal Thomas de Vio Cajetan (1468–1534), who wrote commentaries on Aristotle's *Categories* and *Prior Analytics*, Porphyry's *Isagoge* and a series of texts engaging with (and often critical of) the views of Aquinas, as well as several texts on the nature of essence and being; and the flamboyant Italian scholar Girolamo Cardano (1501–76), an authority on metaphysics and physics who provided new interpretations of the Aristotelian concepts of matter and the four elements of hot, cold, wet and dry in several treatises including 'On subtlety' (*De subtilitate*, 1550), 'On nature' and 'On the one' (*De natura* and *De uno*, both written in 1560) and 'On the variety of being' (*De rerum varietate*, 1557).[95] The *Exercitationes* of the Italian emendator and naturalist Julius Caesar Scaliger (1484–1558) is also frequently referenced, primarily because it was written to condemn the innovations of Cardano's 'On subtlety' and was thus useful for providing a series of opposing viewpoints for disputation. By far the most mentioned secondary author is the Paduan philosopher Jacopo Zabarella (1533–1589), whose main aim was to appraise critically and expand the understanding of Aristotle's logical system within its own limits, and who produced a considerable body of knowledge on the nature of logic alongside commentaries on many of Aristotle's works. Although Catholic, Zabarella's ideas on natural philosophy, scientific methodology and the theory of knowledge were highly influential among Protestant intellectuals in the early seventeenth century.[96] One of his central ideas, that logic was an instrumental discipline or tool that formed the basis of a method for empirical reasoning rather than a science or art in its own right, was frequently discussed and interrogated by many of the Scottish regents, although their views of him ranged from muted praise to outright condemnation.

---

[95]　See John P. Doyle, 'Fonseco, Pedro da', Edward P. Mahoney, 'Cajetan (Thomas de Vio)', and Eckhard Kessler, 'Cardano, Girolamo', in Edward Craig (ed.) *The Routledge Encyclopaedia of Philosophy* (10 vols, London and New York, 1998). Other authors cited only once include Rudolph Goclenius (whose theory of the use of *sorites*, a linked chain of syllogisms, in term logic is referred to in Strang, theses logicae 26 and 41), Francesco Piccolomini, Girolamo Fracastoro and Fortunatus Crell.

[96]　Eckhard Kessler, 'Zabarella, Jacopo', in Craig (ed.), *Routledge Encyclopedia of Philosophy*.

These authors represent a wide spectrum of opinion on early modern logic, philosophy, and science, but the most important thing linking them for our purposes is that they worked fundamentally within the traditional inherited Aristotelian system. Although many of them, particularly Cardano and Zabarella, offered implicit criticisms of several aspects of Aristotelian logic and philosophy, none of them wished to alter radically or simplify this world-view in the way that Ramus and other sixteenth century humanist logicians had. If anything, they wished to explore and enhance its nuance and complexity. Their regular citation within the record of teaching shows clearly that in the Scottish universities the experiment of humanist logic was one that was no longer welcome, and that the main foci of the curriculum was to augment and bolster student knowledge within a thoroughly scholastic framework.

Another indication that intellectual life in the Scottish universities of the early seventeenth century was ossifying in more conservative forms was the restoration of metaphysics, and indeed of topics that would have been strictly demarcated under the heading of theology in the immediate post-reformation era, within the ambit of the set philosophy curriculum. Melville removed all traces of metaphysical study from his reform programme, in part because, in its attempts to speculate rationally on the nature of matter, of being, and of reality, it inquired directly into areas that impinged upon divine mysteries best left hidden, and in part because Catholic theology was so enmeshed with Aristotelian metaphysics that to study it could potentially lead to students succumbing to Catholic doctrine. However, by the beginning of the seventeenth century metaphysics had begun to reassume prominence within reformed seminaries on the Continent, as part of a wider resurgence of all branches of scholastic thought in the codification of Protestant systematic theology.[97]

Only one of the theses of the late sixteenth century, those of the Edinburgh regent James Adamson in 1600, featured a section of *theses metaphysicae*. However, of the eight theses extant for St Andrews between 1608 and 1625, four have a dedicated section on metaphysics. It is surely no coincidence that all four of these examples occur in the theses printed between 1611 and 1613, when Gledstanes, who had already demonstrated his support for traditional areas of the curriculum with the restoration of canon law in 1611, was at the height of his power in St Andrews as both archbishop and university chancellor. Metaphysics also began to reappear in dedicated sections within the theses of James Reid at Edinburgh in 1622 and 1626, and in Aberdeen in the theses of John and William Forbes in 1623 and 1624, and more generally we find that theses relating to strictly

---

[97]   Armstrong, *Calvinism and the Amyraut Heresy*; Muller, *After Calvin*; Trueman and Clark (eds), *Protestant Scholasticism, passim*.

metaphysical questions make an increasingly regular appearance in the *theses logicae* and *physicae* of the early seventeenth century.

Perhaps most importantly, although philosophical and theological study had tended to be strictly demarcated into 'lower' and 'higher' disciplines in the later sixteenth century (as witnessed most clearly by the strict separation of *theses theologicae* and *philosophicae* at St Andrews between 1595 and 1602), the theses of the early seventeenth century show many regents interested in exploring the affinities between the two disciplines, and incorporating scriptural and biblical arguments into their philosophical reasoning, and vice versa. Thus in the theses of John Strang (St Leonard's, 1611) we find the usage of Aristotle to defend an attack on a Catholic interpretation of free will and a defence of God as the creator of all things against Plato's explanation of the origins of the world in his *Timaeus*;[98] and in a series of *theses ethicae* by Andrew Aidie, we find a condemnation of Catholic ceremony and liturgy underpinned by the physical arguments of Aristotle himself in relation to time:

> The matters of those in the future pertain in such a way to the dead that in no way do they change the state of the former or the latter for worse or for better. In vain, therefore, are solemn Masses celebrated for individual souls. In vain, also, was purgatory built up by the Popes (if we believe Aristotle), since the souls there are unable to be freed by the work of men living here.[99]

In the series of theses by William King at Edinburgh, he notes in 1616 that a comet witnessed in 1577 has parallels with similar comets described in Ezekiel and Joshua, and in 1624 states that God creates new stars as a sign of his divine power, a fact which is attested by scripture.[100] King is

---

[98]   Strang, 'theses ethicae' 13.1–3: '1. Si ergo Arist. in doctrina de Libero arbitrio defecit, quatenus Spirituales virtutes ignoravit, at quanto melius ipse quam alii omnes. 2. Nos veo ut Dogma Pontificium de Libero arbitrio tanquam execrabile abjuramus, ita Arist. hac de re doctrinam utcunque imperfectam agnoscimus, nihil tamen fidei repugnans continere asseveramus.'; 'theses physicae' 13.1–2: '1. Solus Deus absolute aeternus & immortalis. 6. [*sic*] Coelos divina voluntate indissolubiles, egregiè divinus Plato censuit, In Timaeo, suâ vero naturâ nequaquam nec nos aliter de mente humana aut Angelis censemus.'

[99]   Aidie, 'theses ethicae': [Ex Arist.] 'Res posterorum ad defunctos, ita pertinere ut statum nullo modo horum aut illorum mutent in pejos aut in melios. Frustra igitur Missae solennes pro distinctis animabus [*sic*] celebrantur. Frustra etiam Purgatorium a Pontificus fuit aedificatum si Aristoteli credimus quum hominum hic viventium opera liberari inde nequeant animae.' I am very grateful to Giovanni Gellera for this reference.

[100]   King (1616), 'theses astronomicae' 7: 'Cometam a.d. 1577. tribus fere mensibus conspicuam, ex uniformi ejus motu tardiore Lunari, ex ductu maximi circuli quem proprio motu designavit, ex Parallaxi minori Lunari, & interdum vix sensili: plerique magni nominis Astronomi in aetheris regione Lunâ superiori constitisse evidenti & firmâ demonstratione collegerunt. App. 1: Non solù, sacrae literae, quae testantur Solem pugnante JOSUA tribus

most striking, however, in the fascinating discussion that he provides in 1616 of the origins of language and terms, where he notes that God by his own will gave fitting names to every created thing, which Adam then began to understand with God's approval. Man then made the decision through his own sense of pride to speak in multiple languages rather than retain the primal *lingua franca* of Hebrew at the building of the tower of Babylon.[101] King's fellow regent James Fairley stated in 1618 that the ideas of 'the eternal, infinite and other predicables', although stemming from God alone, are only adequately demonstrated by Arisotelian logic, and in 1621 described Moses as a 'divine amanuensis' to God, and stated in his *theses physicae* that giants are attested by scripture.[102]

The connection of scripture with philosophy is seen most clearly, however, in the series of theses by James Reid. In his theses of 1622, while exploring the thesis 'Divine disciplines are of God, and created of God: yet human disciplines have these same features', he gives a resounding argument for the importance of biblical study as part of the course of philosophical learning:

> Where therefore is dispute held more vigorously and logically, where are falsehoods and sophistical reckonings displayed more straightforwardly, than in the book of Job? ...Where is a more exquisite art, not of made up but true rhetoric, than is contained in the prophets and apostles? Where, truly, are more abundant and consummate moral precepts than in Exodus, in Deuteronomy, the wisdoms of Solomon, and finally in the Gospel? Was there ever a philosopher who dealt with nature more completely than Moses, was there ever a philosopher more wise? Finally, those Metaphysical things which ought to be brought together with Holy Scripture, which begin with God, end

---

horis constitisse, ad optionem EZECHIAE 15. gradibus regressum esse, stellam novam magis apparuisse: sed etiam novorum siderum, & cometarum procreatio, inordinatae in Coelo mutations eius mutabilitatem arguunt.' King (1624), 'theses physicae' 14: 'Non solum Sacrae literae, quae testantur ☉ pugnante Iosua 3. horis constitisse, ad orationem Hezekiae 15. grad. Regressum esse, Stellam novam Magis apparuisse: sed etiam novorum syderum procreatio, unius, Anno 1600, in Cygno juxta eam stellam quae in ejus pectore lucet, alterius, quod Anno 1604, in ♐ visum est: Cometarum etiam in Aetherea regione supra ☽ situs, coeli mutabilitatem arguunt. 1. *Certum igitur posse Deum, qui universum ex nihilo architectatus est, nova sydera ubi, quando, unde & qualia velit, efficere: quo autemmodo, quove sine, homini incertum.*'

[101]   Reid (1616), 'theses logicae' 13: 'SACRA SCRIPTVRA testator DEUM primum fuisse ... libera sua voluntate quibusdam rebus à se creatis proprias & conuenientes appelationes attribuisse, quas posteà ADAM tacito consensu usurpare coepit, & pro sua sapientia etiam ac libero arbitrio singulis animantium speciebus propria nomina imposuit. Similiter ante aedificationem turris BABYLONICAE sola HEBRAICA lingua fuit in usu, posteà verò in paenam superbiae, linguae aedificantium fuerunt confusae, & nova linguarum idiomata extitêre.'

[102]   Fairley (1615), 'theses logicae' 17; Fairley (1623) 'theses logicae' 1.6; 'theses physicae' 11.

with God; and those things concerning God and the divine are always spoken of most divinely.[103]

This sentiment is captured 'hieroglyphically' in King's 1626 theses, where he lays out a series of overlapping circles linking the various philosophical disciplines, all embraced within the circle of theology, and notes that the 'learned Egyptians' and 'more ancient Greeks' understood that these disciplines were all thoroughly interlinked.[104] These ideas are also given full narrative form in the work of Robert Barron, who had taken up a post as professor at Marischal College following several years as regent in St Salvator's College. In his *Philosophia Theologiae Ancillans* (1621), he recounts the inherent links between the disciplines and the benefits of studying them holistically.

The preceding discussion aside, there is limited evidence of the engagement with ideas that stood outside the twin spheres of Aristotle and scripture. Plato is mentioned sparingly in these texts, usually only to be criticised in comparison with Aristotle. However, there is clearly a growing level of engagement with his works, particularly at St Andrews. John Strang and William Wedderburn (St Salvator's, 1608) cite the *Timaeus* and Plato's ideas on visual sense impression and several other physical issues, and Andrew Bruce had read *Hippias* and discusses Plato in relation to several points alongside his biblical exposition.[105] William Lammie (St Salvator's, 1613) was exceptionally well read, citing references to Empedocles, Plato, Epicurus, Augustine, Seneca, Anaxagoras, Democritus and Ausonius, among others.[106] There is also fleeting citation of more contemporary authors on empirical reasoning and early science. The theses of James Wemyss (St Leonard's, 1612) briefly mentions the *systema logicae* of Bartholomew Keckermann, whose work would become a set text on

---

[103] Reid, 'theses de disciplinis in genere', 1: 'Disciplinae divinae de Deo sunt, & dei creatures: de iisdem sunt humanae.' 1.7: 'Ubi igitur nervosiùs logicè disputatur, ubi fallaces & captiosae rationes aperiuntur enucleatiùs, quàm in libro Iob? ... Ubi exquisitior ars non fictae sed verae Rhetoricae, quàm in Prophetis, quàm Apostolis conspicitur? Quaenam moralia praecepta copiosiora & consummatiora visuntur, quàm in Exodo, in Deuteronomio, Solomoniacis dogmatis, & demum in Evangelio? Quis unquam Philosophus de natura absolutiùs Mosa tractavit, quis unquam sapientiùs? Quae denique Metaphysica cum S. Scrip. Conferenda, quae à Deo exordiuntur; in Deum finiunt semperque de Deo & divinis divinissimè loquuntur.'

[104] Reid (1626), 'theses de disciplines in genere' 3.

[105] Wedderburn, 'theses physicae' 5.2, 9.2, 20.2; Bruce, 'theses logicae' 1.2.1: 'Ergo *Hippias* ille non eo magis fuit Philosophus, quia & calceos, & strigiles, & lecythum a se facta singular ostentavit'; 'theses physicae' 2.2, 14.3, 18.2.

[106] Lammie, 'positiones logicae' 10, 24; 'positiones ethicae' 5, 8, 9, 10, 16; 'positiones physicae' 2, 3, 6, 8, 13, 16, 34, 'astronomicae & cosmographicae' 7.

the revised 1641 curriculum at the united colleges of Aberdeen.[107] There is also the slightest evidence that the Ptolemaic world view was being questioned by the regents, when Copernicus is mentioned in the theses of Lammie, and is even described by William King as 'very learned'.[108] However, although it is clear that the new ideas relating to science and motion were at least under discussion in the Scottish universities in the early seventeenth century, they appear within an overwhelming image of Aristotelianism and Biblicism which would not be broken until well into the 1660s. While these two elements did reflect parts of the curriculum laid down by Melville it is clear that his attempts to bring a radically new humanist ethos to the universities, one that embraced controversial thinkers and educationalists such as Ramus alongside traditional areas of study, had largely been overturned.

Conclusion

The removal of the Protestant re-foundations of King's College and St Andrews was enacted in 1619 and 1621 with royal and parliamentary support, and in their place the original pre-reformation collegiate constitutions at both universities, 'so far as the same may stand with the estate of true religion', were to be restored.[109] Although the *Nova Erectio* of Glasgow continued to act as that university's constitutional basis, these acts can be seen as bringing about a formal end to the 'Melvillian' experiment in educational reform. However, the evidence of political and intellectual life at the Scottish universities in the two decades prior to 1620 suggests that this was merely a reflection and confirmation of a much wider trend away from Melville's unified educational ideal, as each of the universities developed along very different paths shaped by a range of local and national interests. Following Melville's removal from St Andrews the crown and its ecclesiastical supporters, along with the disaffected masters who had been unhappy with the 'New Foundation' from the beginning, seized the opportunity to re-assert control of the university and systematically purge it of his influence, particularly in the sphere of divinity teaching. This was not an entirely smooth process, and a range of internal grievances persisted among the masters requiring outside monitoring and resolution, while the masters themselves faced a struggle with the royal will over rights of presentation and staffing. However, it is remarkable how quickly all the elements of religious and intellectual controversy

---

[107] Wemyss, 'theses logicae' 14.4. *Fast Aberdonenses*, pp. 230–231.

[108] Lammie, 'astronomicae & cosmographicae' 7. King (1616), 'theses astronomicae' 8.

[109] *RPS*, 1621/6/117 [accessed 30 March 2010]; see also Conclusion.

connected to Melville were abandoned or removed, and how widespread the consensus attached to this removal was. As the universities developed in the 1610s, royal intervention remained focussed on St Andrews, where the king's experiences of Oxford and Cambridge inspired him to redevelop it as a centre espousing the defence of civic and religious orthodoxy, a trend reflected in the focus on redeveloping the ceremonial elements of university life. However, the crown did take steps to ratify and uphold the landed settlements of all the university foundations, and did intervene with support and disciplinary oversight when required, particularly at Glasgow with the purging of Patrick Sharp from office. The greatest success story in Scottish education in this period was the unparalleled growth and investment of the new institutions at Edinburgh and New Aberdeen, where the local community rallied behind both 'town' foundations as a means of providing cheap and effective education to their children in a way that was not matched at the older universities, despite some well-timed gifts of financial intervention from the crown elsewhere. Finally, and perhaps most importantly, the intellectual spirit that Melville had tried to introduce to the Scottish universities, one that embraced new and experimental approaches to humanist studies alongside the traditional Aristotelian curriculum and separated and elevated the study of a strongly Presbyterian form of divinity above all other subjects, was clearly in abeyance from very early in the seventeenth century. While the universities would once again become embroiled in disputes over the form and content of the Scottish Kirk in the later 1620s (particularly among the circle of theologians at Aberdeen), and while severe disruption to the wider university settlement would again arise as a result, the era of 'Melvillian' reform at the university died out quietly in the final decades of the reign of James VI and I, and ushered in a period of limited equilibrium and peace.

Conclusion

On 4 August 1621, an Act of Parliament formally brought to an end the tenure of the 'New Foundation' over the University of St Andrews. Noting that the alterations made to the university had 'bred such uncertainty in profession of sciences and observation of orders appointed by the first founders', all the original constitutions were to be restored 'so far as the same may stand with the estate of true religion', with all the traditional roles of the principal masters and regents re-established. The only exception to this revocation was St Mary's, which was to 'keep still the profession of divinity within their schools as presently is and has been used'.[1] A similar process of restoration was undertaken at King's College Aberdeen in November 1619 under Bishop Patrick Forbes of Corse, where in a visitation tackling the decay caused by the widespread lack of reform since the 1580s he ordered a sweeping return to the original structures of faculty and staffing established by William Elphinstone.[2] Although Forbes' radical action at the university resulted in another period of conflict and confusion that lasted until his death in 1635, the restoration of the old foundation was officially recognised by Charles I in 1633.[3] Only at Glasgow, where the streamlined *Nova Erectio* had saved the university from collapse, was the 'Melvillian' re-foundation established on a permanent footing, and remained the basis of the university's constitution until the Universities (Scotland) Act of 1858.

The central aim of this book has been to create a narrative of Andrew Melville's involvement in the Scottish universities after the reformation, and by extension to show how the universities came to grips with a new Protestant identity. By any standard of judgement that is applied, the constitutional revolution that Melville attempted to implement largely failed; yet the universities still adapted successfully to a reformed settlement, and ultimately thrived in the increasingly gloomy intellectual climate of the early seventeenth century. Melville is certainly due a portion of the credit for this success, but hopefully the preceding discussion has shown that a range of factors outside his control, and often acting in direct opposition to him, contributed to the process.

---

[1] *RPS* 1621/6/117 [accessed 30 March 2010].

[2] Stevenson, *King's College*, pp. 63–70.

[3] Stevenson, *King's College*, pp. 70–79.

It is often assumed that there was some great forward momentum transforming the Scottish universities into Protestant institutions after 1560 that made them look and feel fundamentally different from their Catholic predecessors. In truth, the process of Protestant reform and expansion that engulfed the Scottish universities was more akin to a slow-moving wave, with tides of activity that advanced and retreated in line with the rhythms of local and national politics. Support for the forces of Catholicism and conservatism at King's College meant that almost two decades passed before it fully engaged with Protestant reform in 1582–3, when it had the bad fortune of picking a period of particularly fraught relations between the crown and the Presbyterian wing of the Kirk to attempt the implementation of a 'Melvillian' re-foundation, and which subsequently resulted in the long-term abeyance of any meaningful reform. Glasgow, meanwhile, was effectively and swiftly reformed by Melville in his time as principal, but while the *Nova Erectio* remained in place after his departure the university lost direction during Thomas Smeaton's disruptive term as principal and the lengthy period of inertia that followed under Patrick Sharp.

St Andrews has more evidence than any of its 'ancient' counterparts relating to this transitional period, and it is clear that soon after 1560 a Protestant institution emerged there that was recognisably different from the Catholic one that had existed before the reformation. However, the continuity between these two institutions was far greater than their differences. The original university structure remained intact, and none of the major proposals for reform – whether those put forward in 1560/61 by the *First Book of Discipline*, those in 1574 and 1576 by the Regent Morton, or those in 1579, 1588 and 1597 by Melville and the Scottish government – ever had more than a limited impact. Far more effective were the small-scale reforms enacted by the masters themselves. The interim statutes promulgated in the early 1560s removed the aspects of the university's Catholic heritage that were most incompatible with its new Protestant identity, but were flexible enough to allow the university to continue its business unimpeded at a critical time of uncertainty. Similarly, St Leonard's operated more effectively than its counterparts in the decade after the 'New Foundation' as it ignored the full reform plan and made only moderate changes and improvements to the existing foundation. Conversely, the 'New Foundation' appears to have been most damaging to St Salvator's because of the protests raised at the intrusion of two new masters into the college against the old foundation, and because it radically altered the ancient rights and privileges accorded to the provost.

It is surprising that there was such a lack of input from the General Assembly to the reform process, and that there was such an extensive role played by the royal government. Admittedly, the dividing line between those who were masters pursuing internal reform at the universities and those who were connected with the General Assembly was often blurred, particularly in the case of Melville. However, it is still remarkable that after the bold plans put forward in the *First Book of Discipline* the assembly were so content to leave the universities to their own devices, save for the occasional involvement in commissions of visitation and the ratification of the new foundations at King's and Marischal. By contrast, it is clear that both national and local government recognised the importance of education for shaping and improving the 'godly' commonwealth. While they did not enact sweeping reform, the royally-sponsored visitations to Aberdeen and St Andrews in the mid-1570s, to St Andrews in 1588, and to Glasgow in 1602 and 1614 intervened at critical junctures in the development of each of these institutions and ensured that they maintained minimum standards of education and discipline. This process reached its zenith at St Andrews in the politically charged atmosphere of the later 1590s, when the visitations not only removed Melville from his position of authority but tried to take far-reaching steps to make university masters and affairs more accountable to government. This intervention continued to shape the university's relationship with the crown for the following two decades.

By the same token, it is highly unlikely that the new institutions at Edinburgh and New Aberdeen would have survived and thrived without the continued support of both their respective town councils and their local citizenry. The complex early battles for control of these institutions between the councils and a range of ministers and magnates, mirrored by a similar clash between the masters of Glasgow and the civic government, shows that a range of interests in Scottish urban society were waking up to the benefit of locally-controlled and sponsored higher education in the closing decades of the sixteenth century. The contrast between the fortunes of Marischal and Edinburgh with those of the abortive foundation at Fraserburgh also shows how crucial sustained support from the local citizenry was in maintaining this benefit, particularly in terms of finance.

In terms of teaching, there was ultimately little in the way of radical change in the post-reformation period. At Marischal College Melville's call for professorial specialisation was at least partially heeded by the masters; however, elsewhere regents continued to take their class through the entire four-year degree, and it was only in the 1620s that specialist professors began to appear at the other Scottish universities. Evidence for the processes of lecturing, examination and discipline show that the key components of university life did not alter in form or content from their medieval antecedents although, as the visitation records show, these processes were occasionally not carried out at each university with sufficient rigour or quality. Most importantly, the texts that the masters read in arts did not fundamentally change. There was no great uptake of radical new Continental learning or authors. The fierce resistance to Ramus and the continued adherence instead to Aristotle and a broad range of commentators serves to check the idea that Melville introduced a sweeping transformation to the intellectual content of education post-1560. In many ways, this continuity is one of the most significant findings of this work. Like most of the universities in Northern Europe, there was no great rejection of Aristotle or the medieval intellectual heritage in Scotland. Rather, there was a gradual incorporation into this tradition of the Renaissance focus on *ad fontes* study of classical texts, and some limited (and judging from the evidence of the reaction towards Ramus at St Andrews and Edinburgh, sceptical) engagement with sixteenth-century humanist reforms in logic and rhetoric. The most significant change was the focus on Greek and on advanced Latin, discernible in scattered fashion in the various lecture notes and printed theses for each university, in the College Orator's Book at St Andrews, and in the record of teaching at King's College in the early 1600s. It is impossible, from our sources, to say who brought about that change and when it occurred, but the evidence points to this too being a gradual process, in development long before Melville's arrival and continuing to develop long after his removal.

While religion played a part in university developments after the reformation, it was only part of a wider range of issues that motivated change. For Melville and his supporters in the universities, religion was everything. There was a clear identification of St Mary's under Melville with the broader aims of the Kirk and the Presbyterian party, and the college held particular ideological significance for him as an 'anti-seminary' to combat Jesuits and recusants. A major part of the tension between Melville and the royal government stemmed from him using St Mary's to spread Presbyterian ideas among his students, a tension which was reflected in the backlash against Melville's allies at King's College and Glasgow in the 1580s. For men like John Rutherford, James Martine and Patrick Sharp, however, religion was of minimal importance, and in many ways their conception of what a university was and its function must have been very different to Melville's. The feud between Martine and William Welwood serves to exemplify this. On one level it came about because the former was nominally Presbyterian and the other nominally Episcopalian. On another it was because of what those factional affiliations meant in terms of the wider kin network and politics of the burgh, and on still another was related purely to the financial situation of both men within the college. Further to this, the example of St Salvator's generally in the post-reformation period serves to counter the belief that all universities in this period were lofty ivory towers heavily engaged with the latest intellectual movements. For Martine, Rutherford and their colleagues, they fulfilled their basic job of educating students with the minimum of innovation and expected to be rewarded accordingly. Problems only became apparent when monetary rewards were not evenly distributed, and only then, when the masters turned on one another, did the quality of teaching come in for criticism.

Melville's intellectual vision for the Scottish universities was highly advanced for its time, revolutionary in nature and, if fully implemented, would have made Scotland one of the pre-eminent centres for reformed higher education in Europe. He made considerable progress in fulfilling this ideal as principal of Glasgow where he had a free rein in teaching, and one of his greatest achievements was rescuing the university from near collapse. He was clearly effective in teaching divinity students to expound Calvinist dogma at St Mary's, thanks partly to the Ramist 'method' which formed a central part of his pedagogy, and teaching evidence shows he provided students with a clear grasp of the underlying philology and history of scripture. However, positive achievements need to be set against the fact that, although he took his responsibilities as a 'doctor' of the church seriously, his involvement in Kirk politics detracted from his work in educational reform. Although Melville should be given the credit for the transformation of St Mary's into Scotland's first Protestant seminary, James Melville, Robert Howie and the supporting cast of masters in the college arguably played a much larger and more important role in its development and stabilisation. Melville's uncompromising dogmatism and legendary temper also meant that while the government was keen to see widespread reform undertaken across the universities, they were never truly willing to rely solely on him to achieve it. There is no doubt that Melville's intellectual programme, which so intriguingly blended together a range of humanist, Aristotelian and Ramist elements and was so highly pragmatic in approach, was something never before seen in Scotland when it was first disseminated at Glasgow. This programme clearly found its way into some elements of teaching at the other universities as well, albeit in a largely diluted form. Yet while Melville did contribute intellectually to the settlement of education in post-reformation Scotland, his contribution forms only part of a much longer and gradual process of reform and expansion, where the broader practicalities were achieved by a much wider body of local and national interests, and by Melville's more conservative fellow academics.

Appendix
Student Matriculations and
Graduations, 1559–1625

Background and Data Issues

There is a greater wealth of surviving material relating to student matriculation and graduation at St Andrews than there is for any other British university. The graduation roll for the university recorded in the Acta Facultatis Artium dates to what may be assumed to be the first formal graduations at the university in 1413. This starts some 36 years before the commencement of the surviving list at Oxford in 1449, while the matriculation roll recorded in the first volume of the Acta Rectorum begins in 1473.[1] For the period under consideration in this book the rolls were consistently maintained and, despite occasional gaps,[2] provide a wealth of data on the student populace. Both matriculation and graduation lists were recorded after 1577/78 in the Acta Rectorum up to 1738.[3] While the rolls as they stand capture a large percentage of the students at the university in this period they do not tell the whole story, and there are a number of issues relating to their record-keeping that mean they must be treated with caution.

Firstly, there are issues relating purely to the nature of the entries in the rolls themselves.[4] The date of graduation, but especially matriculation, fluctuated according to circumstances from year to year, in the case of the latter usually taking place between October and March in the academic year of entry but sometimes later than this.

Secondly, the recording of student names were by no means confined to these rolls, and many students are found in other university and archival sources that are not found in the matriculation and graduation registers. For example, there are names of graduating students found in the Bursar's Book and appended to the printed *theses philosophicae* throughout the period under consideration which are not recorded in the matriculation

---

[1] *Early Records*, pp. xxvii–xlii.
[2] Primarily 1559–61, and 1579–82.
[3] Acta Rectorum, vol. 2, 3–120; vol. 3, 26–378.
[4] For a full discussion of these issues, see *Early Records*, as above.

and graduation rolls, and there are students noted as studying at various colleges in Pringle's Book, the Balcarres Papers and the College Orator's Book.

Thirdly, this problem becomes particularly pronounced in the initial period following the 'New Foundation', when St Mary's was re-founded exclusively as a divinity college. In addition to no longer recording its students in the matriculation roll alongside those of St Salvator's and St Leonard's, the college ceased to award any formal degrees in divinity until they were instituted under Robert Howie between 1607 and 1616. Instead, students were recorded in a separate volume (known now as Howie's Book) which did not begin until 1588 and which does not account for all divinity students, as is proven by the names of additional students found in other sources such as the printed *theses theologicae* produced under Melville between 1595 and 1602. Divinity students did not undertake a fixed period of study at the college, but appear to have spent as many years as they either deemed necessary or could pay for, with students staying from one to six years, so reliance on a date of entry as a fixed point by which to generate the number of the students at the college in any single year is also misleading. Many of these divinity students came to St Mary's from the other colleges in a postgraduate fashion, but many came from outside the university and so there is no way of knowing their exact background. These is further compounded by the fact that there are several instances when divinity students are recorded as matriculating from St Mary's after 1579, but are not recorded in the formal register of divinity students.

The fact that there is so much material has in one sense actually impeded any systematic analysis of student data for the post-reformation period. The surviving matriculation and graduation rolls from the foundation of the university to 1579 and the matriculation roll for the period 1747–1897 were transcribed and published by the university librarian and first keeper of the university muniments, James Maitland Anderson, in the early twentieth century. However, a volume covering the intervening period, though planned and partially transcribed, was never completed owing to the range and complexity of the sources involved.[5] Further work on this project by the university historian Ronald Cant, which comprised much more detailed and extensive transcripts of the rolls and their cross-referencing with other sources, was also left unpublished at Dr Cant's death.[6]

---

[5]   *Early Records*; J. Maitland Anderson, *The Matriculation Roll of the University of St Andrews 1747–1897* (Edinburgh, 1905); UYUY306/1, UYUY306/2.

[6]   See St Andrews University Library Special Collections, Cant Papers.

Approach and Methodology

Following the publication in 2004 of his *Biographical Register of the University of St Andrews, 1747–1897*, Dr. Robert Smart turned his attention to the period 1579–1747. He attempted to create from the above sources as full as possible a register of students for the period, with their matriculation and graduation dates, postgraduate studies, and further careers where known. While these registers give students in alphabetical order with a wealth of prosopographical information they do not provide lists of student matriculations and graduations for each year or from each college, or allow for an easy analysis of student numbers in any given period.[7] Conversely, while Maitland Anderson's *Early Records* provides lists of student matriculation and graduation for each year up to 1579, it makes no attempt to match up the names in these lists in a prosopographical fashion. With both these issues in mind, an Excel dataset was created for this book where every student for the period 1559–1625 was entered with information, where known, under the following headings: name; college; date of matriculation; date of BA (if known); date of MA (if known); other/ further degrees (including divinity studies); further career information. This involved cross-referencing Maitland Anderson's published matriculation and graduation lists with one another to establish which students between 1560 and 1579 went on to further BA and MA studies, entering the data under the headings above, and converting Dr Smart's prosopographical data for students after 1579 and up to 1625 into tabular format. These two data sets were then combined, cross-referenced and checked for any duplication. They were also rationalised so that where there were a range of multiple matriculation dates during any one academic year they were all assumed to notionally date from the beginning of that same academic year (for example, 10 November 1613, 5 January 1613/14 and 1 March 1614 would all be notionally dated to the beginning of the academic year in 1613). The same approach was taken with graduation dates where they were only given in the manuscripts for the approximate academic year to ensure consistency. Although this approach hides some occasional ambiguities in the dataset, it made it far easier to construct an overall model of trends in graduation and matriculation from a range of very disparate data. The entire dataset, which produced over 3,600 separate student entries for the period 1559–1625, was then entered into a series of pivot-tables to produce the analyses outlined below.

---

[7]   Despite these minor issues, Dr Smart's *Registers* are works of first-rate research and importance for the history of the University of St Andrews, and I am very grateful to Dr Smart for allowing me free access to the manuscript of the *Register* for 1579–1747.

The data for St Andrews was then compared with the surviving records of matriculation and graduation published for Edinburgh, King's College, Marischal College and Glasgow, to try and establish some sense of the comparative numbers of entrants and graduates at each institution prior to 1625.[8] This is a necessarily limited exercise. Edinburgh has no printed matriculation records for the period but has a reasonably comprehensive list of graduates, while the records for King's and Marischal begin in 1600 and 1605/06 respectively, and are by no means complete for the period under examination. While there have been limited analyses of the student numbers at the Scottish universities in the seventeenth century,[9] this is the first set of numbers that takes into account a detailed and comprehensive account of those at St Andrews. Divinity students have been recorded from the first year they appear in the records, usually as a divinity student in the register but there are several separate entries where a student is simply noted as matriculating from St Mary's with no corresponding entry in the divinity register. Finally, a word of caution is required for anyone wishing to cite these numbers as definitive: while every attempt has been made to check and double-check them from the existing records, it would be impossible from the extant sources to construct a full and complete account of student numbers in this period. Both Dr Smart and I are reasonably confident there is less than a five per cent margin of error in the account of St Andrews students from the existing sources, but these charts should be taken as providing indicators of the broader trends of the evolution of the Scottish student populace in the post-reformation period, rather than providing an exhaustive year-by-year account.

---

[8]   *A Catalogue of the Graduates in the Faculties of Arts, Divinity, and Law, of the University of Edinburgh*; FMA, vol. 2, pp. 186–204; *Munimenta*, vol. 3. pp. 3–16, 60–79; *Roll of Alumni in Arts of University and King's College of Aberdeen*.

[9]   Analyses of student numbers and socio-geographic origins of students at King's and Marischal between 1600 and 1860 were undertaken by Rachel Hart in Colin A. McLaren, *Aberdeen Students 1600–1860*: tables relating to the period 1600–1639 can be found at pp. 24–51. Christine Shepherd also produced an analysis of student numbers from the sources outlined above, but with the numbers of St Andrews students taken solely from graduation theses. Shepherd, pp. 398–411. Both these studies make use of the data available for the institutions at Marischal and Glasgow that show the numbers in each class – bajan, semi, tertian and magistrand – in the period under consideration. I have chosen to focus solely on entrants and recorded graduates.

Table 1   Recorded Matriculations in Arts at St Andrews, 1559–1625

	College				
Year	St Leonard's	St Mary's	St Salvator's	Unknown	Grand Total
1559	12	11			23
1560	4	7	16		27
1561	7	8	5		20
1562	15	12			27
1563	14	15	12		41
1564	3	13			16
1565	17	11	15		43
1566		29	8		37
1567		19	9		28
1568	21	18	11		50
1569	24	10	9		43
1570	17	22	9		48
1571	18	13	11		42
1572	9	21	9		39
1573	19	22	13		54
1574	33	23	10		66
1575	20	9	14		43
1576	40	13	15		68
1577	23	8	7		38
1578	16	8	4		28
1579	36	15	17	5	73
1580	28		9	1	38
1581	43		17		60
1582	32		31	1	64
1583	41		19	1	61
1584	25		12	1	38
1585	21		1	1	23
1586	19		2	9	30
1587	23		18		41
1588	7		3		10
1589	24		24	1	49
1590	36		10		46
1591	20		16	1	37
1592	26		1		27
1593	21		16		37

1594	1			31	32
1595				39	39
1596				46	46
1597				37	37
1598	14		11	1	26
1599	32		30	3	65
1600	21		18	2	41
1601	41		16		57
1602	26		25		51
1603	22		25	1	48
1604	31		29		60
1605	2		20	1	23
1606	49		30	1	80
1607	27		26	1	54
1608	22		32		54
1609	42		30	1	73
1610	43		17		60
1611	52		31	1	84
1612	38		29	2	69
1613	58		46	3	107
1614	31		33		64
1615	13		41	2	56
1616	45		34	1	80
1617	32		54	3	89
1618	26		39	1	66
1619	26		27	1	54
1620	24		22	2	48
1621	25		27	1	53
1622	16		26		42
1623	31		29		60
1624	29		21		50
1625	12		9	22	43
Grand Total	1545	307	1150	224	3226

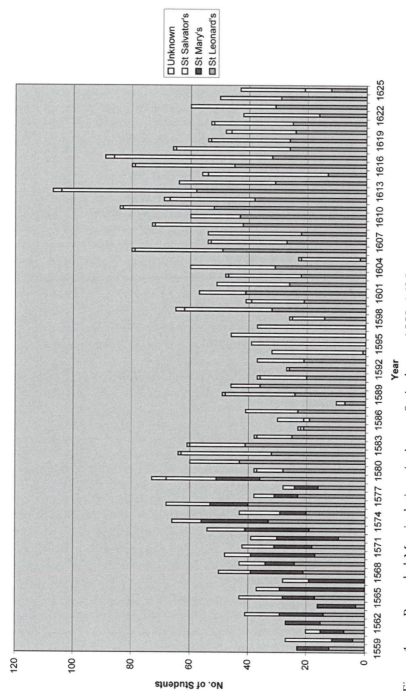

Figure 1   Recorded Matriculations in Arts at St Andrews, 1559–1625

Table 2　　Recorded Number of MA Graduates in Arts at St Andrews, 1563–1625

| College | | | | | |
Year	St Mary's	St Leonard's	St Salvator's	Unknown	St Mary's PG	Grand Total
1563		8				8
1564	1	1	1	2		5
1566	12	11				23
1568	7	6	8			21
1570	11	11	14	1		37
1572	16	10	9			35
1573	3	10	1			14
1575	18	17	11			46
1576	9	3	7			19
1578	5	14	7			26
1579		1				1
1580	5	13	9	4		31
1581	8	15	5	8		36
1582	2	17	4	6		29
1583	8	21	12	15		56
1584		20	8	6		34
1585		23	10	8		41
1586		15	11	7		33
1587		22	10	5		37
1588		12	7	3		22
1589		14		3		17
1590		17	1	13		31
1591		6	8	6		20
1592		6	1	18		25
1593		13	7	3		23
1594		21	6	5		32
1595		17	7	3		27
1596		15	3	11		29
1597		14	5	7		26
1598				22		22
1599			1	25		26
1600		2	1	27	1	31
1601		3		20	3	26
1602		10	8	4		22
1603		25	19	6	1	51

1604		6	13	4		23
1605		12	10	2		24
1606		13	9	1		23
1607		11	3	1	1	16
1608		18	35	4		57
1609		1	13	2		16
1610		32	13	2		47
1611		20	11	5		36
1612		20	16	2		38
1613		27	17	2		46
1614		23	16	1		40
1615		33	14	4		51
1616		12	20	3	1	36
1617		30	26	2		58
1618		22	22	6	1	51
1619		17	29	4		50
1620		26	21	5		52
1621		17	34	2		53
1622		14	22	5		41
1623		14	16			30
1624		17	13			30
1625		17	14	7		38
Grand Total	105	815	588	302	8	1818

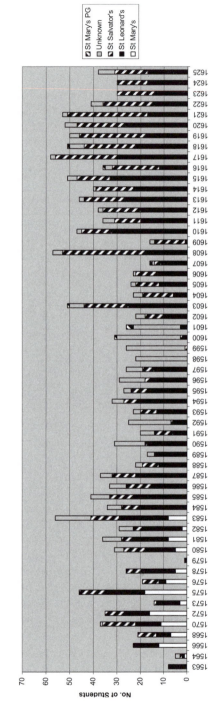

Figure 2   Recorded Number of MA Graduates in Arts at St Andrews, 1563–1625

Table 3   Recorded Number of Entrants to Divinity at St Andrews
               (Broken Down by College Where Known), 1582–1625

Year	College				
	St Leonard's	St Mary's PG	St Salvator's	Unknown	Grand Total
1582			1		1
1583				1	1
1586		3			3
1587	2		2	2	6
1588	4		4	6	14
1589	3	5		3	11
1590	2		1	5	8
1591	5	1	4	3	13
1592	2	2	3	1	8
1593	5		1	4	10
1594	1		1	1	3
1595	2	2	1	5	10
1596	2		1	6	9
1597	2	3	1	2	8
1598		1		4	5
1599		9		5	14
1600		8	2	5	15
1601	2	7		8	17
1602		3	4	4	11
1603	2				2
1604	1	1	2	2	6
1605	1	2	2		5
1606	5	2	2	3	12
1607	4	2	7	1	14
1608	3	1	3		7
1609	2	6	5	3	16
1610	3	3	3	3	12
1611	4	3	8	2	17
1612	4	5	10		19
1613	3	6	3	2	14
1614	7	1	5	1	14
1615	6	8	6	4	24
1616	1	6	8	2	17
1617	4	10	10	6	30
1618	8	20	7	2	37

1619	9	8	9	4	30
1620	8	4	9	1	22
1621	2	6	18		26
1622	2	5	5	7	19
1623	6	9	8		23
1624	3	8	7	1	19
1625	8	2	5	3	18
Grand Total	128	162	168	112	570

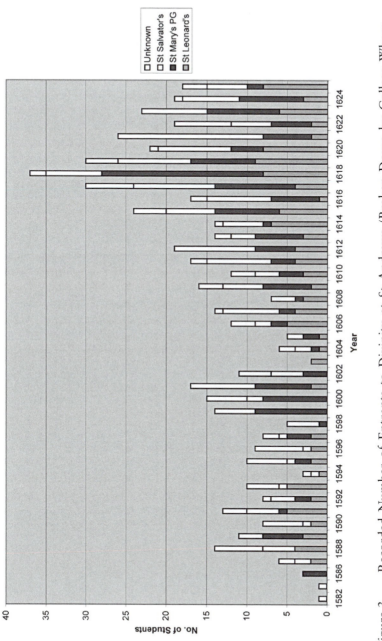

Figure 3   Recorded Number of Entrants to Divinity at St Andrews (Broken Down by College Where Known), 1582–1625

Table 4   Recorded Number of Entrants to Arts at All Scottish Universities (Where Known), 1601–1625

	College/University					
Year	Glasgow	King's	Marischal	St Leonard's	St Salvator's	Annual Total
1601	38	14		41	16	109
1602	19	12		26	25	82
1603	0	12		22	25	59
1604	30	38		31	29	128
1605	43	11	11	2	20	87
1606	11	21	25	49	30	136
1607	26	14	6	27	26	99
1608	23	32	0	22	32	109
1609	29	17	19	42	30	137
1610	28	14	28	43	17	130
1611	30	17	15	52	31	145
1612	30	25	15	38	29	137
1613	13	20	9	58	46	146
1614	26	29	17	31	33	136
1615	30	26	21	13	41	131
1616	32	11	22	45	34	144
1617	44	16	16	32	54	162
1618	36	14	18	26	39	133
1619	27	17	0	26	27	97
1620	31	16	24	24	22	117
1621	45	21	18	25	27	136
1622	26	24	21	16	26	113
1623	37	15	21	31	29	133
1624	34	21	22	29	21	127
1625	33	23	22	12	9	99
Grand Total	721	480	350	763	718	3032

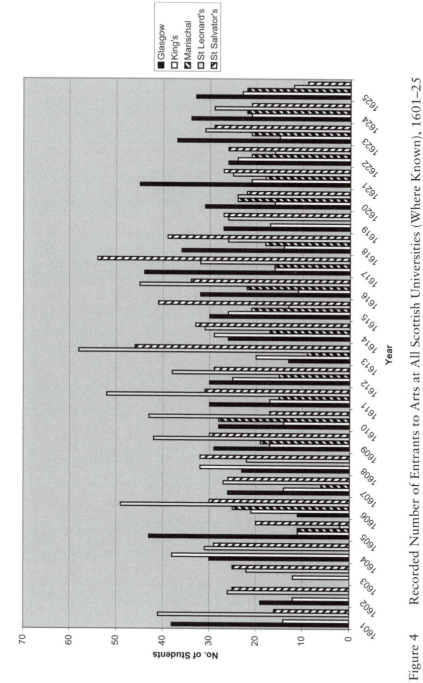

Figure 4   Recorded Number of Entrants to Arts at All Scottish Universities (Where Known), 1601–25

Table 5   Recorded Number of Graduates in Arts at All Scottish Universities (Where Known), 1587–1625

	College/University					
Year	King's	Marischal	Edinburgh	St Leonard's	St Salvator's	Annual Total
1587			48	22	10	80
1588			30	12	7	49
1589			0	14		14
1590			13	17	1	31
1591			0	6	8	14
1592			28	6	1	35
1593			19	13	7	39
1594			20	21	6	47
1595			29	17	7	53
1596			24	15	3	42
1597			34	14	5	53
1598			32			32
1599			34		1	35
1600	9		32	2	1	44
1601	10		20	3		33
1602	6		32	10	8	56
1603	6		23	25	19	73
1604	11		25	6	13	55
1605	8		24	12	10	54
1606	7		28	13	9	57
1607	8		27	11	3	49
1608	16		0	18	35	69
1609	6		33	1	13	53
1610	12		26	32	13	83
1611	8		22	20	11	61
1612	17		24	20	16	77
1613	10		31	27	17	85
1614	10		28	23	16	77
1615	8		34	33	14	89
1616	17	7	27	12	20	83
1617	15	11	46	30	26	128
1618	16	8	34	22	22	102
1619	20	8	34	17	29	108
1620	8		34	26	21	89
1621	13		42	17	34	106

1622	8		34	14	22	78
1623	11	10	30	14	16	81
1624	8		27	17	13	65
1625	9	11	36	17	14	87
Grand Total	277	55	1064	599	471	2466

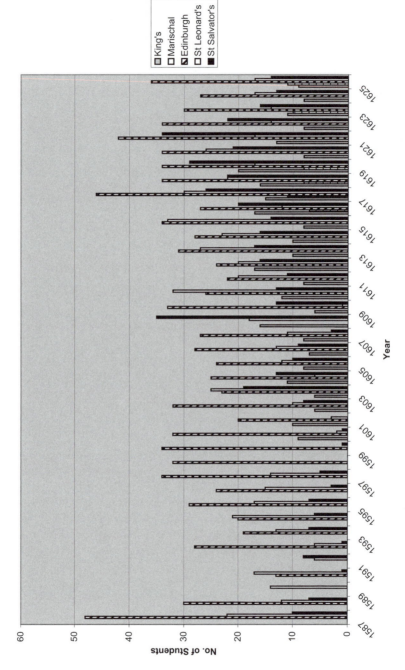

Figure 5   Recorded Number of Graduates in Arts at All Scottish Universities (Where Known), 1587–1625

Bibliography

Manuscript Sources

Aberdeen City Archives

Council Register, 1590–94 (vols 33–5), and Index

Aberdeen University Library

MS 113, 116, 150 (Student Notebooks)
MS K225/2
Vaus, John, *In Primam Doctrinalis Alexandrini Partem Commentarii* (1522) (MS Lambda2 Vau C)
Vaus, John, *Rudimenta Puerorum in Artem Grammaticum* (1531) (MS Lambda2 Vau R3)

Bodleian Library

Letters between Andrew Melville and Stephen Powle, 30 April 1583–1 March 1584 (MS Tanner 168, ff. 203v–204v)

British Library

Andrew Melville to Jean Castoll, Berwick, 23 February 1584 (Cotton MS Caligula D IX)

Edinburgh University Library

Melville, Andrew, *Melvini Epistolae* (MS DC6.45)
Student Notebook (EUL Dc.10.37)
Student Notebook (MS La. III. 155)

Glasgow City Archives

Glasgow Presbytery Minutes 1592–1608 (CH2/171/1–3)
Glasgow Presbytery Minutes (Transcripts) 1592–1603 (CH2/171/31–4)

National Archives of Scotland

Papers relating to the University of St Andrews (PA10/1)

National Library of Scotland

Student Notebook (Advocates MS 5.2.3)
The Balcarres Papers (Advocates MS 29.27), vols 7–8
Andrew Melville to Theodore Beza, 10 November 1579 (Wodrow Folio 42, fos. 11r/v)
Melville, Andrew, *Floretum Archiepiscopale* (Wodrow Folio 42, fos. 47r/v)

St Andrews University Library

Echline, John, *Capitula quaedam eorum quae a Porphyrio imbecillitati non parum utilia* (MS36226)
Malcolm, John, *DIANETICA Ad Aristotelis Scientiam non ad Rami Opinionem Continuatam* (MSBC59)
Papers relating to the lands and privileges of St Leonard's College, St Andrews (UYSL100)
Pringle's Book (UYSL156)
The St Leonard's College Orator's Book (UYSL320)
Papers relating to the lands and privileges of St Mary's College, St Andrews (UYSM100)
Papers relating to the lands and privileges of St Salvator's College, St Andrews (UYSS100)
St Salvator's College Papers, Cartulary 'B' (UYSS150/2)
Papers relating to the provosts and principals of St Salvator's College, St Andrews (UYSS200)
Papers relating to executive proceedings in St Salvator's College, St Andrews (UYSS400)
Howie's Book (UYUY152/2)
Matriculation and Graduation Rolls (UYUY305–6)
Acta Rectorum of the Rector of the Faculty of Arts (3 vols, UYUY350)
The Faculty of Arts Bursar's Book (UYUY412)

Printed Primary Sources

Adamson, J. (Praeses), *Theses philosophicae* (Edinburgh: 1600, 1604)
Adamson, P., *Assertiones Quaedam, ex aliis eiusmodi innumeris erroneae, per Andream Melvinam*, in Adamson, *Opera*, ed. T. Wilson (1620)
Aidie, A. (Praeses), *Theses philosophicae* (Edinburgh, 1616)

Anderson, P.J. (ed.), *Officers and Graduates of University and King's College, Aberdeen*, New Spalding Club (Aberdeen, 1893)

Anderson, P.J. (ed.), *Roll of Alumni in Arts of University and King's College of Aberdeen, 1596–1860* (Aberdeen, 1900)

Anderson, P.J., and Kellas Johnstone, J.F. (eds), *Fasti Academiae Mariscallanae Aberdonensis*, New Spalding Club (3 vols, Aberdeen, 1889–98)

Aristotle, *The Complete Works of Aristotle: the Revised Oxford Translation*, ed. J. Barnes (Princeton, 1984)

Aristotle, *De Generatione et Corruptione*, trans. and ed. C.J.F. Williams (Oxford, 1982)

Bannatyne, R., *Memorials of Transactions in Scotland, A.D. MDLXIX–A.D. MDLXXIII*, ed. R. Pitcairn, Bannatyne Club (Edinburgh, 1836)

Bertram, C., *In Linguae Hebraicae and Aramaicae Comparationem* (Geneva, 1574)

Botfield, B. (ed.), *Original Letters Relating to the Ecclesiastical Affairs of Scotland, 1603–1625*, Bannatyne Club (2 vols, Edinburgh, 1851)

The British Union: a Critical Edition and Translation of David Hume of Godscroft's De Unione Insulae Britannicae, trans. and ed. P.J. McGinnis and A. Williamson (Aldershot, 2002)

Brown, K., and others (eds), *The Records of the Parliaments of Scotland to 1707* (St Andrews, 2007–10) (www.rps.ac.uk)

Bruce, A. (Praeses), *Theses aliquot logicae, ethicae, physicae, sphaericae* (Edinburgh, 1614)

Bucholtzer, A., *Isagoge Chronologica* (In Officina Sanctandreana, false imprint, 1596); copy consulted annotated by Andrew Melville and held at NLS, E.84.f.16

Burton, J.H., and others (eds), *The Register of the Privy Council of Scotland* (Edinburgh, 1877–)

Calderwood, D., *History of the Kirk of Scotland by Mr David Calderwood*, ed. T. Thomson, Wodrow Society (8 vols, Edinburgh, 1842–49)

Cameron, J.K. (ed.), *The First Book of Discipline* (Edinburgh, 1972)

Cameron, J.K. (ed.), *The Letters of John Johnston and Robert Howie* (St Andrews, 1963)

Carr, J. (Praeses), *Theses aliquot logicae, ethicae, physicae & astronomicae* (Edinburgh, 1617)

Craig, W. (Praeses), *Theses philosophicae* (Edinburgh, 1599)

Craufurd, T., *History of the University of Edinburgh from 1580 to 1646* (Edinburgh, 1808)

Deeds Instituting Bursaries, Scholarships, and other Foundations, in the College and University of Glasgow, Maitland Club (Glasgow, 1850)

Dalzel, Andrew, *History of the University of Edinburgh from its Foundation*, ed. David Laing; with a memoir of the author by Cosmo Innes (2 vols, Edinburgh: Edmonston & Douglas, 1862)

Dunlop, A.I. (ed.), *Acta Facultatis Artium Sancti Andreae* (single volume edition, Edinburgh, 1961)

Evidence, Oral and Documentary, Taken by the Commissioners Appointed by King George IV, for Visiting the Universities of Scotland (4 vols, London, 1837)

Fairley, J. (Praeses), *Theses philosophicae* (Edinburgh: 1615, 1619, 1623)

Ferme, C., A Logical Analysis of the Epistle to the Romans, Translated by William Skae: and a Commentary on the same Epistle by Andrew Melville, in the Original Latin, ed. W.L. Alexander, Wodrow Society (Edinburgh, 1850)

Fuller, T., *The Church History of Britain*, ed. J. Nichols, 3 vols (London, 1837)

Geddie, P., *De iustificatione hominis coram Deo, theses theologicae* (Edinburgh, 1600)

Hamilton, Archibald, *Calvinianae confusionis demonstratio, contra maledicam ministrorum Scotiae responsionem* (Paris, 1581).

Hamilton, Archibald, *De confusione Calvinianae sectae apud Scotos ecclesiae nomen ridiculè vsurpantis, Dialogus* (Paris, 1577).

Hannay, R.K. (ed.), *The Statutes of the Faculty of Arts and the Faculty of Theology at the Period of the Reformation* (St Andrews, 1910)

Hay, Archibald, *Ad ... D. Jacobum Betoun ... pro collegii erectione ... oratio* (Paris, 1538)

Hay, Archibald, *Ad ... D. Davidem Betoun ... de foelici accessione dignitatis cardinalitiae, gratulatorius panegyricus* (Paris, 1540)

Hay Fleming, D. (ed.), *Register of the Minister, Elders and Deacons of the Christian Congregation of St Andrews, 1559–1600*, Scottish History Society (2 vols, Edinburgh, 1889–90)

Henderson, A. (Praeses), *Gymnasma philosophicum de rebus logicis, ethicis, physicis, sphaericis, metaphysicis* (Edinburgh, 1611)

Innes, C. (ed.), *Fasti Aberdonenses: Selections from the Records of the University and King's College of Aberdeen*, Spalding Club (Aberdeen, 1854)

Innes, C. (ed.), *Munimenta Alme Universitatis Glasguensis*, Maitland Club (4 vols, Glasgow, 1854)

Jansen, C., De *Praedestinatione, sive de causis salutis et famnationis aeternae disputatio* (Edinburgh, 1595)

Johnstone, A. (ed.), *Delitiae Poetarum Scotorum* (2 vols, Amsterdam, 1637)

King, W. (Praeses), *Theses philosophicae* (Edinburgh: 1612, 1616, 1620, 1624)

Kingdon R.M., and Bergier, Jean-Francois (eds.), *Registres de la Compagnie des Pasteurs de Genève* (Geneva, 1962–)

Kirk, J. (ed.), *The Second Book of Discipline* (Edinburgh, 1980)

Kirk, J. (ed.), *Stirling Presbytery Records, 1561–1567*, Scottish History Society (Edinburgh, 1981)

Knox, J. (Praeses), *Theses philosophicae* (Edinburgh: 1601, 1605)

John Knox's History of the Reformation in Scotland, ed. W. Croft Dickinson (2 vols, London, 1949)

Lachrymae Academiae Marischallanae sub obitum moecenatis & fundatoris sui munificentissimi: nobilissimi et illustrissimi Georgii, comitis Marischalli (Aberdeen, 1623)

Laing, D. (ed.), *A Catalogue of the Graduates in the Faculties of Arts, Divinity, and Law, of the University of Edinburgh, since its Foundation* (Edinburgh, 1858)

Lammie, W. (Praeses), *Positiones aliquot logicae, ethicae, physicae, metaphysicae, astronomicae & cosmographicae* (Edinburgh, 1613)

Leslie, J., *History of Scotland*, ed. E.G. Cody, Scottish Text Society (2 vols, Edinburgh, 1895)

Livingstone, M., and others (eds.), *Registrum Secreti Sigilli Regum Scotorum* (Edinburgh, 1908–)

Lundie, T., *Utrum episcopus Romanis sit Antichristus necne?* (Edinburgh, 1602)

Luther's Works, ed. H.T. Lehman and J. Pelikan (55 vols, St Louis, Missouri and Philadelphia, Pennsylvania, 1955–86)

Macfarlane, W., *Genealogical Collections Concerning Families in Scotland*, ed. J.T. Clark, Scottish History Society (2 vols, Edinburgh, 1900)

MacIlmaine, R., *The Logike of the Moste Excellent Philosopher P. Ramus Martyr* (London, 1574)

Malcolm, J., *Commentarium Acta Apostolorum* (Middleburg, 1615)

Maitland Anderson, J. (ed.), *Early Records of the University of St Andrews: the Graduation Roll 1413–1579 and the Matriculation Roll 1473–1579*, Scottish History Society (2 vols, Edinburgh, 1926)

Maitland Anderson, J. (ed.), *The Matriculation Roll of the University of St Andrews 1747–1897* (Edinburgh, 1905)

Marwick, J.D. (ed.), *Charters and Other Documents Relating to the City of Glasgow A.D. 1175–1649* (2 vols, Glasgow, 1894–97)

Marwick, J.D. (ed.), *Extracts from the Records of the Burgh of Glasgow A.D. 1573–1642* (Glasgow, 1876)

Masson, J., *De libero arbitrio theses theologicae* (Edinburgh, 1597)

Melanchthon, P., *Orations on Philosophy and Education*, ed. S. Kusukawa and trans. C.F. Salazar (Cambridge, 1999)

Melville, A. (Praeses), *Scholastica diatriba de rebus divinis ad anquirendam et inveniendam veritatem* (Edinburgh, 1599)

Melville, A., and Adamson, P., *Viri clarissimi A. Melvini Musae et P. Adamsoni vita et palinodia et celsae commissionis cue delagatae potestatis regiae in causis ecclesiasticis brevis & aperta descriptio*, ed. T. Wilson (Netherlands, 1620)

Melville, J., *The Autobiography and Diary of Mr James Melvill*, ed. R. Pitcairn, Wodrow Society (Edinburgh, 1842)

Mierbeck, T., *Theses physicae De Generatione et Corruptione* (Edinburgh, 1600)

Morgan, A. (ed.), *University of Edinburgh Charters, Statutes, and Acts of the Town Council and Senatus 1583–1858* (Edinburgh, 1937)

Morton, A., *Theses theologicae de Sacramentis et missa idololatrica* (Edinburgh, 1602)

Moysie, D., *Memoirs of the Affairs of Scotland, 1577–1603*, Bannatyne Club (Edinburgh, 1830)

Petrie, J. (Praeses), *Theses aliquot philosophicae* (Edinburgh, 1603)

Plato, *Complete Works*, ed. J.M. Cooper (Indianapolis and Cambridge, 1997)

The Political Poetry of George Buchanan, trans. and ed. P.J. McGinnis and A. Williamson, Scottish History Society (Edinburgh, 1995)

Porphyry, *Introduction*, trans. and ed. J. Barnes (Oxford, 2003)

Ramus, P., *Dialectique* (1555), ed. M. Dassonville (Geneva, 1964)

Ramus, P., *P. Rami Regii Professoris Dialecticae in Libri Duo* (Paris, 1572)

Reid, J. (Praeses), *Theses philosophicae* (Edinburgh: 1610, 1614, 1618, 1622, 1626)

Renwick, Robert (ed.) *Abstracts of Protocols of the Town Clerks of Glasgow* (10 vols, Glasgow, 1894-1900)

Robertson, G. (Praeses), *Theses philosophicae* (Edinburgh, 1596)

Row, J., *History of the Kirk of Scotland from the Year 1558 to August 1637*, ed. D. Laing, Wodrow Society (Edinburgh, 1842)

Scaliger, J.C., *Iulii Caesaris Scaligeri viri clarissimi poemata in duas partes divisa* (n.p. 1574)

Scharp, J., *Theses theologicae de peccato* (Edinburgh, 1600)

Scot, W., *An Apologetical Narration of the State and Government of the Kirk of Scotland since the Reformation*, ed. D. Laing, Wodrow Society (Edinburgh, 1846)

Scott, W., and Laing, D. (eds), *Bannatyne Miscellany*, Bannatyne Club (3 vols, Edinburgh, 1827–55)

Select Works of Robert Rollock, ed. W. Gunn, Wodrow Society (2 vols, Edinburgh, 1849 and 1844)

Stelling-Michaud, S. (ed.) *Le Livre du Recteur de l'Académie de Genève*, (6 vols, Geneva, 1959–1980)

Strang, J. (Praeses), *Theses ex uberrimis logicae, physicae, geometriae, astronomiae, metaphysicae* (Edinburgh, 1611)

Stuart, J. (ed.), *Extracts from the Council Register of the Burgh of Aberdeen 1570–1625*, Spalding Club (2 vols, Aberdeen, 1844–8)

Stuart, J. (ed.), *The Miscellany of the Spalding Club*, Spalding Club (5 vols, Aberdeen, 1841–52)

Thomson, J.M. and others (eds), *Registrum Magni Sigilli Regum Scotorum: The Register of the Great Seal of Scotland* (11 vols, Edinburgh, 1882–)

Thomson, T. (ed.), *Acts and Proceedings of the General Assemblies of the Kirk of Scotland from the year MDLX*, Maitland Club (3 vols, Glasgow, 1839–45)

Wedderburn, W. (Praeses), *Theses aliquot logicae, ethicae, physicae, sphaericae* (Edinburgh, 1608)

Welwood, W., *Guilielmi Velvod de aqua in altum per fistulas plumbeas facile exprimenda apologia demonstrativa* (Edinburgh, 1582)

Wemyss, J. (Praeses), *Theses philosophicae à generosis quibusdam adolesecentibus* (Edinburgh, 1612)

Wied, H. von, *A simple, and religious consultation of us Herman by the grace of God archbishop of Colone ... by what meanes a Christian reformation ... may be began* (London, 1548)

Wilkie, D. (Praeses), *Theses philosophicae quaedam* (Edinburgh, 1603)

Wodrow, R. *Collections upon the Lives of the Reformers and Most Eminent Ministers of the Church of Scotland*, ed. William J. Duncan (2 vols, Glasgow, 1834–35)

Wodrow, R., *Selections from Wodrow's Biographical Collections: Divines of the North-East of Scotland*, ed. R. Lippe, New Spalding Club (Aberdeen, 1890)

Wood, M. (ed.), *Extracts from the Records of the Burgh of Edinburgh, A.D. 1589 to 1603* (Edinburgh, 1927)

Wood, M. (ed.), *Extracts from the Records of the Burgh of Edinburgh, A.D. 1604 to 1626* (Edinburgh, 1931)

Young, A. (Praeses), *Theses philosophicae* (Edinburgh, 1617)

Secondary Sources

Adams, John, 'Gabriel Harvey's *Ciceronianus* and the Place of Peter Ramus' *Dialecticae libri duo* in the Curriculum', *Renaissance Quarterly*, 43 (1990): 550–69

Allen, P.S., *Erasmus: Lectures and Wayfaring Sketches* (Oxford: Clarendon Press, 1934)

Anderson, Robert, Lynch, Michael and Phillipson, Nicholas, *The University of Edinburgh: An Illustrated History* (Edinburgh: Edinburgh University Press, 2003)

Backus, Irena, 'L'Enseignement de la Logique à l'Académie de Genève entre 1559 et 1565', *Revue de Théologie et Philosophie*, 111 (1979): 153–63

Backus, Irena, *Reformation Readings of the Apocalypse: Geneva, Zurich, and Wittenberg* (Oxford: Oxford University Press, 2002)

Barnes, Jonathan (ed.), *The Cambridge Companion to Aristotle* (Cambridge: Cambridge University Press, 1995)

Bernstein, Hilary, *Between Crown and Community: Poitiers and Civic Culture in Sixteenth-Century Poitiers* (Ithaca and London: Cornell University Press, 2004)

Blanchard, Ian, and others, 'The Economy: Town and Country', in Patricia Dennisoun, David Ditchburn and Michael Lynch (eds), *Aberdeen Before 1800* (East Linton: Tuckwell Press, 2000)

Boissonnade, Prosper, *and others, Histoire de l'Université de Poitiers, passé et present (1432–1932)* (Poitiers: Imprimerie Moderne, Nicolas, Renault & Cie, 1932)

Borgeaud, Charles, 'Cartwright and Melville at the University of Geneva, 1569–1574', *American Historical Review*, 5.2 (1899): 284–90

Borgeaud, Charles, *Histoire de l'Universite de Genéve: L'Academie de Calvin* (Geneva: George & Co., 1900)

Bower, Alexander, *The History of the University of Edinburgh* (3 vols, Edinburgh: Waugh and Innes, 1817–30)

Brian G. Armstrong, *Calvinism and the Amyraut Heresy: Protestant Scholasticism and Humanism in Seventeenth-Century France* (Madison and London: University of Wisconsin Press, 1969)

Broadie, Alexander, *The Circle of John Mair: Logic and Logicians in Pre-reformation Scotland* (Oxford: Clarendon Press, 1985)

Broadie, Alexander, 'Philosophy in Renaissance Scotland: Loss and Gain', in John MacQueen (ed.), *Humanism in Renaissance Scotland* (Edinburgh: Edinburgh University Press, 1991)

Brockliss, Laurence, 'Curricula', in Hilde De Ridder-Symoens (ed.), *A History of the University in Europe, volume 2: Universities in Early Modern Europe (1500–1800)* (Cambridge: Cambridge University Press, 1996)

Bruyere, Nellie, *Méthode et Dialectique dans l'Oeuvre de la Ramée* (Paris: Vrin, 1984)

Burnett, Amy, *Teaching the Reformation: Ministers and their Message in Basel, 1529–1629* (Oxford: Oxford University Press, 2006)

Cairns, John, 'Academic Feud, Bloodfeud, and William Welwood: Legal Education in St Andrews, 1560–1611', *Edinburgh Law Review*, 2 (1998): 158–79, 255–87

Cameron, Euan, 'Archibald Hay's *Elegantiae*: Writings of a Scots Humanist at the College de Montaigu in the Time of Bude and Beda', in J-C. Margolin (ed.), *Acta Conventus Neo-Latini Turonensis* (Paris: Vrin 1980)

Cameron, James, 'Andrew Melville in St Andrews', in D.W.D. Shaw (ed.), *In Divers Manners: A St Mary's Miscellany* (St Andrews: St Mary's College, 1990)

Cameron, James, 'Aspects of the Lutheran Contribution to the Scottish Reformation 1528–1552', *Records of the Scottish Church History Society*, 22 (1984): 1–12

Cameron, James, 'The Re-foundation of the University in 1579', *St Andrews Alumnus Chronicle*, 71 (1980): 3–10

Cameron, James, 'St Mary's College 1547–1574 – The Second Foundation: the Principalship of John Douglas', in D.W.D. Shaw (ed.), *In Divers Manners: A St Mary's Miscellany* (St Andrews: St Mary's College, 1990)

Cameron, James, 'Some Aberdeen Students on the Continent in the Late Sixteenth and Early Seventeenth Centuries', in Paul Dukes (ed.), *The Universities of Aberdeen and Europe: The First Three Centuries* (Aberdeen, 1995)

Cameron, James, 'A Trilingual College for Scotland: the Founding of St Mary's College' in D.W.D. Shaw (ed.), *In Divers Manners: A St Mary's Miscellany* (St Andrews: St Mary's College, 1990)

Cant, Ronald, *The College of St Salvator: Its Foundation and Development* (Edinburgh: Oliver and Boyd, 1950)

Cant, Ronald, 'The New Foundation of 1579 in Historical Perspective', *St John's House Papers*, 2 (1979)

Cant, Ronald, 'The St Andrews University Theses, 1579–1747: A Bibliographical Introduction', *Edinburgh Bibliographical Society Transactions*, 2.2 (1941): 105–50 and 'Supplement', ibid., 2.4 (1945): 263–73

Cant, Ronald, *The University of St Andrews: A Short History* (4th edn, St Andrews, 2002)

Castor, Grahame, *Pléiade Poetics: A Study in Sixteenth-Century Thought and Terminology* (Cambridge: Cambridge University Press, 1964)

Chaix, Paul, and others, *Les Livres Imprimés à Geneve de 1550 à 1600* (Geneva: Droz, 1966)

Collinson, Patrick, *The Elizabethan Puritan Movement* (London: Cape, 1967, 1982)

Cowan, Ian, *The Scottish Reformation: Church and Society in Early Modern Scotland* (London: Weidenfeld and Nicolson, 1982)

Craig, Edward (ed.) *The Routledge Encyclopaedia of Philosophy* (10 vols, London and New York: Routledge, 1998)

Crawford, Barbara (ed.), *Church, Chronicle and Learning in Medieval and Early Renaissance Scotland* (Edinburgh: Mercat Press, 1999)

Curtis, Mark, *Oxford and Cambridge in Transition, 1558–1642* (Oxford: Clarendon Press, 1959)

Dawson, Jane, *Scotland Re-formed, 1488–1587* (Edinburgh: Edinburgh University Press, 2007)

Doelman, James, *King James I and the Religious Culture of England* (Cambridge: D.S. Brewer, 2000)

Donaldson, Gordon, 'Aberdeen University and the Reformation,' *Northern Scotland*, 1 (1972–3): 129–42

Donaldson, Gordon, *All the Queen's Men* (London: Batsford, 1983)

Donaldson, Gordon, *James V–James VII* (Edinburgh: Oliver and Boyd, 1965)

Donaldson, Gordon, 'The Relations between the English and Scottish Presbyterian Movements to 1604' (unpublished PhD thesis, University of London, 1938)

Donaldson, Gordon, 'Scottish Presbyterian Exiles in England, 1584–8', *Scottish Church History Society Records*, 14 (1960–62): 67–80

Donaldson, Gordon, *The Scottish Reformation* (Cambridge: Cambridge University Press, 1963)

Dunbar, Linda, *Reforming the Scottish Church: John Winram (c. 1492–1582) and the Example of Fife* (Aldershot: Ashgate, 2002)

Dunlop, Annie, *The Life and Times of Bishop James Kennedy* (Edinburgh: Oliver and Boyd, 1950)

Durkan, John, 'Early Humanism in King's College', *Aberdeen University Review*, 163 (1980): 259–79

Durkan, John, 'Early Humanism in Scotland', *Innes Review*, 4.1 (1953): 4–24

Durkan, John, 'The Early Library of St Salvator's', *The Bibliotheck*, 3 (1962): 97–100

Durkan, John, 'Henry Scrimgeour: Renaissance Bookman', *Edinburgh Bibliographical Society Transactions*, 5 (1978): 1–31

Durkan, John, 'John Rutherford and Montaigne: an Early Influence?', *Bibliotheque d'Humanisme et Renaissance*, 41 (1979): 115–22

Durkan, John, 'The Royal Lectureships under Mary of Lorraine', *Scottish Historical Review*, 62.1 (1983): 73–8

Durkan, John, and Kirk, James, *The University of Glasgow, 1451–1577* (Glasgow: Glasgow University Press, 1977)

Durkan, John, and Ross, Anthony, *Early Scottish Libraries* (Glasgow: J.S. Burns, 1961)

Elsmann, Thomas, 'The Influence of Ramism on the Academies of Bremen and Danzig: A Comparison', in Mordechai Feingold, Joseph Freedman and Wolfgang Rother (eds), *The Influence of Petrus Ramus: Studies in Sixteenth and Seventeenth Century Philosophy and Sciences* (Basle: Schwabe, 2001)

Feingold, Mordechai, 'English Ramism: A Reinterpretation', in Mordechai Feingold, Joseph Freedman, and Wolfgang Rother (eds), *The Influence of Petrus Ramus: Studies in Sixteenth and Seventeenth Century Philosophy and Sciences* (Basle: Schwabe, 2001)

Feingold, Mordechai, 'The Humanities', in Nicholas Tyacke (ed.), *The History of the University of Oxford, volume 4: Seventeenth-Century Oxford* (Oxford: Clarendon Press, 1997)

Feingold, Mordechai, Freedman, Joseph and Rother, Wolfgang (eds), *The Influence of Petrus Ramus: Studies in Sixteenth and Seventeenth Century Philosophy and Sciences* (Basle: Schwabe, 2001)

Forbes-Leith, William, *Pre-Reformation Scholars in Scotland in the Sixteenth Century* (Edinburgh: James MacLehose and Sons, 1915)

Fincham, Kenneth, 'Oxford and the Early Stuart Polity', in Nicholas Tyacke (ed.), *The History of the University of Oxford, volume 4: Seventeenth-Century Oxford* (Oxford: Clarendon Press, 1997)

Fletcher, J.M., 'Change and Resistance to Change: A Consideration of the Development of English and German Universities during the Sixteenth Century', *History of Universities*, 1 (1981): 1–36

Fraenkel, Pierre, 'De l'Ecriture à la Dispute: Le Cas de l'Académie de Genève sous Théodore de Bèze', *Cahiers de la Revue de Théologie et Philosophie* (Lausanne, 1977)

Freedman, Joseph, 'The Diffusion of the Writings of Petrus Ramus in Central Europe, c. 1570– c.1630', in Freedman, Joseph, *Philosophy and the Arts in Central Europe, 1500–1700* (Aldershot: Ashgate, 1999)

Freedman, Joseph, 'Melanchthon's Opinion of Ramus and the Utilization of their Writings in Central Europe', in Mordechai Feingold, Joseph Freedman and Wolfgang Rother (eds), *The Influence of Petrus Ramus: Studies in Sixteenth and Seventeenth Century Philosophy and Sciences* (Basle: Schwabe, 2001)

Freeman, T.S., '"The reik of Maister Patrik Hammyltoun": John Foxe, John Winram, and the Martyrs of the Scottish Reformation', *Sixteenth Century Journal*, 27 (1996): 43–60

Frijhoff, Willem, 'Patterns', in Hilde De Ridder-Symoens (ed.), *A History of the University in Europe, volume 2: Universities in Early Modern Europe (1500–1800)* (Cambridge: Cambridge University Press, 1996)

Gilbert, Neil, *Renaissance Concepts of Method* (New York: Columbia University Press, 1960)

Gill, Mary, and Pellegrin, Pierre (eds), *Blackwell Companions to Philosophy: A Companion to Ancient Philosophy* (Massachusetts and Oxford: Blackwell, 2006)

Goodare, Julian, 'The Attempted Scottish *Coup* of 1596', in Julian Goodare and Alasdair MacDonald (eds), *Sixteenth-Century Scotland: Essays in Honour of Michael Lynch* (Leiden and Boston: Brill, 2008)

Goodare, Julian, *The Government of Scotland, 1590–1625* (Oxford: Oxford University Press, 2004)

Goodare, Julian, *State and Society in Early Modern Scotland* (Oxford: Oxford University Press, 1999)

Goodare, Julian, and Lynch, Michael, *The Reign of James VI* (East Linton: Tuckwell Press, 2000)

Grafton, Anthony, *Joseph Scaliger: A Study in the History of Classical Scholarship, vol. 1: Textual Criticism and Exegesis* (Oxford: Clarendon Press, 1983)

Grafton, Anthony, *Joseph Scaliger: A Study in the History of Classical Scholarship, vol. 2: Historical Chronology* (Oxford: Oxford University Press, 1993)

Grafton, Anthony, and Jardine, Lisa, *From Humanism to the Humanities: Education and the Liberal Arts in Fifteenth- and Sixteenth-Century Europe* (London: Duckworth, 1986)

Graham, Michael, *The Uses of Reform: 'Godly Discipline' and Popular Behaviour in Scotland and Beyond, 1560–1610* (Leiden: Brill, 1996)

Grant, Alexander, *The Story of the University of Edinburgh During its First Three Hundred Years* (2 vols, London: Longman and Co., 1884)

Grant, Ruth, 'The Brig o' Dee Affair, the Sixth Earl of Huntly and the Politics of the Counter-Reformation', in Julian Goodare and Michael Lynch (eds), *The Reign of James VI* (East Linton: Tuckwell, 2000)

Greenslade, S.L., 'The Faculty of Theology', in James McConica (ed.), *The History of the University of Oxford, volume 3: The Collegiate University* (Oxford: Oxford University Press, 1986)

Haag, Emile, *La France Protestante*, 5 vols (Paris: Sandoz et Fischbacher, 1877–96)

Henderson, George, *The Founding of Marischal College* (Aberdeen: Aberdeen University Press, 1947)

Herkless, John and Hannay, Robert, *The Archbishops of St Andrews* (5 vols, Edinburgh: William Blackwood and Sons, 1907–15)

Herkless, John, and Hannay, Robert, *The College of St Leonard* (Edinburgh: William Blackwood and Sons, 1905)

Hewitt, George, *Scotland under Morton, 1572–1580* (Edinburgh: John Donald, 1982)

Heyer, Henri, *Catalogue des Theses de Théologie Soutenues à l'Académie de Genève Pendant les XVIᵉ, XVIIᵉ et XVIIIᵉ siècles* (Geneva: Georg et Cie, 1898)

Horn, David, 'The Origins of the University of Edinburgh', *University of Edinburgh Journal*, 22 (1967)

Horn, David, *A Short History of the University of Edinburgh, 1556–1889* (Edinburgh: Edinburgh University Press, 1967)

Hotson, Howard, *Commonplace Learning: Ramism and its German Ramifications, 1543–1630* (Oxford: Oxford University Press, 2007)

Hotson, Howard, 'The Historiographical Origins of Calvinist Millenarianism', in Gordon, Bruce (ed.), *Protestant History and Identity in Sixteenth-Century Europe, volume 2: the Later Reformation* (Aldershot: Ashgate, 1996)

Houwen, L.A.J.R., MacDonald, Alasdair and Mapstone, Sally (eds), *A Palace in the Wild: Essays on Vernacular Culture and Humanism in Late-Medieval and Renaissance Scotland* (Leuven: Peeters, 2000)

Howell, Wilbur, *Logic and Rhetoric in England, 1500–1700* (Princeton: Princeton University Press, 1956)

Hoyle, David, *Reformation and Religious Identity in Cambridge 1590–1644* (Woodbridge: Boydell Press, in association with Cambridge University Library, 2007)

Jardine, Lisa, 'Humanistic Logic', in Charles Schmitt and Quentin Skinner (eds), *The Cambridge History of Renaissance Philosophy* (Cambridge: Cambridge University Press, 1998)

Jardine, Lisa, 'Inventing Rudolph Agricola: Cultural Transmission, Renaissance Dialectic, and the Emerging Humanities', in Anthony Grafton and Ann Blair (eds), *The Transmission of Culture in Early Modern Europe* (Philadelphia: University of Pennsylvania Press, 1990)

Johansen, Karsten, *A History of Ancient Philosophy, from the Beginnings to Augustine*, trans. Henrik Rosenmeier (London: Routledge, 1998)

Jones, Leonard C., *Simon Goulart, 1543–1628* (Geneva; Georg & Cie, 1917)

Kearney, Hugh, *Scholars and Gentlemen: Universities and Society in Pre-Industrial Britain, 1500–1700* (London: Faber and Faber, 1970)

Kellas Johnstone, James, 'Notes on the Academic Theses of Scotland', *Records of the Glasgow Bibliographical Society*, 8 (1930): 81–98

Kingdon, Robert, *Geneva and the Consolidation of the French Protestant Movement, 1564–72* (Geneva: Droz, 1967)

Kingdon, Robert, *Myths about the St Bartholomew's Day Massacres* (Cambridge, Mass.: Harvard University Press, 1998)

Kirk, James, 'The Development of the Melvillian Movement in Late Sixteenth Century Scotland' (2 vols, unpublished PhD thesis, Edinburgh University, 1972)

Kirk, James, 'John Knox and Andrew Melville: A Question of Identity?', *Scotia*, 6 (1982): 14–22

Kirk, James, '"Melvillian" Reform in the Scottish Universities', in Alasdair MacDonald, Michael Lynch and Iain Cowan (eds), *The Renaissance in Scotland: Studies in Literature, Religion, History and Culture* (Leiden: Brill, 1994)

Knox, Samuel, *Walter Travers: Paragon of Elizabethan Puritanism* (London: Methuen, 1962)

Lee, John, *Lectures on the History of the Church of Scotland, from the Reformation to the Revolution Settlement* (2 vols, Edinburgh: William Blackwood, 1860)

Lee, Maurice, *John Maitland of Thirlestane and the Foundation of Stewart Despotism in Scotland* (Princeton: Princeton University Press, 1959)

Lefranc, Abel, and others, *Le Collège de France 1530–1930* (Paris: Le Presse Universitaires de France, 1932)

Legrand, Emile, *Bibliographie Hellénique des XVe et XVIe Siècles* (Paris : E. Leroux, 1962)

Lewis, Gillian, 'The Geneva Academy', in Andrew Pettegree, Paul Duke and Gillian Lewis (eds), *Calvinism in Europe 1540–1620* (Cambridge: Cambridge University Press, 1994)

Lewis, John, *Adrien Turnèbe (1512–1565): A Humanist Observed* (Geneva: Droz, 1998).

Loach, Jennifer, 'Reformation Controversies', in James McConica (ed.), *The History of the University of Oxford, volume 3: The Collegiate University* (Oxford: Oxford University Press, 1986)

Lohr, Charles, 'Metaphysics and Natural Philosophy as Sciences: the Catholic and the Protestant Views in the Sixteenth and Seventeenth Centuries', in Constance Blackwell and Sachiko Kusukawa (eds), *Philosophy in the Sixteenth and Seventeenth Centuries: Conversations with Aristotle* (Aldershot: Ashgate, 1999)

Lynch, Michael, *Edinburgh and the Reformation* (Edinburgh: John Donald, 1981)

Lynch, Michael, 'The Origins of Edinburgh's "Toun College": A Revision Article', *Innes Review*, 33 (1982): 3–14

Lynch, Michael, *Scotland: A New History* (London: Pimlico, 1992 edition)

Lynch, Michael, and Dingwall, Helen 'Elite Society in Town and Country', in Patricia Dennisoun, David Ditchburn and Michael Lynch (eds), *Aberdeen Before 1800* (East Linton, 2000)

Maag, Karin, *Seminary or University? The Genevan Academy and Reformed Higher Education, 1560–1620* (Aldershot: Ashgate, 1995)

M'Crie, Thomas, *Life of Andrew Melville* (2 vols, Edinburgh: William Blackwood, 1819); (1 vol, Edinburgh: William Blackwood and Sons, 1856)

McCallum, John, *Reforming the Scottish Parish: The Reformation in Fife, 1560–1640* (Aldershot: Ashgate, 2010)

MacDonald, Alan, 'Best of Enemies: Andrew Melville and Patrick Adamson, c.1574–1592', in Julian Goodare and Alasdair MacDonald (eds), *Sixteenth-Century Scotland: Essays in Honour of Michael Lynch* (Leiden and Boston: Brill, 2008)

MacDonald, Alan, *The Jacobean Kirk: Sovereignty, Polity and Liturgy, 1567–1625* (Aldershot: Ashgate, 1998)

MacDonald, Alan, 'James VI and the General Assembly', in Julian Goodare and Michael Lynch (eds), *The Reign of James VI* (East Linton: Tuckwell Press, 2000)

MacDonald, Alan, 'James VI and I, the Church of Scotland, and British Ecclesiastical Convergence', *The History Journal*, 48.4 (2005): 885–903

MacDonald, Alasdair, 'Florentius Volusenus and Tranquillity of Mind: Some Applications of an Ancient Ideal', in Alasdair MacDonald, Zweder R W.M. von Martels, and Jan R. Veenstra, *Christian Humanism: Essays in Honour of Arjo Vanderjagt* (Leiden and Boston: Brill, 2009)

Macfarlane, Ian, *Buchanan* (London: Duckworth, 1981)

Macfarlane, Leslie, 'The Library of Bishop William Elphinstone', *Aberdeen University Review*, 37 (1958): 253–71

Macfarlane, Leslie, *William Elphinstone and the Kingdom of Scotland 1431–1514: The Struggle for Order* (Aberdeen: Aberdeen University Press, 1985)

McLaren, Colin, *Aberdeen Students 1600–1860* (Aberdeen: Aberdeen University Press, 2005)

McLennan, Bruce, 'The Reformation in the Burgh of Aberdeen', *Northern Scotland*, 2 (1974–77): 119–144

Macneill, William, 'Scottish Entries in the *Acta Rectoria Universitatis Parisiensis* 1519 to c. 1633', *Scottish Historical Review*, 43 (1964): 66–86

Mack, Peter, *Renaissance Argument: Valla and Agricola in the Traditions of Rhetoric and Dialectic* (Leiden: Brill, 1993)

Mackie, John, *The University of Glasgow, 1451–1951* (Glasgow: Jackson, 1954)

Mapstone, Sally, and Wood, Juliette (eds), *The Rose and the Thistle: Essays on the Culture of Late Medieval and Renaissance Scotland* (East Linton: Tuckwell Press, 1998)

Mason, Roger, *Kingship and the Commonweal: Political Thought in Renaissance and Reformation Scotland* (East Linton: Tuckwell Press, 1998)

Meerhoff, Kees, *Rhétorique et Poetique au XIVe Siècle en France: Du Bellay, Ramus et les Autres* (Leiden: Brill, 1986)

Meerhoff, Kees, and Magnien, Marcel (eds), *Ramus et l'Université* (Paris: Editions Rue d'Ulm, 2004)

Mellon, Pierre, *L'Académie de Sedan* (Paris: Librairie Fischbacher, 1913)

Methuen, Charlotte, 'The Teaching of Aristotle in Late Sixteenth-Century Tübingen', in Constance Blackwell and Sachiko Kusukawa (eds), *Philosophy in the Sixteenth and Seventeenth Centuries: Conversations with Aristotle* (Aldershot: Ashgate, 1999)

Molland, A.G. 'Duncan Liddell (1561–1613): An Early Benefactor of Marischal College Library', *Aberdeen University Review*, 51 (1986): 485–99.

Morgan, Victor, and Brooke, Christopher, *A History of the University of Cambridge, volume 2: 1546–1750* (Cambridge: Cambridge University Press, 2004)

Mullan, David, *Episcopacy in Scotland* (Edinburgh: John Donald, 1986)

Muller, Richard, *After Calvin: Studies in the Development of a Theological Tradition* (Oxford: Oxford University Press, 2002)

Notker-Hammerstein, Helga, 'Relations with Authority', in Hilde De Ridder-Symoens (ed.), *A History of the University in Europe, volume 2: Universities in Early Modern Europe (1500-1800)* (Cambridge: Cambridge University Press, 1996)

Notker-Hammerstein, Helga, 'The University of Heidelberg in the Early Modern Period: Aspects of its History as a Contribution to its Sexcentennary', *History of Universities*, 6 (1986): 105–33

Ong, Walter, Ramus, Method and the Decay of Dialogue: From the Art of Discourse to the Art of Reason (Cambridge, Mass.: Harvard University Press, 1958)

Ong, Walter, *Ramus and Talon Inventory* (Cambridge, Mass.: Harvard University Press, 1958)

Oxford Dictionary of National Biography (Oxford, 2004) (www.oxforddnb.com)

Pearson, A.F. Scott, *Thomas Cartwright and Elizabethan Puritanism, 1535–1603* (Cambridge: Cambridge University Press, 1925)

Plattard, Jean, 'Scottish Masters and Students at Poitiers in the Second Half of the Sixteenth Century', *Scottish Historical Review*, 21 (1924): 82–6

Prewitt, Kendrick, 'Gabriel Harvey and the Practice of Method', *Studies in English Literature, 1500–1900*, 39 (1999): 19–39

Reid, H.M.B, *The Divinity Principals in the University of Glasgow 1545–1654* (Glasgow: MacLehose, 1917)

Reid, Steven, 'Aberdeen's "Toun College": Marischal College, 1593–1623', *Innes Review*, 58.2 (2007): 173–95

Reid, Steven, 'Andrew Melville, Sacred Chronology and World History: The *Carmina Danielis 9* and the *Antichristus*', *Innes Review*, 60.1 (2009): 1–21

Reid, Steven, 'Early Polemic by Andrew Melville: The *Carmen Mosis* (1574) and the St Bartholomew's Day Massacres', *Renaissance et Réforme*, 30.4 (Autumn 2006/07): 63–82

Ridder-Symoens, Hilde de (ed.), *A History of the University in Europe, volume 2: Universities in Early Modern Europe (1500–1800)* (Cambridge: Cambridge University Press, 1996)

Robinson-Hammerstein, Helga (ed.), *European Universities in the Age of Reformation and Counter Reformation* (Dublin: Four Courts Press, 1998)

Rogers, Charles, *Three Scottish Reformers* (London: English Reprint Society, 1874)

Rother, Wolfgang, 'Ramus and Ramism in Switzerland', in Mordechai Feingold, Joseph Freedman and Wolfgang Rother (eds), *The Influence of Petrus Ramus: Studies in Sixteenth and Seventeenth Century Philosophy and Sciences* (Basle: Schwabe, 2001)

Rummell, Erika, *The Humanist–Scholastic Debate in the Renaissance and Reformation* (Cambridge, Mass.: Harvard University Press, 1995)

Ryrie, Alec, 'Reform Without Frontiers in the Last Years of Catholic Scotland', *English Historical Review*, 119 (2004): 27–56

Ryrie, Alec, *The Origins of the Scottish Reformation* (Manchester: Manchester University Press, 2006)

Salmond, James, and Bushnell, George, *Henderson's Benefaction: A Tercentenary Acknowledgment of the University's Debt to Alexander Henderson* (St Andrews: W.C. Henderson and Son, Ltd, 1942)

Schmidt-Biggemann, Willhelm, 'New Structures of Knowledge', in Hilde De Ridder-Symoens (ed), *A History of the University in Europe, volume 2: Universities in Early Modern Europe (1500–1800)* (Cambridge: Cambridge University Press, 1996)

Schmitt, Charles, 'Philosophy and Science in Sixteenth-Century Universities: Some Preliminary Comments', in J.E., Murdoch and Edith Sylla (eds), *The Cultural Context of Medieval Learning* (Dordrecht and Boston: Reidel, 1975)

Schmitt, Charles, 'Towards a Reassessment of Renaissance Aristotelianism', *History of Science*, 11 (1973): 159–93

Senebier, Jean, *Histoire Littéraire de Genéve* (3 vols, Geneva: chez Barde, Manget & Compagnie, 1786)

Sharratt, Peter, 'Peter Ramus and the Reform of the University: the Divorce of Philosophy and Eloquence?' in Peter Sharratt (ed.), *French Renaissance Studies, 1540–1570: Humanism and the Encyclopedia* (Edinburgh: Edinburgh University Press, 1976)

Sharratt, Peter, 'The Present State of Studies on Ramus', *Studi Francesci*, 16 (1972): 201–13

Sharratt, Peter, 'Ramus 2000', *Rhetorica*, 18 (2000): 399–445

Sharratt, Peter, 'Recent Work on Peter Ramus (1970–1986)', *Rhetorica*, 5 (1987): 7–58

Shaw, Duncan, *The General Assemblies of the Church of Scotland, 1560–1600: Their Origins and Development* (Edinburgh: St Andrew Press, 1964)

Shepherd, Christine, 'Newtonianism in the Scottish Universities in the Seventeenth Century', in R.H. Campbell and Andrew Skinner (eds), *The Origins and Nature of the Scottish Enlightenment* (Edinburgh: John Donald, 1982)

Shepherd, Christine, 'Philosophy and Science in the Arts Curriculum of the Scottish Universities in the Seventeenth Century' (unpublished PhD thesis, University of Edinburgh, 1975)

Skalnik, James, *Ramus and Reform: University and Church at the End of the Renaissance* (Kirksville, Missouri: Truman State University Press, 2002)

Smart, Robert, 'Draft Biographical Register of Students at the University of St Andrews, 1579–1747' (n.p)

Smith, Mark, 'The Presbytery of St Andrews 1586–1605: A Study and Annotated Edition of the Register of the Minutes of the Presbytery of St Andrews' (unpublished PhD thesis, University of St Andrews, 1985)

Stevenson, David, *King's College, Aberdeen, 1560–1641: From Protestant Reformation to Covenanting Revolution* (Aberdeen: Aberdeen University Press, 1990)

Stevenson, Katie, *Chivalry and Knighthood in Scotland, 1424–1513* (Woodbridge: Boydell Press, 2006)

Thomas, Andrea, *Princelie Majestie: The Court of James V of Scotland, 1528–1542* (Edinburgh: John Donald, 2005)

Thorndike, Lynn, *The Sphere of Sacrobosco and Its Commentators* (Chicago: University of Chicago Press, 1949)

Trueman, Carl R. and Clark Scott R. (eds), Protestant Scholasticism: Essays in Reassessment (Carlisle: Paternoster Press, 1999)

Veitch, John, 'Philosophy in the Scottish Universities', *Mind*, 2 (1877): 74–91, 207–34

Verbeek, Theo, 'Notes on Ramism in the Netherlands', in Mordechai Feingold, Joseph Freedman and Wolfgang Rother (eds), *The Influence of Petrus Ramus: Studies in Sixteenth and Seventeenth Century Philosophy and Sciences* (Basle: Schwabe, 2001)

Waddington, Charles T., *Ramus: Sa Vie, Ses Ecrits, et Ses Opinions* (Paris: Librairie de Ch. Meyrueis et Co., 1855)

Watt, Donald E.R., and Murray, A.L. (eds) *Fasti Ecclesiae Scoticanae* (Edinburgh: Scottish Records Society, 2003)

Watt, W.S., 'George Hay's Oration at the Purging of King's College, Aberdeen, in 1569: A Translation', *Northern Scotland* 6 (1984–5): 91–6, and commentary by Durkan, John, ibid.: 97–112

White, Allan, 'The Menzies Era: Sixteenth-Century Politics', in Patricia Dennisoun, David Ditchburn and Michael Lynch (eds), *Aberdeen Before 1800* (East Linton, 2000)

White, Allan, 'Religion, Politics and Society in Aberdeen, 1543–1593' (unpublished PhD thesis, University of Edinburgh, 1985)

Williams, Penry, 'Elizabethan Oxford: State, Church and University', in James McConica (ed.), *The History of the University of Oxford volume 3* (Oxford: Oxford University Press, 1986)

Williamson, Arthur, *Scottish National Consciousness in the Age of James VI* (Edinburgh: John Donald, 1979; repr. 2003)

Winning, Thomas, 'Church Councils in Sixteenth-Century Scotland', *Innes Review*, 10 (1959): 311–37

Woltjer, J.J., 'Introduction', in Th.H. Lunsingh Scheurleer, G.H.M. Posthumus Meyjes and others, *Leiden University in the Seventeenth Century: An Exchange of Learning* (Leiden: Brill, 1975)

Wormald, Jenny, *Court, Kirk, and Community: Scotland, 1470–1625* (Edinburgh: Edinburgh University Press, 2001 edn)

Wormald, Jenny, 'The Headaches of Monarchy: Kingship and the Kirk in the Early Seventeenth Century', in Julian Goodare and Alasdair A. MacDonald (eds), *Sixteenth-Century Scotland: Essays in Honour of Michael Lynch* (Leiden: Brill, 2008)

Wormald, Jenny (ed.), *Scotland: A History* (Oxford: Oxford University Press, 2005)

Index

Where known, connections of an individual to a specific university and their most important role there are given. Peers are listed by surname, not title.

St Andrews Studies in Reformation History

*The Shaping of a Community: The Rise and Reformation of the English
Parish c. 1400–1560*
Beat Kümin

*Seminary or University? The Genevan Academy and Reformed Higher
Education, 1560–1620*
Karin Maag

Marian Protestantism: Six Studies
Andrew Pettegree

Protestant History and Identity in Sixteenth-Century Europe
(2 volumes) edited by Bruce Gordon

*Antifraternalism and Anticlericalism in the German Reformation:
Johann Eberlin von Günzburg and the Campaign against the Friars*
Geoffrey Dipple

*Reformations Old and New: Essays on the Socio-Economic
Impact of Religious Change c. 1470–1630*
edited by Beat Kümin

Piety and the People: Religious Printing in French, 1511–1551
Francis M. Higman

The Reformation in Eastern and Central Europe
edited by Karin Maag

John Foxe and the English Reformation
edited by David Loades

The Reformation and the Book
Jean-François Gilmont, edited and translated by Karin Maag

The Magnificent Ride: The First Reformation in Hussite Bohemia
Thomas A. Fudge

Kepler's Tübingen: Stimulus to a Theological Mathematics
Charlotte Methuen

'Practical Divinity': The Works and Life of Revd Richard Greenham
Kenneth L. Parker and Eric J. Carlson

Belief and Practice in Reformation England: A Tribute to Patrick Collinson by his Students
edited by Susan Wabuda and Caroline Litzenberger

Frontiers of the Reformation: Dissidence and Orthodoxy in Sixteenth-Century Europe
Auke Jelsma

The Jacobean Kirk, 1567–1625: Sovereignty, Polity and Liturgy
Alan R. MacDonald

John Knox and the British Reformations
edited by Roger A. Mason

The Education of a Christian Society: Humanism and the Reformation in Britain and the Netherlands
edited by N. Scott Amos, Andrew Pettegree and Henk van Nierop

Tudor Histories of the English Reformations, 1530–83
Thomas Betteridge

Poor Relief and Protestantism: The Evolution of Social Welfare in Sixteenth-Century Emden
Timothy G. Fehler

Radical Reformation Studies: Essays presented to James M. Stayer
edited by Werner O. Packull and Geoffrey L. Dipple

Clerical Marriage and the English Reformation:Precedent Policy and Practice
Helen L. Parish

Penitence in the Age of Reformations
edited by Katharine Jackson Lualdi and Anne T. Thayer

The Faith and Fortunes of France's Huguenots, 1600–85
Philip Benedict

Idols in the Age of Art
Objects, Devotions and the Early Modern World
edited by Michael W. Cole and Rebecca E. Zorach

Local Politics in the French Wars of Religion
The Towns of Champagne, the Duc de Guise, and the Catholic League,
1560–95
Mark W. Konnert

Enforcing Reformation in Ireland and Scotland, 1550–1700
edited by Elizabethanne Boran and Crawford Gribben

Philip Melanchthon and the English Reformation
John Schofield

Reforming the Art of Dying
The ars moriendi *in the German Reformation (1519–1528)*
Austra Reinis

Restoring Christ's Church
John a Lasco and the Forma ac ratio
Michael S. Springer

Catholic Belief and Survival in Late Sixteenth-Century Vienna
The Case of Georg Eder (1523–87)
Elaine Fulton

From Judaism to Calvinism
The Life and Writings of Immanuel Tremellius (c.1510–1580)
Kenneth Austin

The Cosmographia *of Sebastian Münster*
Describing the World in the Reformation
Matthew McLean

Defending Royal Supremacy and Discerning God's Will in Tudor
England
Daniel Eppley

Adaptations of Calvinism in Reformation Europe
Essays in Honour of Brian G. Armstrong
Edited by Mack P. Holt

The Monarchical Republic of Early Modern England
Essays in Response to Patrick Collinson
Edited by John F. McDiarmid